ageing
societies

A

ageing
societies:
myths, challenges and opportunities

Sarah Harper

Hodder Arnold

A MEMBER OF THE HODDER HEADLINE GROUP

Distributed in the United States of America
by Oxford University Press Inc., New York

First published in Great Britain in 2006 by
Hodder Education, a member of the Hodder Headline Group,
338 Euston Road, London NW1 3BH

www.hoddereducation.co.uk

Distributed in the United States of America by
Oxford University Press Inc.
198 Madison Avenue, New York, NY 10016

The advice and information in this book are believed to be true and
accurate at the date of going to press, but neither the author nor the publisher
can accept any legal responsibility or liability for any errors or omissions.

British Library Cataloguing in Publication Data
A catalogue record for this book is available from the British Library

Library of Congress Cataloging-in-Publication Data
A catalog record for this book is available from the Library of Congress

ISBN-10: 0 340 51756 5
ISBN-13: 978 0 340 51756 7

1 2 3 4 5 6 7 8 9 10

Typeset in 10/14 Gill Sans Light by Servis Filmsetting Ltd, Manchester
Printed and bound in Great Britain by CPI Bath.

What do you think about this book? Or any other Hodder
Education title? Please send your comments to the feedback
section on www.hoddereducation.co.uk.

Contents

List of figures

List of tables

Preface

Demographic ageing is a reality. Most western-style countries have aged continuously over the past century. By 2030 half the population of Western Europe will be aged over 50, with a predicted average life expectancy at age 50 of a further 40 years, i.e. half Western Europe's population will be between 50 and 100 years of age.

However, as governments and policy makers have become aware of the implications of population ageing, so the demographic burden hypothesis has spread. Public rhetoric in many western countries at the turn of the century, perpetuated by media dramatisation, has focused on four pervasive myths in particular: dramatic population ageing in developed countries over the next 30 years will cause national health care systems to collapse, economies to crumple under the strain of pension demands and disintegrating families to buckle under increasing care commitments; it is also presumed that the developing world will remain young. *Ageing Societies: myths, challenges and opportunities* shows why these are contemporary myths and highlights the real challenges and some of the opportunities of a mature society – a demography which will be with us but for a short time this century.

Ageing Societies can be considered a sandwich book. If you wish to learn briefly about the reality of ageing societies you can simply read Chapters 1, 10 and 11. Chapter 1 introduces, questions and shows why the four pervasive myths of ageing societies can be refuted. Chapters 10 and 11 look at the real challenges and opportunities of a mature society – age discrimination, intergenerational integration and the vital necessity of addressing ageing with the development agenda. However, if you also wish to understand the processes and evidence behind these notions, then Chapters 3 to 9 take you through the dynamics of societal ageing – the demography and notions of age and ageing itself, and the impact of this on our work and family lives.

Combining biodemography with sociological theory, Chapters 2 and 3 explore the dynamics of falling fertility and mortality, the drivers behind population ageing, and the biological determinants behind ever increasing longevity. The concept of age is examined, identifying it as an indicator only of biological and psychological changes, and yet socially a determinant of individuals' allocated roles, independent of their biological or psychological capacity.

Chapters 4 to 7 consider the current evidence for the realities of ageing in developed countries. First is the growing necessity for extending economic activity into later life, and the implications of societal ageing for the intergenerational contract and provision of social security. Second is the changes within modern families, and the implications of this for the provision of support and care for the increasing older population. Chapters 8 and 9 present evidence for the real demographic challenge, the ageing of the developing world. Faced with one billion older adults within 30 years, with little or no infrastructure to provide long-term care or public social security within many of these societies, older people will remain dependent on families and communities for support.

Developing an understanding of future mature societies is to recognise that while age and cohort-related behaviours should be added into future equations, these are not fixed and will change over a cohort's lifetime, as well as within and between cohorts. However, the role of *age integration* and *intergenerational relationships* has a pervasive dynamic, and it is this aspect of mature societies, *the possibility of increased interaction between successive cohorts and generations,* which may prove to be the consistent and stable force within all societies as they mature.

Sarah Harper
July 2005, Oxford

Acknowledgements

I am indebted to family, friends, colleagues and students who have contributed to the ideas in this book.

I owe particular gratitude for the intellectual stimulus and encouragement provided by Andrew Achenbaum, Vern Bengtson, Linda Waite, Gunhild Hagerstad, Bob Michael, Bob Willis, Hal Kendig, John McCallum, Elizabeth Sundersand, Dale Lund, Richard Connelly, Richard Suzman, Pat Thane and Margot Jeffreys, several of whom also provided the intellectual and actual space to enable me to find the time to write. I am indebted to Anthony Tomei and Todd Peterson, whose passing comments provided the catalyst to take up the book and finish it!

I also wish to thank Philip Walters, who saw an idea and grasped it for Edward Arnold, and Marion Kerr and Bill Neely. Jan Ayres and Joanna Migdal always believed I would finish. I am particularly grateful to George Leeson, who helped me see the myths of societal ageing, and who guided me through the demography, and to my father, Robert Harper, for his detailed research and advice on the emergence of retirement. I wish to thank Carole Newbigging, Sue Marcus, Daphne Harper and Pavel Ovseiko for their editorial assistance, and Jamilah Ahmed, the Arnold editor who finally brought the book to publication.

Finally, my sincere gratitude goes to Peter, Imogen, Giles and Caroline, who have all patiently supported my occasional absences and endless discussions on demographic change. This book is dedicated to my three children, who were conceived, born and brought up during the far too long writing of *Ageing Societies*.

For Imogen, Giles and Caroline

1
Ageing societies

Demographic ageing is a reality. Most Western-style countries have aged continuously over the past century, the measure of ageing being an increase in the percentage of those over 60 years, and a decrease in those under 15 years. By 2030 half the population of Western Europe will be aged over 50, with a predicted average life expectancy at age 50 of a further 40 years, that is half Western Europe's population will be between 50 and 100 years of age. One quarter of this population will be over 65, 15 per cent over 75. Indeed, it has been suggested that half of all baby girls born in the West today will live into the next century, approaching a predicted 5 million centenarians within Western Europe alone. Yet, already two-thirds of the world's older population live in developing countries, with the absolute numbers of older people in these regions estimated to double to reach some 900 million within 25 years. In 45 years time, well within the predicted lifespan of many of this book's readers, there will exist 2 billion older people.[1] Of course, many of us reading this book will be part of that 2 billion. Something we sometimes overlook. We – hopefully – are tomorrow's elderly population.

The power behind this demographic change is a combination of a decline in the numbers of children being born with a lengthening of life of those already born. This process is set to spread throughout the world this century, with increasingly ageing populations, until equilibrium is reached as we approach the twenty-second century, when a more balanced profile will, it is predicted, emerge and be maintained. This is truly something to aspire to. For a society to have achieved a long and healthy lifespan, with a high probability that most individuals born will live to achieve the natural human lifespan in good health, and with limited frailty, must surely be a major achievement of civilisation. Indeed, to have achieved this throughout the world would surely be *the* achievement of civilisation. For then we would have also conquered poverty, disease, famine and war throughout the world – these still being the major killers for most people.

Society's view of ageing

The common public concept of 'ageing' has been one of an increased requirement to provide health and social service delivery to older people. Yet demographic change will also have significant implications for labour supply, family and household structure, health and welfare service demand, patterns of saving and consumption, provision of housing and transport, leisure and community behaviour, networks and social interaction, and even, it has been suggested, the geopolitical order of the new century. However, as governments and policy makers have become aware of the implications of population ageing, so the *demographic burden hypothesis* has spread. Public rhetoric in many Western countries at the turn of the century, perpetuated by media dramatisation, has focused on four pervasive myths in particular:

- Health services thoughout the Western world are collapsing under the strain of growing numbers of older people.

- The dependency ratio, that is workers to non-workers, will become so acute that the economies of many western countries will collapse.

- We are all going to live in loose, multigenerational families which will face increasing emotional strain as large numbers of older people become reliant on decreasing numbers of children to care for them in their dependent old age.

- Ageing is a feature of the developed world, and has little relevance for developing countries.

However, these problem laden scenarios are in fact myths. It is not ageing populations that are the main explanatory factor for pressure on health care services, rather the wider effects of income, lifestyle characteristics and new technology. Similarly, the forecast dependency ratio is not due so much to the presence of large numbers of older people who are unable to work because of their age, but labour markets which have used retirement as a regulating mechanism in times of labour over-supply, and pension systems which have allowed healthy active individuals to withdraw from economic activity. We may be seeing an increase in alternative family structures, and the widespread provision of public forms of care, but there is little evidence that kin do not continue to ensure that their family members are cared for and supported. Indeed, the ageing of the developing world is the *real* demographic challenge, which will face one billion older adults within 30 years, with little or no infrastructure to provide long-term care, or public social security.

This is not to suggest that there are not *challenges* ahead as we adjust to a more mature society. There is a growing necessity for extending economic activity into later life, and for rethinking the mechanisms of the intergenerational contract and provision of social security; health care systems throughout the world will need to adjust to a reduction in acute diseases and infant and child-related medicine and increase in non-communicable disease and long-term care; the bastion of institutionalised age discrimination needs to be tackled; and the reality of the experience of disease and disability at the very end of a normal lifespan acknowledged and appropriate social care and support frameworks established. However, there are also real *opportunities* presented by a mature society – age-integrated flexible workforces, intergenerational integration, age equality, and politically stable, age-integrated societies are all potential benefits of a demography which will be with us but for a short time this century.

The following thus provides an overview of the main theories, arguments and debate over societal ageing. The study of population ageing has burgeoned considerably over the past decade, with the recognition by mainstream economists, sociologists and demographers that this will have significant implications for their area of research. The discussion aims to synthesise the prevailing debate in each of the areas concerned, and to indicate specialist texts that will enable the reader to explore the issues in more depth.

We also consider the dynamics of falling fertility and mortality, the drivers behind population ageing, before turning to examine the concepts of age and ageing. Drawing on ideas from biodemography, the biological determinants behind ever increasing longevity are explored. The concept of *age* is also examined. This is identified as an indicator, as opposed to a determinant, of biological and psychological changes, and yet remains a social determinant of individuals' allocated roles, independent of their biological or psychological capacity. Age also has *analytical value* as a descriptive variable, and it identifies at any given time *birth-cohort membership*, and thus potential life-shared cohort experiences. In addition, the intersection of age with gender, race and class is producing specific life experiences for men and women across the life course.

An ageing world

The population ageing experienced in the developed countries of the world in the twentieth century – and particularly the latter half of that century – is unprecedented in demographic history, and furthermore the trend is expected to continue well into the twenty-first century. Demographically, age 60 or 65 is taken to represent old age, those under age 15 are generally taken as young. (Though, as we shall see later in Chapter 3, such chronological ages have little reality.) In global terms, only 8 per cent of the population was aged 60 years and over in 1950. This had increased to just 10 per cent by the end of the century but is expected to increase even further to 22 per cent by the year 2050[2] by which time globally the number of older people will outnumber the number of young people. At the turn of the twenty-first century, there were approximately 610 million people aged 60 and over in the world corresponding to almost three times the number in 1950, and by 2050 the absolute figure is expected to reach 2 billion, more than a tripling over just 50 years. There will be an even more marked increase in the number of people aged 80 years and over, namely from 70 million to a staggering 394 million in the year 2050.

The world's oldest countries

Table 1.1 shows the proportion of the population aged 65 and over in the world's oldest countries at the turn of the twentieth century. As is clear (with the exception of Japan), the top 20 are all European. Globally, Italy has the highest proportion of persons aged

Table 1.1 *The world's oldest countries at the turn of the twenty-first century*

Country	Proportion of the population aged 65 and over
Italy	18.2
Japan	17.7
Greece	17.3
Sweden	17.2
Spain	16.9
Belgium	16.9
Germany	16.2
France	16.1
United Kingdom	15.6
Portugal	15.5
Austria	15.5
Switzerland	15.4
Norway	15.1
Finland	15.0
Croatia	15.0
Latvia	15.0
Denmark	14.8
Serbia	14.8
Hungary	14.6
Estonia	14.5
Luxembourg	14.3
Slovenia	14.3
Ukraine	13.9
Czech Republic	13.9
Netherlands	13.6
Canada	12.7
Australia	12.4
United States	12.3
Iceland	11.6
Ireland	11.2

Source: United Nations, 2005.

65 years and over, a consequence of its low fertility levels, as we shall see later. Of the European Union countries, Italy at 18.2 per cent has the highest proportion of older people while Ireland at 11.2 per cent has the lowest. Australia, Canada and the United States are at the lower end of this scale with between 12 and 13 per cent of their popu-

lations aged 65 years and over. Interestingly, even the former Eastern European countries have higher percentages than Canada, Australia and the USA. However, these proportions represent very different numbers of older people. The largest elderly population in the developed world is in the USA, with 35 million people aged over 65 (50 million over 60), followed by Japan with nearly 23 million (31 million over 60), and Germany with around 13 million (20 million over 60).

The percentage shifts can be dramatic over a very short period. In the early 1990s the Northern Europeans headed the table, with Sweden and Norway at 17.9 per cent and 16.3 respectively. Italy, Greece and Spain were at 14–15 per cent. Most remarkable has been the rise in the table of Japan, ranked nineteenth in 1992 with 12.8 per cent of its population over 65. The early 'agers' of Northern and Western Europe have thus been caught up by the rest of Western Europe and are now experiencing a double ageing of the population – the aged population is ageing itself with increasing proportions aged 75 and over – while Japan has caught up with and is preparing to overtake the rest of the aged world.

Indeed, it is the pace of population ageing that can be most significant (Fig. 1.1). While it took France, for example, 115 years to move from 7 per cent to 14 per cent of its population over 65, the UK achieved this in 45 years, and Japan in 26. It is the developing countries which will face extreme rapidity of ageing. It is predicted, for example, that the Latin American countries of Brazil and Colombia will age in this manner within 20 years.

Ageing index[3]

Another important measure of age structure is the ratio of young to old, defined as the number of people aged 65 and over per 100 children of age 14 and under. Figure 1.2 shows selected countries from 2000. Already at the turn of the twenty-first century, five countries, Germany, Greece, Italy, Bulgaria and Japan, had more older people than young people, that is had become a *mature society*, with other European countries including the UK joining the list by 2001. As is clear, though, by 2030 all listed countries from the developed world will have this structure. In the developing world, South Korea will have more old than young by 2030, and several other Asian countries will be approaching this ratio. Asia as a whole will be *mature* by 2040.

We can explore this age breakdown in more detail taking the example of the UK. The 2001 Census noted the official *maturing* of the UK population, as the number of individuals aged over 60 was greater than those aged under 15. The proportion of the UK population aged over 60 had reached 21 per cent by 2001. Of these, 36 per cent were aged over 75, corresponding to 7.5 per cent of the total population, and 9 per cent were aged over 85, comprising 2 per cent of the total UK population. However, the numbers of older people in the UK are predicted to increase significantly over the next 25 years (Table 1.2). Growth will be particularly significant among the oldest old – by 2025 more than one quarter of the UK's population will be aged over 60 years, with more than a third of these aged over 75 years.

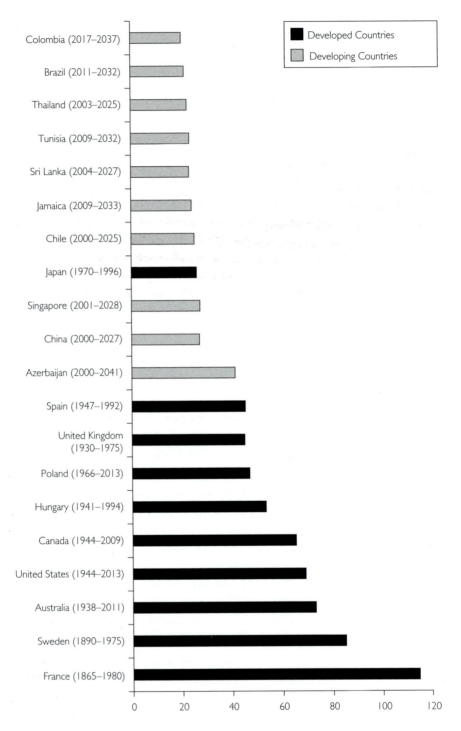

Figure 1.1 *Speed of population ageing.*
Source: Kinsella and Velkoff, 2001.

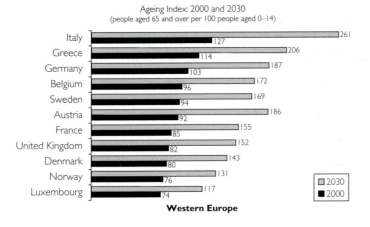

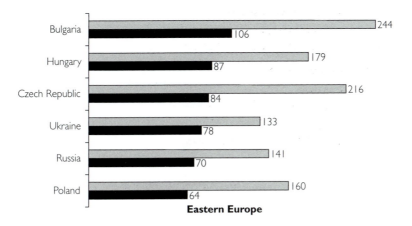

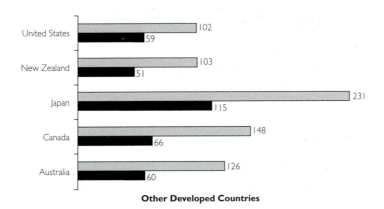

Figure 1.2 *The Ageing Index, 2000 and 2030.*
Source: Kinsella and Velkoff, 2001.

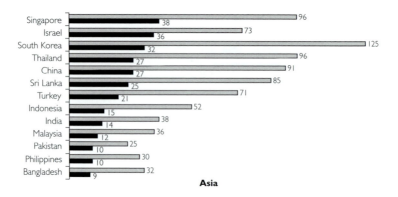

Asia

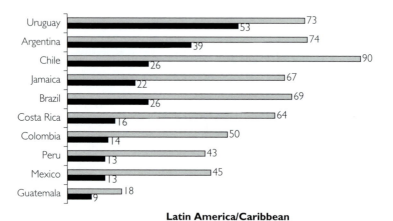

Latin America/Caribbean

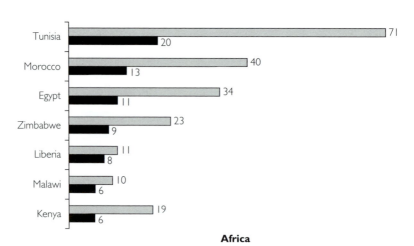

Africa

Figure 1.2 (cont.)

Table 1.2 Census and projected population of the UK, 2001 and 2025 (thousands)

Age group	2001		2025	
	Number	**Percentage**	**Number**	**Percentage**
0–14	11105	18.9	10788	16.9
15–29	11077	18.8	11117	17.1
30–44	13271	22.6	12910	19.9
45–59	11115	18.9	12672	19.5
60–74	7816	13.3	11234	17.3
75+	4405	7.5	6392	9.8
Total	58789		64837	

Source: Census 2001 and National population projection 2000-based

Median ages

Another measure is to consider a society's median age, that is the age that divides the population into numerically equal parts of younger and older people. In the 52 countries study mentioned above (Fig. 1.2), all the countries in the developed world had median ages over 32, while in the developing world they were all under 25. As is clear from the examples in Fig. 1.3, median ages will increase markedly in some countries over the next 25 years. Italy, Brazil, China, Mexico and Thailand, for example, will all see over a ten-year increase in median ages. Italy is currently predicted to have the highest median age at 52. Japan will reach 50, with most other developed countries, and some Asian countries, over 40.

Oldest old

Of equal significance is the growth rate of those over age 80. The group aged 80 years and over is the fastest growing age group in the world with an annual growth rate of 3.9 per cent.

This is partially explained by the rates of declining mortality among this cohort, but is also due to the low fertility around the time of the First World War, so that those people reaching age 80 in the mid-1990s were part of a relatively small birth cohort. Within a few years fertility had increased again, so at the turn of the twenty-first century a much larger birth cohort was reaching age 80. The growth rate of the world's 80+ age group thus increased from 1.3 per cent to 3.5 per cent in just four years. The projected annual growth rate of this age group is 3.9 per cent until 2010, remaining at approximately 3 per cent until at least 2020. This is in comparison with 2.6 per cent rising to 3 per cent for the over-60 age groups as a whole. By the year 2050, it is predicted that 20 per cent of persons aged 60 and over will be in this group. Currently 44 per cent of those aged over 80 live in Asia, some 17 per cent in China alone (a reflection in part of the very large proportion of the total world population in this country), 30 per cent are in Europe and 13 per cent in the USA. By 2030 it is predicted that Japan

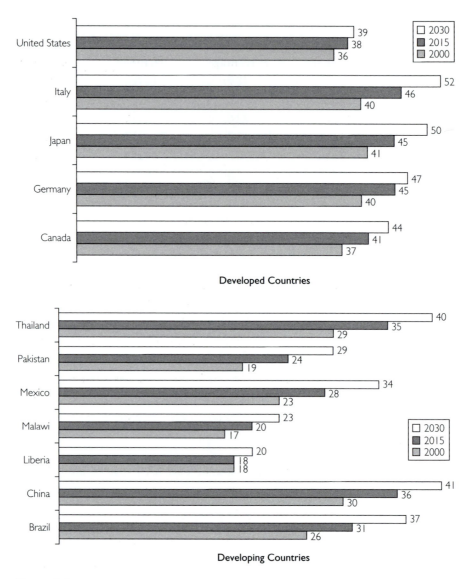

Figure 1.3 *Median ages in 12 countries, 2000, 2015 and 2030.*
Source: Kinsella and Velkoff, 2001.

will have 35 per cent of its older population aged 80 or over. In recognition of this increase in the oldest old the UN Population Division is now producing population projections with a final age category of 100+.

World population pyramids

As is clear from Fig. 1.4, it is predicted that by 2030 the population pyramid for the developed world will move towards population parallel lines, with more or less 10 per

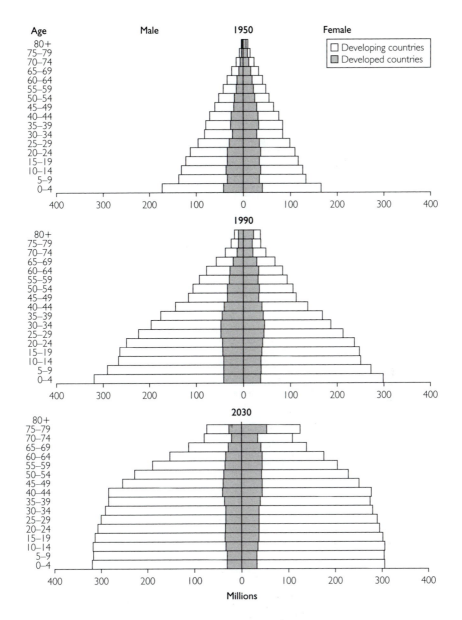

Figure 1.4 *World population pyramids.*
Source: United Nations 2003.

cent of the population in each age decade between birth and 100, that of the developing countries will straighten considerably. Over the next 40 years, however, we shall continue to see a top-heavy pyramid, with a large bulge of mature and then older adults moving up as the dominant population.

This is illustrated by the graphs in Fig. 1.5 which show the current and predicted UK

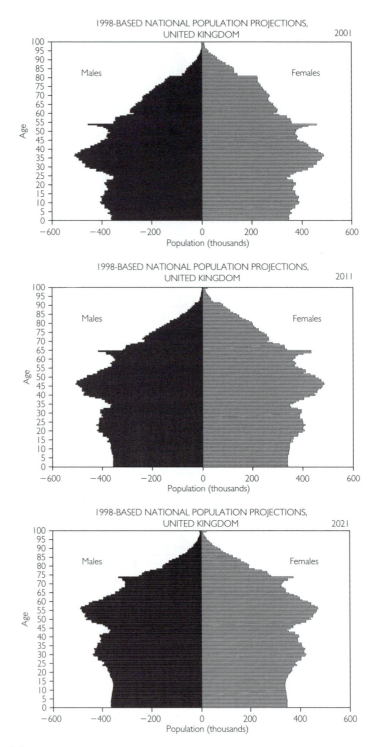

Figure 1.5 *Current and predicted UK population pyramids.*

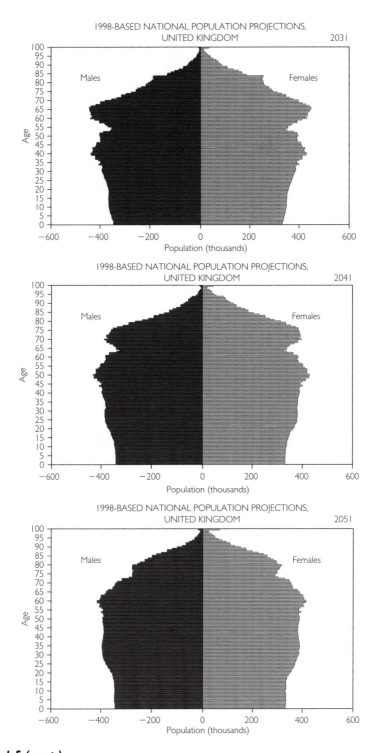

Figure 1.5 (cont.)

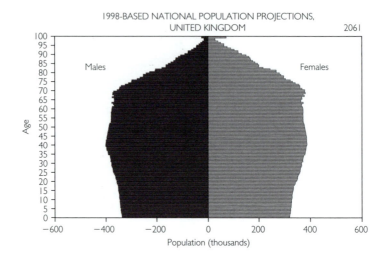

1998-BASED NATIONAL POPULATION PROJECTIONS, UNITED KINGDOM 2061

Figure 1.5 (cont.)

population pyramids. Note the immediate post-Second World War baby boom of 1946, followed by a rapid fall in birth rate, with its nadir in 1957. The second and main UK baby boom occurred from then until the mid-1960s. Thus the UK will experience a mini shelf of older people who will advance test the health and pension systems prior to the main boom some ten years later.

We can also demonstrate this for the USA (Fig. 1.6). In 1960 the largest age cohort was the under-14s. By 1990 this bulge had reached the 20–40 age group, and these cohorts will continue to represent the majority population as they age to between

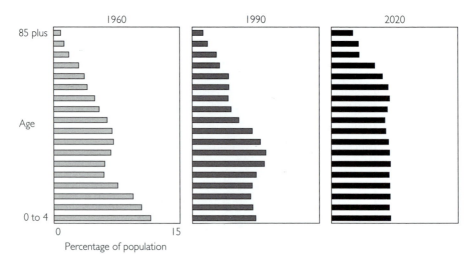

Figure 1.6 *Altering age profiles in the USA.*

50–70 by 2020. If we continued this to 2040, it is clear that, given continuing low levels of fertility, those aged 70 to 90 will continue to hold a dominance over the pyramid. Yet as is also clear from the parallel lines following the bulge up the graph, by 2050 the USA will have achieved an age-balanced society.

Tables 1.1 and 1.2 and Figures 1.1–1.6 illustrate demographic ageing at the societal or population level. This then allows us to consider the national and international context of these demographic changes, the social, economic, political implications of this mature age structure. An alternative view is to consider the impact at the individual level, as life expectancy has risen significantly over the past few decades.

Lengthening lives

What is most striking from the life expectancy rates from birth (Fig. 1.7) is not only that everyone born in the developed world, with the exception of the former Eastern European countries, can now expect to live for more that 75 years, but also the high life expectancies now expected from birth in much of Asia and Latin America. Indeed, with the exception of Africa, many countries in the developing world now have life expectancies at birth of 70 years or older.

Overall, however, life expectancy in the developed regions in 2005 was 76 years compared with 65 years in the developing regions. Continued declines in mortality are expected to push these figures to 82 and 74 years respectively by the year 2050, thereby reducing the gap between developed and developing regions. It is the speed of the demographic transition over the past century that is particularly striking. In 1880 a female baby could expect to live until age 47, her great-granddaughter born 100 years later could expect to live until age 78. Her baby brother had a life expectancy of 44 years, his great-grandson can expect to live until age 71.

This is most dramatically illustrated in Fig. 1.8, which reveals the considerable shift in the survival curve, for US women, over the last century. The ultimate aim is to achieve a complete rectangular shape, so that approaching 100 per cent of the population survive with limited disability until their nineties. We can see this scenario – the compression of mortality and disease and disability morbidity – in Fig. 1.9 which shows that by 2011 the majority of the UK population are predicted to survive until age 86. In both the UK and US cases, current evidence suggests a compression of morbidity, at least for current cohorts, in old age.

Current predictions for Europe and the USA thus suggest a rise in healthy active life expectancy, forecasting that both men and women in their early seventies can expect to live well into their eighties, enjoying most of those years disability-free. What is the impact on individuals as they realise the potential of lifespans which may take them well into their ninth or even tenth decade? As we shall see later in Chapter 6, there is a clear *ageing of life transitions*, with all Western-style ageing societies displaying an increase of age at first

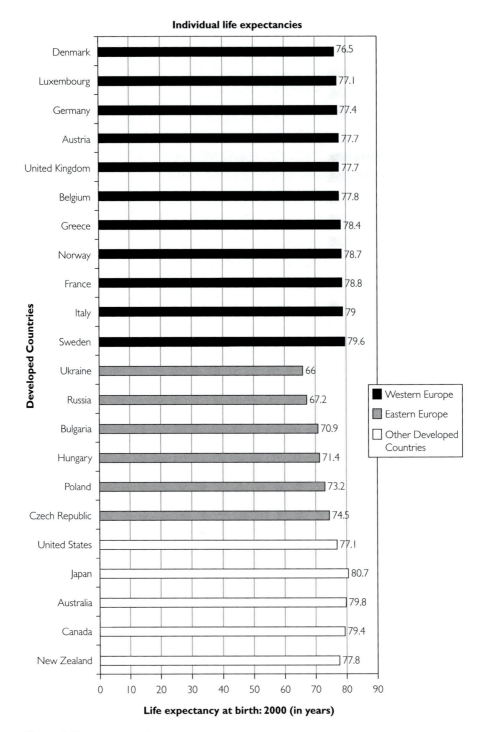

Figure 1.7a *Individual life expectancies.*
Source: Kinsella and Velkoff, 2001.

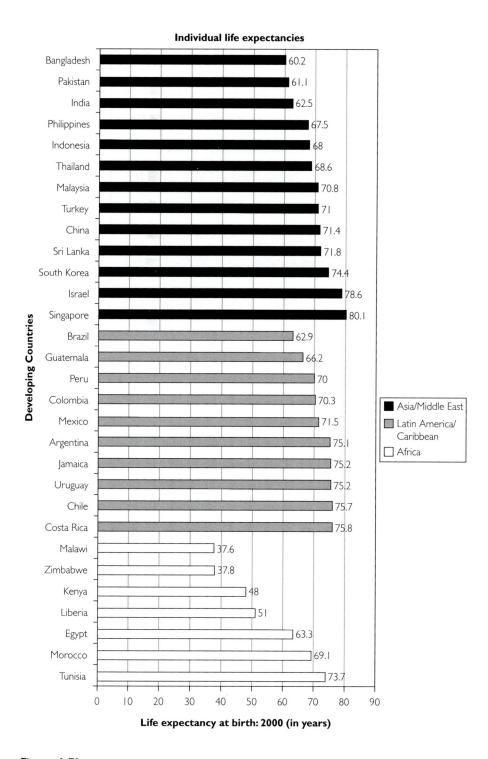

Individual life expectancies

Developing Countries

Bangladesh	60.2
Pakistan	61.1
India	62.5
Philippines	67.5
Indonesia	68
Thailand	68.6
Malaysia	70.8
Turkey	71
China	71.4
Sri Lanka	71.8
South Korea	74.4
Israel	78.6
Singapore	80.1
Brazil	62.9
Guatemala	66.2
Peru	70
Colombia	70.3
Mexico	71.5
Argentina	75.1
Jamaica	75.2
Uruguay	75.2
Chile	75.7
Costa Rica	75.8
Malawi	37.6
Zimbabwe	37.8
Kenya	48
Liberia	51
Egypt	63.3
Morocco	69.1
Tunisia	73.7

Legend:
■ Asia/Middle East
▨ Latin America/ Caribbean
□ Africa

Life expectancy at birth: 2000 (in years)

Figure 1.7b

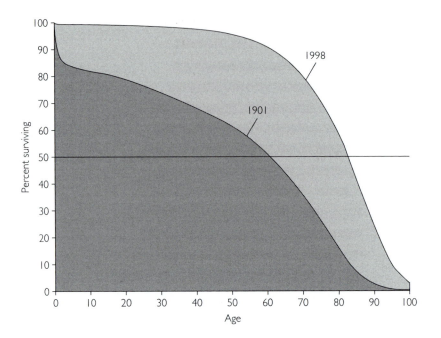

Figure 1.8 *Survival curve for US females 1901–98.*
Source: Adapted from An Aging World, 2001.

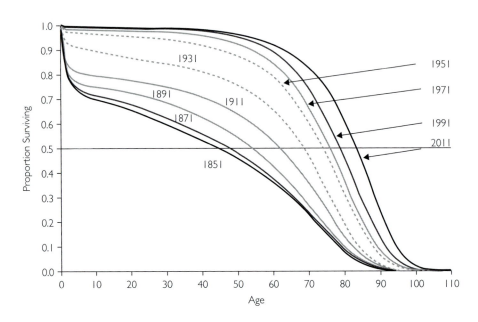

Figure 1.9 *Rectangularisation of UK survival curve 1851–2011.*
Source: Adrian Gallop, Government Actuaries Department, UK.

marriage and at remarriage, at leaving the parental home, at first childbirth. While public and legal institutions may be lowering the age threshold into full legal adulthood, individuals themselves are choosing to delay many of those transitions which demonstrate a commitment to full adulthood – full economic independence from parents, formal adult union through marriage or committed long-term cohabitation, and parenting. It can be argued, for example, that because early death through disease, war, famine and (for women) reproduction is no longer the common experience, individuals feel more comfortable about establishing marital unions later in life and bearing children later.

Ageing societies/Ageing individuals

Falling fertility and increasing longevity have led to the demographic ageing of all Western industrialised societies. As discussed earlier, this awareness of demographic ageing of the developed world has brought with it the *demographic burden hypothesis*, leading to a variety of public myths. For, as the press is constantly reminding us, dramatic population ageing over the next 30 years will cause national health care systems to collapse, economies to crumple under the strain of pension demands, and disintegrating families to buckle under increasing care commitments. The following discussion examines the evidence behind these myths. It is important that both individuals, who are facing increasing life expectancies within demographically ageing societies, and governments and policy influencers understand the reality of the demographic issues in order to plan and develop societal frameworks and policies appropriate for the demographic challenges and opportunities ahead.

For example, the provision of health care for older people is but one component of the future. In contrast to much public belief, many of us will live out much of the remainder of our lives in reasonable health, with limited disability. Indeed, around 90 per cent of individuals can expect to live out their lives without significant disability or need for help with daily activities.[4] A mature society then is not a society of long-term care beds and nursing homes, though there will clearly be some increased demand for these as the demographic bulge referred to earlier passes through the population but this will then settle. A mature population is one of healthy, active mature individuals able to contribute actively to their society, its productive and reproductive activities. Let us briefly consider the myths, before turning to the challenges and opportunities which lie ahead, in particular in relation to the two issues that provide a framework for most people's lives – work and family relationships.

Demographic ageing and health care provision

It is a component of current political rhetoric that health services thoughout the Western world are collapsing under the strain of demographic ageing. In the late 1990s, industrialised countries devoted quite large proportions of GDP to health care, ranging from 7 per cent in the UK to 14 per cent in the United States. However, there is a universal desire to limit government and private expenditures for health care while improving health care outcomes, thereby ensuring that health care productivity is an important policy issue as we move into the twenty-first century.

Policy makers in much of Europe have expressed deep concerns with regard to the increasing pressure on health and social care costs arising from the demographic ageing of their populations.[5] In the United States too, the fear of ageing baby boomers and their health and social care needs has been a recurrent theme of debate and research.[6] Long-term US forecasts predict that by the year 2030 almost 33 per cent of GDP will be accounted for by health care.[7]

However, as Leeson[8] has pointed out, although a number of cross-national studies have considered the determinants of health care costs, only one has found that the *age structure* of the population, that is the proportion of population aged 65 and over being taken as the age structure indicator, is an explanatory factor alongside the effects of *income*, *lifestyle characteristics*, and *environmental factors*. Grimley-Evans goes as far as to suggest that longevity achieved by the right mechanisms will actually reduce the cost of care in later life.[9] Part of the false rhetoric lies with the methodologies used in some research studies.[10] As Seshamani and Gray[11] have shown, attempts to investigate the effects of demographics on health care expenditure have often simply linked chronological age and the use and/or cost of health care services. These patterns are then applied to the demographics of a population changing over time to assess the effect of these changing demographics on the use and cost of health care services. The results imply that age contributes between 0.3 and 0.8 per cent of annual expenditure growth.[12] This simple and illustrative way of assessing the age-cost effects, however, ignores the fact that age-specific utilisation patterns among different age groups change over time. Changing demographics is not the only dynamic factor in the equation.

Analysis of OECD data[13] reveals that in developed countries, per capita health care costs for those aged 65 years and over have increased at the same rate as for those aged less than 65 years. Actual health care expenditures have increased disproportionately among the very old.[14] As Seshamani and Gray,[15] however, point out, a number of studies have emphasised that the observed relationship between health care expenditure and age can be explained by the concentration of health care expenditure in the period immediately prior to death.[16] In other words, the higher health costs associated with older age groups need not be linked to age but rather to the increasing proximity of death.

If we turn to examine individual countries, we see that there are different dynamics operating within different systems. Within the USA, a growing elderly population means particularly large increases in both Medicaid and Medicare expenditure. Hospital and physician expenses relating to those over age 65 are covered almost universally by Medicare. A second means-tested programme, Medicaid, provides medical care to eligible persons of all ages and is a major contributor to nursing home expenses for the elderly population. The forecast large public expenditure is due to the high level of health care expenditures in the USA in general, and the private–public division of health care insurance provision that shifts most of the population from private to public sources of payment at age 65.[17] The feared Medicare crisis in the USA, therefore, can be attributed not to the increasing numbers of old people *per se* but increasing per capita health care expenditures, combined with a policy framework which makes these a public liability. Furthermore, forecasters predict a long-term decline in the prevalence of disability in the USA.[18] Measuring future rates of disability is controversial, yet if these predictions are correct, then there will be significant savings in the Medicare budget from this factor alone.[19]

Age-related health care costs form an even smaller component of the explanation for rising health care costs in the UK. The UK does not exhibit the general OECD pattern of per capita health care costs for those aged 65 years and over increasing at the same rate as for those aged less than 65. Rather, there is a disproportionately smaller increase in per capita costs for the older ages compared with younger age groups.[20] In contrast to the findings of previous studies, for example, Seshamani and Gray found that in the period 1985–87 to 1996–99 in England and Wales, the older age groups, 65 years and over, did not have larger increases in their health care costs than the middle age groups. On the contrary, for combined National Health Service care costs and for hospital and community health service costs, the oldest old, aged 85 years and over, actually had *decreases* in their real per capita costs.

This means that the proportion of National Health care expenditure allocated to the older age groups has decreased over time. The authors point out that this levelling out of expenditure allocation is mainly a result of moving costs away from the older population for non-acute hospital care. They argue that the different patterns of cost-change for different age groups among the health care sectors reflect differing health service needs of the different age groups, different patient management schemes in the different sectors, decreased access to care for older patients, and a shifting of older patients from non-acute hospital and community health services to other social care settings such as residential and nursing homes. This is substantiated by other research which shows that the market value of the nursing and residential care sector for older people increased by 43 per cent from 1988 to 1998 while the value of long-stay hospital care in the National Health Service decreased by 52 per cent.[21] As Leeson concludes,[22] costs have been reduced through service substitution out of the National Health Service. Baily and Garber[23] thus argue that the UK governmental system of health care financing and provision is relatively well positioned to implement integrated programmes for managing chronic diseases, while under-investment in new (and old) technologies may impair productivity. They suggest that flexibility in the organisation of care, together with competition among providers and appropriate incentives, is likely to promote productivity.

Finally, there is the argument that medical spending is highest in the last few years before death. So, as a population ages, most of the lifespan beyond age 65 mirrors that of those adults under age 65, and so it is not the number of people over the age of 65 that is of importance, but the number in the last years of life.[24] The ageing of the population thus shifts the costs into progressively older ages, rather than significantly increasing total medical care expenditure.[25]

To conclude, the predicted increases in medical and health care costs are not as a result of growing numbers of older people *per se*, but as a result of *current policy frameworks* within which these costs will occur. This is a recurrent theme throughout the book – we need to assess current frameworks to allow adaptation to a shifting in the demographic composition of the population.

Demographic ageing and the economy

There is real concern that the ageing of populations will bring with it serious fiscal issues. As Peter Heller of the International Monetary Fund notes, many studies suggest that the ageing of industrial populations will add greatly to the burden of public expenditure, principally through a sharp growth in real spending on pensions, health care and long-term residential care.[26] However, he then goes on to state:

> Although some of the rising burden can be attributed to the underlying dynamic, in many countries, of slowing real economic growth accompanied by a shrinking labour force . . . the fiscal pressures in fact originate from *the existing framework of social insurance* in many countries.[27] (Harper emphasis)

As with health care costs, it is not demographic ageing *per se*, but current policy frameworks and other social and economic factors associated with these which are the real factors here:

> One dimension of this is . . . the commitment to generous public pensions . . . structured to facilitate retirement at or around age 65, if not earlier (despite rising longevity), and starting pension benefits are roughly indexed to wage at retirement.[28]

Many studies rely on the current measures of dependency ratios, that is workers to dependants, and current retirement rates,[29] rather than acknowledging that these are period- and cohort-specific and can themselves be changed. The argument is reiterated by Dalmer Hoskins, Secretary-General of the International Social Security Association:

> Demographic ageing is causing considerable concern, if not alarm, in many circles. Yet the public debate about the future of social security is often lacking in accurate and objective information. It is easier to focus on the 'burden' of ageing on society than attempt to better understand the complex, interrelated nature of the issues involved, especially the rising number of persons of working age who are inactive and contributing neither taxes nor social security contributions.[30]

A further concern is a slowdown in growth due to fewer younger people working and consuming. However, as will become clear, if individuals continue to be economically active, then their consumption rates and patterns will also change. Currently, considerable consumption behaviour of those over age 50 is centred on leisure activities rather than on consumable goods. If an individual remains within the labour market throughout their sixties, then it is very likely that they will choose to spend later life income on household consumable goods. For example, consumer goods which they purchased in their twenties and thirties will have a limited lifespan. Again, there needs to be a change in societal perceptions of older cohorts and their predicted patterns of behaviour, which can then be capitalised upon by marketing avenues. Already key marketing and consumer organisations are beginning to realise this.

The main concerns, therefore, that exist in relation to demographic ageing and the economy are high public spending on pensions; high dependency ratios between workers and non-workers; and a slowdown in consumption due to an increase in older people and a decrease in younger people.

All three concerns, however, are dynamics of current cohorts and the current time period, they are not fixed. Two factors in particular are worth noting – generous public pension systems which allow healthy active potentially productive individuals to retire, with the expectation that they will be supported in this retirement for up to 40 years, and a society which discriminates on stereotypical grounds against older workers, increasingly defined as those over the age of 50, and not only allows but encourages them to withdraw from economic activity up to 40 years before the expected end of their lives. Both these are recent phenomena, and both can and need to be constructively tackled so that limited resources can be effectively used to support frail late life individuals at the end of their lives.

This relates to another linked myth, one which compounds the policy challenge – that older people are unproductive potential burdens on society, and that this commences at age 50. Indeed, several authors contend that the high levels of early withdrawal by workers is partially motivated by continued negative perceptions of older workers.[31] Despite the fact that there is little practical evidence to support the view that those over age 50 are consistently less able to perform modern economic activity than those younger,[32] such stereotypically views remain, are widely published in the popular press and other outlets,[33] and appear to impact upon employer behaviour.[34] Slow work speed, low adaptability, particularly to new technologies, low trainability, low skills uptake, and too cautious, are all stereotypes expressed by employers.[35] The perception that age and characteristics are related appears embedded in our current societal perceptions. North American research,[36] for example, reports that while older workers are rated more highly in terms of academic skills, ability to get along with co-workers, willingness to take directions, work ethic, productivity and supervisory skills, younger workers are rated more highly in terms of computer skills, stamina and energy, flexibility and ability to learn quickly. Such stereotypical attributes are similarly described by Arrowsmith and McGoldrick[37] for the UK in terms of qualitative and quantitative characteristics. Older workers are perceived to retain the former, such as high quality of service, pride in job, cheerfulness, reliability, while younger workers exhibit so-called quantitative characteristics, such as fast pace of work, trainability, adept at handling new technology.

As Harper has pointed out for the UK,[38] and Bird and Fisher for the USA,[39] these stereotypical attitudes within the two nations have shown no improvement since research carried out in the 1950s. In reality, laboratory-based research suggests there is negligible decline in physical and mental activity which would impact upon activities of daily living, between the ages of 20 and 70 and, in general, variations *within* age groups far exceed those *between* age groups.[40] However, there are clearly fixed stereotypical attitudes towards older workers and a general perception that they are unproductive in relation to younger cohorts. We shall return to this again in Chapter 10.

The dynamics we need to address are why healthy active adults are retiring from work when they can contribute (something we shall examine in detail in Chapter 4), and how countries can respond most effectively to the need to reform their pension systems so that the resources are available to support the most needy in society. We shall assess some of the required fiscal policy changes in more detail in Chapter 5, but the message is clear – industrialised countries will not be burdened by the changing demographics *per se* but by *their inability or unwillingness to acknowledge the necessity of adapting fiscal and social policies to the changing social and cultural attributes and health profiles of upcoming cohorts.*

Complex policy measures are difficult to implement. However, research in the 1990s was already indicating the impact quite simple adjustments would make. For example, increases in the early and normal retirement age can have a significant effect on the long-term costs of public pensions. Thus increasing the US early retirement age from 62 to 67, and the normal retirement age to 70, would eliminate the long-term deficit in the US public pension system.[41] While simple to calculate, such adjustments, as we shall see in Chapter 5, are of course more complex to implement.

Indeed, as Heller argues, governments should carefully calculate the long-run implications of their existing programmes, focusing on core public goals; existing programmes in the areas of pensions and medical care must adapt to changing circumstances. That much of this is reliant on government will become clearer when we examine national policies in more detail. The European Commission, for example, has highlighted a projected public spending increase from 4 per cent to 8 per cent GDP over the next 40 years.[42] However, as it admits, several countries are already introducing comprehensive strategies in response to forthcoming demographic predictions, while others are failing in their policy response by applying only piecemeal approaches, so that currently Germany and France will face debt levels which exceed 200 per cent GDP by 2050, while by the same year the UK and Sweden will have actually accumulated net general government assets exceeding their respective GDP.

By seeking to change the time path of future programme expenditures, governments have a better chance of being time consistent in their policies and can focus on those commitments they can reasonably honour, and thus create sufficient fiscal leeway to adapt and respond to uncertain challenges. Heller, for example, notes Swedish and Italian efforts to incorporate self-activating adjustments in the parameters of their pension programmes to respond to increases in life expectancy as important examples.

What is clear is that countries have many long-term problems in common and this requires a consideration of the global macroeconomic imbalances which could arise. How industrial economies address their demographic problems will have important consequences for the global economy. Yet, as we shall see, these issues are not of concern just to ageing industrial countries. Of particular interest is how large changes in national age distributions will affect wider economic issues such as national saving patterns, capital requirements and international capital flows, particularly between the developed and the developing world.[43]

> They will be very much on the policy agenda of emerging markets, transition economies and developing countries in every region of the world. Certainly the issues to be faced, the strategic approaches that will work, and the weight to attach to policies affecting different generations will differ across the regions and countries as their incomes differ. But the gathering force of these long-term developments[44] is worldwide in its scope and it is a force that the world community cannot any longer ignore.[45]

Demographic change and families

The third public fear is that we shall all increasingly live in loose, multigenerational families, as individuals becoming emotionally distant from our kin as we lose our range of horizontal relatives. In addition, emotional strain will rise within these families as large numbers of older people become reliant on decreasing numbers of children to care for them in a dependent old age. We have already indicated that the stereotype of old age as a long period of inactive disability is false, so let us now briefly examine some of the realities of modern families.

Firstly, it is true that the emphasis on the family as a mode of social organisation has been significantly reduced over the past century by a combination of economic, social and ideological developments. This model whereby kin groups pooled their resources and related to the community as an intact unit, has been replaced by greater emphasis on the individual as a unit of social control. As Fry[46] has summarised, in small-scale egalitarian societies, parents and children remain interdependent all of their lives, with kinship networks and their economic activity providing individuals with a safety net. Parents control children in the interest of their kin units. In contrast, within large-scale capitalist societies based on wage labour and market economies, families are only a part of a wider safety net. Relationships between parents and children are thus transformed from those based on economic interdependence to those of companionship, friendship and intimacy. As Waite[47] notes, the shift from family-based to wage-based employment has loosened the kin connection to property and marriage, encouraging individual autonomy in many of these decisions. In addition, urbanisation and technological change have produced new forms of communication, social intercourse and entertainment, reducing the significance of that provided by the family.

Similarly, within the family unit itself, the roles and responsibilities of kin members have been questioned in the light of the widespread emergence and consolidation of a variety of new family forms within many industrialised societies. Within Europe, for example, the nuclear family now represents around three-quarters of kin-based households, alongside reconstituted or recombinant stepfamilies, single parent families and cohabiting couples. There is also increasing recognition of the growing number of ethnic minority families, whose kinship roles and relationships differ from those of the majority white populations.

In addition, the ageing of the population itself has implications for both family structure and individual kinship roles. Early work on ageing and the family was clearly focused on the demographic implications of early demographic predications.[48] In other words, increasing longevity equalled increasing numbers of older people requiring care. At the same time, declining fertility was perceived as shrinking the reservoir of family care for the old, and placing increasing pressures on the middle-aged coping both with dependent children and ageing parents. The complexity of the equation is now clearer, as well as the recognition that the environments which were producing ageing societies were also producing new family situations, and that the demise or shrinking of the family due to ageing societies was too general a concept – rather more heterogeneous family forms were emerging. We have long recognised that historically the extended family and the household are not the same,[49] and it is unlikely, in Western industrial societies at least, that the increase in living generations will result in a return to the multigenerational households seen early last century. We now need also to acknowledge that the nuclear family and household are increasingly disjointed units. Even within conventional nuclear family units, there are a growing number of family/household combinations, and the life course experience of family roles and relationships for any individual is fragmented into many possible combinations.

As the nuclear family structure becomes increasingly replaced by alternative structures, proponents of the theory of family disintegration argue that the social institution of the family as an agent of socialisation for younger members and a source of nurture and companionship for all is also being destroyed.[50] However, this has been questioned by both feminist and post-modern writers, and family sociologists, who point out that the traditional nuclear family is actually ill-suited for a post-modern society,[51] and alternative forms are emerging which include an increase in multigenerational relationships[52] and members not formerly defined as kin.[53] Thus, as Waite[54] has recently pointed out, in contemporary industrial societies, the family still retains responsibility for reproduction, socialisation, co-residence and transmission of property across the generations. It

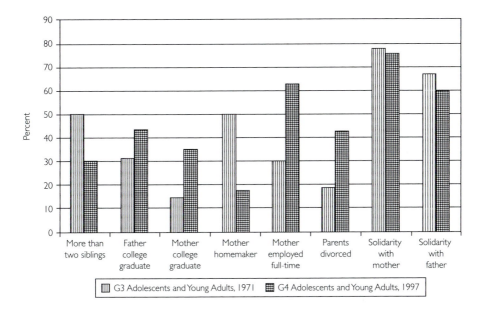

Figure 1.10   *Historical changes in family structure and parental attributes: generation X compared with their baby-boomer parents at the same age.*
Source: Bengtson, 2001.

is also a major unit of consumption, and still provides the majority of support and care to older adults,[55] and almost all the financial, emotional and instrumental support to children. Similarly, as we shall explore, extensive work in the USA[56] and Europe[57] continues to reveal the strong sense of obligation held between the generations, despite significant changes in family structures.

Questions do arise, however, concerning the roles and responsibilities for individuals within these new family forms, in particular the manner in which social and economic resources are being transferred between the generations, and the effect these new structures have on the negotiation and carrying out of reciprocal care between individuals, especially care for dependent adults.

In terms of the first concern, longitudinal work in the USA has revealed that intergenerational transmission from parents to children remains strong. Bengtson draws on the 30-year Longitudinal Study of Generations[58] to explore the effects of changing family structures on intergenerational influences. As Fig. 1.10 illustrates, Generation X (G4), i.e. those aged 18–22 in 1997, experienced different family structures and characteristics from baby boomers (G3) at the same age in 1971.

Generation X were more likely to have grown up in a home with less than two siblings, with a father and a mother who were both college graduates, and with a mother who was working full-time. Twice as many grew up in divorced households. Despite these differences, however, the results of analysis of how the two generations compared in terms of family solidarity suggested that they were surprisingly similar on these measures. In particular, family transmission processes, social learning and parental affirmation occur in a strikingly similar manner between the two cohorts, with maternal attachment remaining especially strong. Indeed, among nuclear families these appear to have increased. Bengtson and colleagues thus concluded that, despite changes in family structure and socio-economic context, intergenerational influences remained strong, and alternative and multi-generational families were performing the functions of nuclear families where necessary.[59]

The second concern, over failing obligations between generations to care for dependent adults, has been widely studied in various European countries. Although sophisticated studies, able to examine cohort, age and period effects, are limited, there are indications from cross-sectional work of at least an intention to maintain future family obligations towards older kin. In France, for example, despite government fears of a breakdown in family solidarity, 80 per cent of middle-aged children said they would provide for needy parents and parents-in-law through the provision of housing, or care in the parents' own house.[60] Scandinavian research has highlighted the importance of kinship within a modern welfare state, reporting that there was both increased contact with family members and a significant move towards a more positive view of the family as a supportive institution.[61] Similarly, studies in southern European countries[62] have all highlighted that women are motivated by the strong moral imperative within society to take care of older kin, with indications that this is being transferred to younger generations.

We can explore this in more detail using the Danish Longitudinal Future Study (a panel study running since 1987) as an illustration. While most people in Denmark feel that the care and support of older people is a public sector responsibility, the family continues to contribute practical help and support. During the post-war period, many aspects of the caregiving role of the family in Denmark were professionalised and became the responsibility of the public sector. An increasing proportion of the country's resources was needed to provide care, security and social support for its citizens. Towards the end of the twentieth century, privatisation took on an ever increasing role, with private pension schemes, privatisation of care and health insurance.[63] There has been an expectation that the high profile role adopted by the state might reduce the propensity of the family to care. However, a supportive familial network can be crucial for an older person's ability to cope, and even in well-developed welfare states the family can have a supportive role for older people.[64]

Drawing on data from the Danish Longitudinal Future Study, Leeson outlines the patterns of children, siblings, contact and support (see Table 1.3). The study started with four cohorts aged 40–44, 50–54, 60–64 and 70–74. In 1997 these had reached 50–54, 60–64, 70–74 and 80–84 years respectively and a new 40–44 year old cohort was added.

Nearly one-third of the youngest cohort (40–44) are childless,[65] compared with only 18 per cent of the oldest (70–74). However, those in this latter cohort that do have children have large families, with just under one half having three children or more compared

Table 1.3 *Danish Longitudinal Future Study,[66] 1987–2003 (Wave 1 (1987) and Wave 2 (1997) – characteristics, family contactonel attitudes.*

	Cohort			
	40–44	**50–54**	**60–64**	**70–74**
Born in	1953–57	1943–47	1933–37	1923–27
Average no. of annual live births	77000	92000	65000	72000
Population size (millions)	4.4	4.0	3.7	3.4
Total fertility at age 25 years	1.54	2.03	2.53	2.58
Life expectancy at birth M/F	69.8/72.6	65.6/67.7	62.0/63.8	60.3/61.9

	Cohort			
	70–74	**60–64**	**50–54**	**40–44**
Contact with child:				
At least once a week				
1987		40	48	68
1997	73	77	84	83
Less than once a week				
1987		60	52	32
1997	27	23	15	17

	Cohort			
	70–74	**60–64**	**50–54**	**40–44**
The family can provide better support than is available elsewhere:				
1987		84	84	81
1997	89	90	87	79

Source: Leeson, 2005.

with only 13 per cent of those aged 40–44. As further reflection of the changes in family formation patterns, 26 per cent of the three younger cohorts have children from a previous relationship compared with only 13 per cent of the oldest cohort. The cohort-specific differences are equally striking with regard to spouse's/partner's children from a previous relationship, where the proportion ranges from 21 per cent of the youngest to only 5 per cent of the oldest cohort having such children in their family. Of equal interest is the presence of siblings. Cohort fertility and mortality levels determine the number of (surviving) siblings. Mortality over the life course determines that 22 per cent of the 70–74 year olds have no (surviving) siblings compared with less than 11 per cent among the other three younger cohorts. On the other hand, both mortality and fertility determine that 12 per cent of the 70–74 year olds have a large number of surviving siblings, five or more, twice the percentage of the youngest cohort of 40–44 year olds.

The study also reveals an increase in contact with both non-resident children and siblings between 1987 and 1997 and, perhaps most surprising in the light of the strong welfare state paradigm, a significant move towards a more positive view of the family as a supportive institution. Indeed, all cohorts have moved towards more contact and a more positive attitude indicating that this represents a general move in the population as a whole and not just in specific cohorts or age groups – in other words, we are seeing a period effect. As Leeson points out, given the highly diverse range of adult unions in Denmark, and the prevailing fear that such familial complexities may not provide the supportive networks required for elder caregiving and support, such findings are reassuring. While there may be a trend towards looser-knit, divorce-extended families, the importance of the family in Denmark as a supportive institution is not weakening – on the contrary it appears to be strengthening.

Such evidence then questions the growing public concern that families are becoming less willing to provide care for older relatives. Research suggests an adaptation by kin to the more fluid family structures, a continuation of close kin and intergenerational ties, and even in some cases an increase in attachment. As we shall see in Chapter 11, there are various other indications that families are remaining strong supportive networks. Indeed, given that grandparents occupy an 'expanding' position within the family,[67] reciprocal caregiving by kin is, if anything, increasing.

Demographic change and development

We return to our fourth myth, that it is the developed world which will face the biggest burden of increased population ageing. In reality, it is the developing countries who are truly facing the massive challenge of unprecedented ageing (Fig. 1.11). While the industrialised countries do have the social and economic infrastructure to support those frail and dependent elderly people who are unable to support themselves economically, albeit one that needs to be modified, developng countries are confronting a rapid expansion of their older populations with few or no public institutions or regimes to support them.

The massive scale of ageing facing these countries is potentially devastating with 1 billion older people predicted within 15 years. Currently almost two-thirds of the world's older population live in developing countries, with the absolute numbers of older people in these regions estimated to more than double to reach some 1 billion in 2030. The numbers are truly staggering – there are 47 million Africans over the age of 60, 49 million live in Latin America and the Caribbean and already 370 million live in the Asian/Pacific region. Perhaps most significant of all is the speed at which these countries are ageing. The demographic transition which took between 100 and 150 years in the developed world will occur in less than 50 years in these countries. As Fig. 1.1 illustrates on p. 6, while it took around 50 to 70 years for most of the countries in the developed

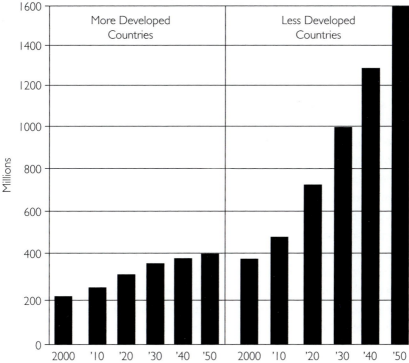

World population 60 and over: 2000—2050

world to move from 7 per cent to 14 per cent of their population over age 65 (in the case of Sweden, 85 years and France, 115 years), many developing countries will achieve this in half the time, averaging 23 or 24 years. In 45 years time there will be 2 billion older people, three-quarters of whom will live in the developing world. Such countries will be faced not so much with supporting large numbers of active healthy retired people, but frail dependent elders in real need. Many of these countries are yet to establish even minimal social insurance schemes, and face real challenges.

Yet, older people are among the poorest in every developing country. They have the lowest levels of income, education and literacy, they lack savings, assets and land, have few skills or capital to invest in productive activity, and have only limited access to labour, pensions or other benefits. They are often in poor health, with high levels of frailty, and face inadequate or inaccessible health services. In addition, depending on their personal circumstances, local cultural norms or specific national factors, they may have large numbers of dependants, or alternatively lack family and community support. While there has long been a recognition that in a context of limited resources and programmes, highest priority must be given to older people who are alone and vulnerable,[68] the numbers in such circumstances are considerable, and beyond current available resources. Particularly vulnerable, for example, are those living in areas ravaged by war or civil unrest, who find themselves isolated and displaced, their families dislocated, and themselves without access to basic needs such as pensions or health and welfare services. In addition, while older people are especially vulnerable in times of environmental crisis or civil strife, post-emergency programmes often focus on younger people, at the expense of older adults. While older people may be among the most vulnerable populations in the world, governments confronted with huge challenges of mass poverty and deprivation have little capacity to shift scarce resources.

Health care provision for this population will therefore present a real challenge. In particular the *epidemiological transition* is now under way in all regions of the world, with a shift from predominantly infectious and parasitic diseases to chronic and degenerative diseases. One of the factors related to declining mortality rates in the developing world is a growth in long-term non-communicable diseases such as cardiovascular disease and cancer, and an increase in disability. Contrary to common perceptions, disabilities tend to be more prevalent in developing regions.[69] Indeed, almost half the disease burden in high-mortality regions of the world, is already attributable to non-communicable diseases, *the epidemic of non-communicable disease*[70] being accelerated by population ageing. In addition, most developing countries will have to face the double burden of communicable and non-communicable diseases.

The World Health Report 2003 vividly states the situation confronting the developing world, and the challenge to cope with the impact of demographic ageing alongside so many other existing demands on economies and social structures:

> For millions of children today, particularly in Africa, the biggest challenge is to survive until their fifth birthday, and their chances of doing so are less than they were a decade ago. This is a result of the continuing impact of communicable diseases. However, a global increase in non-communicable diseases is simultaneously occurring adding to the challenges . . . of the 45 million deaths among adults aged 15 and over in 2002, 32 million, or almost three quarters, were caused by non-communicable diseases, which killed almost four times as many people as communicable diseases and maternal, perinatal and nutritional conditions . . . 3 in 4 adult deaths in Latin America and the developing countries of Asia and the Western Pacific are caused by non-communicable disease, reflecting the relatively advanced stage of the epidemiological transition achieved in these populations and the emergence of the double burden of disease.[71]

The World Health Report, 2003 identifies cardiovascular disease and lung cancer as two new major global epidemics, brought on not only by environmental factors, in particular smoking and diet, but also due to the fact that individuals are now living sufficiently long to develop them. These diseases are often perceived as developed world diseases brought on by Western lifestyles, yet more deaths from cardiovascular disease now occur in developing countries than in the developed world. These are being encouraged in part by the global marketing of tobacco and processed food products high in saturated fat, sugar and salt. As individuals live longer, they are more likely to develop these diseases. Yet, most health systems in these regions are struggling to address the heavy burden of acute diseases, including HIV/AIDS and tropical diseases, and tackle infant, child and maternal mortality, and have no spare capacity for developing much needed preventative and public health programmes, let alone long-term care strategies.

The second area of real concern is material security. Most people in developing counties have no prospect of a secure and sustainable income in their old age. Few, for example, have any access to public benefits. Even among workers few are covered by any public programme. In contrast to the 84 per cent of those over age 60 in OECD countries who receive a pension, the proportion drops to less than 20 per cent in many Latin American countries, less than 10 per cent in South-east Asia, and under 5 per cent in parts of Sub-Saharan Africa. It is not only political impetus that is missing; there are substantial practical problems in extending formal insurance coverage to workers in both rural and informal sectors, ranging from lack of adequate record keeping enabling the identification of appropriate participants in these schemes through to the logistics of actual delivery of the cash benefits to such populations.[72] For while nearly every country has some form of social security coverage of older people, even in those countries with more developed systems there tend to be large sections of the workforce who are excluded from coverage.[73]

In summary, due to the rapid acceleration of ageing in developing countries, the demographic challenges, which European societies addressed over some 150 years – allowing time for the development of appropriate institutional frameworks and policies – will simultaneously confront governments in developing countries. Regions afflicted with acute poverty, famine and lack of access to basic sanitation and fresh water, are still grappling with high levels of infant and maternal mortality, and acute infectious diseases, while at the same time confronting the challenges of growth in non-communicable disease and the need for long-term care and economic security for a growing older population. Many of these countries have only scant public institutions and welfare regimes to cope with the current demographic profile of predominantly children and young adults, and are now facing the urgent necessity of developing appropriate institutions and regimes for the 1 billion older adults who will be surviving over the next 25 years.

Mature societies

There are clearly challenges ahead as we adjust to a more mature society. However, within the developed world, it is not ageing populations *per se* that are the main explanatory factors for pressures on the family, economy and health care services, rather the wider effects of rapid growth in standards of living, increased awareness of and demands for technology to assist in every aspect of our lives, and contemporary lifestyle characteristics. Furthermore, these changes are also occurring within specific policy frameworks, established at a time when the demographic composition of the population was different. As we shall argue, these policy frameworks need to be adjusted, and indeed already are being adjusted, to reflect the upcoming demographic shift.

While there are clearly numerous questions to be addressed concerning the maturing of societies, the following are particularly pertinent for our understanding of the reality behind the forthcoming predicted changes. In the following chapters we shall examine the available evidence:

- How did mass retirement, and in particular early retirement, evolve, how extensive is it, and is it likely to be reversed in the near future?

- What are the financial arrangements for supporting retired people in western countries, how do they vary, how dependent are they on the intergenerational contract and what are the likely future scenarios?

- How are western family structures, roles and relationships changing in response to demographic change?

- What are the current and future health and social care needs of ageing populations in the developed world, how dependent will these be on the provision of family and other informal care, and will families be able to sustain any increased demand due to changing individual life course trajectories and dispersed kin networks?

- What are appropriate strategies for providing health, social care and material security for older populations in the developing world in the context of existing family and community structures and severe competition for limited resources?

- Finally, how can we harness the experience, expertise and creativity of such an historically large number of older people, and create a mature age-integrated society?

The next two decades will provide a significant opportunity for governments to put in place a framework for a mature society. The reality of demographic ageing may be approached in different ways. We can accept that we shall have issues concerning increasing numbers and proportions of older people in our society over the next 40 years, introduce ameliorative policies and wait for a more age-symmetric population to arrive. We can attempt to manipulate our population structure by increasing births or immigration. Or, we can explore the many advantages of a society with a mature population, adapt to take full advantage of these opportunities, and work towards creating the framework for an age-symmetric society. It is this latter approach that governments should surely be pursuing – the opportunity to harness the experience, expertise and creativity of such an historically large number of older people.

Notes

1 HAI, 2002.
2 United Nations, 2005.
3 Much of the information on the age index, median ages and oldest old is provided by Kinsella and Velkoff, 2001.
4 Jacobzone, 1999.
5 Leeson, 2004b; Howse, 2005.
6 Lee and Skinner, 1999; Shoven et al., 1994; Howse, 2005.
7 Burner et al., 1992; Warshawsky, 1994.
8 Leeson, 2004b.
9 Grimley-Evans, 2003.
10 Petrou et al., 2000.
11 Seshamani and Gray, 2002.
12 OECD, 1988; Gerdtham, 1992; Barer et al., 1987.
13 Seshamani and Gray, 2002.
14 Gerdtham, 1992; Mendelson and Schwartz, 1993; Cutler and Meara, 1999; Barer et al., 1987.
15 Seshamani and Gray, 2002.
16 Lubitz and Riley, 1993; McGrail et al., 2000; Himsworth and Goldacre, 1999; Zweifel et al., 1999; O'Neill et al., 2000.
17 Henretta, 1998; Bosworth and Burtless, 1998.
18 For example, Manton et al., 1997; Freedman and Martin, 1998.
19 Leeson, 2004b.
20 Seshamani and Gray, 2002.
21 Laing and Buisson, 1999.
22 Leeson, 2004b.
23 Baily and Garber, 1997.
24 Grimley-Evans, 2003.
25 Heller, 2003.
26 ibid., Lee and Tuljapurkar, 2000; OECD, 2001a; European Commission, 2002.
27 Heller, 2003, p. 14.
28 ibid.
29 OECD, 2001a.
30 Hoskins, 2002.
31 Casey et al., 1992; Forte and Hansvick, 1999; Taylor and Walker, 1994.
32 Lindley, 1999.
33 Engineering Employers Federation, 2004; Lester, 2001; Gaster, 2002.
34 Taylor and Walker, 1994.
35 Casey et al., 1992.
36 Forte and Hansvick, 1999.
37 Arrowsmith and McGoldrick, 1996.
38 Harper, 1989.
39 Bird and Fisher, 1984.
40 Warr, 1994.
41 Bosworth and Burtless, 1998.
42 European Commission, 2002.
43 Bosworth and Burtless, 1998; Heller, 2003.
44 Heller is also considering in his analysis global climate change and terrorism.
45 Heller, 2003, p. 230.
46 Fry, 1999.
47 Waite and Bachrach, 2000.
48 Harper, 2004a.
49 Laslett and Wall, 1972.
50 Popenoe, 1993; Popenoe, 1996.
51 Stacey, 1996.
52 Bengtson, 2001.
53 ibid.
54 Hughes and Waite, 2004.
55 Logan and Spitze, 1996.
56 Bengtson, 2001.
57 Leeson, 2004c; Leeson, forthcoming.
58 Bengtson et al., 2002.
59 ibid.
60 Chwalow et al., 2001.
61 Leeson, 2004c; Leeson, forthcoming.
62 Larizgoitia-Jauregi, 2001; Figueiro and Sousa, 2001; Triantafillou and Mestheneos, 2001.
63 Leeson, 2005b.
64 Daatland, 1997.
65 Leeson, 2005b.
66 The study reveals similar patterns of cohort childlessness as the US Health and Retirement Survey (HRS, 2004).
67 Roberto and Stroes, 1995.
68 ESCAP, 1987.
69 WHO, 2003.
70 ibid., p. xii.
71 ibid., pp. 1, 13.
72 Schulz, 1999; see also ISSA, 1980.
73 SSA, 1997.

2
The dynamics of population ageing

Population ageing is the inevitable consequence of the classical demographic transition which began in Europe in the eighteenth and nineteenth centuries[1] and entailed first a decline in mortality over almost 150 years followed by a dramatic and fairly rapid decline in fertility. This was destined to age the populations of Europe. Clearly, an understanding of demographic ageing presupposes an understanding of past development and characteristics of the population. A population's contemporary characteristics are the result of past demographic behaviour in terms of fertility, mortality, migration, marriage patterns and the like. As well as the pure demographics of population development, there are short-term social or global events, war and the massive displacement of populations, for example, which can affect populations quite dramatically.

The demographic transition

Demographically, global development has become increasingly uneven since the onset of the demographic transition in Europe – beginning in France shortly after the French Revolution. In the eighteenth and nineteenth centuries, populations of the known world were characterised by high levels of both mortality and fertility and subsequently low levels of population growth. It was in this demographic climate towards the end of the eighteenth century, that Malthus put forward his theory of population,[2] whereby excessive growth would meet with checks in the form of epidemics and famines due to the limitations for food production. However, Malthus stood at the gateway of a revolution the implications of which he was unable to predict. Mortality was declining as a result of advances in medical science and improved sanitation, hygiene and housing. However, now populations across Europe could continue their geometric growth due to the industrialisation of agriculture and the opening up of the North Americas. Malthus's checks were thwarted. Food production could now grow geometrically, rather than arithmetically as Malthus had claimed, and was therefore able to keep up with population growth.

By the end of the nineteenth century, most of Europe's populations were experiencing the beginning of the demographic transition's continual fertility decline,[3] which would have dramatic and far-reaching consequences. By the 1930s–1940s, European fertility levels had fallen to replacement levels of 2.1 while mortality continued its decline. Natural

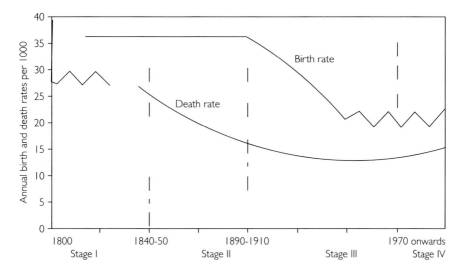

Figure 2.1   *The classic model of the four stages of demographic transition in Western Europe.*

population growth was approaching zero again and across Europe fertility declined even further in what has been termed the second demographic transition.[4]

As a result of this modern demographic cycle, over some 200 years European populations multiplied fourfold, life expectancies increased from approximately 35 years to approximately 75 years, total fertility rates declined from five to less than two, and crude birth and death rates declined from levels of 30–40 per thousand to only 10 per thousand population.

The process is best illustrated in the form of a graphic abstract model of transition (see Fig. 2.1). The mortality decline precedes the fertility decline, and in this phase the natural rate of increase reaches a maximum. As the fertility decline begins and accelerates, the two curves converge again and the natural rate of increase returns to a low level. As shown by the graphic illustration, it is implicitly assumed that once the continuous declines in mortality and fertility begin, they do not reverse.

There are some fundamental differences in the demographic transition in developing countries as illustrated in Fig. 2.2. The crude birth and death rates in stage I of the transition are at higher levels, and stage II (the decline to low mortality levels) appears to be much shorter.

The type A countries have experienced a mortality decline and a fertility decline, both of which are continuing in stage III. Type B countries, however, still have a high birth rate although their death rates have declined and are levelling off (but at a higher level than the type A countries).

Thus while the classical demographic transition has been completed in the developed countries of the world – and indeed some have begun a second demographic transition[5]

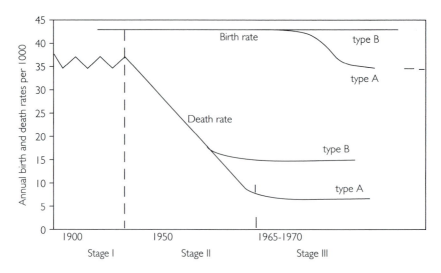

Figure 2.2   *The demographic transition model in developing countries.*

– developing countries find themselves at different stages of the transition: some have experienced continued fertility declines, others are just beginning and yet others show few if any signs of fertility decline.

The secular shift in ageing

The demographic transition throughout the Western world has consisted of falling fertility and mortality rates; the ageing of these populations during demographic transition is a second-order demographic effect. Falling mortality leads initially to an increase in the proportion of younger people in a population because it tends to impact first on infant mortality. Falling infant mortality then becomes a contributory factor to falling fertility. A large continuous fall in fertility leads to an increase in the proportion of older adults. Continuing falling mortality leads later to an increase in longevity. Furthermore, life expectation increases proportionately as individuals age from birth, and the proportions of those in later and later ages increases as societies age.

The trends towards longer life expectancy and higher proportions of older people are described in Table 2.1. While the dramatic ageing of populations is a quite recent phenomenon, having commenced in the twentieth century, the increase in life expectancy is not new. It is the speed of recent changes which is striking. More modest and less rapid increases from the ages in the low thirties in the seventeenth century to those in the low fifties took as long as 300 years.[6] In England life expectancy at birth increased during the twentieth century by around two-thirds for both men and women.[7] During this time the proportion of adults who were aged over 60 increased twofold. If we take the statistics back to 1540, the earliest reliable data available for

Table 2.1 *Expectation of life at birth and proportion over age 60, England 1541–1991*

Year	Expectation of life at birth		% over 60	
1541	33.75		8.67	
1591	35.51		7.93	
1641	33.70		8.27	
1691	34.87		9.06	
1741	31.70		8.11	
1791	37.33		7.41	
1841	40.28		6.58	
	Male	**Female**	**Male**	**Female**
1891	41.9	45.7	6.9	7.8
1911	49.4	53.4	7.3	8.6
1931	58.4	62.4	10.7	12.3
1951	66.2	71.2	14.6	17.7
1971	68.8	75.0	15.9	21.9
1991	70.1	78.3	16.5	23.1

Source: Data provided in Laslett (1995) using data from Wrigley and Schofield, 1981.

England, we find a doubling of life expectancy at birth, and a trebling of the proportions over age 60.[8]

Much of our detailed understanding of the impact of declining mortality and population ageing has come from the meticulous work of the population historian Peter Laslett. He identified a *secular shift in ageing*[9] whereby populations moved from a low plateau in terms of ageing to a high one (Fig. 2.3).

While the early and future years are reconstructions and projections, it is clear from the actual English data analysed (1530–1990s) that the steepest climb in both graphs took place between the 1920s and 1950s.

As Laslett concludes:

> Although they were subject to quite sharp fluctuations in life expectancy at birth – and here the effects of epidemics, wars and food shortages spring to mind – our ancestors never seem to have been subject to ageing changes on anything like the scale that has been experienced by the populations going through the secular shift. Recovery in duration of life was rapid after episodes of disasters . . . proportions of elderly persons in the population remained fairly constant, showing the same tendency to revert to the average after rises and falls, for centuries on end.[10]

However, as the analysis by Wrigley and Schofield[11] reminds us, between the 1540s and the end of the nineteenth century, the proportion of people over age 60 fluctuated

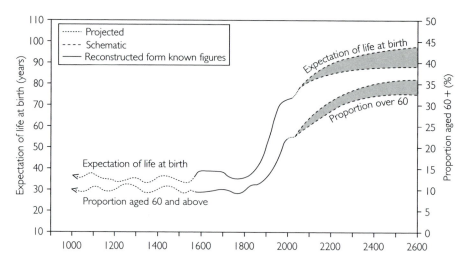

Figure 2.3 *Secular shift in ageing, England 1000–2600.*
Source: Laslett, 1975.

between 7 per cent and 10 per cent of the total population, but this depended crucially on falls and rises in fertility, which in turn appear to have been related to fluctuations in the age of marriage. As a percentage of the adult population, those over age 60 ranged between 12 per cent and 20 per cent during these centuries. Similarly, Weiss[12] noted in the early 1980s that in terms of life expectancy, the actual years added to late life since primitive times have been around 12 years for a 50 year old.

It is interesting to note that life expectation increases proportionately as we age from birth. As we see from Table 2.2, life expectancy for men in 2000 was 75 more years, that is to age 75; at age 50, 28 more years, to age 78, at age 60, 20 more years, to age 80, and at age 80, 7 more years, to age 87. The longer we live, the longer we can expect to live! In addition, since the early 1980s there have been advances in extending later years.

Another key factor here is the apparent compression of morbidity at the end of life. While still debated, recent work, especially by Manton in the USA, has significantly added to the data supporting this hypothesis. During the time before the secular shift, sickness and death were distributed across the whole life course; since the secular shift, there has been a tendency towards postponement, and, if we follow Fries' theory, when societies settle in the high plateau sickness and death will be concentrated in a very short period before death. If this model was to occur, the survival curve would eventually become rectangular (see Chapter 1, Fig. 1.9). The point being made here is that, while caution needs to be taken, the consistent and upward trend in both societal and individual late life ageing is clearly established for Europe at least.

Kreager has recently highlighted the need to consider demographic ageing not only as the outcome of fertility and mortality decline, but also in terms of *age structural transi-*

Table 2.2 *Life expectancies at certain ages in the United Kingdom, males and females, 1980–2000*

	Age 0		Age 50		Age 60		Age 80	
	M	**F**	**M**	**F**	**M**	**F**	**M**	**F**
1980	70.8	76.9	24.1	29.2	16.3	20.8	5.8	7.5
1985	71.7	77.6	24.9	29.8	16.8	21.2	6.0	7.8
1990	72.9	78.6	26.0	30.6	17.7	21.9	6.4	8.2
1995	74.0	79.2	26.7	31.1	18.4	22.3	6.5	8.4
1999	75.0	79.8	27.6	31.6	19.2	22.8	6.8	8.5
2000	75.3	80.1	27.9	31.8	19.5	23.0	7.0	8.6

Source: Recent Demographic Developments in Europe 2000, Council of Europe and Office of National Statistics.

tion.[13] Drawing on the work of Pool,[14] he notes that *structural ageing*, the shift to higher proportions of the population at older ages, should be seen as a final phase of the wider and more complex process of demographic transition, which is a major set of social and demographic determinants in its own right:

> Once we consider a transitional population's changing age structure as a whole, rising proportions of elderly are only one of a number of alterations in relative cohort size which interact with each other. Significantly smaller and larger birth cohorts, for example, may be expected to have 'wave' or 'echo effects' as their size comes to be reflected in fertility patterns when they reach childbearing years. Long-term oscillations in cohort size are only one issue.[15]

World population prospects

Of course the population of the world is not only ageing, it is also increasing in size, with a concentration of this growth in the developing countries. By 1990, the world's population was approximately 5.3 billion, and while fertility in the developed world was well below replacement levels, in the developing world it was substantially more. By mid-2000, world population had reached 6.1 billion and this figure is increasing by approximately 1.0 per cent, corresponding to 75 million people per year,[16] and by 2050 the world's population is expected to be between 7.7 billion and 11.7 billion, depending on the UN variant with the UN medium variant predicting 9.1 billion. Historically, a population growth of 1 billion is nothing new. The pace of the growth is historically without precedence, however. The world's population increased from 1 to 2 billion in the course of 100 years from around 1830 to 1930. What had taken 100 years then only took another 30 years – world population reached 3 billion in 1960. The next billion took only 15 years, and the next again only 12 years. The next again just 12 years.

The most striking feature of the regional development illustrated in Table 2.3 is the

Table 2.3 World population development, 1990–2050, UN medium-range forecast, by region (millions)

	1990	**2005**	**2025**	**2050**
Europe	721	728	707	653
Africa	636	906	1344	1937
Asia	3169	3905	4728	5217
Oceania	27	33	41	48
North America	283	331	388	438
Latin America	444	561	697	783
Total	**5279**	**6465**	**7905**	**9076**

Source: United Nations, 2005.

Table 2.4 World population development, 1990–2050, UN constant scenario, by region (millions)

	1990	**2005**	**2025**	**2050**
Europe	721	728	696	606
Africa	636	906	1490	3099
Asia	3169	3905	4968	6487
Oceania	27	33	42	55
North America	283	331	392	454
Latin America	444	561	733	957
Total	**5279**	**6465**	**8321**	**11658**

Source: United Nations, 2005.

declining population of Europe together with the dramatic increase in the populations of the African continent and Asia – and to a lesser extent Latin America. While the European population is expected to decline by 10 per cent in the next 45 years, those of Asia and Latin America are expected to increase by 33 per cent and 40 per cent respectively. Growth from 2005 to 2050 in Africa will amount to a staggering 114 per cent.

There is, however, a great deal of uncertainty in population forecasts and the United Nations chooses to illustrate this by working with a series of different scenarios based on different assumptions regarding developments in fertility and mortality. Although the medium scenario is most often taken as the most likely development, it too is based on fertility and mortality assumptions which may be unrealistic. The fertility assumption, for example, dictates that fertility levels globally will decline/increase to around 1.85 during this century. For many developing countries this corresponds to a 50 per cent reduction over just two generations. Equally unrealistic may be the assumption for developed countries that fertility levels will actually increase to this level. But what if fertility cannot be controlled in either direction? The extreme forecast of the United Nations assumes unchanged fertility levels globally. The results of such reproductive behaviour are presented in Table 2.4.

Table 2.5 *World population development, 1800–2050, UN medium scenario, by region (millions)*

	1800	**1939**	**2005**	**2050**
Europe	195	573	728	653
Africa	102	175	906	1937
Asia	631	1162	3905	5217
Oceania	2	11	33	48
North America	5	143	331	438
Latin America	19	131	561	783
Total	**954**	**2195**	**6465**	**9076**

Source: United Nations, 2005 and Bourgeois-Pichat, 1989.

Table 2.6 *World population development, 1800–2050, by region (percentage)*

	1800	**1939**	**2005**	**2050**
Europe	20	26	11	7
Africa	11	8	14	22
Asia	66	53	60	59
Oceania	0	1	1	1
North America	1	6	5	5
Latin America	2	6	9	9
Total	**100**	**100**	**100**	**100**

Source: United Nations, 2005 and Bourgeois-Pichat, 1989.

In world regions with high levels of fertility (Latin America, Asia and Africa), the long-term consequences of not reducing fertility levels are overwhelming. By 2050, world population will reach about 12 billion, with 3 billion on the African continent. In India alone, constant fertility would give growth from just over 1 billion persons today to 2.2 billion by 2050. In the course of 45 years, the population of Europe will dwindle to just over 600 million persons.

This extreme scenario only serves to illustrate the dramatic growth potential in the populations of developing countries if fertility levels do not decrease. The future development of global population lies probably somewhere between the medium and constant scenarios.

The demographic development through the nineteenth and twentieth centuries saw a shift in the global distribution of population, and this is expected to continue, as illustrated in Tables 2.5 and 2.6. The population of today's developed regions (Europe, North America and Oceania) constitute 17 per cent of world population today, but this is expected to fall to just 13 per cent by 2050. The most dramatic development is expected in Africa. While the world population increases by 40 per cent from 2000 to 2050, Africa's population is predicted to more than double reaching 21 per cent of the world's population. In that same period, the population of Europe declines by 10 per cent to 653 million persons.

The mechanics of population change

Fertility

Fertility remains a key driver of demographic change. As we discussed, in general, the countries of Europe have come through the demographic transition and entered what some demographers call the second demographic transition.[17] According to Day,[18] fertility is the most evasive demographic component as far as finding universal explanations for its historic development over time is concerned, thereby precluding accurate predictions. Despite this, understanding fertility and the mechanisms of its change has attracted an enormous amount of research interest.

When fertility levels reached replacement levels in the 1930s and 1940s in most of Europe, it was widely believed that they would fall no lower. However, apart from a short-lived baby boom in the mid-1960s, fertility moved below the replacement level plateau and began a more or less uninterrupted decline comparable to that seen in the final stage of the classical demographic transition. When the countries of Northern Europe reached fertility levels of around 1.5 or below in the mid-1980s, it was predicted that these would increase – and that such low levels were a unique demographic phenomenon. The fertility experience of Spain and Italy has proved such predictions wrong. Today, most of these countries have fertility levels below replacement levels, the only exceptions being Turkey and the United States (Table 2.7).

The total fertility rate for the UK and its development since 1960 is illustrated in Table 2.8 and it is clear that fertility levels have been insufficient to reproduce and replace the population since the mid-1970s – and there is no evidence of sustained upswing in levels.

It is important to view these trends in terms of cohort measures (fertility rates per cohort) rather than calendar measures or fertility rates per year. Thus calendar measures of fertility suggested a plateau at replacement level in the 1930s and 1940s at what was seen as the end of the classical demographic transition, with subsequent further decline to levels significantly below replacement levels. Cohort measures of fertility, however, indicate that fertility levels had simply been undergoing a continuous smooth decline since the decline of the transition had begun. In some countries this downward trend had certainly been interrupted by periodic increases (during and immediately after the Second World War and in the mid-1960s), but these were by no means indicators of new lasting trends. Indeed period total fertility levels, which reflect the extent to which each generation that reaches the mean age of childbearing reproduces itself, suggest that European cohorts born after 1960 will no longer reach replacement level in most countries.[19]

The causes of these trends are unclear. Standard *demographic transition theory* explains fertility reduction as a result of infant and juvenile mortality – fertility reduction is *an equilibrating response to maintain population stability in the face of changing mortality regimes*.[20] Capital-investment theory suggests that the need to invest in education as skill-based

Table 2.7 *Total fertility rates in selected countries, 1985 and 2003*

Country	TFR		Country	TFR	
	1985	**2003**		**1985**	**2003**
Northern Europe			**Southern Europe**		
Finland	1.64	1.76	Greece	1.67	1.27
Ireland	2.48	1.98	Italy	1.42	1.29
Norway	1.68	1.80	Portugal	1.72	1.44
Sweden	1.74	1.71	Spain	1.64	1.29
United Kingdom	1.79	1.71			
Western Europe			**Eastern Europe**		
Austria	1.47	1.39	Bulgaria	1.98	1.24
Belgium	1.51	1.66	Czech Republic	1.96	1.18
Denmark	1.45	1.73	Hungary	1.85	1.30
France	1.81	1.89	Poland	2.32	1.24
Germany	1.37	1.74	Romania	2.32	1.27
Netherlands	1.51	1.75	Russian Fed.	2.05	1.33
Switzerland	1.52	1.41	Turkey	3.59	2.46
Elsewhere					
Australia	2.50	1.75	Canada	2.00	1.50
Japan	2.10	1.38	United States	2.00	2.10

Note: For Russian Federation, Australia and Canada 1999, Turkey 1998.

Source: Recent demographic developments in Europe 2000, Council of Europe and United Nations, 2003 and 2005, Eurostat Data base.

Table 2.8 *Total fertility rate (TFR) in the United Kingdom, 1960–2003*

	Year						
	1960	**1970**	**1980**	**1990**	**1995**	**2000**	**2003**
United Kingdom TFR	2.71	2.43	1.89	1.83	1.71	1.65	1.71

Note: The total fertility rate is the average number of children that would be born alive to a woman during her lifetime if she were to pass through and survive her childbearing years conforming to the age-specific fertility rates of a given year.

Source: Recent Demographic Developments in Europe 2001, Council of Europe and Eurostat Data base.

labour markets arose during the industrial revolution resulted in parents lowering fertility to invest more in fewer high quality children – fertility decline is seen as a response to changing economic systems. Cultural theories suggest that fundamental norms and values with regard to the need and desire to have children have changed radically as societies and their members have become increasingly hedonistic. Thus self-actualisation, freedom of choice, emphasis on quality of life and leisure, and a retreat from commitments, may all act against the notion of investment in offspring. There is, however, conflicting evidence. Wealthy nations – with welfare levels more than sufficient to induce childbearing – would face population decline if not for the compensation of international migration. Similarly, a country such as Pakistan in the midst of an economic recession seems to be on the verge of a fertility transition despite the economic climate.[21]

It has also been argued by Easterlin that fertility is influenced by generation size and relative economic status.[22] This would mean that the baby bust generations as they enter adulthood would enjoy increased relative economic status thereby giving rise to increased levels of fertility – in theory at least. Easterlin's models, however, did not take into account the influx of women into the workplace since the 1970s, and the high opportunity costs of leaving the workplace to have and bring up children. Indeed, one of the driving theories behind fertility fall focuses on increased female labour participation, suggesting that increased female education and autonomy, increased desire for consumption requiring second incomes and increased female investment in careers have all led to increased female economic activity and a subsequent decline in childbearing.

However, new patterns of fertility appear to be emerging in Europe which suggest that we have moved beyond the former relationship of fertility and female employment. Cultural change has resulted in young women prioritising economic employment over childbearing, so that, given the choice, a growing number will remain childless. Consequently, those countries which make it easier for women to combine economic activity and childbearing are seeing a rise in fertility, those in which it is still difficult to combine the two, are seeing a dramatic decline. For example, southern Europe has both low fertility levels, and relatively low female labour force participation. In part this is because it is difficult for mothers to maintain economic activity and so many withdraw. In Italy, for example, where total fertility is 1.29 1, only 60 per cent of females aged 25–49 are active in the labour force compared with 84 per cent of women in this age group in Denmark where fertility is 1.76. The experience of Sweden shows that extensive social policy measures to reduce the opportunity costs of having children, and help women to remain in employment after giving birth, maintain or even increase fertility levels.

The postponement of childbearing is also a contributory factor. This operates in two broad ways. First, is the argument that current low fertility cohorts will eventually increase their cohort level though late reproduction. Second, it is asserted that postponement of childbearing reduces the actual number of children born. In England and Wales, almost 10 per cent of the 1946 generation of women were childless by age 40. This had risen to almost 20 per cent for the 1960 generation. For Denmark, the corresponding figures are 8 per cent and 15 per cent respectively; for the Netherlands, 12 per cent and 20 per cent. Lesthaeghe's[23] detailed analysis of six Western European countries (Germany, Switzerland, Netherlands, Austria, Belgium and France) examines the influence of postponement on cohort fertility rates. This study points out that all six countries reached period total fertility levels of 2 or below (that is replacement) by 1975. From then onwards a new pattern of fertility emerged, characterised by postponement at younger ages, with varying degrees of catch-up at later ages. Indeed, those countries in which current cohorts postponed first birth, had a rapid catch-up during their thirties, while those who had earlier first births, had much lower rates of births post-30. This accounted for the very similar period total fertility rates of between 1.3 and 1.7 for all six countries. Clearly, then, the drivers behind fertility change are complex.[24]

Mortality

Across the Western world, and increasingly in parts of the developing world, the shadows of mortality and morbidity have been lifting throughout the twentieth century so that new cohorts can expect to live longer and healthier than previous cohorts. Average life expectancy at birth has increased globally by twenty years over the past half century, from 46.5 years in 1955 to 66.5 years in 2005, representing a global average increase in life expectancy of five months per year throughout this period.[25] During this time there was also a shift in the global pattern of mortality. In the middle of the twentieth century, the countries in the developed world had relatively low rates of mortality, and those in the developing world relatively high. By the turn of the twenty-first century, three broad categories had emerged: countries of the developed world with low rates of mortality and high life expectancy; countries of the developing world with high mortality, namely Sub-Saharan Africa, and some parts of Asia, Latin America and the eastern Mediterranean; and countries of the developing world with low mortality (Table 2.9)

While Africa retains high levels of child mortality, and very high levels of adult mortality, Asian and eastern Mediterranean regions have made significant reductions in mortality rates, so that while there are countries with high adult and child mortality, these

Table 2.9 *Mortality stratum by region*

	High Child, Very High Adult	High Child, High Adult	Low Child, High Adult	Low Child, Low Adult	Very Low Child, Very Low Adult
Africa	X	X			
Latin America*			X	X	
South-east Asia		X		X	
Eastern Mediterranean		X		X	
Europe			X	X	X
North America*				X	X
Western Pacific				X	X

*Note: * WHO combines these two sub-regions into The Americas.*

Source: Adapted from WHO, 2003.

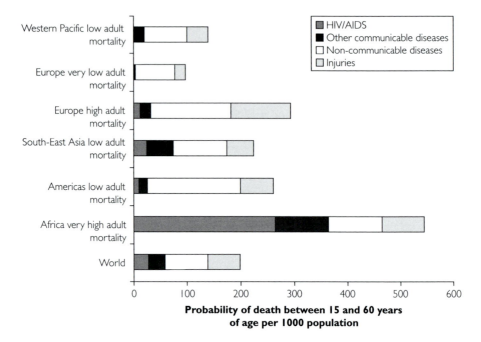

Figure 2.4 *Adult mortality: probabilities of death between 15 and 60 years of age by cause, selected epidemiological sub-regions, 2002.*
Source: WHO, 2003.

regions also now contain countries with low child and adult mortality. Latin America and Eastern Europe have achieved low child mortality, though retaining countries with high adult mortality, while Western Europe, North America and the Western Pacific now have very low adult and child mortality rates in most of their countries.

As a result of the above patterns, there is a striking difference in the number of deaths beyond age 70. Sixty per cent of deaths in the developed world occur after age 70, compared with only 30 per cent in developing countries. While child mortality plays a big part here, there is also a difference between regions in the proportion of deaths among young adults. In developing countries 30 per cent of all deaths occur between the ages of 15 and 59, compared with 20 per cent in the developed world[26] (Fig. 2.4).

As illustrated by Figs 2.5 and 2.6, both fertility and mortality rates in the developed and developing countries are predicted to converge by the middle of the century.[27]

Throughout Western Europe, improvements in public health, especially in the early years of the twentieth century, led to falling mortality at all ages. As the century progressed, mortality rates increasingly appeared to be related to lifestyles and behaviour. In the United Kingdom, for example, mortality levels continued to decline throughout the post-war period at almost all ages, and with the exception of decreases in infant mortality, the mortality decline at around age 40 was the most significant in the 1970–90

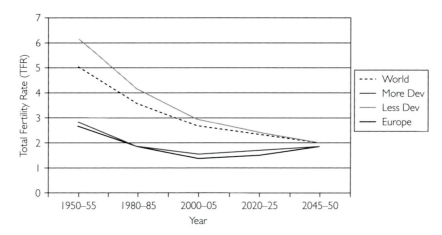

Figure 2.5 *Fertility rates, 1950–2050.*
Source: United Nations, 2005.

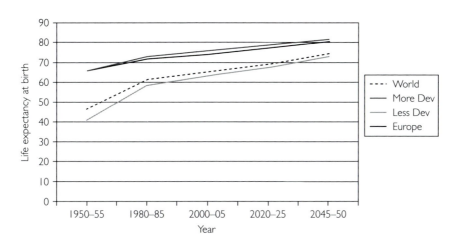

Figure 2.6 *Mortality rates, 1950–2050.*
Source: United Nations, 2005.

period. Table 2.2 presents the development in life expectancies at certain ages over more recent years. Life expectancies at birth in the United Kingdom, for example, increased throughout the period and for both sexes as mortality declined at almost all ages. In fact, in the United Kingdom, it is particularly the scale of the decline in adult and old age mortality which contributes to the observed increases in life expectancies at birth. For infant mortality, although declining, is already so low in this country that the contribution of this decline to the increase in life expectancy at birth is modest. Towards the end of the twentieth century, almost all of the increase in life expectancy at birth in the United Kingdom can be attributed to decreases in mortality at relatively high ages. However, late-age mortality is an increasingly important component of overall mortality and it is changes in these mortality levels that could still confound population forecasts, as they have done in the recent past.[28]

The decline of mortality in Europe over the twentieth century provides an interesting illustration of this process in the developed world. In the post-war years, European countries fell into a two-tier classification as far as life expectancies were concerned, with the more developed northern countries leading the way ahead of the less developed southern and eastern countries.[29] In 1950, female life expectancy in Norway was around 74 years and male expectancy 71 years, compared with just 55 years and 50 years respectively for Albania – the Albanian figures being the approximate life expectancies for Norwegians at the turn of the twentieth century, some 50 years earlier. European life expectancies began to converge, however, in the course of the next 20–25 years especially as high mortality countries in the south and east experienced quite dramatic declines while the low mortality countries of the north had slowed their rate of decline. Thus, by the 1970s, female life expectancy in Albania had increased to 70 years, now within ten years of Norwegian levels, and male life expectancy in Portugal – at 64 years the lowest in 1970 in the West – was within ten years of the highest European country, Sweden.

By the turn of the twenty-first century, the situation had changed again, as illustrated in Table 2.10. While the countries of the European Union continued their overall mortality declines and increasing life expectancies at birth,[30] the Baltic States and the Eastern European countries are falling noticeably behind again. Male life expectancy in the Russian Federation, for example, is alarmingly low. Other Eastern European countries such as Poland, Hungary, the Czech and Slovak Republics and Bulgaria also show signs of a stagnating development in life expectancies, especially for males.

As an example, life expectancy at birth for Hungarian males fell from approximately 67.5 years in 1965 to 65 years in 1990 managing to increase to 68.4 years by 2005. Bulgaria, Poland and the Czech and Slovak Republics have experienced similar trends in life expectancy with stagnation or, at best, only slight improvements. Australia, Canada, Japan and the United States all lie in the Western Europe area of life expectancies.

To date, there have been no comprehensive studies of the (sub)geographical variations in mortality throughout Europe, but national studies would indicate that there are interesting points of issue. For example, there is no strong relationship between life expectancy at birth and national wealth. In 1998, Luxembourg had the highest gross domestic product at market prices per capita in the European Union – higher even than the United States and Japan – but ranked only eleventh in terms of life expectancy at birth for females and eighth for males. On the other hand, France which ranked top in terms of female life expectancy at birth ranks only number twelve in terms of GDP per capita. Nor does there seem to be a clear relationship between mortality and the qual-

Table 2.10 Life expectancies at birth in selected countries, latest figures

Country	Life expectancy		Country	Life expectancy	
	Male	Female		Male	Female
Northern Europe			**Southern Europe**		
Denmark	74.9	79.5	Greece	75.6	80.8
Finland	75.1	81.8	Italy	76.9	82.9
Iceland	78.7	82.8	Malta	75.8	80.7
Ireland	75.1	80.3	Portugal	74	80.5
Norway	77.0	81.9	Spain	77.2	83.7
Sweden	77.9	82.4	Cyprus	76	81
United Kingdom	76.2	80.7			
			Eastern Europe		
Western Europe			Albania	70.9	76.7
Austria	76	81.8	Bosnia	71.3	76.7
Belgium	75.7	81.9	Belarus	62.4	74
France	75.8	82.9	Bulgaria	68.8	75.6
Germany	75.5	81.3	Croatia	71.3	78.4
Luxembourg	75.1	81.4	Czech Republic	72	78.5
Netherlands	76.1	80.8	Estonia	65.4	76.9
Switzerland	77.6	83.1	Hungary	68.4	76.7
			Latvia	65.5	76.8
Other developed countries			Lithuania	66.3	77.7
Australia	77.6	82.8	Poland	70.5	78.9
Canada	77.3	82.4	Romania	67.5	74.1
Japan	77.6	84.3	Macedonia	70.4	74.5
United States	74.0	80	Moldova	64.2	71.5
			Russian Fed.	59.1	72.2
			Slovak Republic	70	77.9
			Slovenia	72.6	77.9
			Ukraine	60.1	72.5
			Turkey	66.3	70.9
			Armenia	67.9	74.6
			Azerbaijan	63.2	70.5

Source: Recent demographic development in Europe 2000, Council of Europe 2003 and United Nations, 2005.

ity of health care and social provision. Some southern European countries, which score poorly on this quality rating, have low mortality levels.[31]

The increases in life expectancy in Europe in the first half of the twentieth century, were primarily the result of rapid declines in infant and maternal mortality, and that caused by infectious diseases in childhood and early adulthood. Access to improved housing, sanitation and education, reduction in family size, increased income and better public heath measures such as mass immunisations, all contributed to this *epidemiological transition.*[32]

Since the mid-twentieth century, however, mortality rates seem increasingly to be related to lifestyles and behaviour, such as smoking, alcohol consumption and the consumption of animal fats. For instance, alcohol-related cancer mortality is six times greater in the north-west of France than in southern Italy, and lung cancer mortality is much higher in the United Kingdom and Germany as well as the Benelux countries, where smoking has long been widespread. Mortality from cardiovascular diseases is generally higher in Northern Europe, where the use of animal fats is extensive compared with the southern European countries where such consumption is lower.

Understanding the laws of mortality

Behind the public health understanding of mortality, statisticians and biodemographers have been attempting to understand the relationship of age and mortality. As early as 1825, the British actuary, Benjamin Gompertz,[33] observed a law of geometrical progression in relation to human life tables. The subsequent 'Gompertz Equation' described the exponential rise in death rates between sexual maturity and old age, and for nearly two centuries the proposition that human mortality rises exponentially with age was generally accepted. As Olshansky and Carnes[34] point out, however, what Gompertz actually discovered was that for various human populations aged between 20 and 60 (and under certain circumstances 10–80), living in the eighteenth and nineteenth centuries, arithmetic increases in age were consistently accompanied by geometric increases in mortality. Outside these ages, the law does not neatly apply. This fact has led some researchers to reject the law in total. Yet, so long as causes of death are restricted to those having a biological origin, the *Gompertz Equation* does produce a biologically-based law of mortality for populations across species[35] and should be respected for its usefulness in this respect.

More recently, evolutionary biologists have introduced arguments concerning genetic mutations which might account for the consistent rise in human mortality with age. The *evolutionary theory of senescence* is based on the concept that natural selection clears away genes that compromise reproduction or survival up to and through the ages of reproduction. The mathematical interpretations of this, such as *mutation-accumulation theory*, suggest that mutations detrimental to post-reproduction ages lead to a rise in hazard rates[36] with age. A similar effect is seen with *antagonistic pleiotropy*, which occurs if there are genes which have a positive effect on net reproduction and negative effect on post-reproduction survival. In his key work, *Evolution in Age-Structured Populations,*[37] Charlesworth develops the concept of mutational collapse, whereby the force of gene mutation gains dominance over selection. Put simply, evolution will select out and remove those mutations which have a detrimental effect on younger age groups, for those carrying them will have a lower chance of surviving to reproduce themselves, and thus these detrimental genes. Gene mutations, however, which only detrimentally affect those of post-reproductive age, will survive within the population, for those carrying them will have already reproduced and passed on the mutation before the mutant gene starts to have a negative effect. In addition, some of these mutations which have a negative effect in old age, may well have a positive effect in younger life, and are thus likely to have a high chance of selection into subsequent generations. Under these circumstances, genes with a detrimental effect only in later life will be successfully passed on through the generations, allowing a clustering of such detrimental effects in late life, and thus increases in the rate of mortality.

Other work by evolutionary biologists has shifted the debate from populations to focus on gene selection and expression within individuals. One of the key scientists in this field is Tom Kirkwood[38] with his *disposable soma theory*. This suggests that there is an energy play-off in the body between those cells responsible for reproduction, and those for maintenance. According to evolutionary theory, our primary purpose is to reproduce, thus the reproductive cells win in the trade-off. One outcome is that the body needs to be maintained only sufficiently long to successfully reproduce and raise our children. Ageing is therefore an accumulation of a series of cellular breakdowns as the body concludes its primary evolutionary role.

Kirkwood has recently tested aspects of this theory drawing on fertility records of British aristocratic families, which revealed that those with the lowest fertility also lived longest.[39] There are clearly various interpretations of this study. One may be that families are genetically predisposed towards low fertility/high longevity or vice versa. Another, which has particular relevance for this current discussion, is that the trade-off happens more quickly within an individual's lifetime. Thus as the energy put into reproduction by women so rapidly declined last century, so there was more available for body maintenance, affecting the rapid rise in life expectancy of women in particular over the past 100 years. Empirical evidence shows, for example, that the current cohort of women in old age had far smaller families than their own mothers, and are currently living far longer.[40] However, while there may well be an association between falling reproduction and increasing longevity (in part because the public health and educational influences affecting fertility also impact upon mortality), this does not of course in any way imply a causal association for individuals themselves. In another area, recent work by Partridge[41] on *Drosophila*, has suggested that, among fruit flies, delaying reproduction delayed the ageing process. In other words, reproduction in fruit flies in some way triggers the ageing process.

Gains in life expectancy and limits to the human lifespan

As already discussed, twentieth-century western industrialised nations saw dramatic rises in life expectancy. Yet there remains a widely accepted belief that there exists a maximum human lifespan[42] of around 120 years. This has, if anything, been confirmed in the public imagination by the death in 1997 of Jeanne Calment, a Frenchwoman of 122 years – the world's reliably verified oldest living human. The fact that the reliably verified oldest man died around the same time at 115 years of age also confirms another widely held belief that women are in some way programmed to live longer than men. There are therefore a number of questions concerning this pace of increasing life expectancy, and whether there exists a limit to the span of a human life. In particular, can the gains in human longevity be maintained? Will the increase in active life expectancy continue throughout this century? Are we reaching the point of diminishing returns? Considerable research has been carried out in this area by Carnes and Olshanksy, who conclude that humans are not built to last much beyond the lifespans we are currently observing.[43]

The demographic debate concerning longevity and the human lifespan, has broadly drawn on three main hypotheses:

- *compression rectangularization* – addressing the variability in individual lifespans

- *limit distribution* – concerning the age pattern of human mortality; and

- *limited lifespan* – the maximum age attainable by humans.

The compression rectangularization hypothesis proposes that the variation in age of human death should decrease over time. This has been supported by some empirical studies which have suggested that decreasing variability in human lifespans has already been observed. Ryder's[44] analysis of life-model tables, for example, revealed that as life expectancy increased, the coefficient of variation declined. From this Ryder extrapolated that the variability in age at death should diminish to nothing around the mid-eighties, reflecting a process of convergence towards a characteristic human lifespan of around 85 years.[45] According to the limit distribution hypothesis there exists a statistical limiting distribution that mortality curves may approach, but not surpass. Simply stated, the limited lifespan hypothesis proposes that there is a specific age beyond which no one can survive. This thesis has been supported by two broad arguments. First, as Weiss and others have shown, there has been no increase over time in the maximum age observed at death for human populations,[46] and second, the exponential increase in mortality rates with age eventually results in a finite lifespan.[47]

All three hypotheses, however, have recently been questioned by Wilmoth,[48] who draws together a variety of evidence to argue that among some populations at least:

- there has been a slow-down in the rectangularization of the human survival curve;

- there has been an acceleration in rates of mortality decline among older age groups; and

- maximum age at death has in fact risen over the past century or so.

Referring to the compression rectangularization hypothesis, Wilmoth introduces evidence from the USA, Sweden and Japan,[49] which suggests that while there has been rectangularization of the survival curve during most of the last century, there was a slow down, and even scattering, after the mid-1950s. Thus compression and rectangularization are by no means universal aspects of mortality decline. In relation to the limit distribution hypothesis, he queries the underlying assumption that all large human populations in all environments should be subject to the same universal mortality limit.[50] Similarly, in relation to the limited lifespan hypothesis, an assumption that it is possible to survive to some maximum age, but not to this age plus one day, is clearly intuitively unappealing.[51]

Declining mortality rates at extreme old age

Recent empirical evidence challenging the notion of constant increases in mortality rates with age points to a rethink of current hypotheses concerning longevity and the human lifespan. In contrast to the reported stability in maximum age at death, produced for example by Olshansky,[52] Swedish data reveal that the maximum age at death for both men and women has risen steadily for the past 130 years[53] (Fig. 2.7).

Part of this trend, and that seen in data collected in France, England and Wales and Japan, is due to population growth,[54] which is of course also a product of the decrease

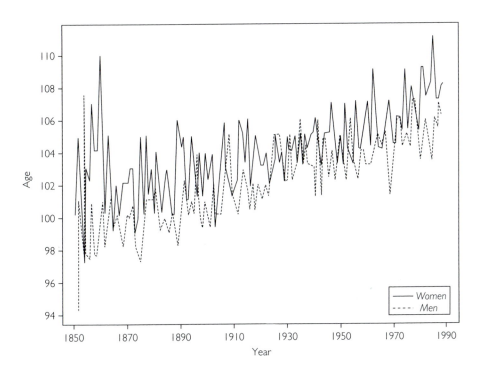

Figure 2.7 *Maximum reported age at death in Sweden, 1850–1990.*
Source: Wilmoth and Lundstroem, 1996.

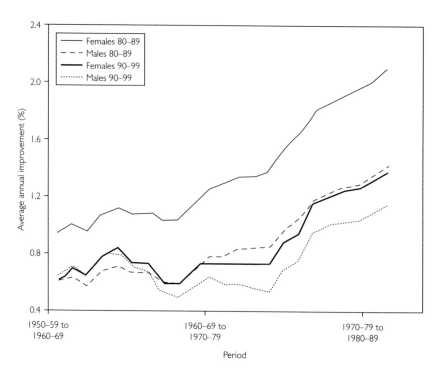

Figure 2.8 *Average annual rates of mortality decline.*
Source: Wilmoth and Lundstroem, 1996.

in mortality. There is, in addition, an acceleration of mortality decline at older ages. In some populations these older ages are now characterised by the fastest age-specific rates of decline currently experienced.

Human death rates are falling in developed societies even among the oldest old, with a variety of multi-species studies suggesting that in fact hazard functions (probability that an individual surviving to a specific age will die at that age) level off at extreme old ages. Both laboratory observations on a variety of non-human species, and human population studies on Western European countries, the USA and Japan,[55] suggest that for many non-human species mortality actually decreases with age, while for humans the rate of increase in mortality continues but at a much slower rate in the eighth and ninth decades and beyond[56] (Figs 2.8 and 2.9).

This increase in the age of those groups with the most pronounced mortality decline has been termed the ageing of mortality decline.[57]

A similar picture is produced from data gathered on some 70 million people who reached at least 80 years, and 200,000 centenarians,[58] which revealed that mortality rates decelerate after 80 years, reaching a plateau at around 110 years (Fig. 2.10). The current data after this is so limited that one can only hypothesise as to whether the rate increases or decreases.[59]

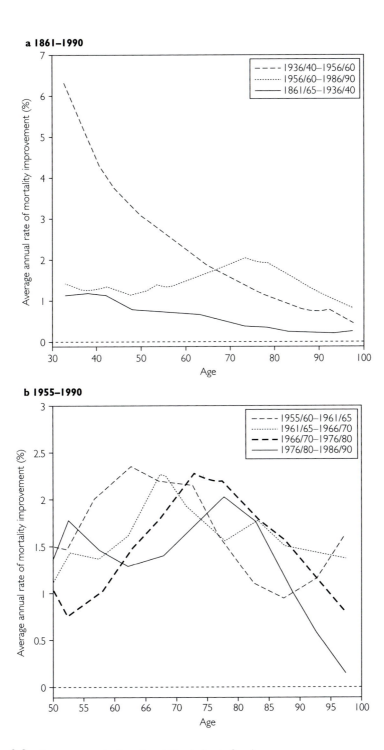

Figure 2.9 *Average annual rates of mortality decline in Sweden.*
Source: Wilmoth and Lundstroem, 1996.

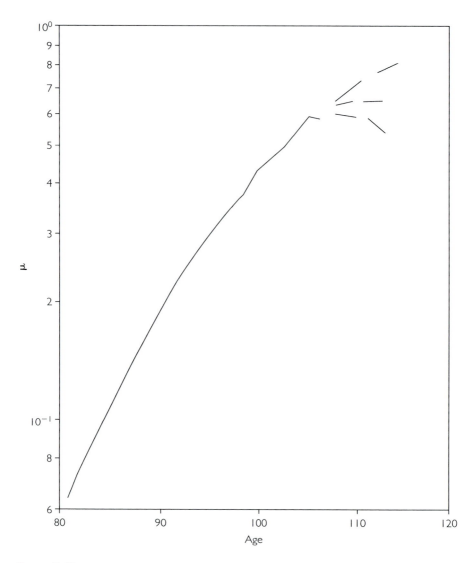

Figure 2.10 *Mortality at age 80 and over.*
Source: Vaupel, 1997.

Evidence of this consistent and widespread deceleration in mortality rate at old ages came as a surprise to many.[60] Arguments as to why this should occur are complex. What is of particular interest is the relative contribution of genetic, developmental and environmental selectivity to this process. Some initial work on non-human species, for example, has suggested that population density might be a factor,[61] theorising that lowering of the population density through death of its members might produce a more conducive environment for survival, thus enhancing the life expectancy of those still alive. In practice, of course, populations tend to strive for equilibrium whereby lost members through death are replaced by births or immigrants. In addition, subsequent research has indicated that, regardless of density, in some populations mortality rates rise with age, level and then decline.[62]

The *compositional change* of the population – the premise that those who survive to old age are systematically different from those who die at younger ages, and this might also impact upon death rates in later life – has also been examined.[63] However, while statistically this is a factor in the explanation,[64] as Vaupel points out, the degree of heterogeneity required to make this a mathematical artefact is so large that it is unlikely that this accounts for all of the observed decline in mortality. Nevertheless, there is some indication from geneticists that much of the flattening of mortality rates at the end of life, could indeed arise from the genetic heterogeneity among humans.[65] *Increased population size* has also been identified as another factor. As Finch and Pike have argued,[66] population size does not have a major effect on maximum lifespan during the *Gompertz acceleration of mortality*. However, when the rate of mortality rise slows down at advanced old ages, population size then becomes a greater determinant of maximum lifespan.

Indeed, there may well be a slow-down in the rate of mortality rise not only at the population level, but also at the individual level. These changes may be concerned with *behavioural and psychological changes* which occur with old age, and may be associated with declines in reproductive activity, or with repair mechanisms which compensate for damage at younger ages.[67] Other explanations have focused on *environmental change*, pointing out, for example, that very old people in today's modern societies tend to live in relatively protected environments, which might decrease their vulnerability to mortality and morbidity relative to the exogenous factors affecting those in midlife and early late age.[68] In addition, as we discussed earlier, modern lifestyle modification, such as diet and exercise, pharmaceuticals and medical interventions, are all having a current impact on life extension at old ages.[69] These modifications:

> have led many to believe that continued progress can be made in improving life
> expectancy, particularly at older ages. When extended, this perspective suggests that
> there is no biological limit to life because there is no limit in the development of new and
> effective life-extending technologies. On the other hand, the emergence of new strains
> of bacteria, viruses and parasites . . . suggest that the modern advances in public health
> can have both positive and negative effects in human longevity.[70]

If we are willing to allow ourselves to be progressively multidisciplinary and inventive in our sweep of thought, then we can turn to Vaupel who merges ideas from engineering, biology and demography in his discussion of *bio-reliability theory*. Quoting Dawkins,[71] he argues that some biologists in particular have been influenced by the 'one-hoss shay' model of Oliver Wendell Holmes that ran perfectly until one day all of its pieces fell apart simultaneously! This, he argues, is a supposition used to justify the belief in species-specific maximum lifespans. Yet, *engineering reliability theory* highlights the inherent viability of complex machines to operate successfully long after the time for which they were designed to function, and this is supported by empirical observations. As Vaupel describes, equipment is often engineered with a high probability of survival up to a specific point, yet such designs generally also result in substantial spans of life after the target age. Thus the Pioneer space probe designed to reach Mars was still functioning when it left the solar system; washing machines and refrigerators may be designed to last until the end of the warranty period yet some continue to function successfully long after their warranty period has expired (never mine). A body design that gives human beings a good chance of surviving long enough to reproduce successfully may be sufficiently robust a design that some humans survive and flourish long after their sell-by date.[72] Furthermore, Vaupel produces evidence from death rates of US automobiles to suggest that both behavioural and physiological factors of the very old car population lead to a decline in the rate of increase in car death rates similar to that observed in biological species (Fig. 2.11). If we wish to explore even further afield in our search for answers, then Rose introduces us to the analogy of *relativistic mechanics* in physics, and in particular the slowing down of velocities as they reach the speed of light.[73] But enough.

To sum up, current demographic theory concerning human longevity appears to have significant explanatory limitations. Variability in age at death may be increasing rather than decreasing; deceleration in the rate of mortality decline appears to suggest that we are not currently approaching a statistical lower limit in mortality rates; we may now be seeing an increase in maximum ages at death. One view is that we are asking the wrong set of questions. Just as intuition tells us that it is unlikely that it will be possible to survive to some maximum age, but not to this age plus one day, so it also tells us that it is unlikely that humans will ever achieve infinite life. As Wilmoth himself concludes,[74] it is possible that there does indeed exist a maximum human lifespan. However, this is likely to be at a point well beyond current experience, and we presently have no way of theoretically or empirically verifying this. Our current demographic confusion may simply be indicating that we are not currently close to a limit in human longevity. It does not, however, suggest that no ultimate limit exists.

The future: genetic influences

Of increasing significance as we enter the new century, is our growing understanding of the role of genes in controlling lifespans, and how they interact with environmental factors. There is thus active scientific debate over the question of increasing life expectancy, and whether there are indeed limits to human longevity.

According to Kaplan contemporary human populations represent 'an ancient, but flexible response system in a very novel environment'.[75] The conventional view of evolution processes is that within each environmental context, natural selection favours certain genetic variants. Populations thus adapt, and importantly remain adapted, to specific environmental conditions through selection:

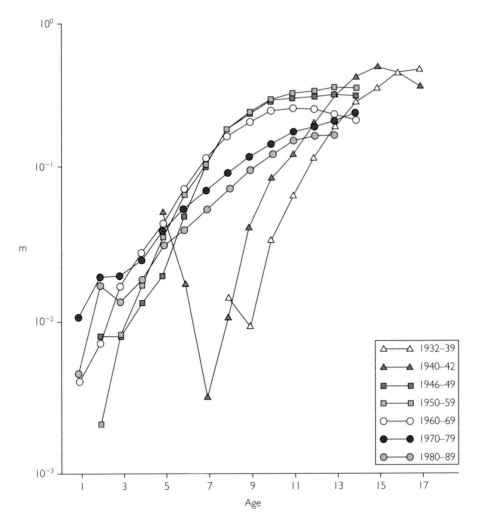

Figure 2.11 *Central death rates for automobiles.*
Source: Vaupel, 1997.

> In general it can be expected that organisms will respond flexibly and adaptively to environmental variation commonly experienced in the evolutionary history of the organism, and respond less adaptively to environmental variation outside the range of common experience.[76]

This leads to the key question of how a species which has evolved slowly over many hundreds of thousands of years, will adapt to the sudden transformations of modern environmental stimuli. Given that the most basic features of the psychological and physiological mechanisms underlying our responses to the environment evolved in the context of a hunting and gathering ecology, most people today live under very different conditions.

For example, as Kaplan points out, access to food resources is virtually unlimited for many people today:

> This food availability is outside the range of anything experienced by traditional peoples in the past. This availability may mean that our evolved allocation mechanisms are not designed to respond to unlimited food access. Perhaps the increases in longevity and the increased health of the very old people that have occurred in the last several decades are at the bounds of our energy adaptive flexibility.[77]

Kaplan continues by arguing that our evolutionary history may not have designed us to respond adaptively to a modern environment containing a virtually unlimited food supply and an ability to combat illness through contemporary western medicinal advances:

> It may be that large future increases in the healthy human lifespan will require major manipulation of our evolved allocation system, either through genetic engineering or chemical interventions.[78]

Yet, if anything, new advances in biodemography are questioning former theories of programmed senescence and specific limits to life expectancy, advancing instead models that treat lifespans as highly plastic,[79] i.e. with the ability to change and react to environmental stimuli. Finch describes this approach as follows:

> The available evidence from different species shows that organisms of whatever body construction have the potential for widely varying patterns of senescence, with respect to the intensity of any particular pathophysiological age change and its time course of occurrence. This enormous plasticity is completely consistent with the recent increases of human lifespans.[80]

Finch draws on the example of Alzheimer's disease to expand upon this concept of plasticity, exploring the idea that while complex gene–environment interactions may well lead to the vulnerability of particular organ systems for degeneration during ageing, the age at which the impairment is manifested will be subject to considerable variability. As he concludes:

> [T]his plasticity challenges traditional beliefs that the lifespans of higher organisms are rigidly pre-programmed by their genes . . . there may be statistically distinct life-history trajectories within a given human population which are subject to myriad gene-environment interactions, including lifestyle choices.[81]

Longevity genes

We now return to the question of genetic predisposition to ageing and the identification and mapping of genes determining longevity. The past twenty years or so have seen growing interest in longevity assurance genes or *gerontogenes*:[82]

> The gene is the basic unit of inheritance; typically a gene makes a protein. A gerontogene
> . . . makes a protein involved in ageing, and more precisely, a protein involved in
> determining lifespan.[83]

Johnson and Shook continue by identifying the four distinct categories of geronto-genes:[84]

- *deleterious genes* have evolved as a result of mutation accumulation, described earlier;

- *pleiotropic genes* are similar but have the capacity to affect several aspects of the phenotype – or physical signs of the gene function (pleiotropic and deleterious genes are predicted by the evolutionary theory of ageing);

- *ageing genes* actively attack the organism; and

- *longevity genes* promote survival.

It is thought that most genes are of this latter type. While it is believed that these gerontogenes do exist, and identification of such genes has been achieved in very simple organisms, identifying these in complex organisms such as mammals is far more problematic.

Despite claims to have identified ageing related genes, such as p21, we do not currently have a good understanding of the nature of the complex interactions underlying these complex genetic disorders. If the complexity is largely due to *allelic heterogeneity*,[85] then useful diagnostics, at least based on the more common susceptibility alleles, should be practicable.[86] If, however, the complexity also involves *locus heterogeneity*,[87] but remains largely genetic in nature, *positional cloning* of the genes involved should be feasible, and would facilitate the development of both improved diagnostics (based on gene sequence, or possibly on particular gene products) and improved drug therapies. At the other extreme, if most or all of the complexity derives from complicated multi-locus gene-environment interactions, then progress on either diagnostics or interventions, based on genomics, will be elusive at best. Yet despite the current lack of understanding, there are clearly broad social implications which would follow should at least some of the more common genetic conditions associated with ageing fall at the more accessible end of the complexity scale.

To add to the complexity, it is not only the genetic blueprint which needs to be unravelled, the environmental factors referred to earlier are also myriad and complex, and go back to the prezygotic environment,[88] and beyond. Finch gives us an idea of the kind of timespans that could be involved:

> the ova from which we arose were formed in our mother's ovaries while she was a
> foetus in our maternal grandmother's uterus, which allows environmental effects that
> span at least three generations, and could have profound influences on characteristics of
> one or more ensuing generations.[89]

In conclusion

While there have always been older people, the revolution of the twentieth century was the rapid increase in the numbers of those in later life, so that the percentage surviving to old age, and extreme old age, within each cohort has increased significantly over the past 100 years. As interest has turned to the question of human longevity, so our understanding of the processes behind ageing and senescence has increased. There is currently active scientific debate over the question of increasing life expectancy, and whether there are indeed limits to human longevity. Gerontologists and biodemographers are becoming interested in the phenomenon of the extensive physiological postreproductive lifespan found in humans, and how this is related to modern environmental factors. Of increasing significance as we enter the new century, is our growing understanding of the role of genes in controlling lifespans, and how they interact with environmental factors.[90]

Notes

1 Van de Kaa, 1987; Bourgeois-Pichat, 1989; Coleman, 1996; Livi-Bacci and Ipsen, 1992.
2 Malthus, 1798.
3 Livi-Bacci and Ipsen, 1992.
4 Van de Kaa, 1987.
5 ibid.
6 Wrigley and Schofield, 1981.
7 Taking life expectancy at age 15 as a more accurate level, given the high mortality in early childhood, this increase is around one half, and life expectancy at age 50, the increase is one half for men and two-thirds for women since 1880.
8 Kertzer and Laslett, 1995.
9 Laslett, 1976.
10 Kertzer and Laslett, 1995, p. 21.
11 Wrigley and Schofield, 1981.
12 Weiss, 1981.
13 Kreager and Schroeder-Butterfill, 2003.
14 Pool, 2000.
15 Kreager and Schroeder-Butterfill, 2003.
16 United Nations, 2005.
17 Livi-Bacci and Ipsen, 1992; Van de Kaa, 1987.
18 Day, 1995.
19 Lesthaeghe, 2001.
20 Kaplan, 1997, p. 202.
21 Sathar and Casterline, 1998.
22 Easterlin, 1980.
23 Lesthaeghe, 2001.
24 Lesthaeghe, 2001; Lesthaeghe and Neels, 2000; Kreager, 2004 Kreager and Schroeder-Butterfill, 2003.

25 WHO, 2003.
26 ibid.
27 United Nations, 2005.
28 Leeson, 1981.
29 Mesle, 1996; Leeson, 2002.
30 The exception being Portuguese males.
31 Kunst et al., 1988.
32 WHO, 2003.
33 Gompertz, 1825.
34 Olshansky and Carnes, 1997.
35 Carnes et al., 1996.
36 Hazard rate or hazard function is the probability that an individual surviving to age x will die at that age.
37 Charlesworth, 1994.
38 Kirkwood, 1977; Kirkwood, 2005a; Proctor et al., 2005; Drenos and Kirkwood, 2005; Kirkwood, 2005b; Kirkwood et al., 2005.
39 Kirkwood, 1999.
40 Grundy, 1999.
41 Sgro and Partridge, 1999.
42 Life-span of an individual referring to his or her age at death; of a species referring to the maximum potential length of life for the most robust members; the mean life span of a group of individuals referring to the group life expectancy (after Wilmoth, 1997).
43 Carnes and Olshansky, 2001; Olshansky et al., 2002a; Olshansky et al., 2002b; Olshansky et al., 2003; Carnes et al., 2003.
44 Ryder, 1975 quoted in Wilmoth, 1997.
45 See also Fries, 1980.

46 Weiss, 1981; Olshansky *et al.*, 1990.
47 Fries, 1980.
48 Wilmoth, 1997.
49 Wilmoth and Lundstroem, 1996.
50 Wilmoth, 1997.
51 See also Gavrilov and Gavrilova, 1991.
52 Olshansky *et al.*, 2002a.
53 Wilmoth and Lundstroem, 1996.
54 This is because the extreme values of a sample from any probability distribution are partly a function of sample size.
55 Vaupel and Lundstroem, 1994; Lundstroem, 1995; Wilmoth and Lundstroem, 1996.
56 Kannisto, 1994; Wilmoth, 1995.
57 Horiuchi and Wilmoth, 1995.
58 Thatcher, 1997; Vaupel, 1997.
59 Vaupel, 1997.
60 ibid.
61 Kowald and Kirkwood, 1993.
62 Vaupel, 1997.
63 Kowald and Kirkwood, 1993; Olshansky *et al.*, 1993.
64 Vaupel and Carey, 1993; Vaupel, 1997.
65 Johnson and Shook, 1997.
66 Finch and Pike, 1996.
67 Vaupel, 1997; Kowald and Kirkwood, 1993.
68 Partridge, 1997.
69 Olshansky and Carnes, 1997.
70 ibid.
71 Dawkins, 1995.
72 See also Hayflick, 1994.
73 Rose, 1997.
74 Wilmoth, 1997.
75 Kaplan, 1997, p. 204.
76 ibid., p. 200.
77 Kaplan, 1997, p. 202.
78 ibid.
79 Wachter, 1997.
80 Finch, 1997, p. 261.
81 Finch, 1997, p. 246.
82 Rattan, 2004; Butler *et al.*, 2003; Vijg and Suh, 2005; Warner, 2005.
83 Johnson and Shook, 1997, p. 109.
84 Described by Vijg and Papaconstantinou, 1990.
85 Allelic heterogeneity is where many different mutations within a given gene can be seen in different patients with a certain genetic condition.
86 Although even in this, almost certainly, over-optimistic scenario, the problems with implementing diagnostics on a large scale with the hereditary cancer genes BRCA1 and BRCA2 provide very salutary lessons.
87 Locus heterogeneity is where the same clinical phenotype can result from mutations at any one of several different loci.
88 The uterine environment in which the ova were formed.
89 Finch, 1997.
90 Recent developments include: telemorase (enzyme used to make human cells replicate indefinitely *in vitro*), gerentogenes (genes linked to longevity have been manipulated in experiments with animals), hormone therapies (hormones such as DHEA have been linked to ageing), caloric restriction (animal experimentation has shown a link between a diet low in calories and increased lifespan; an ingredient of red wine – resveratrol – seems to mimic the age-enhancing effects of caloric restriction).

3
Understanding age and ageing

While concepts of class, race and gender have been explored fully, the variable age is less well understood. Indeed, beyond a small group of academic gerontologists, knowledge of the full theoretical construct appears limited, and the public perception of age and ageing is generally one of biological ageing resulting in old age. However, just as our understanding of race and gender are now multifaceted, so the concepts of age and ageing need to be explored at various dichotomous levels: historically and contemporarily; individually and societally; biologically and socially; and in terms of the concepts of age, generation and cohort.

Age and ageing through time

Our notion of the historical reality of later life sits somewhere between images of a time:

> in which the old were treated with respect, when they occupied positions of power by virtue of their control over family holdings, and when they were surrounded and supported by married children, and grandchildren . . .

and one:

> in which old people crowd meager public charitable facilities in search of a miserable lodging, or a piece of bread, to allow them to survive in a society that gave no quarter to those lacking the brawn or the health to earn their daily living . . .[1]

In the first scenario, modernisation is heralded as the tragic perpetrator/executor of doom, with older people as the victims of progress. In the second, modernisation brings with it welfare reforms, and older people are the beneficiaries of social programmes and intergenerational transfers. In reality, while demographic transition might have been relatively consistent in its progress across Western Europe and akin societies, the social and political arrangements for older adults varied considerably between and within societies, and over time, and were moderated by factors such as class and gender.

The most pervasive view, however, is that old age was a rarity:

> It is believed that 'in the past' . . . few people lived to old age. In consequence, old people had a rarity value which meant that not only were they financially less costly, they were culturally more valued and respected than in the present. Families took for granted that

they cared for older relatives and so they imposed little or no charge on public welfare . . . older people had skills and knowledge which were still useful to and valued by the young.[2]

This notion arises due to the confusion, highlighted in Chapter 2, between life expectancy at birth and life expectancy from adulthood. In the nineteenth century, those who survived childhood had a life expectation of 50 or 60 years, especially women. Indeed the proportion of those aged over 60 living in England and Wales was 9 per cent in the late seventeenth century, rising to 10 per cent in the early eighteenth century, and only falling to 7 per cent in the nineteenth century due to a rise in the birth rate.[3] The other notion is that old age began much earlier, probably around 40, with stereotypical images of frail white-bonneted 40-year-old grannies bent over in fireside chairs.[4] Yet, as Thane argues, while it is likely that people *looked* older earlier, the ages of 60 and 70 have been consistently used as the official age for withdrawal from public duties.

Thus military service in ancient Greece was compulsory, if required, until age 60;[5] in Rome 60 was recognised as the year of achieving the status of old age;[6] and in Medieval England compulsory work under the labour laws for both men and women was obligatory until age 60.[7]

There have been several analyses of the experiences and representations of age and ageing over time.[8] Pictures which emerge from these suggest a clear understanding of the heterogeneity of later life and a recognition that the experience of ageing and old age was acutely different for men and women. There was also a recognition that old age could be broadly divided into a more active span and a more frail one, but also that capacity varied in later life, and was not necessarily in line with chronological age. Old age has long been divided into what, in early Modern England, was called the 'green old age', a time of fitness and activity, albeit with some failing powers, and a final phase of decrepitude and frailty.[9] This division is still recognised today in the notions of Third and Fourth Ages – with the Third now being associated with healthy active retirement (and as such even conceived as commencing at age 50(!)[10]), and the period of increasing disability that may occur sometime between the ages of 80 and 100,[11] noted as the Fourth Age.

Age

While there has been extensive literature on the meaning of *old age,* analysis of the notion of *age per se* has been less well rehearsed.[12] Yet, in western societies, the naturalness of the use of *chronological age* in the marking of our lives is instilled within us from our early socialisation. So culturally immersed are we that the widespread view is that there is no satisfactory alternative to chronology as an indicator of age. This is reflected in a spectrum of ways: from the social recognition of the importance of annual ageing, with the emphasis on anniversaries such as birthdays, to the legal entrenchment of chronological age as a marker for a series of life transitions – age of consent, age of majority, age of retirement, etc.

One standpoint,[13] however, is that age *per se* explains very little, perhaps nothing of abiding interest. Age itself is not a cause of anything: it is part of the trait description of persons, a classification variable, the title of a set of categories in a particular classification system. Even its use as a social marker tells us very little about any contemporary individual of that age. The fact that individuals are enfranchised in many European countries at 18 tells us little about the maturity of a particular 18 year old, other than that they live in a society which regards 18 to be the norm for the population of attaining some level of political maturity. Similarly, the fact that the pensionable age for many individuals throughout the West is 65 again does not inform us about any particular 65 year old, other than that they live in a society which regards 65 to be the age at which the majority of the working population require some kind of supplementary assistance to maintain an income. Indeed, as we shall discuss later, this is based on an historical model which, in most cases, is now bereft of any relevance to contemporary health or capability status. One could argue that the ages of 18 and 65 simply tell us that the particular individuals have survived for 18 and 65 years respectively.

Hazelrigg notes:

> Age as a classification variable is causally significant insofar as the dynamics of a given process are sensitive to the age states of persons involved in that process . . . [a]n apparent sensitivity to age might be to age state as such, but it could be instead a sensitivity to some other variable or variables with which age is correlated.[14]

We can use one of Hazelrigg's examples to explore this idea further. Mate selection appears to be age-sensitive to some degree. First, it is age-sensitive in that the sexual intercourse component of mating behaviour is proscribed in most western societies until an age-eligibility threshold has been reached, though this age varies between societies. It also appears to be age-sensitive in that the ages of most couples fall within a short chronological range, on average within a five-year band. This may be an outcome of selection on age, or it may be a proxy for other traits such as fecundity or congruent life expectancy. Alternatively, it may be a factor of proximity and availability, for at the time of initial mate selection younger people are legally inaccessible and those older fall outside the range of normal social interaction as delimited by education, or have been already selected. Analysis of age variation among couples in second and subsequent marital and cohabiting unions reveals greater variance than in first unions, on average up to 15 years.

Age as a variable

A key question is whether age has the same analytical coherency as race, class or gender. Hazelrigg argues that beyond its use by individuals and groups to date events, a simple marker in the regulation of the process of living, age itself is of little importance. This notion is strongly contended by Riley who regards age as a classification variable of social status,[15] highlighting the fact that *age stratification theory*[16] (which we discuss later in the chapter) was developed to be comparable to class stratification theory. There are, however, important differences between these variables. First, all such descriptive variables lie along a spectrum of potential mobility. While on the whole, sex, race and ethnicity are fixed, class and religion have the potential to be mobile, while mobility across age strata is universal. This factor has been taken up recently by those working on age discrimination (see Chapter 10). Class is based on unequal power relationships. Alternatively, while neither sex, or rather its socially constructed variable gender, nor age emerged through such inequality, during particular historic periods, and in relation to other personal characteristics and circumstances, individuals can find themselves in such unequal power relationships by virtue of their association with a particular age or gender. Indeed, Minkler and Estes[17] go so far as to deny that age *per se* has any salience as an analytical variable, arguing instead that it is only through its association with gender and class that we can understand its relationship to power structures and access to resources. What is clear, however, is that this can be stated to varying degrees in relation to all descriptive variables. There are hierarchies of power where gender is the determining factor, others where class is dominant, and yet others, as we shall see, where age is key.

Age and the individual

From the perspective of the individual, age classification introduces signposts which Hazelrigg describes as 'linking memory and anticipation, an iteratively remembered past and an iteratively expected future'.[18] Age classification is therefore integral to the normal organisation of consciousness. As Mead's extensive work on life history, reminiscence and autobiography[19] informs us:

> one interacts retrospectively with one's younger selves, recalling earlier states of selfhood in the productive functioning of memory, and interacts prospectively with one's older selves, anticipating conditions, actions, goal realizations and the like of later states of selfhood.[20]

What is of interest is how we as individuals are able both to conceptualise age as an internal process, a marker, a lived experience, and a regulator of consciousness and memory, and at the same time accept the reality of age as an institutionalised series of sequences and an externally articulated attribute.

As Hazelrigg describes, modern life is lived in two separate registers. On the one hand, most of a life experience is formed directly and indirectly in a highly standardised sequence of institutionalised events – schooling, work, parenting, retirement. These events are regulated by procedural rules and recognised routines, with predictable durations and regulated transitions between events. On the other hand, those aspects of life experiences that are not institutionalised and structurally stabilised in recognised life course sequences, tend to have little or no connection to status dimensions or specific locations in the life course. These would include self-image, personal satisfaction, existential aesthetics, etc.

Tensions arise when the two registers fail to coincide – that is the internal register falls out of sync with that regulated by society. This may be referred to as *off-time*.[21] Examples include middle-aged couples falling in love and publicly exhibiting displays of physical affection and romance, or older people adopting student-style lives. This concept has been extensively explored by Hagerstad.[22] Off-time may also include the experience of being externally forced, through illness for example, to fall outside the normal behaviour range as defined for one's age.[23] There are also occasions where society takes an individual and places them within a situation which is unusual for their chronological age. For example, a very young person being rapidly promoted within an institution which is very highly age regulated, such as a university, and taking on a professorial mantle.[24] William Hague, who became leader of the UK Conservative Party in his thirties during the 1990s was seen by many as *off-time*.

Age and society

For both the individual and society, age conveniently dissects the life course into more manageable components. Several authors have argued, for example, that the life course was institutionalised in response to the movement of individuals from domestic units to bureaucratically organised corporations.[25] Hazelrigg comments:

> Chronological age is clearly associated with state-level societies. Age defined chronology becomes the basis for universalistic (in contrast to particularistic) norms in regulating large populations. Age defines the responsibilities of citizenship. With capitalism and industry, age has further been used to define adulthood and labour force participation. . . . Legal norms gauge the life course and calibrate a social clock of role entrances and exits.[26]

As Hazelrigg goes on to describe, for each age-related transition there is a stage of preparation, a stage of participation, and a stage of retirement:

> Preparatory stages are ones of enculturation and skill acquisition for an adult life of work and career in the labour market. Children are launched into adulthood once they have completed their schooling and have attained the chronological age demanded by legal norms of adult privilege. Especially relevant are the norms concerning work and age of marriage as thresholds into the stage of adult preparation. Retirement from participation in the labour force is similarly guided by chronological legal norms, most notably the eligibility for state security programs or pensions.[27]

Fry[28] is even more explicit on the role of the labour market:

> When adulthood is organized by labour force participation, life courses are staged. Where participation in labour markets is marginal to sporadic, generational principles organize life.

Chronology and chronological age became a useful tool for coping with the need for rationalisation, succession, social control and integration. It is impartial, easily operationalised, and avoids complicated testing and examinations. The fact that it is in reality an incorrect proxy for most of the variables it claims to represent[29] has, until recently, been conveniently ignored! Fortes[30] takes a more individualistic view, suggesting that the task of the individual is to build and maintain a stable identity. Institutionalised life course is one way to regulate this individual change over time; it arrays ages of selfhood into a predictable sequence of states and transitions that satisfies many of the demands of population management on a societal scale.

Age stratification

Age stratification theory was proposed by Riley and colleagues[31] in the 1970s. Age is perceived to be both a process and a structure. Originally devised along social lines, Riley[32] later refined the argument to include biopsychosocial processes, thus conceptualising individual ageing as comprising psychological and biological development alongside the experience of entering and exiting social roles. Riley and colleagues argued that the ageing process influenced the structure of age-related acts or capabilities. Using the dual concepts of *allocation*, the process whereby individuals are assigned and reassigned to roles, and *socialisation*, the instructing of individuals as to how to perform new life course roles, they suggested that these two concepts moderate between social structures relating to individuals of given ages, and to social structures relating to roles open to individuals of given ages and age related expectations and sanctions. Developed to be comparable to class stratification theory,[33] age stratification theory promoted the idea that societies organise the distributions of rewards and opportunities and develop sets of behavioural expectations based on the stratifying characteristics of their members, with chronological age as a central element in the system.[34] Thus societies are structured and individuals stratified on the basis of age. Over time, two separate processes occur as the age structures change and individuals themselves age. These processes are both independent and separate and also, at some level, inter-dependent.

In summary, age is an *indicator*, as opposed to a determinant, of biological and psychological changes; it can be a *determinant* of individuals' allocated roles, independent of their biological or psychological capacity; it has *analytical value* as a descriptive variable; and it identifies at any given time point *birth-cohort membership*, and thus potential life shared cohort experiences.

Generation

The role of generation has long excited the minds of philosophers and historians. In his historical analysis of the study of generations, Jaeger[35] identifies Comte[36] as producing the first scientific study of generations in history. During the 1830s he systematically examined the succession of generations as they moved through history, arguing that social progress required death as the renewer of human society. Other German scholars, Dromel,[37]

Ferrari[38] and Rümelin,[39] took up the theme, the former two attempting to impose, via an arithmetic bridge, a biological-genealogical thirty-year rhythm onto the chronology of collective historical events.[40] A shift away from mass historical development to a more specific group-oriented approach occurred with the writings of Dilthey. Focusing on writers, artists and philosophers, he noted that many of the important contributors to German Romanticism were born in adjoining years (1767, 1768, 1770, 1773), leading him to theorise that:

> Those who receive the same impression during their formative years form a generation. In this sense, a generation consists of a close circle of individuals who make up a holistic unit through their dependence upon the same historical events and changes which they experience during their formative years in spite of other differences. [Dilthey, 1875][41]

The stereotype that impressions received in younger years cannot be easily discarded in later life, no matter how convincing these later contrasting impressions may be, was cast.

The interwar years saw a regular flow of dissertations on generations from across the humanities and beyond: Ortega[42] for the philosophy of culture; Muller[43] for history; Pinder[44] for art history; Lorenz[45] for the history of music and literary historians Kummer;[46] Alewyn[47] and Petersen;[48] Wechessler[49] for Romantic languages; Drerup[50] for classics; and Scheidt[51] for biology. While most confine their thoughts to concepts of groups of thematically orientated generations emerging in the arts or literature for example, some writers, such as the philosopher Ortega, still pushed the idea of universal historical generations, while others such as Pinder, Lorenz, Muller and again Ortega, remained convinced of the idea of rhythmic historical generations tied into biological laws. Pinder and his development of *entelechy* provides an example of this. For Pinder entelechy denotes an intellectual formative tendency characteristic of a certain historic period. Examples of specific groupings of apparently associated births which Pinder finds remarkable include the three years 1683–87 which saw the births of Rameau, Berkeley, Watteau, Bach, Handel, Scarletti, Asam and Neumann, or the single year 1813 in which Verdi, Wagner, Hebbel, Buchner and Ludwig were all born.

What all these theorists had in common was the search for a general law which would express the rhythm of historical development, in terms of a biological law relating to the limited human lifespan and the continual overlap of current and subsequent generations.[52] While few scholars subsequently accepted the logic of historical change being tied to biological laws, the underlying concept of conservative older generations being superseded by creative younger ones as a driver of social change and historical development remained embedded in social thought.

But there were voices of dissent. Febvre, for example, pointed out that these were but segments of generations, identifiable literary generations might cross-cut in time political generations, and even if they were to coexist the forces producing them might well be different. This was articulated in the classic theory of Karl Mannheim, who declared that:

'the social phenomenon of generations represents nothing more than a particular kind of identity of location, embracing related age groups embedded in a historical-social process'.

For Abrams,[53] however, there was an internal coherency to these age groups, perceiving generations to be age groups that not only repudiate norms established by their seniors but carry that repudiation with them through life and seek to transmit it through their successors. He continues with a definition of *generational solidarity* as the collective consciousness crystallised within an age span, creating meaningful, linked or disassociating, relationships between it and other age spans.

What defines one generation will influence another existent at the same time. For example, our artist generation coexists at roughly the same time and is defined by the same age boundaries as a political generation. The two may have very different attributes and be formed through very different processes. Inevitably, however, they will cross-influence each other. Similarly, we are able to *understand* aspects of the later behaviour of an entire generation by reference to an early experience of some members of that chronological age set. For example, all Europeans currently in their seventies and eighties lived through the Second World War. Identification of that experience remains at some level with this generation. What we must avoid, however, is the extrapolation of this single cultural category generation to *explain* broader social processes. Spitzer[54] refines this to point out a further subtle distortion. While it is acceptable to identify generation units as clusters of attributes that distinguish groups chronologically, it is not acceptable to then explain the behaviour of these groups with reference to a chronological definition constructed out of the evidence of that behaviour. For example, if an historically significant cohort is defined by all those whose experience of the First World War decisively affected their political behaviour in 1939, we cannot then expect to use this to address the generational consequences of the First World War, except by definition.

Of interest is that a so-called generation – a generation of artists for example – despite differences in the socialisation and life experiences of coevals may be sustained for 50 years.[55]

In his key paper on 'The Problem of Generations'[56] Mannheim set out to explore a key question of the time, the link between the replacement of generations and social change. Producing the first framework for a systematic study of generations, he introduced the three key concepts of generational location, actual generations and generational units:

> The fact that people are born at the same time, or that their youth, adulthood and old age coincide, does not in itself involve similarity of location; what does create a similar location is that they are in a position to experience the same events and data, and especially that these experiences impinge upon a similarly stratified consciousness.[57]

Contemporaneity becomes significant only when it also involves participation in the same historical and social circumstances. Youth experiencing the same historical events may be part of an *actual generation*, but within this larger grouping, individual groups or *generational units* may work up the material of these common experiences in different ways. Linking concepts of class location with generation location, Mannheim argued that both endow the individual sharing in them with a common location in the social and historical process, thereby limiting them to a specific range of potential experiences.

Furthermore, argues Mannheim, we have to take the phenomenon of stratification into consideration:

> Some older generation groups experience certain historical processes together with the young generation and yet we cannot say that they have the same generation location. The fact that their location is a different one, however, can be explained primarily by the different stratification of their lives.[58]

Refining Dilthey's concept[59] to consider early life experience as providing a *framework* for later experiences, Mannheim argued that childhood impressions form the first strata upon which subsequent later life impressions are embedded. Early impressions form a natural view of the world, all later experiences receiving their meaning from this original set. Older generations will always interpret current events in the light of those early impressions which they absorbed in their youth and thus the two generations can never experience the same historical process in the same manner.

However, further refining this concept in the light of social and historical change, Mannheim goes on to assert that, under certain conditions, older generations become more receptive to influences from the young, to the extent that:

> with an elasticity of mind won in the course of experience, the older generation may even achieve greater adaptability in certain spheres than the intermediary generations, who may not yet be in a position to relinquish their original approach.

Mannheim used these ideas to explore the creation of society through the continuous emergence of new age groups or generations:

> Our culture is developed by individuals who come into contact anew with the accumulated heritage. In the nature of our psychical make-up a fresh contact . . . always means a changed relationship of distance from the object and a novel approach in assimilating, using and developing the proffered material.

If the cultural process were always carried on and developed by the same individuals then, once established, any fundamental social pattern attitude or intellectual trend would probably be perpetuated. Following shifts in historical and social situations, the changes in thought and practice necessitated by the changed conditions could only be brought about if individuals had perfect elasticity of mind, minds capable of experiencing all that there was to experience, knowing all that there was to know, and able to start afresh at any time:

> . . . the continuous emergence of new human beings certainly results in some loss of accumulated possessions . . . [but] it facilitates re-evaluation of our inventory and teaches us both to forget that which is no longer useful and to covet that which has yet to be won.

In illustration of this, Mannheim recalls Hume's notion[60] that the succession of human generations was configured to resemble that of a caterpillar or butterfly, so that the older generation disappears at one stroke and the new one is born all at once. Here each successive generation starts afresh, creates its own social institutions, decides its own moral and legal frameworks, defines good and evil anew. Mannheim adjusts this to ask what the human social life course would be like if one generation lived forever and none followed to replace it. Here lies a world in which the concept of generation is absent, there are no young to challenge the ideas of the old, where, once all have grown to adulthood, children exist only as memories. Indeed a world where the 'history of the social and the biography of the individual occupy the same time line'.[61] In an alternative scenario, James[62] envisages a situation when, after a history of generational replacement, the human race is faced for the first time with no new children, the youngest generation closing human time behind them with each year.

The concept generation has spawned several associated concepts. Though *generation gap* is an often colloquially used term, Spitzer provides a clear definition.[63] Life cycle behaviour is recurrent behaviour appropriate to the chronological phases of each individual's lifespan. Generational consciousness or behaviour is an articulated shared consciousness (sometimes referred to as a generational ideology) by a specific age group due to a shared historical experience. If the division (however perceived) between generations is greater than that normally attributed to life stage differences, we have what is called a generation gap. Generation gaps are by no means fixed and do not necessarily lead to a permanent cultural change. For example, generational conflicts may fade with time as the younger age group take on the lifestyles, goals and obligations of their parents. Alternatively, changes which emerge first as a generational break may remain, to be transmitted through successive age groups until they characterise the population. Many people see the emergent liberal views of the youth of the 1960s as representing such a generational change. What is still not clear, however, is whether these changes emerged from within a specific generational grouping and then spread, or whether they were forces which impacted upon the entire population at the same time, but were taken up rapidly by the younger age groups due to their life stage, and at a slower, but steady rate by older age groups.

Linking individual time with historical time

The length of individual lifespans which overlap does indeed bring a contextual rhythm to history, along the lines of '*I danced with a man who danced with the Queen of France*', a narrative of the 1970s from an elderly woman in her nineties who claimed that as a young girl she had in 1880 danced with an elderly man in his nineties, who claimed that as a very small lad he had danced with Marie Antoinette. Similar tales abound. As Achenbaum[64] points out, the death of the last US Civil War pensioner occurred in the 1970s. A soldier from the 1860s married a young woman just before his death early in the 1900s. She, entitled to a Civil War widow's pension, lived on until the 1970s. There is a real sense of loss each time the last soldier in a particular First World War battle dies. In June 2004 at the 60th anniversary of the D-Day Landings, there was a potent public desire to fully commemorate this historic event as the last major anniversary before all but a handful of the veterans die. A sense that somehow through individual lives history has reality.

Cultural categories and age

At one level we can define single cultural categories in which age differences do matter. Before the age of mass media, multi-channelled television, personal commuters, electronic games and video recordings, there existed a short period when large numbers of the UK population would experience together national media events on a regular basis. In that short period of mass television ownership with only two terrestrial channels and no means of television home recording, the majority of the population would sit down each evening and across the nation jointly enjoy the same media experience. Particularly popular were large costume dramas, and when these were showing local community events were at times curtailed due to lack of attendance.[65] There also exists a 'generation' of adults, born in the UK between the mid-1950s and mid-1960s, who twice weekly en masse viewed a particular children's television programme and are still adept 30 years on at making anything you care to name out of a plastic bottle. While these children experienced very different regional, parental and educational milieux, the subtle educational and behavioural messages transmitted by the makers and presenters of this programme were at some small level internalised by all these children. With the advent of multi-terrestrial channels from the 1970s onwards, followed swiftly by home video recording, such mass devotion by children to one television programme was quickly diluted. Yet while membership of this cultural generation provides a useful reminiscent conversational gambit in adulthood, it is unlikely to have had any deep impact on many future lives, nor is it likely to be of any significant help in understanding broad behaviour patterns of this adult population.

Furthermore, it clearly does not preclude other ways of identifying further cultural categories for these adults. On this scale, however, we can identify many 'generations.' In terms of potential health impacts, for example, there are numerous examples: the generation of almost exclusively bottle-fed adults born in the UK between 1960 and 1975 when breastfeeding was not encouraged; the generation of adults born in the UK who benefited from free NHS care, free dentistry, free school milk; the generation of women given free breast screening and cervical smears; and so on.

Spitzer raises an equally pertinent question. How does one specify the boundaries of generations in a seamless continuum of daily births? As with many social categories, there is an inevitable blurring or ambiguity at the boundaries. Yet demographers routinely manipulate categories handed down by the arbitrary decision of the Census Bureau to allocate precedence to the decades. We are left with groupings defined by birth or age at the commencement of a specific decade – pyramids describing the number of girls born between 1950 and 1960, 1960 and 1970, 1970 and 1980, etc, or fertility rates in clean ten-year intervals each defined as starting with years ending in a 0. In instances where there is evidence or theoretical justification that some perceived age-specific differences may be historically significant, it is appropriate to cut age groups out of the continuum to explore whether their collective behaviour can contribute to explanations,[66] though even then the inevitable blurring may lead to indistinct variation between these and those older and younger ages on either side.

Alternatively, instead of asking how long a generation really is, or how many generations usually coexist, or what points in an individual's life cycle are decisive, or whether ageing has more profound political consequences than early socialisation, we should ask whether and in what respects age related differences matter in a given historical situation.

An alternative way of tackling this is to control for the age-related variable. For example, if we wish to understand the impact of ageing and diet on tooth decay using longitudinal data it is necessary to control for the impact of increased national dental care which affected different groups at different times of their lives. The fact, for example, that 20 year olds may have less dental decay than 10 year olds may well be related to the provision of free National Health dental care throughout the childhood of the 20 year olds, and not for the 10 year olds. It clearly does matter when you were born. The baby boom generation of the USA – those born between 1946 and 1966 – have lived their lives in competition with their fellow age peers for education, jobs and (soon) Social Security. Those born in later decades, face less competition for employment, but an increased necessity to support late life programmes such as Medicare and Social Security. Similarly, those born in the early 1960s in the UK faced massive unemployment as they were entering the labour market, fundamentally affecting their lifelong earning opportunities; those born in the 1990s will enjoy the opportunities of a labour shortage when they reach labour market age. We shall explore aspects of this in more depth below.

In summary, we have two broad contemporary frameworks within which the concept of generation is interpreted. Those scholars within theoretical sociology and social history who perceive individuals born within the same time period as having a shared history, a common biography, view generation as the link between an individual life course and the social changes that occur during the historical time of that life course. A generation may thus be thought of as *embodied history*.[67] The problem then for quantitative social scientists is how to disentangle those factors pertaining to the individual life course from those emerging from the historical context. It is here that the concept of cohorts, and cohort analysis has been refined by some to form a more analytical tool in the understanding of age and generational change.

Cohort

While historians had been using the concept of generation for some time, the socio-logical concept of cohort appears to have been introduced by Ryder[68] in 1965;[69] Cohort location then became established as a central variable in sociological analysis.[70] Cohort flow was identified as a ubiquitous social process that gave a new dynamism to the understanding of the constitution of societal age structure,[71] as well as to the forces impinging on individuals as they moved through the life course. As Dannefer and Uhlenberg[72] point out, the reliance of human development on social relations and the importance of social interaction as a key determinant of human growth is recognised in the young, but often overlooked in the older population. Yet it remains decisively impor-tant. Social structure entails the explication of social forces as regular, systematic influ-ences on individuals of all ages at any given point in time. One only need compare patterns of ageing in different historical periods or across cultures to recognise the pro-found significance of social structure:

> These two social relations and social structure describe the features of human dynamics
> that render cohort analysis so necessary because they provide order to the diversity in
> human life course trajectories.

Uhlenberg[73] introduces a key question for those interested in age and ageing societies. Why does each cohort arriving at old age have a particular composition and why does its composition differ from preceding and succeeding cohorts? At one level this is easily addressed. A cohort begins with a particular demography at birth, that is its sex, race and economic composition. Differential mortality may lead to a higher proportion of some subgroups surviving to old age; social mobility may lead to changes in cohort social status composition; and different historical periods will allow or enhance differential migration in and out of specific cohorts.

A more sophisticated analysis places cohorts within specific historical contexts. This approach also attempts to determine intra as well as inter cohort variability. Elder and O'Rand's historical work, for example, identifies linking mechanisms between cohort variability and historical events.[74] The *life-stage principle* suggests that disruptive social changes have enduring consequences on subsequent lives, and a particularly marked effect on those vulnerable at the time of occurrence. The concept of *interdependent lives* diffuses impacts to others not necessarily intimately affected by the initial event. Under a control cycle, disruptive social change produces adaptation effects which influence future actions by individuals. *Situational imperatives* refer to the wider cohort changes that may occur in response to the initial event. Finally, new situations are responded to by both individuals and cohorts in respect of the characteristics developed by each in response to the initial event, the *accentuation principle*.

Then there is the question of *cohort accounting*. Uhlenberg and Miner[75] provide a clear synthesis of the argument. In many western countries a system of public *intergenerational transfer* occurs whereby money is transferred from the working population, usually via taxation, to older people in the form of old age-related benefits. In the USA, for example, most of the revenue collected for the Social Security payroll tax in a particular year is not retained for the benefit of the current workers, but is paid out to the current older population. This system operates due to an implicit understanding – a *social contract*, in this case an *intergenerational contract* – that cohorts paying Social Security taxes throughout their working years will subsequently receive benefits in their old age, which in turn will be funded by payroll taxes from the then working cohorts. However, the balance between what any specific cohort gives and what it receives over its entire lifetime will vary:

> If successive cohorts did not change in size and composition, if no change occurred in life expectancy, and if no change occurred in the rules governing transfers between age groups, it would not be difficult to develop an accounting schema to answer the question of lifetime taxes and benefits for each cohort.

Each cohort, however, has a specific demography – they vary in size and gender and racial composition, and each moves through its life course in the context of varying economic, political and social events, with different policy outcomes. While it is theoretically possible to produce an accurate system of cohort or generational accounting,[76] estimating lifetime consequences of specific policies for each cohort in relation to economic growth is a complex system, and its merits are still unclear.[77]

Age and the life course

Like gender and ethnicity, both age and life course are socially constructed. The life course in complex societies is based on a combination of generational and chronological age.[78] As we discussed earlier in relation to age as a variable, we need to combine age with other social characteristics, so the intersection of age with gender, race and class produces specific life experiences for men and women across the life course. In addition, the life course perspective promotes a holistic, as opposed to an age segmented, approach, focusing on pathways and transitions, rather than on differences across or within certain age groups.[79]

A starting point for life course analysis is the acknowledgement of the historical context within which different cohorts experience different aspects of the life course.[80] Currently, most older people in western societies carry with them distinctive life course experiences. In this way, many older women experienced their younger lives within a framework of primary domestic duties, supplemented by intermittent economic activity. Most older men experienced a long period of economic activity, with supplemental, if any, domestic duties, followed by abrupt retirement. As a result, most older women replaced low earning capacity or economic dependence in younger life, with low incomes in old age. Cohorts in midlife, however, have had very different social and economic frameworks within which to live out their lives. Half the labour force in many countries is now female, and full-time economic employment, with or without domestic, in particular childcare, responsibilities, is becoming a widespread experience for women. Despite this, there is still considerable income disparity in the earning capacity of mid-life men and women. However, it is likely that future cohorts of older women will have higher incomes relative to previous cohorts, and a lower gender income disparity will emerge.

Within this historical context, Elder[81] identifies two life course themes – *timing* and *process*. Timing relates to the incidence, duration and sequence of roles throughout the life course.[82] Thus understanding an individual's life course employment history is more useful than understanding their employment position at any one point. *Process* focuses on ageing as a series of life transitions. Each phase of life is understood in relation to prior phases, and is mediated by other variables of gender, class and race. The transition from student to employed, for example, produces different life experiences and trajectories depending on whether the individual leaves full-time education at 16 and moves into unemployment, or at 25 and moves into a high income profession. Similarly, the transition to parenthood is experienced very differently by men and women, and the transition to parent of a non-dependent child, the so-called *empty nest syndrome*, is mediated both by gender and by the experience of active parenting itself. This view has been expanded by Dannefer,[83] drawing on theories of *cumulative disadvantage*.[84] Thus initial inequalities arising from gender, class or race, for example, both place the individual on a trajectory, and serve to constrain the individual over the life course. As a result, such early inequalities are accentuated over time.

In addition, these life course trajectories are also influenced by personal characteristics:

> Individuals traverse a variety of distinctive tracks through their lives: life course pathways consisting of various role transitions and trajectories, and developmental pathways, including transitions and trajectories related to physiological health and psychosocial characteristics, such as identity, efficacy and happiness.[85]

Another perspective has explored the life course in terms of the differentiation of activities. The stereotypic model is to perceive ageing as moving through a period of youth involved in education, midlife involved in production and reproduction, and late life in rest and leisure. However, as Riley has pointed out,[86] age differentiated social structures separating life into such age-graded phases is incompatible with current demographic and social changes. As we shall discuss in Chapter 6, along with ever lengthening longevity we are also seeing a general delaying of life transitions. As a result, such age graded phases as education, production and leisure are now occurring concurrently rather than sequentially, resulting in diverse individual trajectories.

Alternative perspectives

We explored earlier the concept of age as an indicator of biological and psychological changes, and a determinant of individuals' allocated roles, independent of their biological or psychological capacity, acknowledging that age identifies at any given time potential life shared cohort experiences. In addition, we now see that the intersection of age with gender, race and class produces specific life experiences for men and women across the life course. This is, of course, all very much driven by our understanding of western societies. We shall conclude our discussion of age, generation and life course with a brief illustration from non-Western society. The connection of life course with age is far weaker in traditional societies, though of all societies, East Africa is known for its age sets and age grading. Almagor provides a detailed analysis and ethnography of the intricate system of ritual transitions members have to pass through in order to progress from one age grade to another.[87]

Various anthropological studies[88] have highlighted alternative ways in which the life course might be structured, though by the late twentieth century the influence of the state and penetration of chronological age as an ordering variable was evident in most of the research sites. In Stroeken's study of the Sukama of north-west Tanzania, for example, rather than individuals being marked by a physical body, they were defined by a zone, incorporating the large network of life course events. This emphasises the social status of elderhood, measured by the wealth of alliances, offspring and livestock, which cannot be diminished through ill health or loss of mental capacity. The Gussui of south-western Kenya[89] have a similar notion of elderhood. However they have adapted this traditional seniority gradation based on networks and affiliations to modern demands, incorporating such aspects as the role of entrepreneur to the criteria for achieving successful seniority status. As a consequence, elders no longer have a precise measure by which to gauge their successful attainment of elderhood.

In the AGE study,[90] neither the !Kung nor Herero, hunter-gatherer and Bantu pastoralist peoples respectively of Botswana, had a concept of chronological age, and while they were able to sort members of the community into apparently age related groups when requested to do so by the researcher, they were unable to perceive similarities between members of these groups, neither could they understand why there should be:

> . . . neither terms for life stages nor chronological ages have much function in daily life. Rural Herero is a face-to-face society, and there is little or no reason to resort to age categories, or any other type of category for describing people or groups of people.[91]

This view was also reflected in the concept of ageing, which was regarded as a slow inexorable process of physical decline, but the tempo of which varied widely among individuals:

> . . . as people age, their activities gradually become more and more restricted, but there are no standard or stereotypical activities of the elderly. A person who retains health at age 70 does much the same thing every day as a 50 year old.[92]

Herero or !Kung mark age by physical transitions – physical decline is a significant marker because it is so related to survival, though this is moderated by kin support. Alternatively, for the Tuareg, a semi-nomadic peoples in northern Niger, social transitions – courtship, marriage, childbirth and grandchildren – mark ageing, not number of years survived.[93] In an added twist, then, life transitions defining the ageing process are predominantly social rather than biological. A girl becomes a woman not at menstruation, but at marriage; a woman becomes an older woman not at menopause, but on having a child marry. These social transitions are expressed in both public and private conduct and religious ritual: forms of dress, song and dance, and use of public space are carefully delimited by social age, and form the structure to Tuareg society. Prominent in Tuareg ideology is the didactic relationship of youth and old age with secularism and music, prayer and peace respectively. These are further enhanced by metaphors of kinship and social stratum; Tuareg society is acutely hierarchical. Thus rituals surrounding life transitions serve not only to change the status of the individual but also to realign roles, and reaffirm and integrate social relationships, particularly between social cohorts.

The contrast between the ethnographer, Rasmussen,[94] and the peoples she is recording, vividly captures the social construction of age as a marker of time and life. The question raised by Rasmussen is, how would our image and relationship with later life change if we lived in a culture in which *biological and social transitions* measured our progress through the years? Defined by US western codes she is an unmarried mid-life western woman. Yet by Niger reckoning she is still in the full flush of youth, having yet to pass through the rites of passage of marriage and childbearing. At the same time she is a social contemporary, of some 20 years standing, of a cohort of Niger women who are now attaining later life through grandparenthood. There is particular pathos in the description of the rapid physical decline of many of her friends. In previous times she and they danced together as young maidens. Now, while she still biologically has the physical body of a young woman, some of her contemporaries have died, and most are old women with grandchildren, scarred by the physiological disease and decay of the harsh Niger environment.

Taking a different regional example, Japanese society applies a wide variety of terms to different points of the life course. Traphagen's lexicon[95] of commonly used terms illustrates the complexity of the relationship between chronological age and life transitions. These he divides into relational age terms and periodic age terms. Three terms divide all individuals into categories based upon relative rank – *senpai* (senior), *kohai* (junior) and *doryo* (colleague). This pertains to both kin terms and the public work of school, work and community. In addition, kin-based terms denoting age or status will be used to apply to non-kin. For example, mid-life men and women, whether they are married with children and regardless of their relationship to the namer, will commonly be referred to as uncle and aunt (*oji-san* and *oba-san*). Similarly, old men and women are frequently given the name of grandfather or grandmother (*ojii-san* and *obaa san*) regardless of the presence or otherwise of grandchildren.[96] In all cases the use of the term is related to a combination of chronological age and physical appearance.

In addition, there are a series of terms through which all individuals transition. Broadly speaking, these flow for males from new born baby (*aka-chan*) to weaned or toddling boys (*boya*), to elementary (*shogakusei*) middle (*chugakusei*) and high (*kokosei*) school students. On entry into work, a ritual transition occurs (*seijinshiki*) enabling the term *shakaijin* to be used. Those who reach age 18 and pass onto college rather than the world of work are perceived to be in a liminal state between childhood and adulthood. This further emphasises the close correlation of life stages with age in defining points on the life course, and is in strong contrast to the purely chronological definition of attainment of a set age used in most western societies, such as the 18 years of age used in the UK. The term young adult (*otona*) is used to refer to those who have emerged from the liminal state and/or have confirmed themselves as adults, again emphasising the complex association between age and life course. This period of young adulthood (*seinen*) continues until between the ages of 30 and 40, when a man enters the prime of manhood (*sonen*). Again, the combination of life course and age defines this. While marriage or birth of first child may signal the transition into this stage, unmarried men in their fifties are unlikely to be seen as still in young adulthood. The two most common names for old people are old person (*rojin*) or upper years (*otoshiyori*), though, as seen previously, many prefer the term grandfather (*ojii-san*). In addition, the term mature years (*jukunen*) is apparently preferred by some to *rojin,* due to the negative connotation of 'old' in the latter.

It is, therefore, clear that the domination of chronological age has less salience in some cultures than others. The Japanese skilfully combine life course transitions and age, in a manner that is sometimes subconsciously learnt rather than fixed by rigid rules. Other cultures, such as those of the Herero and !Kung, place emphasis on physical deterioration while others, illustrated by the Tuareg peoples, place emphasis on social transitions.

Understanding old age/Understanding post-reproductive life

While there have always been older people, the revolution of the twentieth century was the rapid increase in the numbers of those in later life, so that the percentage surviving to old age, and extreme old age, within each cohort has increased significantly over the past 100 years. As interest has turned to the question of human longevity, so our understanding of the processes behind ageing and senescence has increased. As we have seen, there is currently active scientific debate over the question of increasing life expectancy, and whether there are indeed limits to human longevity. Of equal interest, and currently debated by biologists and anthropologists, is the phenomenon of the extensive physiological post-reproductive lifespan found in humans, and how this is related to modern environmental factors. We shall conclude our chapter on understanding age and ageing with a discussion of the debate concerning the emergence and role of old age as defined as post-reproductive life.

Is post-reproductive life evolutionary or a modern artefact?

Women in modern societies can expect to live nearly one third of their adult lives in a post-reproductive state. Whether this phenomenon is relatively new in human experience, or whether it represents something that has been part of human life for millennia may be relevant to understanding medical and social issues surrounding post-menopausal life.[97]

A series of questions are now gaining particular focus in relation to the phenomenon of the menopause and the long period of post-reproductive life experienced by humans. Is this an adaptive consequence of natural selection, in other words did it arise through evolution, or a non-adaptive consequence of the rapid increase in longevity associated with modernity?[98] If this long post-reproductive lifespan was formed through evolution, what is its role? And, given the very rapid changes in modern environments, what kinds of responses and variability might occur?

The widespread existence of an extensive post-reproductive life in humans has inspired an, at times, heated debate between biologists and anthropologists interested in this experience. The discussion can be simply put as follows. Some believe that the female menopause is an adaptive consequence of natural selection, probably as a solution to the trade-off between investing in additional offspring, or in existing offspring and their children.[99] Others argue that this post-reproductive life of human females is a modern effect due to environmentally induced increases in longevity.[100] In other words, the protection offered by our current environment has enabled us to live much longer than the period within which natural selection has moulded our reproductive capacity. Empirical evidence from both non-human species, and from a variety of studies of living and prehistoric non-technological people, has been drawn upon to address these questions.

Given the earlier caveat, studies of contemporary non-technological peoples[101] such as the !Kung of the Kalahari Desert and Aché in Paraguay, indicate that high proportions of these women live well into post-menopausal years. Until recently, estimates by paleodemograpers suggested that an extensive post-menopausal life did not occur historically.[102] Lee has now questioned this, producing data showing considerable comparability between contemporary and prehistoric non-technological people, which indicates a significant post-reproductive life for women in prehistoric times. Highlighting some of the difficulties of estimating life expectancies from skeletal data, he produces Table 3.1.

Table 3.1 Post-reproductive females in stationary populations

	Paleo average[a]	High mortality[b]	High mortality[c]	Aché[d]	!Kung[e]	Modern industrial[f]	USA in 2065[g]
Life expecantancy at birth (years)	23	20	20	37	30	79	90
Prop. surviving to age 45 (%)	0.17	0.21	0.18	0.46	0.35	0.96	0.997
Life expectancy at age 45 (years)	14	17	16	22	20	36	45
Pop. 45+ as Prop. of total female pop. (%)	0.10	0.18	0.15	0.28	0.23	0.44	0.50
Prop. surviving to age 65 (%)	0.05	0.08	0.06	0.28	0.17	0.85	0.965
Life expectancy at age 65 (years)	7	8	8	10	9	19	27
Pop. 65+ as Prop. of total female pop. (%)	0.01	0.03	0.02	0.08	0.05	0.20	0.28

Notes: [a] This is interpolated from Weiss (1973) model life tables with survival to age 15 assumed to be 0.6, and with life expectancy at 15 set equal to the average given by Hassan (1981) for the Paleolithic studies he reviews, which was 21.2 years.

[b] Based on Coale and Demeny (1983), model West female life tables and stable populations with growth rate 0.

[c] Based on Preston et al. (1993) model life table for females.

[d] Calculated from data in Hill and Hurtado (1996: 196–8). These data are explicitly for the forest dwelling period, not the later reservation period when mortality was lower.

[e] Based on Howell (1979), which I interpret to mean that is appropriate to use Coale-Demeny model west life table with life expectancy at birth of 30 years to characterise !Kung mortality in the past; recent !Kung mortality has been much lower.

[f] Based on the US female life table for 1990, according to data of the Social Security Administration (1992:34–35).

[g] Based on Carter and Lee (1992), who forecast mortality using statistical time-series analysis and some modeling assumptions; they forecast somewhat larger gains in life expectancy than do either the Social Security Administration or the US Census Bureau.

Note: Pop. = population; Prop. = proportion.

Sources: Weiss (1973), Hassan (1981), Coale and Demeny (1983), Hill and Hurtado (1996), Howell (1979), US Social Security Administration (1992), Carter and Lett (1992).

He concludes that, even in Stone Age populations, the life expectancy of females at age 45 was more than 10 years, and probably in the range of 12–25 years, and that up to 30 per cent of the female population was post-reproductive. Therefore, in our pre-agricultural past, post-reproductive females probably made up a substantial proportion of the population.

Austad[103] introduces a somewhat controversial argument for continuing this exploration. If the menopause is an artefact of modern life, he argues, then one can presume that physiologically it represents a decline in homeostasis associated with senescence, and will not facilitate optimal health. Medical interventions, such as hormone replacement therapy (HRT), should improve post-reproductive health. If, however, it is an adaptive physiological state moulded by evolution to maximise fitness, then natural selection would presumably have fashioned post-reproductive physiology to this condition, and HRT should be approached with more caution.

The evolution of the menopause

If the menopause is considered to be an adaptive consequence of natural selection, and, as we have seen, this is still in debate, then we need to consider the factors behind the evolution of the menopause. Most arguments have accepted the longevity of humans as given, and then asked what type of selective forces would result in the menopause. Selection for the cessation of reproduction has generally been seen as a solution to a trade-off between two broad types of investment. First, a trade-off between early and late reproduction, second, between the reproductive value of existing kin, and the production of additional descendants. Both cases rely on the assumption that the children of older women will be of a lower reproductive value. This is due to the increased chance of less viable children, as a result of genetic abnormalities, or due to the higher probability of the parents dying while the children are still young and vulnerable.

In the first argument, a trade-off between early and late reproduction, the literature focuses on the *physiological cause of the menopause*.[104] This appears to be the depletion of oocytes – developing egg cells – through follicle decay, which occurs throughout a woman's life, leaving no viable oocytes after menopause.[105] Kaplan[106] suggests that perhaps the costs of increasing the length of the reproductive period through increasing follicle number or viability, may decrease energy available for reproduction early in life. Thus selection might favour allocating more resources to the early reproductive period, at the expense of ending this in midlife. In the second argument, two assumptions operate. First, given that the children of older women are assumed to be of a lower reproductive value, the cost of the menopause would consequently be low. Second, by ceasing to reproduce, older people can bring benefits by investing in the reproduction of their offspring and other kin. This has been called the *grandmother hypothesis*. In this way, if the cost of the menopause is low, and the benefits are high, menopause could maximise biological fitness.[107]

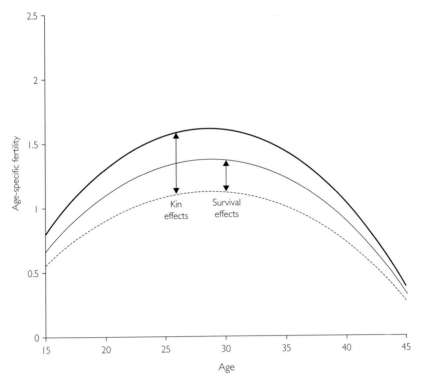

Figure 3.1 *Living longer to invest in descendent offspring.*
Source: Kaplan, 1997.

Kaplan[108] introduces a new slant to the debate suggesting that the question – 'given the human lifespan, what kinds of selective forces could result in the evolution of menopause?' may not be the most helpful. He suggests an alternative question – 'given that humans cease to reproduce in their mid to late forties, why do they live so long?' As Stearns[109] points out, the reproductive biology of today may well represent a genetic history of adapting to previous hostile environments, which almost inevitably led to death before old age. This does not, however, explain why humans retain the capacity to survive long after this reproductive capability has diminished, or failed. Kaplan suggests that perhaps the trade-off here is between living longer to invest in descendent kin and the level of early reproduction. In this case selection might favour allocating more resources to survival and maintenance during younger life, at the expense of a lower reproductive rate. This would, however, be compensated for through increased reproduction of offspring, which would arise from the assistance of older kin. Figure 3.1 displays this.

In Fig. 3.1 the bold line depicts the classic age-specific fertility pattern (in a non-contracepting population without delayed marriage). The dashed line represents the much lower fertility rates that would be achieved without the help of older kin, primarily parents. The difference between the two lines is the increased reproduction due to kin assistance. The solid line represents the higher fertility rate that might be achieved if resources in younger life were not reallocated to ensure survival past menopause, but this would also mean no kin assistance. In other words, while successful reproduction might increase if life ended at menopause, it would not increase as much as it would if assistance from post-menopausal kin were available.

The effect of kin assistance requires the loss of peak reproduction in order to live longer. The costs and benefits are distributed across two generations. The younger generation receives the benefits of assistance from parents and the older generation pays the cost of lower peak reproduction in order to live longer. The older generation received the benefits in turn from their parents. Thus, Kaplan argues, it is possible that a longer lifespan evolved, even though a longer reproductive period did not. He points out that data on the Aché[110] show that men have major declines in fertility after the age of 50; whether this is due to the men not seeking to have their own children or whether they are no longer chosen as partners by younger women, or some other factors, is unclear. However, Kaplan concludes that

> [G]reater focus on the mating and kin investment behaviour of middle-aged and older
> men and on their impacts for survival and reproductive success of offspring and other kin
> in traditional societies is clearly necessary. An understanding of men's behaviour may help
> to solve the riddle of long life and menopause.[111]

The role of post-reproductive life

Regardless of how we phrase the debate, whether we focus on the evolution of a menopause, or on a post-reproductive life, given its current and possibly historical existence for human females, it is appropriate to explore its role. One manner of increasing our understanding of this phenomenon is to examine the circumstances in which it is found in non-human species. Post-reproductive life is found in a variety of mammals; however, it appears that with the exception of some toothed whales,[112] reproductive cessation is an age-related behaviourally imposed cessation, rather than the physiological reproductive cessation found in female humans.[113] In other words, lack of opportunity for mating due to competition from younger animals appears common for both males and females in many mammalian species. Interestingly, however, among mammals kept in captivity, extended life after physiological reproductive cessation not infrequently occurs.[114] Under these conditions, the protected environment ensuring abundant food and protection against predators, enables animals to live much longer than the period over which natural selection has moulded their reproductive capacity.

In a wide-ranging discussion, Carey and Gruenfelder[115] point out that there is clearly some association between extended longevity of a species and complex social structures, and that elderly group members appear to play an important role in sustaining the latter. They present a wide variety of material showing that elderly members of a variety of non-human species play important roles in the cohesion and dynamics of animal populations, serving as guardians, leaders, teachers, caregivers and midwives, sometimes in an apparently altruistic role.[116] Drawing on evidence from toothed whales, elephants and primates, Carey and Gruenfelder reveal how in all three societies older animals undertake specific tasks not performed by the younger animals. For example, both older male and female dolphins frequently guard younger animals. This serves several purposes: the young are protected from predators, monitored so they do not wander, and, possibly, taught adult behaviours by the older dolphins. In addition, the older dolphin is freeing the younger animals to forage for food, an activity that they may not be able to do as efficiently. This, they suggest, is a clear suggestion of reciprocity in work allocation. In addition, older female dolphins may also remain close to their daughters throughout their pregnancies, and assist in the birth, guarding the offspring and allowing the mothers rest after the birth. In contrast, the first major role of elderly elephants is leadership. Elephant size determines dominance and, as elephants continue to grow throughout their lives, is also age dependent. As social organisation is matriarchal, the oldest females are usually the leaders. The matriarch decides both local and seasonal movements, the latter of particular importance because she has retained the knowledge of optimal or long forgotten food and water reserves from her long life. Indeed 'the matriarch is a reservoir of collective wisdom for the community'.[117]

Perhaps the best-known work in this area, is that on primates, with the work of the feminist biologist Hrdy[118] and that of Altman[119] being key. Post-reproductive female life appears common among most primate species, particularly chimpanzees and gorillas.[120] Here we find examples of both leadership and caregiving roles. Both male and female older primates take on leadership of their troops, with the specific gender varying between primate species. In addition, elderly females play an important role in caregiving, with evidence from vervets[121] that the presence of grandmothers can more than halve infant mortality.[122] In addition, as Hrdy[123] points out, in some species, the rank of the older females is passed onto their daughters, thus carrying on into subsequent generations all the advantages or disadvantages that the rank may hold. Finally, Hrdy also highlights the altruistic role some older female primates play in risking their own lives to defend the troop. A similar, apparently altruistic, role is also found in female black bears,[124] who frequently shift their territories away from areas overlapping with their daughters, thereby reducing their own foraging area in favour of their offspring.

It does, therefore, appear that there is considerable evidence from non-human species (and as Carey and Gruenfield point out, a full literature review has never been compiled and synthesised in this field), that elderly members of the population, and in particular grandparents, play an important role in the success of the society, and possibly in ensuring genetic success.

Attempts to test the grandmother hypothesis – that is whether post-reproductive women provide sufficient assistance to offset the contribution of their personal reproduction lost due to menopause – with humans, has been inconclusive. Austad[125] quotes work on late nineteenth-/early twentieth-century Taiwanese farmers,[126] to suggest that the

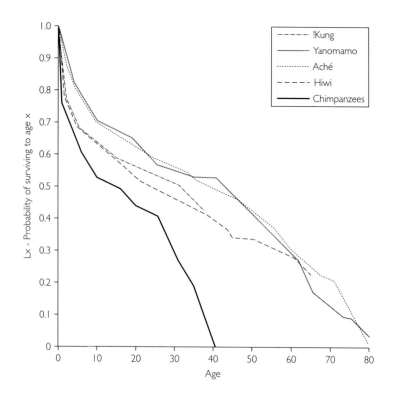

Figure 3.2 *Age-specific probabilities of survival and skill acquisition.*
Source: Kaplan, 1997.

contribution made by the older women as grandmothers did not compensate for their cessation as reproductive mothers. Similarly, Hill and Hurtado's work on the Aché,[127] found a similar hypothesis was not supported by the data. However, they also concluded that in the past older women might have improved the survival of their children, grand-children and other young relatives more than at present, and that maternal mortality might have been higher than observed in contemporary non-technological societies.

The role of elderly adults within contemporary non-technological peoples, can also be illustrated through the work of the anthropologist, Kaplan. Drawing on the fact that, com-pared with all other species, in particular non-human primates, we have a very long post-reproductive lifespan, he gathers material from studies of contemporary non-technological people to suggest that humans developed a very specific type of food gathering which has remained until very recently. Data from the !Kung, Yanomamo, Aché, Hiwi and Hadza hunter-gatherer peoples, reveal diets of large nutrient-dense, low-fibre difficult-to-acquire foods, which have led, he argues, to behaviours and physiology which support long life expectancy. First, the collection of these foods is skill dependent and reliant on skill acquisition. Behind Figure 3.2. is the success of Aché and Yanomamo mid-life men in hunting skill acquisition.

Kaplan argues that these mid-life men, along with other hunter-gatherer groups, have

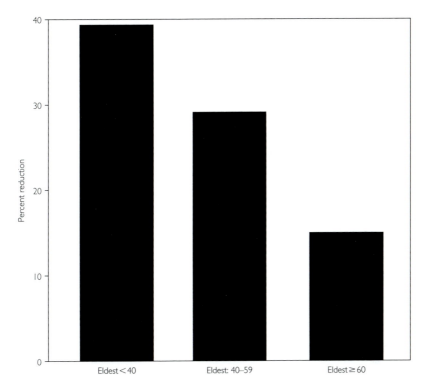

Figure 3.3 *Household profit reduction by presence of elderly person.*
Source: Kaplan, 1997.

acquired detailed knowledge of the reproductive, parenting, grouping, predator avoidance, and communication patterns of each prey species – which takes decades to learn. Thus even men in their late fifties could expect to be significantly more successful at hunting than those in their late teens and early twenties, despite considerable physical inferiority. Maybe, he argues, we evolved a long lifespan because we needed the experience and knowledge of older people to ensure our survival through successful food acquisition. This notion of elderly adults as repositories of knowledge has also been highlighted by demographer and economist Lee. Drawing on Rosenzweig's study of Indian farmers,[128] which explores the relationship between household profit and the presence of an elderly person (Fig. 3.3), he concludes that households in which elderly persons were present were significantly more successful. However, as Lee cautions,[129] we must not presume any causal relationship – as it could well be that good farming practice by the family in general allowed surplus to support elderly parents.

Kaplan's analysis also suggests that the high quality foods consumed by these people may facilitate more effective responses to disease and thus lower mortality, and furthermore that the food-sharing pattern characteristic of these people, may allow sick and injured individuals to recover.[130] However, there is some evidence that death and decline in productivity tend to occur among non-technological peoples at roughly the same time. Extended frailty in old age, currently experienced by a growing number of Westerners, is probably a very recent occurrence.[131] Lee also comes to the same conclusion, commenting on the fact that it is likely that historically the proportion of elderly at or above 65 may have been very low.[132] This may be answered by the findings from contemporary non-technological peoples that frail non-productive elderly are killed. Lee provides a sound summary of our current understanding. Post-reproductive females and older males were probably prevalent in pre-agricultural human populations, and they probably raised the reproductive fitness of their children through leadership, knowledge and food transfers. It is, however, unknown as to whether the longevity of humans can in fact be *explained* by the usefulness of older adults, and the role of post-reproductive life is still unclear.

Notes

1 Kertzer, 1995, p. 364.
2 Thane, 2000, p. 1.
3 ibid., p. 2.
4 See, for example, the pictorial representation of the female life-cycle in the Museum Voor Volkesunde, Belgium reproduced in Walker, 1996, p. 38.
5 Minois, 1989.
6 Parkin, 1992.
7 Thane, 2000.
8 See, for example, Finley, 1984 and Parkin, 1992 on Classical societies; Shahar, 1997 and Pelling and Smith, 1991 on Early Modern and Medieval societies; Minois, 1989, Cole, 1992 and Achenbaum, 1995 more generally.
9 Thane, 2000.
10 UK ERSC New Dynamics of Ageing Programme.
11 Marmot et al., 2003.
12 Kertzer and Schaie, 1989; Kertzer and Keith, 1984.
13 Hazelrigg, 1997.
14 Hazelrigg, 1997, p. 111.
15 Riley, 1987.
16 Riley et al., 1972.
17 Minkler and Estes, 1999.
18 Hazelrigg, 1997, p. 105.
19 Mead, 1934.
20 Mead, quoted in Hazelrigg, 1997, p. 105.
21 Hochschild, 1973.
22 Hagestad, 1986.
23 A personal anecdote illustrates this – Andrew Paterson became Britain's youngest heart transplant patient in 1980 at age 22. Normal experience for a 20 year old in the late twentieth century did not include long-term illness

and disability. Solace was found in the reading of First World War literature, when such experiences were the common experience of many young men.
24 Another personal anecdote – on arrival in Shanghai as an invited academic from the University of London, the Welcoming Ceremony was delayed for some time, until the Head of the Shanghai Bureau asked when Professor Harper was arriving. When I was introduced for the second time, he refused to speak to me or to show me any courtesy for the remainder of the visit. A 30-year-old woman was clearly not an "on-time" prestigious academic visitor!
25 Kohli, 1986; Marshall, 1985; Keith et al., 1994; Thomas, 1979.
26 Hazelrigg, 1997.
27 ibid.
28 Fry, 1999.
29 Neugarten, 1982.
30 Fortes, 1984.
31 Riley et al., 1972.
32 Riley and Riley, 1994.
33 Riley, 1972.
34 McMullin, 2000.
35 Jaeger, 1985.
36 Comte, 1849.
37 Dromel, 1862.
38 Ferrari, 1874.
39 Rüemelin, 1875.
40 Jaeger, 1985.
41 Dilthey, 1875 quoted in Jaegar, 1985, p. 276.
42 Ortega y Gasset, 1923.
43 Müller, 1928.
44 Pinder, 1926.

45 Lorenz, 1928.
46 Kummer, 1922.
47 Alewyn, 1929.
48 Petersen, 1930.
49 Wechssler, 1930.
50 Drerup, 1933.
51 Scheidt, 1929.
52 Mannheim, 1964 [1929].
53 Abrams, 1970.
54 Spitzer, 1973.
55 This example is given by Spitzer to illustrate a slightly different point.
56 Mannheim, 1929.
57 Mannheim, 1929 quoted in Jaeger, 1985.
58 Spitzer, 1973.
59 The work of Dilthy and Mannheim was to serve as the foundation of imprint analysis and the psychological understanding of adolescence and age cohorts.
60 Hume, 1739.
61 Hardy and Waite, 1997.
62 James, 1992.
63 Spitzer, 1973.
64 Achenbaum, 1998.
65 The prime example of this was in the 1960s when the BBC's Sunday evening showing of *The Forsyte Saga* resulted in Sunday evening church services across the country being rescheduled for a few weeks.
66 Spitzer, 1973.
67 Harper, 2004c.
68 Ryder, 1965.
69 According to Dannefer and Uhlenberg, 1999.
70 Elder, 1974.
71 Riley et al., 1972.
72 Dannefer and Uhlenberg, 1999.
73 Uhlenberg and Miner, 1996.
74 Elder and O'Rand, 1995; O'Rand, 1996.
75 Uhlenberg and Miner, 1996.
76 Kotlikoff, 1992.
77 Howse, 2005.
78 Fry, 1999; Elder, 1985; Hagestad and Neugarten, 1985.
79 Moen, 1996.
80 Elder and O'Rand, 1995.
81 Elder, 1985.
82 Moen, 1996.
83 Dannefer, 1987.
84 Merton, 1968.
85 Moen, 1996, p. 178.
86 Riley and Riley, 1994.
87 Almagor, 1978b; Almagor, 1978a.
88 Makoni and Stroeken, 2002.
89 Okemwa, 2002.
90 Keith et al., 1994.
91 ibid., p. 20.
92 ibid.
93 Rasmussen, 1997.
94 ibid.
95 Traphagan, 2000.
96 This is also found in some European based cultures, see Mestheneos and Svensson-Dianellou, 2004.
97 Austad, 1997, p. 161.
98 ibid.
99 Kaplan, 1997; Hill and Hurtado, 1991.
100 Austad, 1997.
101 Hill and Hurtado, 1991; Lancaster and King, 1992.
102 Weiss, 1973; Lovejoy et al., 1977.
103 Austad, 1997.
104 vom Saal et al., 1994.
105 Richardson et al., 1987 quoted in Kaplan, 1997.
106 Kaplan, 1997.
107 ibid.
108 ibid.
109 Stearns, 1992.
110 Hill and Hurtado, 1991.
111 Kaplan, 1997, p. 198.
112 For example, pilot, killer and sperm whales, and dolphins.
113 Clutton-Brock et al., 1988, quoted in Austad, 1997.
114 vom Saal and Finch, 1988, quoted in Austad, 1997.
115 Carey and Gruenfelder, 1997.
116 See also Hrdy, 1981; Rogers, 1987; Altmann, 1980; Hill and Hurtado, 1991.
117 Eltringham, 1982, quoted in Carey and Gruenfelder, 1997, p. 137.
118 Hrdy, 1981.
119 Altman, 1980.
120 Caro et al., 1995, quoted in Carey and Gruenfelder, 1997.
121 Small grey African monkeys.
122 Fairbanks and McGuire, 1986, quoted in Carey and Gruenfelder, 1997.
123 Hrdy, 1981.
124 Rogers, 1987.
125 Austad, 1997.
126 Rogers, 1993.
127 Hill and Hurtado, 1991.
128 Rosenzweig, 1994.
129 ibid.
130 Kaplan and Hill, 1985.
131 Kaplan, 1997.
132 Lee, 1997.

4

Retirement: from rest to reward to right

Current retirement attitudes and behaviour are generally considered to be fixed, when in fact they are period-specific. Indeed, mass retirement at a broadly fixed chronological age is historically new, arising in the second half of the twentieth century to cope with the specific health and socio-economic needs of the then older population, and in response to the changing demands of the labour market. Mass withdrawal by workers at state pension age has been extended to ever younger ages over the past 30 years through the spread of early retirement practices.

Historical trends in late life work and retirement

To put this in an historical perspective, there has been a steady withdrawal in most OECD countries from employment at earlier ages throughout the twentieth century.[1] The British situation provides a good context within which to explore these trends historically. There is some debate among historians of work and old age,[2] as to whether the nineteenth century was indeed unique in its high labour force participation rates of older workers, and whether this may not have been the norm in the preceding centuries.[3] However, all agree that there was a steady decline in participation rates among the over-65s from the end of this century. In 1881, 75 per cent of men over the age of 65 living in the UK were economically active, with the suggestion that this may well have been a stable figure for many centuries.[4] Male life expectancy at this time was 42 years. As Table 4.1 reveals, with a few exceptions,[5] male labour participation rates fell steadily over the next 100 years, though they have now risen slightly since the mid-1990s, By 1931, 70 per cent of those aged 65–69 were still economically active, and 37 per cent of those aged over 70; by 1961 this had fallen to 40 per cent and 10 per cent respectively. Whether coincidental or as a result of the same processes, as life expectancies increased (see Table 4.2), and the population of the UK aged, so older men withdrew from economic activity.

The data for women is far more problematic, and as we shall see later, the issue of female retirement remains complex today, compounded by cohort and period trends. Thane[6] suggests that most older women who had a permanent occupation recorded in the Census continued to work past the age of 65, and they admitted to later retirement ages than men. The 1901 Census, for example, attempted to distinguish between those who were retired from an occupation versus those who were no longer working due to marriage, although, as is clear, there are complexities with the figures. (See Table 4.3.)

Table 4.1 *UK male labour participation rates, 1891–2004, age 65+ (%) (rounded)*

1891	65
1901	61
1931	48
1951	31
1991	8
2001	8
2004	9

Source: ONS, 2004.

Table 4.2 *UK male life expectancies, 1891–2001 (in years)*

1891	41.9
1911	49.4
1931	58.4
1951	66.2
1971	68.8
1991	73.2
2001	75.7

Source: ONS, 2001.

Table 4.3 *UK economically active women, 1901 (%)*

Age	Economically active	Retired
55–64	17	8
65–74	13	28
75+	7	92

Source: Census 1901.

Clearly, for both men and women, it is difficult to obtain accurate figures, and late life work may also have continued far longer as hidden and casual employment, however, the trends to withdrawal from the labour market at earlier ages throughout the twentieth century are present.

Far earlier in the nineteenth century, however, it was widely accepted that large numbers of older men and women were being forced through poverty and need to undertake menial toil merely to survive:

> . . . old factory hands [were] presented with a broom, shovel and wheelbarrow, old farm workers employed at stone-breaking and roadwork, old artisans in repair work, old miners working at odd jobs at the pithead, old dressmakers on rough sewing work, and old servants at daily work and charring . . . in the later nineteenth century [there] was

the emergence of a widely expressed revulsion that old people should be forced to such straits in an increasingly prosperous society. Their employment was seen as a source of degradation rather than of status.[7]

The pattern of life for most working people in rural communities . . . was to go on working for as long as one was physically capable, moving to lighter or casual jobs, at progressively lower levels of pay . . . until rendered completely unemployable by ill health, accident or disability. For those too infirm to work, the final years of life were likely to be a precarious existence: every effort would be made to eke out a meagre living – by obtaining outdoor relief, by appealing to charities, by selling furniture and personal effects, by begging, by moving in with relatives – until all resources were exhausted. The last resort would be the Poor Law Workhouse.[8]

As Thane concludes, it came to be generally accepted that old people, like young children, should no longer be expected to toil for survival. Thus the steady introduction of old age pensions, and the emergence of the concept of a period of retirement prior to death.

Yet, as Thane, in her history of old age in England, points out, the 1881 Census was the first to classify the 'retired' as a separate category, though whether this indicates the emergence of the retired as a separate social group, or merely reflects the practicalities of providing information to describe social structure, is, as Thane comments, debatable. Indeed, she quotes Fogarty's assertion that retirement was not a familiar concept among the late nineteenth-century working class, and it was not until the 1920s that the word and associated concept became widely known, with old men being more commonly referred to as retired, pensioner or superannuated.[9] During the early twentieth century, there was an attempt to divide people of working age into the fully employed, the unemployed and the retired. As the labour market restructured and casual work became less available, retirement and unemployment became common terms.

McNicol's[10] comprehensive analysis of the history of British retirement between 1878 and 1948 argues that from the 1880s onwards older workers were forced from the labour market due to technological intensification and an increasingly specialised seg-mented labour force. McNicol believes this led to the introduction of a state pension, and this loss of work led to loss of status for older people. He therefore suggests that by the end of the nineteenth century a new stage of economic development had been reached. Technological developments in industry began to displace older workers who were judged unable to upgrade their skills or surplus to requirements. McNicol refers to '. . . the need to improve industrial productivity by disciplining the young, able-bodied male worker . . .; and the need to hasten the industrial exit of the older "worn out" worker who was increasingly surplus to the requirements of modern capitalism'.[11]

This political economy approach, has, however, been questioned, most noticeably by Thane[12] and Johnson.[13] While agreeing that the question of retirement is complex, they both argue that sectoral shifts in the economy were most influential at this time. At the turn of the twentieth century older workers were concentrated in agriculture, this being the occupation which had been most readily available to them on entering the labour market in their youth. Yet agriculture contracted from the late nineteenth century onwards. Indeed, Johnson[14] suggests that most of the fall in participation rates between 1881 and 1921 was as a result of this sectoral shift in the economy. Meanwhile younger workers had entered the new heavy industrial sector which had expanded throughout the nineteenth century, only to contract during the interwar years when these workers were themselves old. This explanation is also supported by Thane, who points out that male labour market participation over age 65 did decline at the turn of the twentieth century but that this can almost all be accounted for by a general decline in agricultural employment at that time, there being no significant increase in recorded retirement of older men in industrial or service occupations in England, Wales, Germany or France before the 1920s. In other occupational sectors recorded male retirement remained almost constant in Britain between 1881 and 1921. Furthermore, employment rates of men in their fifties actually increased during 1891 to 1921 with the non-agricultural sectors providing alternative job opportunities for these men at this time.[15]

Another factor is the type of work which many older male manual workers were engaged in. Much of the paid work for older men and women was marginal and casual and its availability was gradually shrinking throughout the late nineteenth and early twentieth centuries.[16] Indeed, there was an attempt early in the twentieth century to remove casual labourers from the labour market in order to eliminate underemployment and low pay.[17] In addition, as Thane[18] points out, as well as agriculture, there were smaller concentrations of older male workers in sales work, clothing manufacture, and labouring jobs, all occupations characterised by weak worker organisations, and thus vulnerable to employer instigated redundancy.

Finally, there is the contribution of new pension legislation. It is possible that the introduction of old age pensions at the beginning of the century may have influenced retirement patterns. However, as both Thane[19] and Johnson[20] point out, the introduction of the old age pension in 1908 appears to have had little actual impact on retirement trends. Furthermore, the reduction in 1925 of the pension age from 70 to 65 came immediately before the Depression of the 1930s, and the subsequent rise in the number of retired older men during the 1930s was probably related more to the difficulty unemployed older men faced in re-entering the labour market following dismissal. The real impact of the pension at this time may have been to enable older workers to give up that portion of their income derived from degrading and often harsh casual work, and this may have been particularly the case for women.[21] If there was an economic impact, however, it was probably more firmly concentrated among the middle and lower middle classes. Here the spread of occupational pensions and other assets allowed these groups to afford the luxury of voluntary retirement after age 65.

During the interwar period, unemployment was concentrated among older industrial workers.[22] Johnson[23] argues that at this time both employers and trade unions conspired to preserve limited jobs for younger workers with family responsibilities. In addition, as noted earlier, given the availability of jobs in this sector at the turn of the century, a large proportion of the then younger workers had entered this occupational sector, and had aged within it. Yet, as with agriculture at the end of the nineteenth century, the heavy industrial sector in the UK now began to decline and with it the jobs now occupied by older men. The figures in the immediate post-Second World War period were confused, however, by the labour shortage, which may well have reduced the withdrawal by older men. Conversely, the introduction in 1948 of public pensions conditional on retirement from full-time employment must have had some negative impact on participation. In addition, the increasing mechanisation of many production processes was beginning to impact upon older workers. Older workers found the increase in pace required for some of these processes more difficult than younger workers. Thus jobs requiring teams of workers operating at a pre-established rate had the highest retirement rate; conversely highly skilled occupations benefiting from experience had the lowest.[24]

Changing attitudes to retirement

The post-war period

It was during the post-war years that a variety of complex factors began to interact. As Harper and Thane[25] have pointed out, the post-war years saw a steady change in attitude towards retirement and retirement behaviour itself. The period from 1945 to the late 1960s is of particular interest, not only because withdrawal spread through all classes and occupational groups, but also because this retirement coincided with unprecedented peacetime employment opportunities.[26] The percentage of men over age 70 who were retired rose between 1931 and 1961 from 63 per cent to 90 per cent. Similarly, the percentage of men aged 65–69 who were retired doubled during this time to reach 60 per cent by 1951. This comparison between 1931 and 1951 is particularly significant as the first census occurred during a period of high unemployment with low labour opportunities for older workers, the second during a time of labour shortage. It is also clear that employers, coping with increasingly bureaucratised organisations with a heavy administrative structure, used a retirement age to regulate the workforce. There was a steady move towards fixed retirement ages during these decades. While surveys[27] suggested that around one quarter of firms had fixed retirement ages in the 1940s and 1950s, this figure had increased to two-thirds by the early 1960s.[28] This was most prevalent in large, technological industries with complex administrative structures.[29] By the mid-1960s, major industries such as chemicals, iron and steel, and the nationalised coal mines and railways, all operated with rigid retirement ages. Alongside this ran growing ageism towards older workers. Already by 1957, there was a recognition that discrimination by employers against men aged over 50 was becoming widespread.[30]

Of particular interest is the fact that attitudes to retirement were generally negative during this time. Indeed, due to an earlier predicted labour shortage, the rhetoric we now hear early in the twenty-first century had already been rehearsed some 50 years earlier.[31] Awareness of the changing population structure of the UK – the percentage of over-65s in the population rising almost fourfold from 3.5 per cent to 12 per cent in the first half of the century – led to concern over population ageing. This was compounded by the perceived increase in retirement rates noted above, the percentage of men aged 65–69 who were retired doubling between 1931 and 1951 alone, from 30 per cent to 60 per cent. Alarm was expressed that the ageing of the population would create an unbalanced ratio of workers to dependants, with severe social and economic consequences, though it was unclear as to what these exactly might entail. Support was expressed for the long-term retention of older workers within the workforce. Both the 1947 Economic Survey[32] and the 1948 Royal Commission on Population[33] called for an increase in older workers, arguing for more flexible practices to encourage this. The Philips Report[34] in 1951, however, forecast little change in the dependency ratio, on the assumption that the same percentage would be employed in each age group, these calculations being based on the temporary increase during 1951–53 in older workers, rather than the overall trend towards earlier withdrawal. However, others also warned that demographic ageing would lead to an increase in elderly dependants. Thus while the overall proportion of dependants to workers would not change, state spending by social services on older dependants would be twice that on children, and therefore overall costs would rise.[35] Data was produced revealing that the proportion of national income transferred to those aged over 65 had quadrupled between 1910 and 1954,[36] and the Government Actuary estimated that there would be a £364 million deficit in the National Insurance Fund by 1979 due to increased pensions. The subsequent recommendation was to raise the pension age for men to 68.[37]

The public debate focused on the dependency ratio, rising pensions costs and a move to retaining older workers, all rhetoric emerging again in the early 2000s.[38] As 50 years later, this was supported by evidence that older workers made an active and valuable contribution to the workforce.[39] While there were changes in capacity with age, these could be overcome through retraining and adaptation of the work environment.[40] Furthermore, an age-integrated workforce was perceived to be a versatile workforce.[41]

The final stream of the debate, however, is absent from current concerns. Supported by the medical profession, the retirement impact hypothesis,[42] having been out of fashion during the depression years, resurfaced:

> The literature is overwhelming in its indications that retirement is detrimental to the health of older men.[43]

> . . . the weight of medical opinion is that sudden demise of mental and bodily functions, previously regularly exercised, such as may happen through retirement is likely to cause atrophy and degeneration which are harmful to the health of older persons.[44]

In fact, the literature far from being overwhelming, was negligible in the UK,[45] and under debate in the USA.[46] Yet, it was clearly useful for the government in its campaign to retain older workers to promote such views. A Ministry of Health Circular of 1954 read as follows:

> After six weeks of this existence, life began to pall. He became unsettled, restless and irritable. He really had nothing to do and longed to be back at work. He was repeatedly asked to take up some hobby, which he readily promised to do but his restlessness prevented him from seriously attempting it and a laissez-faire attitude resulted. . . . Eventually getting up in the morning became an effort, and in a short time all his interest in everything flagged. The peace of death came to him soon.

There was, therefore, widespread public acceptance that retirement led to ill health, deterioration and death.[47]

Within 40 years, however, expectations and attitudes had shifted to a great extent. A period of funded leisure post employment is now generally regarded as everyone's right. Yet the acceptance of mass retirement for all at broadly fixed chronological but increasingly younger ages, in order to carry out a fulfilled leisure and consumption based healthy period of late life is historically very new. It is a post-war phenomenon. Current retirement expectations are a post-1960s' phenomenon,[48] which arose during the second half of the twentieth century in order to cope with the specific socio-economic needs of the growing elderly population, and in response to the changing administrative and personnel management demands of growing corporations.[49]

This situation was not unique to the UK. Similar patterns can be seen in most OECD countries. In Australia, for example, during the 1950s, the effects of the depression birth rate caused a sharp drop in young people entering the workforce and there was general support from employers and trade unions to retain older workers.[50] However by the mid-1970s the flow of younger workers on to the Australian labour market encouraged the removal of older workers.

The 1960s were thus the pivot between a predominantly health-led withdrawal by older workers, combined with labour market declines in sectors dominated by older cohorts – factors which had existed for over a century, and a new style consumerist led retirement. Prior to the 1960s the growth in retirement was primarily based on health and welfare issues and the growth of state support of older people in the form of pensions. That post 1960s took up the new impetus of private pensions, leisure and the growth in healthy active later life. In this way, the introduction of widespread pension support allowed retirement to occur by choice among a healthy active population. In the USA, for example, it was not until the 1970s that the development of the US Social Security system allowed retirement to become a common experience of *choice* for older workers.[51] As in the UK, retirement prior to this was broadly confined to those older workers who were forced to leave paid work and rely on family support following ill health or redundancy.[52]

Within the wider national contexts of a general rise in income and the growth of consumption and leisure within the industrialised world, the increase in late life health status, and spread of private pensions and occupational pensions encouraged the growth of late life consumption and leisure activities. At the micro-level this was also probably encouraged by the rapid growth in pre-retirement courses which were widely introduced in the 1970s and 1980s. These were in reaction to the concerns which had surfaced over the detrimental effects of retirement in the 1950s and 1960s. Pre-retirement planning was introduced to encourage a positive active retirement life-style. It also contributed to the development of a leisure-based expectation of retirement.

The 1990s

In most OECD countries it was the rapid growth in unemployment affecting younger workers that dominated public concern during the 1970s and 1980s. It was not until the 1990s that European countries in particular began to return first to the perceived looming pension crisis and then to the upcoming labour and skills shortage. The final decades of the twentieth century saw a steady retirement of men from OECD countries' labour markets at increasingly younger ages. The effect was most acute in southern and some western European countries (Fig. 4.1). Detailed analysis of labour force statistics reveals that each successive cohort of older men has lower employment rates than the preceding cohort.

As can be seen from Fig. 4.2, which divides working population over 25 by age and gender, female participation rates are lower than male at each age. However, in contrast to men, each successive cohort of older women has *higher* employment rates than the preceding cohort.

Taking the UK as an example, the mean male age of retirement[53] fell from 67.2 in 1950 to 62.7 by 1995. Currently, in the UK one-third of those aged between 50 and state pension age do not work, with the proportion of men of this age (50–64) who are not working doubling in the past 20 years. As we discussed earlier, this is occurring during a time of steady growth in longevity, so that average life expectancy for men aged 65 now stands at 80, with disability-free life expectancy reaching 79, a near three-year increase over 15 years.[54] Retirement rates for women are more complex. Although there was a decline in the mean age of retirement for women from 63.9 in 1950 to 59.7 by 1995, this is compounded by the fact that each successive cohort over the period contained a larger number of economically employed women, as women steadily entered the labour market at all ages during these decades.

Concerns over the forecast dependency ratio

This steady withdrawal of male workers in particular at ever increasingly younger ages, coupled with a general increase in the number and proportion of the population in these later age groups, has raised concerns over predicted dependency ratios in all OECD

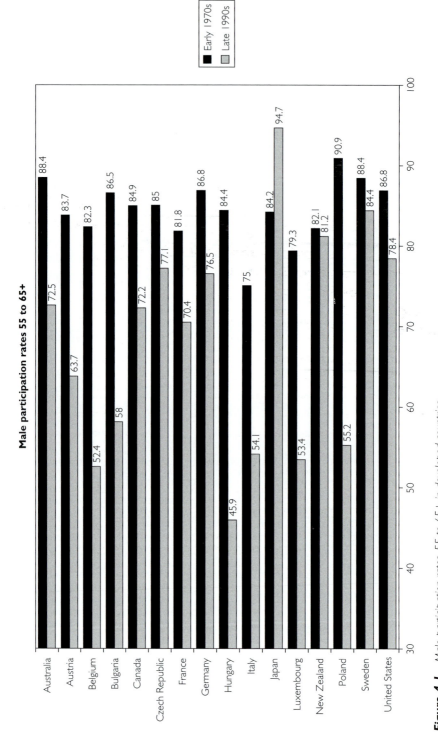

Figure 4.1 Male participation rates, 55 to 65+ in developed countries..

Source: Kinsella and Velkoff, 2001.

Participation rates by age and gender in OECD countries, 2002

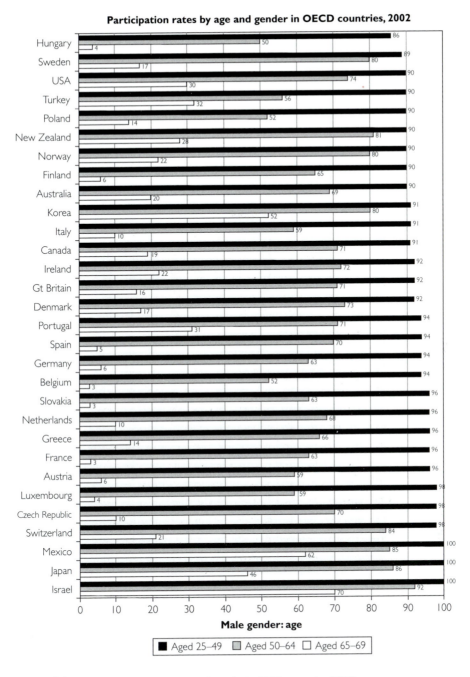

Figure 4.2 *Participation rates by age and gender in OECD countries, 2002.*
Source: OECD 2003.

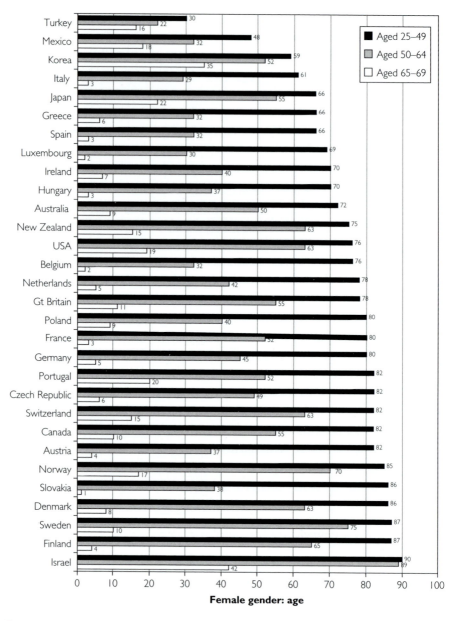

Figure 4.2 (cont.)

countries. The old age dependency ratio is the ratio of the number of people who have retired from economic activity to the number who are economically active. In the mid-1990s, western European countries had the highest level of older populations relative to those of working age. Furthermore, this measure underestimates the proportion of retired as these national level statistics still take 65 as their base age for retirement.

There will be a large increase in the ratio of retired to workers over the next 25 years if retirement rates stay constant. This is a more sophisticated prediction than some, as it is based on average retirement ages which are somewhat lower than standard retirement ages, based on the national pension age, typically 65. Based on these figures, Australia and Japan would see a near doubling in the ratio of male retired to workers, while the Netherlands would see more than a 100 per cent increase.

Over the next 25 years the UK is expected to rise from 21 male pensioners per 100 workers to 33 and from 38 female pensioners to 56. Another way of describing this is that the worker/retired ratio will fall from 3.4 workers per pensioner in 2003 to 2.3 by 2028.[55] While the total demographic support ratio (that is those aged 15–64 to those aged 0–14/65+) is predicted to fall from 1.91 to 1.61, elderly dependants are assumed to cost around three times more than younger ones. By 2010 Japan will have overtaken all other countries in the old age dependency ratios. Beyond 2030, aged dependency will continue to rise rapidly in Japan and Italy, somewhat less in France and Germany, and least of all in Canada and the USA. The UK will experience middle-level growth throughout this period.

Concerns over the forecast dependency ratios comprise two broad themes. First, there is growing concern over a perceived labour shortage. This focuses on the squandering of human resources, both in terms of unused productive capacity among older fit workers, and a perceived increasing skills shortage, especially within Europe. Alongside this runs the economic burden or dependency argument. Here concern at the national level focuses on whether nations can afford to support increasing numbers of older people as a growing proportion of their populations, in particular the inability to sustain either current pension demand or, given the reduced economic productivity and tax income, health and social care costs. There is also some concern for older people as individuals, with research consistently indicating a relationship between withdrawal from economic activity and poverty in old age.

Unused productive capacity and national skills shortage

The concern over unused productive capacity is well illustrated by data from a recent 11 nation study.[56] This uses a measure of foregone productive capacity. Drawing on national data of current labour force participation at ages 50, 60 and 65, they estimate the measure unused productive capacity, this being the proportion of men not working at a given age (i.e. 1 − LFP where LFP is the labour force participation). As described by Fig. 4.3 this ranges from 0.95 in Belgium to 0.4 in Japan. These calculations are easily come by. When the sum of unused capacity (the area above the LFP curve) over all ages in some range is divided by the total area above and below the curve for that age interval, and multiplied by 100, a rough measure of unused capacity over the age interval, as a percentage of the total labour capacity in that range, is produced. This is then plotted for the 55 to 65 age group. As is clear from Figure 4.3, unused capacity varies significantly between developed countries: ranging from 67 per cent in Belgium to 22 per cent in Japan.

According to the UN,[57] this unused labour capacity may lead to a significant skills shortage in the Western world. It is forecasted that an estimated 25 million workers from the developing world will have to immigrate to the EU per year for ten years in order to keep pace with the demand for skilled labour.

Economic dependency

In the mid-1990s, western European countries had the highest level of older populations relative to those of working age. This measure, furthermore, underestimates the proportion of retired as these national level statistics still take 65 as their base age for retirement. In addition, the total demographic support ratio, that is 15–64 to 0–14/65+, needs to be considered. While these age ranges are standard to allow cross-national comparisons, it is acknowledged that they no longer accurately reflect the reality of either educational or retirement ages. This involves adding in the youth dependency ratio, that is the measure of transfers to those under age 15 such as education, childcare, child health, etc. While declining fertility in all industrialised nations leads to a fall in this ratio – predicted to fall from 1.89 to 1.58 between 2000 and 2030 in the UK, for example – elderly dependants are assumed to be significantly more costly than younger ones. The Government Actuaries Department estimates costs for elderly dependants at around three times that of younger ones in the UK. In the USA, the Congressional Budget Office has produced an extreme estimate of seven times.

A third factor to be worked into the dependency equation is how exactly the national pension system is structured and funded. Consider for a moment the differences between the German and British pension systems. In Germany there is a link between benefits and wages that results in social insurance costs rising directly in line with age dependency rates. In the UK, on the other hand, benefits and price increases are offset by increases in real wages. This buffers the working population from the full extent of rising dependency numbers. Furthermore, given the high proportion of workers and current retired who are supported by insurance-based pension schemes, its national pension system has already been structured in a manner which offers some protection against age dependency ratios. By 2030 all G7 countries, with the exception of the UK, are expected to face dramatically raised tax burdens or large budget shortfalls. Figure 4.4 gives the current figures and predicts the future change in per cent GDP to be spent by 2050 on state pension provision alone, which for most OECD countries will be increased. Indeed, it is estimated that Germany will require an increase in contributions to both social security and mandatory health and long-term care insurance from 21 per cent to 34 per cent by 2035.[58] This is, arguably, a fact which is politically unsustainable. Similarly, projections by the OECD suggest that France will have to double the proportion of national income.[59]

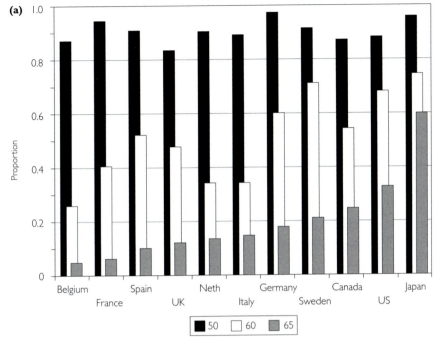

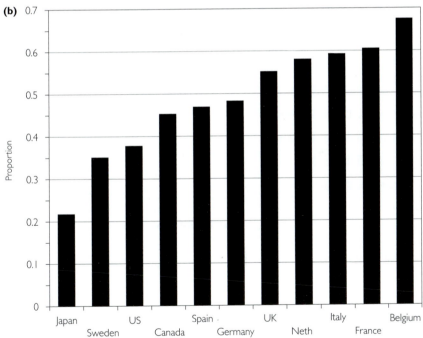

Figure 4.3   *(a) Current labour participation and (b) unused productive capacity in 11 industrialised nations.*
Source: Gruber and Wise, 1998.

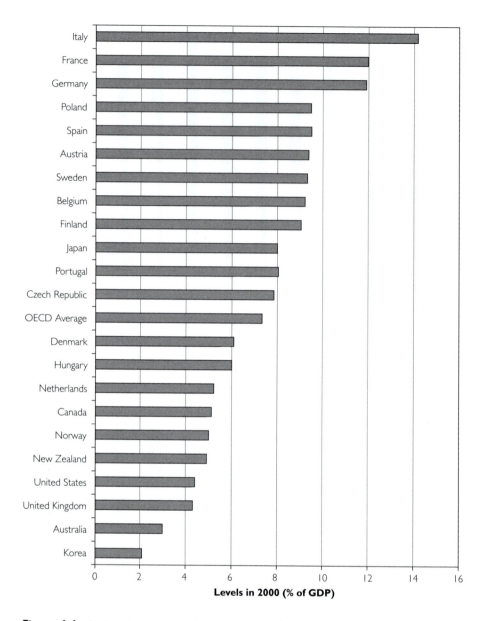

Figure 4.4 *Public expenditure on old age pensions in OECD countries, 2000–2050.*

Individual poverty

The connection between old age, retirement and poverty is well established.[60] Recent dynamic analysis on the British Household Panel Survey, for example, has started to model the transition into poverty at and around the time of retirement. Using the seven waves 1991–97, the work reveals how the event of becoming retired in Britain is strongly associated with a decline in an individual's well-being.[61] Cross-sectional

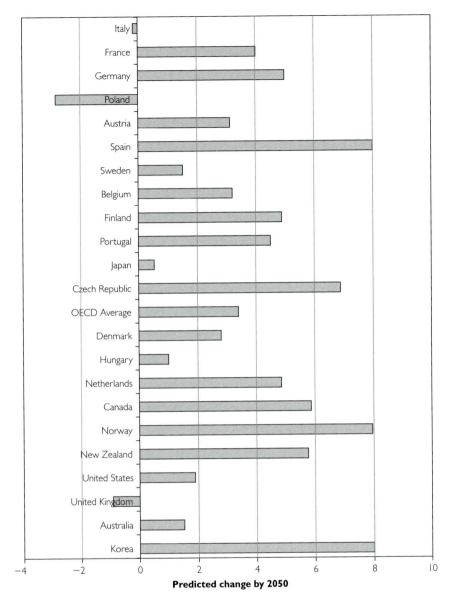

Predicted change by 2050

Figure 4.4 (cont.)

comparisons of retired men with non-retired men and working adults (Fig. 4.5), reveal that around 45 per cent were placed in the poorest third, throughout the 1990s. Furthermore, the oldest cohorts were consistently poorer than younger ones.[62] Indeed, over half those men currently in their eighties remained in the poorest third of the income distribution throughout the decade. The parade of cohorts down-wards reflects both length of time in retirement and the standard of income and

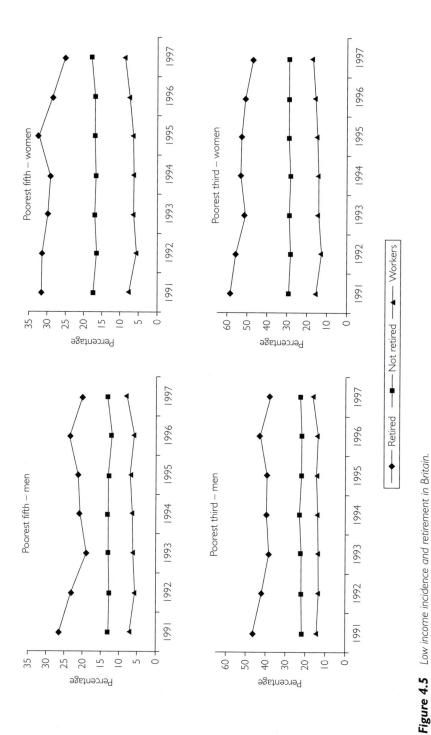

Figure 4.5 *Low income incidence and retirement in Britain.*

Source: Bardesi et al. 2000.

Note: the graphs show the % of each group in the bottom 3rd and bottom 5th of the income distribution in each year.

assets of each subsequent cohort entering the state of retirement. As Fig. 4.5 demonstrates, the income decline effect impacted upon both full and part-time workers. Thus, while few of those in full-time employment were in the bottom third of the income distribution prior to retirement, one third were after being retired for three years. The difference in the proportion with low incomes between those unemployed and already on benefits before retirement, and those in full-time employment, which stood at 40 per cent, had decreased to less than 15 per cent within three years of ceasing work.

Immigration to solve the dependency ratio

As discussed, this unused labour capacity may lead to a significant skills shortage in the Western world.[63] The problem is seen as being more acute in some occupation sectors than others. Of particular concern is the decline in available health and social care workers at the very time when increasing numbers of older people require such services.[64] The work of the United Nations reveals the size of the migration that would be required to counterbalance the predicted population development in a number of countries and maintain the present support ratios (numbers aged 15–64 years in relation to numbers aged 65 years and over). In the case of France, for example, the number of immigrants needed to keep the potential support ratio at its 1995 level would be between 20 and 40 times the annual levels over the past ten years (net immigration was 76,000 per year in the first half of the 1990s, and 39,000 per year in the last half of that decade). It would demand total net immigration of almost 90 million from 2000 to the year 2050, which would result in a total population in France of 187 million in 2050 compared with approximately 60 million today, and of these more than two-thirds would be post-1995 immigrants and their descendants.

Another study of immigration to Western Europe[65] considered a series of scenarios for population development in Western Europe from 1985 to 2050. The scenarios combined different levels of immigration and integration of immigrants' fertility behaviour. Scenarios with low or medium immigration levels and with low or high integration levels lead ultimately to a declining population, so that even medium immigration levels cannot offset the effect of low fertility levels. These scenarios also entail a continuing ageing of the population with at least a doubling of the proportion of the population aged 65 and over. Scenarios with high immigration levels and high, low, or low-low integration levels do lead to population growth. However, even in these scenarios the population will begin to decline ultimately in the face of prolonged low fertility levels. High immigration levels do counteract the ageing of the population, but it is impossible for them to eliminate it. The ageing of the immigrant population would itself, in time, demand even higher levels of immigration if ageing were to be checked continuously. Even with high immigration levels and low-low integration, by 2050 the proportion of the population aged 65 years and over would have increased to 25 per cent, and to 30 per cent with low immigration and low integration. Replacement migration work for the Nordic countries[66] reveals equally daunting immigration levels.

As a recent 2004 OECD report[67] stated, even if immigration can play a complementary role to help solve the situation ahead, it cannot be expected to have more than a marginal impact on the projected disequilibria in the age structure. This is due in part to the convergence in fertility and mortality rates of immigrants with the host population. It is, therefore, clear that immigration levels would have to be unrealistically high to offset Europe's declining population and that demographic ageing cannot be countered by immigration alone. Attention is turning now to selective immigration of skilled/ employable labour to work in specific sectors of the labour market, for example, the health and social care sector, though there are real concerns here that creaming the most highly skilled and qualified personnel from other countries will exacerbate future problems which they may incur in building their own health and social care sectors. We shall return to this later in Chapter 8.

Having discussed the current concerns, let us now consider the drivers behind the trends for increasingly earlier retirement in many OECD countries.

Incentives to retire

Retirement incentives within pension plans

The broad argument presented here is that both private and state pension plans can have a very significant role to play in determining the modal age at retirement and in encouraging early retirement.[68] State social security provision in some countries may offer considerable incentives to early retirement and may account for a significant part of the long-term decline in economic activity rates for older men. In many countries, for example, disability and unemployment programmes have provided early retirement benefits well before the official retirement age.

In a key internationally co-ordinated study directed by the US economists Gruber and Wise (2000), 11 countries collected comparable descriptive data and analytic calculations to model the relationship between social security plan provisions and retirement. The data suggest that there are two features of social security plans which have an effect on labour force participation: the age at which benefits are first available – the early retirement age – and the pattern of benefit accrual. Individuals at every age accrue over time entitlement to future retirement benefits. It is possible to calculate this entitlement, known as social security wealth (SSW), given a person's age. Simply subtract future paid taxes from a person's present discounted value. Key to this calculation is how long a person chooses to remain employed. Wealth will evolve depending upon this factor. Consider for a moment the change in SSW that occurs if a man aged 59 chooses to work for an additional year, rather than simply retire. The difference is SSW accrual. If an accrual is negative to that extra year's net wage earnings, it is an implicit tax on the year's

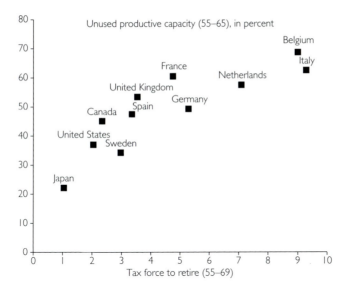

Figure 4.6 *Tax force to retire and unused labour capacity in 11 countries.*
Source: Gruber and Wise, 2000.

earnings; if it is positive, it is an additional subsidy. A negative accrual encourages retirement. Drawing on data from the 11 countries, Gruber and Wise argue that in most countries, due to insufficient actuarial adjustment for the fewer years of pension receipt, combined with generous earnings replacement for retirees, up to 90 per cent, for example in the Netherlands, further combined with high social security payroll taxes for workers, there is an implicit tax on work in later life for older workers and an incentive to leave the labour force. The relationship between this so-called tax force to retire and unused labour capacity in each country studied is shown in Fig. 4.6. There appears to be a strong correspondence between the tax force to retire and unused labour capacity.

Some countries, such as Canada, have even introduced flexible retirement access to state pensions. From 1987 access to a public pension was made possible from age 60, with a 6 per cent reduction per year before age 65. Several authors have seen this as key in encouraging early retirement in Canada,[69] with a tenfold increase in the number of people exiting via this scheme in the 1980s, with the number of those retiring at age 60 increasing from 29.7 per cent in 1991 to 35 per cent by 1995.

Generally, however, the conclusion should be avoided that the association is a causal relationship. It is possible that, either indirectly or directly, in order to encourage labour mobility across ages, such provisions do encourage older workers to retire early. Or it may be that such provisions were necessarily adopted by countries to cope with the redundancies of older workers. Or a combination. What is clear is that in many countries, particularly, for example, Belgium, Italy and the Netherlands, disability and unemployment programmes effectively provide early retirement benefits prior to formal pension age.

Kapteyn and de Vos' study of the Netherlands[70] provides a good example of this process. Here individuals are able to claim a variety of earnings-replacement benefits prior to retirement, such as disability insurance, unemployment insurance, welfare and early retirement support. These can be generous relative to other countries, with unemployment insurance benefits equal to up to 70 per cent of previous earnings, and early retirement support at 70 – 80 per cent, and even up to 90 per cent including after-tax replacement. As described earlier, the Netherlands saw a fall in economic activity for those aged between 60 and 64 from 80 per cent in 1960 to 20 per cent by 1994. During this time there was a trebling in the percentage of men taking up disability benefits. Following the introduction of early retirement benefits in 1981, a further 17 per cent were being supported in this way by 1995. After age 50 male labour force participation falls sharply, while the number on disability rises steadily until age 65, and those on early retirement benefit reaches almost 50 per cent by age 65. Kapteyn and de Vos conclude that the recent dramatic fall in labour force participation over the last four decades can be explained largely by the introduction of the new benefits which created incentives to retire.

Similarly, access to disability benefits in Canada was made easier at the beginning of the 1980s, with the number of claimants aged 60–64 doubling in the ten years following, reaching 99,000 by 1991.[71] Finland and Norway have long used the disability pension scheme as the main early exit route,[72] though this has changed recently with the growth in gradual retirement (see below).

As Blundell and Johnson point out for the UK, benefits designed for the long-term sick and disabled are being increasingly taken up by those in the immediate pre-pensionable ages to allow early withdrawal. In 1994, for example, 25 per cent of all men aged 60–64 and nearly 20 per cent of those aged 55–59 were in receipt of Invalidity Benefit (now Incapacity Benefit), a contributory benefit for the long-term sick or disabled. Quoting data from the UK Retirement Survey,[73] they also point out that there is elastic labour supply behaviour among older men. Thus the fall in demand for lower skilled workers combined with access to benefits in later life may explain the observed fall in labour force participation among older less skilled men in particular. In contrast, those skilled and professional older workers enjoying private occupational pensions, linked to final earnings, especially those with expected pay increases in the immediate pre-retirement years, have incentives to remain in employment.

The Gruber and Wise coordinated study focused on state or publicly funded pension provision. However, a variety of studies have demonstrated that the retirement incentives within occupation or employee-based plans, and private pension plans are also strong and may go some way to explaining some of the differential retirement rates among the occupational groupings.

As Disney[74] illustrates for the UK Retirement Survey (1988/1994), those with an occupational pension scheme had a higher likelihood of retiring before the state retirement age (60 per cent), than those without such a scheme (40 per cent). However, they are also clearly picking up occupational type. While half of those in the skilled and unskilled occupations retire before age 65, two-thirds of those in professional, white-collar activities do so. A supporting finding is reported from the Labour Force Survey data, with those men aged between 45 and 65 in the top half of the wage distribution who held an occupational pension, being significantly more likely to retire than those without.[75] Similarly, work on the BHPS showed that the probability of retirement was 37 per cent higher for workers with an occupational scheme.[76] Similar evidence on the importance of the early exit pension schemes has been reported for the Scandinavian countries.[77]

There is also considerable evidence for North America. While there is little systematic data on early retirement buy-out in Canada,[78] there was significant growth in early exits via private pension schemes in the 1980s.[79] Similarly, studies of self-reported reasons for early exit note the role of early retirement incentives in pension plans.[80] Retirement incentives within US pension policies have also been found to provide a strong encouragement to leave the labour force early.[81] Kotlikoff and Smith[82] have long argued, for example, that the actuarial value of pensions is frequently maximised prior to retirement age, suggesting that 15 per cent of employees could retire at age 55, and 50 per cent at age 62 with no actuarial reduction in pension benefits. Similarly, Herz and Rones[83] point out that changes in social security encouraging individuals to remain in work are offset by countervailing changes in occupational and private pensions. Few of these have adopted incentives to encourage workers to stay in employment, and many have mandatory retirement ages built into the programmes. There is also evidence that private pension schemes encourage individuals to stay on until the early retirement age defined by the scheme, but then provide a strong incentive to retire.[84] Currently, 50 per cent of all US employees work within such a scheme. Furthermore, 75 per cent have defined benefits which provide strong incentives to stick to the early retirement age. The US situation is, however, complicated by the relationship between health insurance, social security, pensions and retirement behaviour. There is much evidence to suggest that employment-based health insurance deters early retirement.[85] Finally, accumulated wealth, savings behaviour, and availability of other sources of income in later life are also influential.[86] What is clear, therefore, is that while pensions and social security systems provide incentives for the population at large to retire, different occupational groups have access to different types of provision and are thus affected in different ways. This has led some to argue that professional, managerial workers are *pulled* out of the labour force by economic incentives and enhanced opportunities for leisure and consumption, whereas those in skilled and unskilled occupations are *pushed* via untenable working conditions and employer attitudes.[87]

Work environment and the labour market

Throughout the last century, older workers were concentrated in older vulnerable activities. At the end of the nineteenth century, they were concentrated in agriculture, and

100 years later they are concentrated in heavy manufacturing. There is an inevitability in this, as the newly trained young people enter the labour market last and take advantage of new industries. Thus the OECD reports[88] that 45 per cent of Japanese men aged over 50 work in agriculture, forestry, or fishing, transport or communications, craft work and manual labour, all sectors that have experienced the greatest decline in total employment. They are under-represented in professional and technical work. Similarly, European Labour Force Statistics reveal that older people are over-represented in these sectors, especially in the Mediterranean countries where they represent over 50 per cent of all workers in manual occupations.[89]

Taking the UK as an example, we can explore this broad framework in more detail. There is some evidence that within the UK there are regional differences in the demand for labour.[90] Several authors have shown that older men tend to be employed in declining industries, under-represented in new growth industries, and especially affected by reduced demand for unskilled workers.[91] McKay and Middleton's secondary analysis of the Working Lives Survey (1994–5), for example, found concentrations of older men and women in manufacturing.[92] This suggests that, in terms of occupational profile by age, between three and four times as many men aged 65 to 69 are in unskilled occupations as those aged 45 to 49. The prevalence of elderly employees in certain occupations is related to regional employment habits. This may explain regional differences in economic activity of the elderly. Between 1971 and 1991, male economic activity of those aged 50–69 fell by 19 per cent in the UK. This decline reached 23 per cent of similarly aged men in northern England, but only 16 per cent of those in the south-east.[93] This reflects the occupational opportunities available in the two regions. Such variations are further compounded by integrated software systems that allow for the international spatial reorganisation of work.

Evidence from throughout the OECD countries, however, also suggests that economic, industrial and organisational changes within both the public and private sectors have provided the circumstances for the decline in labour force participation among older people. Within the public sector, the privatisation of utilities and the introduction of compulsory competitive tendering have altered employment practices, in particular threatening the opportunities for those aged over 50.[94] Similarly within the private sector, the globalisation of markets and the resultant increased competition have led to workforce reduction, which has particularly affected older workers.

Research from both the UK and USA,[95] for example, highlights the selection of older workers for redundancy schemes, with one UK study revealing that older workers had been targeted for early retirement or redundancy packages in nearly 90 per cent of the organisations who were downsizing.[96] A variety of other North American and European research has suggested that (with the exception of Sweden) older workers are likely to be 'first out' in times of recession,[97] unlikely to be targeted for recruitment even in times of labour shortage,[98] and once unemployed, are disproportionately less likely to find new work.[99] Indeed, recent OECD figures reveal that older workers form a disproportionately higher percentage of the unemployed in all countries bar the Slovak Republic.[100]

There is some evidence that this early withdrawal from the labour market is both directly and indirectly encouraged through age discriminatory behaviour by employers[101] and that push factors, such as redundancy or fixed retirement ages, are responsible for a large percentage of early retirements. A comparison of the two waves of the UK Retirement Survey 1988 and 1994, for example, revealed a decline in individually initiated early retirement, and a corresponding increase in employer instigated early retirement. Indeed, of the 40 per cent within this population who quoted redundancy as the main reason for retiring, one-third of this was involuntary.[102] Similarly, Canadian research has highlighted a variety of employers' practices, including the use of occupational schemes as a lever to encourage early retirement.[103]

In addition, there is consistent evidence from a variety of countries revealing a lack of practices aimed at including older workers, lack of training and lack of flexible working arrangements.[104] There is also some evidence that employers are not only eager to push older workers out, they are reticent to employ them. Here again, there are perceived factors which might discourage employers from recruiting older workers: lack of appropriate skills, lack of qualifications and low return on training investment. Evidence from the USA highlights also the role of institutional factors beyond work. Defined benefit pensions schemes[105] and health insurance[106] both deter employers from recruiting and retaining older employees.

Several authors contend that these factors are stimulated by the continued negative perceptions of older workers which we referred to in Chapter 1. As was described, despite the fact that there is little practical evidence to support the view that those aged over 50 are consistently less able to perform modern economic activity than those younger,[107] such stereotypical views remain. The perception that age and characteristics are related appears embedded in our current societal perceptions and appears to impact upon employer behaviour.[108] However, taking simple associational analysis as the basis for age discrimination, and basing one's argument on the standpoint that employers are ageist,[109] is too simple a contention, and hides multiple complexities. Some of these associations are likely to be reflecting proxies for more fundamental problems within the work place. As Casey has argued,[110] with long-term contracts the wages of some older workers may simply exceed their marginal productivity, and it may be considered more cost effective for the organisation to dismiss them, rather than extend equal opportunities to them. Or we can return to the argument promulgated by Hannah in 1986, that large companies in particular desire to manage the retirement process in order to control their own internal labour markets.

Issacharoff and Worth Harris[111] suggest that the US 1967 Age Discrimination Employment Act, which from 1986 allowed no upper limit on employment, has been problematic because it was based on the notion of stereotypical age discrimination as the driver behind employer motivated retirement, and not on the relationship between wages and age. In addition, employers may also be making moral judgements, e.g. that it is preferable for those without young dependants to face redundancy. However, as we shall see later, these practices are age discriminatory and may increasingly become illegal in many countries. We shall return to this in more detail in Chapter 10.

Finally there is the debate over the impact of technological change. Many argue that the requirement for new skills, particularly abilities in information and communication technologies, increasingly excludes older workers, especially men.[112] This is particularly the case given the low level of training commonly offered to older workers. As Fig. 4.7 reveals, without exception, older workers receive less on-the-job training than younger workers in all OECD countries surveyed.

Exploring this in more detail, using the data from the 2002 UK Labour Force Survey as an example, reveals that 18 per cent of the 50–64 age group had received training in the previous three months, compared with 28 per cent of those aged 25–39. This was despite a higher uptake in the 50–64 age group when offered the opportunity. This contradicts OECD data which suggests that many older workers see little benefit to themselves in investing time or effort in training. Similarly, OECD findings that firms are often reluctant to train older workers because it is more efficient to concentrate on younger workers as economic returns are likely to be larger given the longer payback time, contradicts the evidence that older workers are a more stable and loyal workforce. Thus training an older worker will bring returns to the employer, while there is a higher probability that training a younger worker will be for the benefit of a competitor![113] Denying equal training opportunities on age alone is, of course, also age discriminatory.

Returning to the broader debate, others propose that technological innovation and flexible working patterns will increase opportunities for older workers allowing them the possibilities of post-career employment.[114] As I have argued elsewhere,[115] the inherent training component of new technological labour means that future cohorts of older workers will have experience of continual training and skills updating. Bartel and colleagues,[116] for example, have drawn on the US 1966–83 National Longitudinal Surveys of Older Men to argue that workers in industries that are characterised by high rates of technological change, will have later retirement ages as they tend to receive higher levels of on-the-job-training.

Health status, attitudes and expectations of workers

Given that disability benefits are commonly used as a source of pre-retirement age income for the over fifties, it may be argued that increases in disability are driving late life employment withdrawal. While heavy manual labour has decreased, mental stress has grown over the last few decades. Health-related evidence from the USA can be found from across the occupational spectrum and in both pre- and post-retirement surveys.

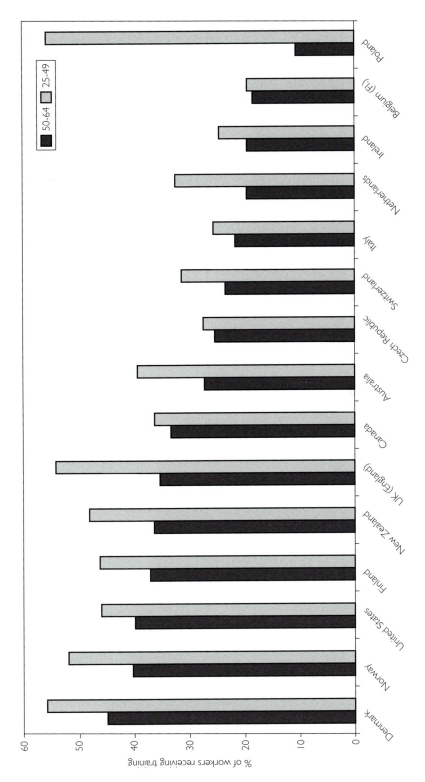

Figure 4.7 *Incidence of job-related training for workers by age in selected OECD countries, 1994–98. Source: OECD, 2001(b).*

For example, in a US study of male academic lawyers,[117] nearly 50 per cent gave health as a primary factor which would shape their retirement decisions. Analysis of both US Health and Retirement data, and the Survey Income and Programme Participation (SIPP) Panel study[118] noted that retirees were more likely to be in poor health or have three or more functional limitations. This was tempered, however, by the caveat that those having health insurance coverage from an employer which would be lost on retirement were more likely to delay their retirement. A range of studies from Scandinavia[119] highlight that health is often stated as a contributory cause of early retirement. As these are mainly small-scale or qualitative, it is difficult to quantify the effect, though generally they were seen to be contributory rather than primary. Jensen's study[120] of those who had retired or who were anticipating retirement also highlights the strong occupational effect operating in Scandinavia. Thus 27 per cent of social workers who were anticipating retirement, and 19 per cent of those already retired, gave health as a reason; contrastingly, poor health was only mentioned by 9 per cent of those anticipating retirement, and 4 per cent of those already retired in the finance sector.

Recent work in the UK[121] supports a higher figure. Data collected on men and women aged 50–64 out of the labour market suggested that only 9 per cent of men and 8 per cent of women were seeking work. Of those not seeking work, around half (58 per cent men and 50 per cent women) gave health as the reason. A similar percentage (53 per cent men and 44 per cent women) also gave health as the reason for retiring. However, it is not always clear as to what the definition of health and disability in these self-reported studies is actually measuring. In particular, younger men and women were more likely to give health as an answer – two-thirds of men in their early fifties gave health-related answers, compared with only just over a third of men in their sixties. Interestingly, for women it was just under one half in their early fifties falling to just over a third in the last five years before their state retirement age, which at the time of measuring was still 55–59. In particular as Casey has pointed out,[122] respondents giving retrospective answers may offer ill health as a socially acceptable reason for retirement. In addition, health may be best regarded as a dichotomous – conditioning – variable. If someone suffers ill health this can be a major factor influencing their decision to retire. If not, health status probably does not enter the equation.[123] Given this, a broad generalised conclusion is that there does seem to be consistent evidence that between one fifth and one quarter of retirements prior to age 65 can be assigned to the category of being promoted by 'ill health'.[124]

Finally, there is evidence that the current older cohorts have internalised the notion of retirement, including early retirement, as an extended period of funded leisure and consumption post-economic activity, and expectations of this are considerably entrenched.[125] Such expectations are now strongly held not only by the employee, but also by his or her partner and wider family.[126] Work, again from the USA, predicting retirement behaviour is of significance here. Analysis of the 1992 and 1994 Waves of Carolina Health and Transitions Study, for example, highlighted the role of social factors in the decision to retire.[127] In particular, both high job satisfaction and having a working spouse decreased the likelihood of retirement, this latter finding being supported elsewhere,[128] including findings that male retirement was nearly twice as likely if the spouse had retired.[129] This suggests social factors are also significant at the individual level of choice. While it might appear counter-intuitive, given that on economic grounds one spouse might be more able to retire if the other was still working, here couples were clearly perceiving retirement as a time of leisure, in which they could carry out jointly shared activities.

This is compounded by the growing responsibilities that many of these cohorts have for kin care and support, especially for their parents.[130] Again we need further research here into the role such commitments play in the decision to withdraw from economic activity, particularly for men. Finally, the understanding of the interaction of all of these factors with health status and disability in these ages is at present limited, though this may account for more than a third of early retirements.[131]

'Push' versus 'pull'

It is a complex story, in that clearly different groups are choosing, or not choosing, to withdraw from economic activity for a range of reasons. There is now considerable evidence that those taking early retirement include two distinct groups.[132] Professional and managerial workers, with high levels of education, and secure well-funded pension plans have a higher than average likelihood of withdrawing from economic activity, especially if their pension plan includes a defined benefit component. This may be tempered, however, by a restraining factor of high enjoyment of work, but also encouraged by increasing levels of stress in these high level occupations. A second group of early retirees comprises those with low levels of education and manual or semi-skilled occupations, who may be being encouraged or forced to take early retirement through employer instigated redundancy schemes. These may be involuntary or nominally voluntary but set in a context of discriminatory and uncomfortable working conditions. Maule, for example, distinguishes between salaried and hourly paid employees, suggesting that those who are paid hourly are more likely to take involuntary retirement due to *push* factors – negative aspects of current job and ill health – while those who are salaried are more likely to choose retirement voluntarily due to *pull* factors – positive potential of new career, jobs, activities.[133]

To sum up, the rapid increase in early retirement has caused considerable concern. The variety of research and sometimes polemic debate has focused on three broad themes. Analysis by economists has revealed that retirement incentives exist within many national pension systems. Changes within the work environment and labour market still both encourage and force workers to withdraw. These include structural, sectoral and technological changes, as well as evidence that employers retain ageist attitudes towards older workers. Finally, health attitudes and behaviours towards disability and frailty, and new expectations emerging with the growth of leisure and consumption opportunities are also now playing a key role in early retirement decisions.

From rest to reward to right

As we asserted at the beginning of the chapter, current attitudes and actions towards retirement are generally considered to be fixed, when in fact they are period specific. Mass retirement at a broadly fixed chronological age is historically new, arising in the second half of the twentieth century to cope with the specific health and socio-economic needs of the then older population, and in response to the changing administrative and personnel management demands of growing corporations. Such labour market withdrawal at state pension age has been extended over the last 30 years through the spread of early retirement. Three broad forces for this phenomenon have been identified here – economic circumstances, employment opportunities, and health and social status, experiences and attitudes. There is now emerging considerable evidence from both the UK and overseas, that part of the diffusion of early retirement practices is motivated by retirement incentives in current pension schemes. Similarly, accumulated wealth, savings behaviour, and availability of other sources of income in later life, including state as well as private benefits, are also influential. There is some evidence that age discrimination by employers encourages early withdrawal from the labour market and that push factors, such as redundancy or fixed retirement ages, are responsible for a large percentage of early retirements. Finally, there is evidence that the current older cohorts have internalised the notion of retirement, including early retirement, as a period of funded leisure, and expectations of this are considerably entrenched, not only for the employee, but also for his or her partner and wider family. This is compounded by the growing responsibilities that many of these cohorts have for kin care and support, especially for their parents.

We can, therefore, see a shift across the twentieth century in the forces driving retirement in OECD countries. Economic security (pensions/savings) operated at the beginning of the twentieth century as a safety net. By the end they had become a catalyst, directly encouraging as well as allowing cessation of economic employment. In contrast, ill health, once the main catalyst of retirement, has become a conditioning variable. That is, so long as an individual remains in good health, then health status is largely irrelevant. However, for individuals with poor health, this can be the catalyst for retirement. Labour market factors have remained constant – older workers, given their career structures, inevitably tend to end up in older and thus more vulnerable labour markets. There are indications however that this may be changing, with a growing increase in mid-life and older workers moving into modern high technological industry. Institutionalised negative attitudes and age discrimination continue. This appears less so in countries such as the USA, Australia and New Zealand where anti-discrimination legislation exists. With widespread government acceptance of the 2006 EU age discrimination directive, European countries may see a more conducive environment ahead. We shall return to this in Chapter 10.

In conclusion

The health and welfare framework which operated in the first half of the century has now been replaced by a different context, which is primarily driven by an economic paradigm: the increasing level of pension provision due to the introduction of occupational and private schemes, the increasing opportunities to purchase leisure goods appropriate to late life, and the market pressure on employers which leads to rationalisation of the workforce with detrimental effects on older employees. The conceptual paradigm associated with this was redefined as the century progressed. Both the Bismarkian and Beveridge systems were founded on a notion of older people requiring a short period of rest as they endured the frailty of old age. The rhetoric behind the Anglo-American programmes of the 1960s and 1970s in particular, such as US Social Security and UK pre-retirement planning, included the notion of reward for contribution to society, which may have reflected the arrival of the Second World War cohort as new retirees. By the 1980s, the internalisation of a period of funded leisure at the end of one's working life had become firmly established. The notion of retirement has thus been redefined from one of *Rest* in the 1940s and 1950s, to *Reward* in the 1970s to a *Right* by the 1980s.[134]

Notes

1 Costa, 1998.
2 Thane, Smith, Johnson and McNicol, for example.
3 Smith, 1984.
4 Riddle, 1984.
5 For example, fluctuations during the Second World War.
6 Thane, 2000.
7 ibid. p. 279.
8 McNicol, 1998.
9 Fogerty, 1992, quoted in Thane, 2000.
10 McNicol, 1998.
11 ibid., p. 59.
12 Thane 2000.
13 Johnson, 1994.
14 ibid.
15 ibid.
16 Thane, 2000.
17 Harris, 1972.
18 Thane, 2000.
19 ibid.
20 Johnson, 1994.
21 Thane, 2000.
22 Thane 2000, queries these figures.

23 Johnson 1994.
24 Le Gros Clark, 1968.
25 Harper and Thane, 1986; Harper and Thane, 1989.
26 Harper, 1989.
27 Ministry of Labour, 1945-55; Shenfield, 1957.
28 Acton Society Trust, 1960; Heron and Chown, 1961.
29 Green, 1988.
30 Shenfield, 1957; Industrial Welfare Society, 1951.
31 Harper, 1989; Harper and Thane, 1986; Harper and Thane, 1989.
32 Central Office of Information, 1947.
33 Royal Commission on Population, 1949.
34 Chancellor of the Exchequer, 1954.
35 Parish and Peacock, 1954.
36 Shenfield, 1957.
37 Chancellor of the Exchequer, 1954.
38 Green, 1963.
39 Warr, 1994.
40 Welford, 1958.
41 Belbin, 1958; Le Gros Clark, 1959.
42 McMahon and Ford, 1955.

43 Anderson and Cowan, 1956, p. 1346.
44 Shenfield, 1957, p. 59.
45 Harper, 1989.
46 Granick, 1952.
47 Emerson, 1959.
48 Harper and Thane, 1986.
49 Harper, 1990; Harper, 1989, Harper, and Thane, 1989.
50 Stoller, 1962.
51 Ransom and Sutch, 1986.
52 Carter and Sutch, 1996.
53 Throughout, however, we must bear in mind the difficulties in definitions and measurement of retirement. In the UK Retirement Surveys, for example, 24 per cent of men who were economically active in 1994 stated that they were retired (Tanner, 1997).
54 ONS, 1999.
55 GAD and ONS, 2001; United Nations, 2000 (UK predictions differ slightly with 4.06 (2000) to 2.61 (2030) but the trend is the same).
56 Gruber and Wise, 1999.
57 United Nations, 2000.
58 Boersch-Supan and Schnabel, 1998.
59 Roseveare et al., 1996.
60 Atkinson, 1995; Johnson and Stears, 1995; Johnson and Stears, 1998.
61 Bardasi et al., 2000.
62 With the exception of the oldest cohort in 1997 – a fact which the authors are hard pressed to explain.
63 United Nations, 2000.
64 Harper and Leeson, 2002.
65 Lutz and Prinz, 1993.
66 Leeson, 2002.
67 OECD, 2004b.
68 Ippolito, 1990.
69 Bellemare et al., 1998.
70 Kapteyn and de Vos, 1998.
71 Firbank, 1997.
72 Gould and Solem, 2000.
73 Meghir and Whitehouse, 1997; Disney et al., 1994.
74 Disney et al., 1997b.
75 Campbell, 1999.
76 Miniaci and Stancanelli, 1998.
77 Gould and Solem, 2000.
78 LeBlanc and McMullin, 1997.
79 Firbank, 1997.
80 Luchak, 1997.
81 Kotlikoff and Smith, 1983; Mitchell, 1992; Luzadis and Mitchell, 1991.
82 Kotlikoff and Smith, 1983.
83 Herz and Rones, 1989.
84 Stock and Wise, 1990.
85 Uccello and Mix, 1998; Quinn et al., 1998.
86 Banks et al., 2002.
87 Maule et al., 1996.
88 OECD, 2004a.
89 OECD, 2003c.
90 Harper and Laslett, 2005.
91 Jacobs et al., 1991; Trinder, 1989.
92 McKay and Middleton, 1998.
93 OPCS, 1992.
94 Burgess and Rees, 1997.
95 Leppel and Clain, 1995; Arrowsmith and McGoldrick, 1997.
96 Arrowsmith and McGoldrick, 1997.
97 Trinder, 1989.
98 Lindley, 1999.
99 Lindley, 1999; Miller, 1966; Hutchens, 1988.
100 OECD, 2001.
101 McKay and Middleton, 1998; Scales and Scase, 2000.
102 Disney et al., 1997a.
103 Bellemare et al., 1998.
104 Bellemare et al., 1998; Gibson, 1993; Lussier and Wister, 1995; David and Pilon, 1990.
105 Hutchens, 1986.
106 HRS, 2004.
107 Lindley, 1999.
108 Taylor and Walker, 1994.
109 ibid.
110 Casey et al., 1992.
111 Issacharoff and Harris, 1997.
112 Briscoe and Wilson, 1991.
113 Neumark, 2001.
114 Arrowsmith and McGoldrick, 1997.
115 Harper, 2002.
116 Bartel and Sicherman, 1993.
117 HRS, 2004.
118 Uccello and Mix, 1998; Quinn et al., 1998.
119 Kilbom, 1999; Jensen, 1999.
120 Jensen, 1999.
121 Humphrey et al., 2003.
122 Casey, 1998.
123 Maule et al., 1996.
124 Maule et al., 1996; Tanner, 1997.
125 Scales and Scase, 2000.
126 Harper, 2004c.
127 Mutran et al., 1997.
128 Uccello and Mix, 1998; Henretta et al., 1993.
129 Henretta et al., 1993.
130 Anderson, 2001; Kodz et al., 1999.
131 Harper and Laslett, 2005.
132 Quinn, et al., 1998; Uccello and Mix, 1998; Mutran, et al., 1997; Humphrey et al., 2003.
133 Maule et al., 1996.
134 Harper, 2004c.

5
Intergenerational contract and social security

Most industrialised countries have a government pension scheme that requires employed workers to pay taxes on their earnings while they work in return for pension benefits when they retire. Through this collective action, governments provide a predictable retirement income to most [older people] in a way that preserves their dignity and self-respect. These contributory programs, which are generally financed on a pay-as-you-go basis, have historically been viewed as valuable institutions that enhance social cohesion.[1]

The intergenerational contract

The provision of these income maintenance programmes has recently been questioned not only in terms of viability, but also in terms of intergenerational relationships. With regard to the first, as we saw in Chapter 4 (Fig. 4.4), without major reforms, many OECD countries can expect to spend over 15 per cent of their GDP on public pension provision alone. We shall address these reforms later. However, behind these figures has been an active debate focused around the notion of the intergenerational contract, that is an implicit understanding between the generations of delayed reciprocal support. Simply put, Generation 1 (G1) provides care and support to G2 while the latter are young dependants. This occurs both privately, typically within the family, and also through public contribution via taxes, for example, to support education programmes. In return G2 provides care and support to G1 in old age, again privately and via taxation programmes. In addition, G2 is at the same time providing care and support to the young and dependent G3. In supporting public pension and health care programmes for G1, G2 is not only reciprocating for the support given earlier by G1, delayed reciprocity, but also trusts that G3 will in turn reciprocate. For this reason G2 fulfils the generational contract and continues to contribute to the well-being of G3, rather than investing directly in their own late life. Pay-as-you-go programmes of pension provision provide a key example of this. Today's workers pay a set tax on their income, in theory to pay for their own old age pension. In practice, their contributions are paying for today's pensioners, and they, therefore, have to trust that tomorrow's workers accept the taxation which will in actuality pay for their old age. We shall return to this in more detail in Chapter 10.

In recent years, however, there has been extensive debate about the necessity and viability of the intergenerational contract. This has been particularly acute in the United States, where there is concern over expensive public programmes providing services and benefits as an entitlement of old age.[2] These programmes are seen as costly and placing a burden on younger generations.[3] Moreover, demographic change may result in these being unsustainable over the long term, and thus unavailable to those younger generations who are currently financially supporting them.[4] In addition, rather than rely on state-provided, worker-financed pension guarantees, an increasing number of adults are choosing, and being coerced by governments, to fund their own late life insurance-based provision.

As Achenbaum[5] notes for the USA, no other public programme[6] has been subject to such public scrutiny as Social Security. Fired by polemic debate, concerns over generational equity emerged in the 1980s. The claims that older adults were receiving too high a proportion of public spending at the expense of younger generations, received widespread coverage in the public press. Older people were not only receiving disproportionately high benefits in relation to their need, but these benefits were being paid for by a poorer working-age population.[7] As the decade progressed, fears of population ageing entered the debate, with images of a smaller and smaller working population funding, through their taxation, a growing older generation. Evidence was produced[8] which suggested that the large tax increases needed to fund the benefits for an increasingly large older population, would have enormous consequences for taxation over the lifetime of younger cohorts. In particular, those cohorts taking up old age benefits before 2000 would receive benefits far in excess of what they paid in taxes, while those entering after this time, the baby boom generation, would have contributed far more in taxation than they could ever expect to receive in benefits.

This debate was also influenced by the wider question of universalism versus means testing; whether it is more equitable to provide benefits for all, or just to those in need – as defined by some means test. This has been further extended to consider whether universalism should be viewed in terms of a *benefit* or a *right* earned by all older people as a group.[9] However, the strongest fuel was provided by those who questioned the use of age as a meaningful criteria in itself. Preston's influential 1984 paper, pointed out that in terms of age stratification and need, it was children who were in greatest poverty, with older age groups now benefiting disproportionately from public programmes. Indeed, such was the rhetoric during this time, and the fear of public programmes for older people swamping the public budgets to the detriment of all other age groups, that scholars such as Achenbaum warned that the intergenerational contract was in danger of collapsing.

Silverstein and colleagues have subsequently examined aggregate change in American attitudes towards public programmes for older people, drawing on three national surveys carried out between 1986 and 1997.[10] They particularly consider whether any such change was related to cohorts or ages. Four factors were identified, which might be leading to intergenerational tensions, three specifically related to age and intergenerational issues, the fourth concerning increasing US opposition to government intervention which was identified at the time.[11]

The three age/intergenerational related factors were:

- Declining intergenerational solidarity identified by the Cato Institute in 1995,[12] which argued that entitlement programmes for the elderly are neither deserved nor in the public interest and therefore should not be a societal obligation.

- Increasing concerns over resource inequality in public programmes along the lines of Preston's 1984 polemic[13] that entitlement programmes for the older population are being funded at the expense of programmes for the very young, and are inherently unfair as they cost more than programmes for younger age groups, and are protected by the disproportionate political power held by older people.

- Increasing concerns over resource inequality in public programmes,[14] and the belief that entitlement programmes, including those for older people, should be targeted at those in need.

Analysis of the survey suggests that, first, the whole population is moving towards being less generous in public programmes to older people, with some three-quarters favouring need over age as determinants of public programmes. Second, the most dramatic cohort shift in this opinion is among those in the transition into young old age, who paradoxically did not generally favour an increase in the very benefits from which they would soon benefit. Finally, the youngest adult cohort was most sceptical about the deservingness of older people. Overall, it seems that Americans are perceiving late life public programmes, less as part of an obligatory social contract between the generations, and more as part of the political process. Furthermore, the emergence of an anti-elderly sentiment coincided with the prosperity of the 1990s, the longest economic expansion in the USA, a time when most younger Americans felt economically secure and were thus more likely to accept the intergenerational contract. The impact of the early twenty-first-century recession, therefore, is likely to wipe out this confidence and impact upon the intergenerational contract. Indeed, the survey results indicated that the general public of the USA already recognises that older people made economic gains during the 1990s, and are now perceived as better off than their children.

There, therefore, appears to be a general shift in public opinion towards reducing, or at least not extending, late life support programmes. Privatising programmes such as Social Security would gain short-term support from the public as it would introduce more individual responsibility in line with American values. However, Silverstein et al sound a note of caution:

> ... the long-term impact will be to further deteriorate the solidarity between generations because the intergenerational function of programmes like Social Security will be compromised in a privatized system where there will be elderly winners and losers.[15]

Furthermore:

> the aging paradox . . . revolves around the twin axes of solidarity and tension. If younger
> adults do not think that the system will work for them when they are older (either due
> to insolvency in the program or program retrenchment due to means testing), then the
> viability of the intergenerational contract will be at risk.[16]

Evidence from Europe, however, is more muted. The continental European model has traditionally been based on notions of a social contract, social solidarity and redistribution. If anything, outside the UK, European pension reform has faced criticism from a variety of national social partners for reducing the redistributional aspect of pension provision, both in terms of income group and age.[17]

Providing late life social security for ageing populations

One of the myths of ageing is that it is increases in longevity *per se* which are causing the potential pension burden. As already discussed, the question of providing late life social security for ageing populations is far more complex than simply equating this with pressure on national budgets due to population trends, though such pressures now have multiple effects. Other drivers for pension reform are compounding the effects of demographic change. First, is the sheer numbers of people now surviving to and beyond pensionable age. Second, is the increasing longevity of this population, so that pension systems designed to support individuals for the last five to ten years of their lives, are now being stretched to cover twenty to thirty years. This is being further compounded by a third factor, the rapidly growing trend of early retirement, which has emerged in all OECD countries. This reduces the numbers of those in economic production who are carrying most of the tax burden. It also increases the demand on occupational and privately invested pensions, and on publicly funded disability pensions.[18] In addition, and fourth, those on pensions increasingly presume to continue the enhanced standard of living now attainable by many individuals during their working lives into their post-employment retirement. This is encouraged by producers, increasingly reliant on late life consumers as the percentage of younger consumers falls. Thus pension systems designed for either subsistence level support or to supplement other forms of late life income, or even Bismarckian-based systems which intended to provide a significant contribution to late life income, are struggling to fund the increasing standard of living demanded by each subsequent cohort of retirees.

Other factors are also operating. As Clark,[19] among others, has pointed out, faith in state-funded welfare has dwindled in recent years, allowing resurgent liberalism combined with public choice theory to counter the view that state provision offers better and more equitable security. Rather, it is perceived that individuals hold the best information about their needs and markets offer the best way of meeting them. Such theories also support the merits of private markets and savings products. Similarly, the widespread adoption of a capitalist market system requiring a flexible, mobile, less protected labour force, lies uneasily with a defined benefit pension system, requiring stability of employment and employer/employee commitment. Defined contribution pension systems based on individual accounts not only shift the commitment away from the employer, but also encourage, it is argued,[20] a mobile responsive labour force.

There is, therefore, an increasing public view, particularly in the USA, that those who can look after themselves in old age through earlier private savings and investments, should be encouraged to do so. This would free public mechanisms to ensure that those in need in old age are provided for. So while demographic trends are set for the near future, governments are attempting to modify the implications of these by encouraging changes in behaviour.

Various authors have suggested ways to relieve some of this predicted burden on the working population, and indeed governments are already acting on some of these modifications. Most of these are tinkering with existing pension systems. Within OECD countries, these pension systems fall into two broad historical models. Much of continental Europe evolved systems based on social insurance or the Bismarckian model. This system covers employed workers, is based on contributions made by the employer and employee, produces benefits which are related to contributions, and has full or partial capitalisation methods of financing.[21] The Anglo-American model of social security is based on the Beveridge model. This covers the entire population regardless of employment status, funds via taxation, and provides minimum subsistence benefits unrelated to contributions. We use the term social security here in the broad sense to cover both these models.

Reforms have focused primarily on the first tier – statutory or public, shifting the balance towards greater reliance on the second tier – occupational and third tier – private or voluntary. These include:

- Moves away from a pay-as-you-go system, heavily reliant on current worker contributions, to advanced funding schemes.

- Moves to remain with pay-as-you-go subject to various modifications. The most popular among authors are the delaying of pensionable age, the reduction in pensions benefits, and an increase in contributions, either individually based or via expanding the national tax base.

- A modification of employment and savings behaviour, e.g. encouraging a longer working life, and encouraging lifelong saving.

- Consideration has also been given to the merits of the increasing shift within occupational second tier schemes from defined benefit to defined contribution schemes.

We shall briefly consider each of these below.

Pension reform

Moving from a pay-as-you-go system

The general consensus over pay-as-you–go appears to be breaking down particularly in the USA where it is now viewed as outmoded and expensive, and in need of reform in order to reflect changes in social and economic views concerning individual responsibility. Particular attention has focused on the broad balance between *pay-as-you-go schemes*, with pensions paid out of current receipts, and *funded schemes* which draw on invested funds, as a response to increased demand. One side of the debate argues that the increase in the tax burden caused with pay-as-you-go schemes through growth in the number of pension drawers is unacceptable both on intergenerational equity grounds and in terms of the financial burden on the nation.[22] It is also argued that pre-funded schemes increase total population saving which is beneficial for the nation, though countries such as the Netherlands and the UK which have introduced such schemes show neither a higher total saving rate nor an increase of total saving during the process of increased capital funding.[23] Furthermore, they produce higher rates of return in periods of demographic ageing. This is because while rates of return in a pay-as-you-go scheme are expected to decrease in part due to the shrinking and ageing population, rates of return in funded schemes are assumed to be unaffected by demographic ageing. This, however, ignores the possibility of negative effects of the ageing of the population on capital markets.[24]

Alternatively, it is suggested that pay-as-you-go schemes are the best way to tackle the problems of demographic ageing as they can be adjusted on the basis of current economic opportunities.[25] It is also argued that across the life cycle there will be an overall reduction in non-pension savings if an individual is forced to increase their pension related savings.[26] Overall, however, it can be argued that the important considerations are not public versus private investment, but rather the amount of money going into and out of the programme, investment strategies, and whether pensions are provided under a defined benefit or defined contribution arrangement.[27]

Modifying the current pension framework

While a variety of technical propositions are being explored, the broad-based reforms focus on the delaying of pensionable age, a reduction in pensions benefits, and an increase in contributions, either individually based or via expanding the national tax base.

Delay pension age

There is a general move in many OECD countries to raise the state pension age. It has been predicted, for example, that the long-term deficit in the US public pension system could be eliminated through immediate and continuous increases in the US normal retirement and early retirement ages to 70 and 67 respectively by 2030.[28] The USA has announced an eventual rise in Social Security age to 67. Similarly, there are calls in the

UK to raise the state pension age to 70 over the next two decades,[29] though the UK government is currently resisting these. There are, however, strong arguments for retaining the state pension age at 65, while providing significant incentives for workers to remain economically active beyond this. But, for the moment, the pressing issue is early withdrawal from economic activity and most reforms are focused here. Several Scandinavian countries, for example, introduced early retirement pension schemes which are now seen as encouraging early withdrawal. Various reforms are being implemented and/or considered, with indications that raising pensions ages within these schemes would have a noticeable impact in reducing early withdrawal.[30]

Reduce benefits

While most public pension systems were originally envisaged as a supplement in old age, many now provide a large proportion of a retired person's income, reaching at least two-thirds of late life income in many European countries. The high benefit level can be seen in the ratio of benefits to pre-retirement earnings, the replacement rate, which is as high as 90 per cent in some countries (Fig. 5.1).

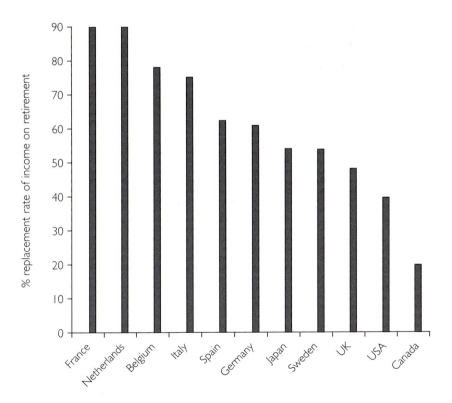

Figure 5.1   *Replacement rate at early retirement age in selected OECD countries.*
Source: OECD 2002.

Several countries have already begun to tackle this, noticeably in Europe where Italy, Belgium and Germany have all recently made changes which have caused the actual average replacement rate (at 65) to fall to around 60 per cent (2001). However, in other countries benefits remain near to or just above the national poverty line. A significant reduction in basic public pension benefits is thus unrealistic. However, an increase in the proportion of flat rate benefits, which carries with it a greater redistributive effect, with high earners receiving a disproportionately lower percentage of their pay in the form of pensions, would reduce public costs.[31] Taken too far, though, it carries the risk of alienating high wage earners. Public pension provision based on means testing at point of retirement is another option, though this also carries with it the risk of discouraging saving in earlier life, as well as encouraging asset transfer to children before retirement.

Increase contributions

Increases in contributions can be achieved through several broad mechanisms.[32] First, there is the possibility of an overall increase in contribution rates for all current contributors. This, however, would require a prohibitively large increase to sustain current pension predictions. An alternative measure is to raise the number of tax contributors, through increasing the number of people in taxable employment. As various authors point out, unemployment and early withdrawal from the labour force over the last few decades of the twentieth century caused considerable financial difficulties for pensions systems. Increasing the number of tax contributors through increasing full-time female employment rates, encouraging immigration, increasing fertility, and discouraging early withdrawal from economic employment are all possible solutions. The USA in particular would benefit from increased female participation rates as dependent spouses receive a highly subsidised pension. Discouraging early withdrawal form economic employment is seen as perhaps the best way to increase contributions. The other possibility is to broaden the tax base from which public pensions are drawn. While this would represent a considerable change in the ideological concept of worker and insurance and compensation, it would enable greater financial flexibility within pay-as-you-go systems.

Modify employment and savings behaviour

Encourage longer working

In Chapter 4, we considered ways in which the population could be encouraged to work longer. In summary, these include removing financial incentives to withdraw from employment, introducing financial incentives to remain economically active, increasing flexible working practices and training opportunities for older workers and tackling ageist behaviour by peers and employers. However, as discussed, the concept of an extended period of leisure-based retirement has been clearly established within western society. Governments may attempt to encourage older workers to remain economically active for longer, but some fear that such policies may not outweigh the increasing affluence of many elderly people, whose financial and political power is grow-ing.[33] Yet, while it may be difficult to deter current cohorts approaching retirement from withdrawing before the pensionable age, subsequent cohorts may well respond to such policies.

Encourage lifelong saving

This is high on many political agendas.[34] However, evidence from both Europe and the USA indicates the difficulties in encouraging individuals to save across the life course.[35]

Move from defined benefit to defined contribution

A defined benefit pension is one to which the employer and employee contribute, with the employer guaranteeing a fixed pension payment on retirement, defined in relation to the employee's age, years of service and income. These are generally not portable between employers. A defined contribution pension is one in which the employer and employee contribute to the employee's pension fund, which is then transferable when the employee leaves the employment. The pension payment on retirement is depend-ent on market investment.

The main shifts are occurring in a move from occupational schemes, most of which are traditionally defined benefit, to personal plans which are defined contribution. In addition, employers in the private sector are switching occupational schemes from defined benefit to defined contribution, mainly for new entrants, though in some cases for existing members. Public service schemes still remain almost exclusively defined ben-efit. However, the introduction of funded schemes into first tier schemes, also introduces the possibility of defined contribution benefits within such schemes. The UK introduc-tion of SERPS is an example, with the 1986 Social Security Act extending the right to contract out of SERPS by allowing individuals to choose instead to save in a defined con-tribution (money purchase) scheme. This is also being discussed in the USA as part of the reforms of Social Security. Current Social Security pensions are defined benefit and fully adjusted for inflation after retirement. Proposals would move part of these to pri-vate accounts, defined contribution plans with benefits dependent on contributions and investment returns.[36]

The debate centres on the fact that defined contribution pensions lead to an inher-ent reduction in income security at and following retirement as such income is depend-ent on the market, and are less redistributive, as such pensions are individual rather than population-based. In addition, there is discussion as to whether such schemes alter other forms of savings, or actually increase overall savings, whether they allow a more flexible withdrawal from the labour market – in part because they are not reliant on final salary figures – and whether they promote labour market flexibility.[37] As previously argued, given that the cohorts coming up are likely to be more flexible and used to changing jobs throughout their lifetime, there may be a strong compatibility between the potential labour market flexibility associated with defined contribution pensions and flexible retirement. There is also some evidence of the influence of pension rights on labour market mobility. An analysis of the effect of pension coverage on labour mobility using the European Community Household Panel Survey (ECHP) in Denmark, the Netherlands and the UK,[38] revealed that pension-covered workers were only less likely to move jobs in the UK, which had a high level of defined benefit provision. There was no effect, for example, in Denmark where the majority of occupational schemes are defined contribution schemes, nor in the Netherlands where schemes are typically arranged at the industry level rather than at the company level. Within the UK, a study of the labour mobility of a group of individuals who were offered the opportunity to join their employer's pension scheme but chose to make their own arrangements,[39] found that 11.6 per cent of employees with a personal account moved within 12 months, twice the mobility of those in a company scheme. It may of course be argued, however, that those who thought they were likely to move on chose not to commit themselves to a company scheme.

Gender implications of pension reform

Much of the literature referred to has an implicit focus on male retirement patterns and pension implications, reflecting the research undertaken. There is considerable recognition, however, of the particular vulnerabilities of women, and the impact of the growth in private-based pension savings on female pension provision. Given the contingent and less secure characteristics of many female employment patterns, personal saving for pensions becomes more difficult to sustain. Indeed, as a recent international review has revealed, the gender gap in pension provision is widest in those countries with the largest current private component.[40]

The issue of providing social security is thus complex and changing rapidly. There exist numerous excellent texts describing individual national schemes and their adaptation to national needs. In order to highlight some of the issues here, the remainder of the discussion will fall into three parts. First, a brief overview of the development of pensions, using the UK as an example. Second, a review of the situation in western European countries outlining the issues, describing the various pension systems in existence at the turn of the century and addressing pension reform. Finally, we shall turn to the USA and address some of the proposals being considered there.

The development of pension provision in the UK

Social historian Thane describes how old age state pensions were 'profoundly to shape the experiences of old people and the ways in which they were perceived by others for the remainder of the twentieth century'.[41]

The 1908 Old Age Pensions Act provided a national non-contributory old age pension for all citizens of good character aged 70 and above whose annual income was less than £21. This pension was intended to contribute to the subsistence of the very old, the very poor and the very respectable, and was, in effect, an amendment of the Poor Law.[42] For the first time the state was to give a cash payment to a group in need as an undoubted right, and for the first time old age was defined by chronological age rather than by other characteristics. Nearly half a million took the first British pension on 1 January 1909, the vast majority at the full rate. While 59 per cent of the population were women, 63 per cent of the pensioners were female. Interestingly, Thane sees the significance of this not as economic, but as a profound social change.

In 1925 a contributory National Insurance pension payable to manual workers over age 65 was grafted onto the original non-contributory scheme, the eligibility for women being reduced to age 60 in 1940. In 1948 this contributory insurance pension was extended as part of the Beveridge social insurance system to include all citizens, not just manual workers, conditional on retirement from full-time employment. The original idea of accumulating a fund was abandoned and reliance on a pay-as-you-go basis was established by the end of the 1950s. This change to complete reliance on workers' National Insurance contributions introduced that which Beveridge had hoped to avoid, employed contributors and income-taking pensioners.[43] In 1959 graduated contributions were introduced for higher earners who in return received a higher state pension. A supplementary state earnings-related pension scheme (SERPS) was introduced in 1978 to provide additional income to those who were not members of an employer pensions scheme. This was replaced in 2002 by the State Second Pension. During this period the percentage of the population who were pensioners increased nearly seven-fold from 3 per cent to 20 per cent.[44]

A system of occupational-based pensions developed parallel to this. In 1810 a non-contributory pension paid from age 60 was extended throughout the civil service. By the end of the century it had spread throughout the rest of the public sector – school teachers, police, Poor Law officials, local government. Private employers were also introducing such schemes, appearing first in the largest and most bureaucratic firms. For example, the Gas, Light and Coke Company paid a discretionary pension from the 1830s; most of the railways had a compulsory contributory scheme by the 1860s; and mining developed mutual aid funds, a combination of employer donations, employee contributions, charitable donations and investment income. Manufacturing was most variable in its pension provision. Much of the industry comprised small firms, and these appeared to be strongly influenced by the needs of the firm for such schemes. As Thane suggests, formal pension schemes were introduced into firms either for paternalistic reasons or because they judged this the best technique for holding on to a loyal and hard working labour force:

> Pensions were generally discretionary and dependent upon a satisfactory work record, and as such they functioned as part of the structure of workplace incentives and

deterrents . . . (they) were usually confined to skilled workers whom firms most wished to retain or attract'.[45]

Though such pensions were introduced primarily on the initiative of employers as a tool of management, they were increasingly sought after by workers as a desirable form of security. At the turn of the century less than 5 per cent of workers were in a company pension scheme, by the 1960s over half the working population were covered,[46] though the time lag between joining a scheme and receiving a pension meant that it was not until the 1980s that half of the retired were actually in receipt of such a pension.[47]

Thane believes that the old age pension in the English context was responsible for constructing a particular image of late life:

> As formal pension schemes gradually became a normal feature of life courses for most English people, they changed these lives by, for the first time, guaranteeing a right to a secure if small income at a fixed age. The fixed pensionable age itself strengthened and universalised a notion long present in English culture that old age began somewhere between 60 and 65. It made this definition more rigid with ambiguous effects. On the one hand it had the beneficial result of rescuing many old people from a desperate struggle for survival . . . On the other hand the pensions paid at a fixed age contributed to the construction of old people as a new and increasingly dominant . . . cultural stereotype, the 'old age pensioner', who was represented as a dependent rather than a contributing member of society once pensionable age was reached, in contrast to older assumptions that people aged and became dependent, if at all, at variable ages.[48]

Pension systems within countries of the European Union

Most EU member states have recently reviewed or are in the process of reviewing their pension systems, as their social security systems come under increasing pressure not only from the demographic ageing of their populations but also the maturing of existing schemes typically established since the Second World War. While distinct national programmes operate, reflecting the different historical timing and emergence of these schemes, there are certain common characteristics. Nearly all countries operate three broad tiers of old age pension cover: first tier – statutory or *public*; second tier – *occupational*; third tier – *private or voluntary*. There is general recognition that future expansion needs to be in the second or third tiers if high quality pension provision is to be sustained for most elderly people. However, while within the Anglo-American model national social security provides only a base level income, intended to be supplemented by employer-based pension funds and individual savings, social solidarity has remained a key factor underpinning many European welfare states, with social security providing the largest part of retirement income.

Philippe Pochet provides an EU perspective on this.[49] Acknowledging that pensions are generally conceived of as national strategies, he notes, however, that current EU aims of increasing cross-national labour mobility and developing Eurozone wide pension markets are key to the future integration of EU markets. The question of pensions has been approached at the European level in three phases, according to Pochet:

> The first is linked to creating the internal market, this centres on promoting labour mobility and on the creation of an integrated financial market. The question of pensions is seen from this point of view as a factor limiting effective freedom of movement. From a normative point of view, *privatization* is the key.[50]

The second phase, he suggests, stems from the adoption of monetary union. Here the objective of maintaining the balance or even slight surplus in public finances is key:

> Since pensions are the costliest item of social expenditure, the pressure to stabilize or even reduce such costs will be reinforced . . . fears have also been expressed about the capacity to finance pensions in the medium term, and the risks involved for the sustainability of the Monetary Union (EMU). Here *sustainability* is central.[51]

The final phase stems from the recent initiatives on social protection, poverty and social exclusion. Here the approach focuses on *redistribution* and the reduction of poverty among older populations.

In terms of the first issue, the European Court of Justice has had an influence in defining the responsibilities of national provision and of the market, particularly in relation to competition law. Currently, basic public pensions are not subject to competition policy, third tier provision is, and there is less clarity over the position of the second tier. Yet, as Pochet points out, second tier provision is currently embedded at a national level, usually compulsory and benefits from protective fiscal arrangements. There are, therefore, strong moves for both second and third tier provision to be subject to European competition policy and to competition from other sectors.

The effect on public debt of pension expenditures is also being actively addressed, with this issue now being seen as a key one for the EMU. In 2000 the Economic Policy Committee recommended reforms aimed at delaying retirement, tighter links between contributions and benefits, and a progressive increase in the role of funded schemes.[52] Unsurprisingly, the third issue, that of social protection, has been less well addressed. The European Council has recently approved three overall objectives in this area: to maintain social cohesion and social solidarity, notably reducing the risk of poverty; to safeguard the financial sustainability of pension systems; and to adapt pension systems to a changing society and labour markets.

As Pochet concludes:

> Rather than radical reform, the discussions taking place at the European level propose incremental change, touching on a range of issues, where efforts are made to reconcile apparently contradictory objectives (collective solidarity and market forces). This, in turn, touches on the close link between the problem of pensions and employment strategies (raising the employment rate and the age of retirement).[53]

So, it is national demographic and financial pressures that are the main drivers for current and future reform, though the three themes identified at the EU level – privatisation, stability and redistribution – are, as we shall see, key elements of national strategies. In addition, there is also early evidence of cross-national interference in national policies. Economic integration and monetary union are making all member states more conscious of neighbouring policies.[54] The recent intervention by Dutch employers seeking reforms to the French and Italian pension systems, because in their view these were potentially skewing capital markets and the subsequent returns to Dutch pension funds, will surely prove to be but an early example.

Given the very rapid review that pensions systems throughout the Western world are currently undergoing, with ongoing reforms and adaptations, the following takes *the last three years of the twentieth century as its benchmark.*[55] This briefly indicates the demographic pressures, the various European schemes in operation at the turn of the century and the ways in which EU governments planned at this time to tackle the upcoming pension crisis. The following thumbnail sketches are intended only to provide an indication of the complexities of the different systems which existed at the turn of the century.[56] These will highlight predicted demographic change and other relevant contexts, and include a brief description of current schemes and potential future developments.

All European social security schemes involve an element of state pension provision with every member state providing a minimum pension for each single person with no other income on reaching a specified age. The 15 member states comprising the EU at the turn of the century, can be divided into two broad groups:[57]

- *Group One* – comprises Denmark, Sweden, Finland, UK, Ireland and the Netherlands. In these countries the statutory pension comprises a universal basic old age pension and a supplementary, earnings-related pension.

- *Group Two* – comprises Germany, Austria, France, Belgium, Luxembourg, Italy, Spain, Portugal and Greece. In these countries pensions are based on occupational status supplemented by universally available minimum benefits.

The funding of these state schemes also varies between the two groups. In Group One, Denmark, Sweden and Finland fund the basic pension from general taxation, with Ireland and the UK relying on a mix of conventional insurance contributions supplemented by general taxation. In Group Two countries, plus the Netherlands, conventional insurance-based principles operate: employees, their employers and the self-employed pay contributions at set rates into the relevant insurance fund, which may be supplemented from general taxation. All these countries are now undergoing reforms, but the division still provides an historically interesting divide.

Group One countries

Denmark

Denmark's population aged 60 or over stands at around 20 per cent, forecast to rise to 26 per cent by 2020 and 29 per cent by 2050.[58] Denmark has already achieved a pension system[59] which most of the rest of the EU is working towards, or even still debating. While the country has a basic state pension funded from taxes, most pensioners now receive their main income from an extensive occupational pension scheme. It is pre-funded, contribution-defined and equivalence-based – so that each contributor receives benefits based on his/her own contribution. This is in contrast to most of Europe which is still largely benefit-defined and financed on a pay-as-you-go system. All Danish pension funds are administered by pension companies or life assurance funds, independent of employers. Denmark has been extending its occupational scheme since the mid-1980s when it was argued: that this would reduce the burden of an ageing population through the increased expenditure from pre-funded schemes; that it was socially unacceptable for most older people to rely on a basic public pension; and that the savings created through the expansion of the pre-funded schemes would increase total savings and thus assist the Danish economy.[60] In particular, the pay-as-you-go pension, funded through taxes, was seen as the main factor behind Denmark's large balance of payments deficit in the 1980s. Despite an active debate over the last few years concerning pension provision and the merits of the alternate systems,[61] the prevailing view is that the expansion of Denmark's pre-funded occupational system, coupled with a move to later retirement, will enable the country to cope with future demographic demands.

Finland

Finland operates a two-tier pension system, with a negligible third tier voluntary or personal pension take-up. The Finnish social security scheme covers all residents in the country, with a basic minimum income of around 38 per cent of the average male industrial worker's net income. However, as it is means tested, a growing number of pensioners are disqualified through the income they receive from the second tier occupational pension. Although the retirement age is 65, anticipatory pensions can be paid at a reduced rate from the age of 60. The pension is financed on a pay-as-you-go basis by contributions from employers, the government and municipalities. Alongside this is a compulsory occupational pension, controlled by insurance companies, pension foundations and pension funds, and fully financed by an insurance premium. Employees pay the same insurance premium according to an annually confirmed payment percentage which the employer collects; the employer's contribution rests on factors such as size of company and average age of employees. Due to the high level of statutory cover, few take up personal or voluntary pension cover. Where it is used, it is usually to allow earlier retirement, or to compensate for missed periods of employment.

Although Finland is facing similar demographic ageing to that of the other member states, its current concern focuses on the rapid growth of early retirement:[62] while retirement age is 65, the average age on retirement is 59. Recent reforms have, therefore, tended to focus on this. Various measures have included raising the age limits of early retirement packages, tightening eligibility and changing the calculations determining pension income, in particular to ensure that even if wages decline in the final few years of employment, particularly for example for manual workers, then this will not affect final pension income. Current moves are for Finland to replace final year's earnings as a basis of pension calculation with average earnings across the working life. Any negative effect for senior executive and professional employees will, it is hoped, be compensated for by increased uptake of private pensions among this group.

Ireland

Ireland is demographically very different to the other member states in that its birth rate remained high until 1980.[63] The percentage of the population aged over 65 thus remains low for a western nation, at around 11 per cent, forecast to rise to around 18 per cent by 2025. In addition, the demographic ageing of the workforce and increase in the number of elderly economic dependants relative to workers is likely to be buffeted by increased female participation rates.[64] However, the Irish state pension is funded on a pay-as-you-go system from current taxation, which is directly affected by small changes in the composition of the labour force. In particular, the current growing entry of women and the coverage of part-time workers will result in additional pension claimants. Current projections predict that the ratio of contributors to pensioners will fall from the 1995 ratio of 6:1 to less than 3:1 by 2035. In addition, the increase in social insurance contributions for employees required to meet the increased cost of pensions will rise from 10.2 per cent to 20.4 per cent during the same period. Income related pensions are not provided under the social security system. While over the past decade the move has been to raise the level of the flat rate pension to bring it up to minimally acceptable cover, more recently interest has turned to examining the need for *supplementary pension provision*. Currently around half of Ireland's employed workforce has some supplementary cover, all on a voluntary basis, and it seems likely that it is the expansion and regulation of these voluntary schemes which will provide the focus of future developments.[65]

The Netherlands

The Netherlands currently has one of the youngest age profiles in the EU.[66] The population aged 60 and over in the Netherlands is currently around 18 per cent, forecast to rise to 37 per cent by 2050, including a 60 per cent increase in the first 20 years of the century. By 2030, the Netherlands will have one of the highest dependency ratios in the EU.[67] In addition, the end of the last century saw a dramatic fall in labour participation by older workers, with the percentage of men aged 60 to 64 who were economically active falling between 1960 and 1994 from 80 per cent to 20 per cent;[68] this early retirement compounding the predicted rapid increase in demographic ageing.

The Dutch system is close to a three-pillar system, with a relatively small third pillar.[69] The *state pension* is a compulsory pay-as-you-go system for all residents. Benefits are flat rate, neither means tested, nor dependent on contributions, and indexed to wages. The social minimum provided under the National Social Assistance Act (1965/1996) coincides with the public pension, and consequently, older people do not draw on social benefits.[70] Replacement is 70 per cent of the statutory minimum wage for single person households, 100 per cent for two person households. The second tier *supplementary occupational pensions* are integrated with the public pension system which together aim to provide 70 per cent of the final salary after a working life of 40 years. In recognition of the increasing fluidity of the Dutch labour market, these occupational pensions are fully portable (as from July 1994), and those over age 40 have a right to state-funded pension contributions during periods of unemployment. Even though there is no legal obligation for employers to provide occupational pensions, most do, and around 90 per cent of the working population are thus covered.

Recent issues of concern have addressed whether to abandon the pay-as-you-go system for the basic state pension, though most commentators think this will be unlikely.[71] Also of debate is whether to broaden the assessment of contributions, currently capped at around 45,000 Dutch guilders. Given that the higher paid would then be paying a much greater part of their income to the financing of a flat rate state pension, this would move against the insurance principle of the old age pension. Other suggestions concern the payment of premiums for the state pension by those over age 65, that is from occupational pension income (unpopular politically) and the raising of the pension age to 66 or 67. Most *occupational schemes* were established in the 1960s and 1970s and are still to mature. However, although they are fully funded, there still remains a concern over the future financing of these.[72] In particular, the most popular schemes operate on a final pay basis, particularly problematic when wage increases are above the indexing of the basic old age pension. There are, therefore, moves to consider either introducing mid-life limits beyond which no further wage increase may be taken into account, or to take career average earnings. There are also changes to the franchise relationship between the state pension and the occupational pension, whereby the supplementary pension takes into account the state pension in building up the 70 per cent salary replacement value of the pension. Increasingly the franchise will use other indicators, such as minimum wage, resulting in future pensions not achieving the 70 per cent value. Finally, the Dutch pension is entitled to be split 50 per cent on divorce, and from 2000 will also cover common law partners.

Sweden

Sweden's recent attempts to control welfare spending have impacted upon all sectors of the population, including older people.[73] Demographically, Sweden has raised its life expectancy by five years since 1970 to 79.5 years.[74] Most people receive pensions under the old Swedish pension system – a three tier system. The pay-as-you-go social insurance system guarantees a basic pension to all those aged 65 and older and a partially funded earnings related supplementary pension – ATP, both administered by the National Social Insurance Board. The basic pension is tied to the consumer price index, and 40 years of residence is required; the ATP requires 30 years of earnings for the full pension with the amount based on the average of the 15 highest earning years. Those eligible for both receive around 65 per cent of their former income (except those on low income who receive supplements, and the high earners who are capped). This is supplemented for some by a series of third tier collectively bargained schemes based on occupation. There are a variety of sliding entry pensions with reduced options from age 60 and enhanced pensions for those who remain in employment until age 70.

From 2000, pensions under the reformed system have been paid out – these reforms were in response to the combination of demographic ageing and increasing early retirement.[75] This new system is based more on insurance principles. The pension is based on earnings in every year from age 16, including earnings after age 65, and will take into account military service, care of children up to the age of four years, and study. Each year the accumulated pension credits of persons aged 65 and over are transformed into a pension. This is decided by using a coefficient determined anew for every cohort of pensioners. The size of the coefficient depends on the expected period for which those who turn 65 will receive a pension. As the expected remaining lifetime increases with each cohort, the coefficient will gradually increase. At present the supplementary pensions are financed only by employers; in future arrangements employees will make a 9.25 per cent contribution in order to enforce the idea that employees are gaining the right to a pension by working for it. In this way it is hoped that work incentives will be strengthened. This new system thus comprises an earnings-related pension and a minimum guaranteed pension. The earnings-related pension consists of a defined contribution pay-as-you-go component and a defined contribution pre-funded component. From age 61 onwards, it is possible to work and draw a pension at the same time. The earnings-related (defined contribution) pension can be drawn at 100 per cent or partially in steps at 75 per cent, 50 per cent or 25 per cent and combined with full or part-time work. Since there is no longer a stipulated retirement age, pension entitlements can be earned for an indefinite period. The minimum guaranteed pension cannot be drawn before the age of 65.

The *collectively bargained schemes* are complex and based on four occupational groups: blue collar in the private sector; white collar in the private sector; central government employees and local government employees. All retain the principle that employees must work until the age of 65; anyone retiring earlier than this receives an annuity which can only be drawn at 65. While the collectively bargained schemes will not meet with serious financial problems in the near future, they too will come under the same pressure as other systems next century. It is likely that these schemes will slowly change from a pay-as-you-go system to a premium reserve system.

As Palme[76] notes, the new system is stable, irrespective of demographic and economic developments. However, the fixed contribution rate is shifting the financial risk on to the retired population, and the future question will be whether pension levels will be seen as offering a decent standard of living to retired people if longevity increases substantially. He concludes that the Swedish reforms maintain the social policy goals of basic income security and redistribution, although the means by which this has been achieved have changed dramatically.

United Kingdom

An excellent overview of the complexities of the United Kingdom's three tier pension system is provided by Carl Emmerson:[77]

- The *first tier* – is mandatory, flat rated and publicly funded on a pay-as-you-go basis, with a significant amount of means-tested benefits available to low income pensioners.

- The state *second tier* pension and the majority of the public occupational pension schemes are financed on a pay-as-you-go basis; private sector occupational schemes, personal pensions and stakeholder pensions are financed on a funded basis.

- The *third tier* consists of voluntary private savings.

The structure of the first tier basic state pension, largely unreformed since its introduction in 1948, is a flat rate benefit. All those earning over the primary earnings threshold, £89 a week (2002–3), pay National Insurance contributions; those earning between this threshold and the lower earning limit, and those unable to work due to disability, sickness or unemployment, have contributions made on their behalf. In order to qualify for the full amount, individuals must have contributed for 44 years, that is 90 per cent of their working lives.[78] The Social Security Act, 1975 linked the basic state pension to the greater of either earnings or savings. Since the early 1980s this has been automatically increased with prices.[79] For a single pensioner, this pension is worth £75.50 per week (April 2002). As the level of means-tested benefit is higher than the basic state pension, no individual should have to rely on the basic state pension for income in retirement.[80] In April 2002 the Minimum Income Guarantee (MIG) was worth £98.15 per week for a single pensioner, some 25 per cent higher than the basic state pension.

The second tier is mandatory to all employees earning above the lower earning limit. Introduced in 1978, individuals pay into either the state earnings-related pension scheme (SERPS), or opt out into a private pension, which initially had to be a defined benefit (final salary) scheme that guaranteed to pay at least as generously as SERPS. From 1988 this could be a defined contribution (money purchase) scheme, taken either through their employers as an occupational pension or as individuals purchasing a personal pension. From April 2000 this could also be a stakeholder pension. From April 2002 SERPS was replaced by the State Second Pension (S2P), initially an earnings-related pension, but with plans to make it a flat rate top up to the basic state pension, which is more generous to lower earners. The State Second Pension and the majority of the public occupational pension schemes are financed on a pay-as-you-go basis; private sector occupational schemes, personal pensions and stakeholder pensions are financed on a funded basis.

The third tier consists of voluntary private savings. Individuals can also make additional contributions to a private pension, up to a limit defined by age and earnings.[81] As Emmerson explains, contributions are made from income before tax and there is no income tax or capital gains tax on any returns to the fund. One quarter of the fund can be taken tax-free on retirement, the remaining three-quarters has to be used to purchase an annuity, the income from which is subject to income tax before the individual reaches age 75. As Emmerson concludes, while the UK pension system provides individuals with a large degree of choice over their pension arrangements, this comes at the expense of an extremely complicated pension system.

Group Two countries

Austria

Currently, most of Austria's population is provided for in later life by the state social insurance system, with occupational schemes being traditionally tied to reward or motivation aspects of the employment contract. This, however, is now changing. While still emphasising the importance of state provision,[82] the government is working to shift the population towards occupational pensions, primarily in response to current demographic trends. At present, around 20 per cent of the population is aged 60 and over. By 2020 this figure will have reached 25 per cent, and some estimates put the figure at 40 per cent by 2050.[83] Predictions indicate an increase in the total dependency ratio to 64.7 per cent by 2015 and 83.9 per cent by 2030. This will be heavily loaded towards older dependants, rising to 58.2 per cent by 2030.[84] The state system is linked to years of paying contributions, the basis for benefits, and the age of retirement. The basis for benefits ensues from the increased value of the respective contribution basis of the best 15 years of the entire time of service, and is maximised by a highest level of basis for benefits. The highest possible pension is 79.5 per cent of the basis for benefits, paid after 45 years of insured service. Occupational pensions date from pre-industrial times, benefit support being given by the rural craft industries, and formalised in the mid-nineteenth century by some employers as a means of securing a minimum income for their employees at end of life. Owing, however, to continued government assurances that the state will provide in old age, only around 10 per cent of the population have taken up occupational pensions. In addition, until 1990 they were regulated by company practice rather than laws, and benefited high income employees. Furthermore, the provision of such pensions is still voluntary and offered more in public companies (around 65 per cent) than private (10 per cent). This should change as Austrians take up the idea that occupational pensions form part of a worker's salary, and they are no longer seen as a reward for faithfulness.

Belgium

The proportion of the population in Belgium aged 60 or over is currently 21 per cent, forecast to rise to 28 per cent by 2020 and approaching 38 per cent by 2050.[85] Dependency ratios will rise from their current 83 per cent, to 92 per cent in 2010 and 119 per cent by 2040, heavily loaded towards the elderly: at 39 per cent currently, 47 per cent in 2010 and 71 per cent by 2040.[86] The Bureau du Plan's projections suggest that, using optimistic projections, the expenditure on state pensions would double as a percentage of GNP by 2040, but would be cushioned by a reduction in the expenditure on unemployment, pre-pensions and family allowances; pessimistic projections suggest that a deficit of −6 per cent of GNP would occur by 2040, with an official debt of 200 per cent GNP. Yet, currently only 8 per cent of all employees (3 per cent manual, 13 per cent white collar) belong to a pension fund, with 20 per cent belonging to group insurance schemes – this latter form of pension provision being provided by some 75 per cent of all firms offering supplementary pensions. Both supplementary schemes were somewhat curbed by the 1994–96 wage restraint imposed by the government that prohibited the introduction or extension of company group schemes. In addition, Belgians are increasingly turning to life insurance, currently accounting for 20 per cent of disposable income. The government, however, appears unwilling to act to increase the use of supplementary pensions.[87] This appears to be due to a certain trust in the existing state scheme to cope with the impending pension demand, combined with the necessity to tackle the large public debt, and thus an unwillingness to grant priority to schemes with budgetary consequences.

France

The French pension system is based on a compulsory social system, financed under pay-as-you-go, providing retirement benefits to those with sufficient contributions.[88] It is a two tier system comprising basic and compulsory supplementary pensions, with a high replacement rate of between 70 per cent and 75 per cent of wages. Consequently, voluntary pensions play a marginal role. The system is managed by pension funds which are independent from the state, and run by administrative councils comprising representatives from both employers and employees.[89] France sees not only demographic ageing *per se* as a problem, but also the ageing of particular occupational groups. Thus in the 1980s it faced its first tranche of retirees as those men who had joined occupations immediately after the Second World War reached retirement age. It is in preparation for the baby boomers coming through early this century, however, that current reforms are directed. The French system has recently responded to impending socio-economic and demographic developments by both reforming the basic pension and consolidating the various compulsory supplementary schemes into two federations: ARRCO and AGIRAC. From 1994 the qualifying period for the age 60 pension was increased from 37.5 to 40 years (that at age 65 continues) and the years for calculation of pension rate increased from the best 10 to the best 25 years, this latter move in particular being estimated to cause a fall in the final pension of up to 3.8 per cent. The creation of the two federations has allowed a more structured approach to extending the remit of supplementary pensions in France. In particular, by raising the compulsory contribution rate to 16 per cent it opened up the possibility of sustained expansion in the funded sector, and signalled a limit to the expansion of the pay-as-you-go pension. Recent debate has also focused on the expansion of voluntary schemes; these are being heavily pushed by the insurance companies with the rationale of encouraging the population to save. The response from the government, employers, trade unions and employees has so far been muted.

In 1999 the Charpin Report was published in response to Prime Minister Jospin's request for possible reforms. This acknowledged a sharp increase in France's ageing population from 2006, with those aged over 60 estimated to reach 30 per cent by 2040. The demographic dependency rate will have almost doubled to 7:10, and the future of pay-as-you-go will be compromised by 2010.[90] The report recommended again extending contribution length to 42.5 years. Two more reports ensued. The Taddei 1999 Study highlighted the contradiction between increasing contribution lengths, increasing time spent in full-time education and increasing earlier retirement (as we saw earlier, real retirement age in France is 57). It was becoming almost impossible to reach the lengths of contributions required. Taddei recommended a system which would encourage a gentle transition to retirement, supported by a mix of employment income and retirement pension.[91] The Teulade Report (2000) also questioned the reality of being able to increase contribution lengths. This suggested that the viability of the pay-as-you-go pensions might be assured through increasing the reserve fund and increasing the state's role in financing non-contributory related pension rights. As Palier[92] has commented, it is politically difficult to reform a generous system of earnings-related benefits covering the majority of the population, financed by social contributions and managed by social partners. He concludes that Jospin will prefer to preserve the pay-as-you-go system by extending the length of contributions required before gaining the right to a full pension. Given that in France there appears no tendency to work longer, there will likely be a progressive reduction in the level of pay-as-you-go pensions, and an increase in private pensions savings.

Bismarckian pension institutions are difficult to reform because they challenge the special interests of various privileged groups of workers. Of particular concern, is that the development of individual pension savings, and for those with insufficient contributions, increased dependence on means-tested benefits, diminishes the level of redistribution, a fundamental goal of Bismarckian systems.

Germany

The German population is covered by a basic state pension, and a range of voluntary supplementary pension schemes with a variable take up.[93] Schmähl[94] provides an excellent overview of the current pensions system:

- The *first tier* is the statutory pension, an earnings related defined benefit scheme, financed by both contribution payments and general tax revenue. Unlike many other European state pensions schemes, this scheme has a low redistributional component, being based on a close link between personal contributions and pension benefits. Alongside this exist other first tier schemes directed at specific occupational groups, such as civil servants, and the self-employed.

- The *second tier* consists of supplementary occupational pension schemes in both the public and private sector. All white and blue collar public workers are covered by collective agreements, and around 50 per cent of private employees are rather unequally covered by voluntary agreements. It is estimated that around only one half of men and one third of women in private industry have some form of supplementary pension.

- The *third tier* comprises a variety of private savings and insurance.

Around 80 per cent of all pension benefits are first tier and thus pay-as-you-go, and 10 per cent each are pre-funded second and third tiers. Furthermore, prior to reforms, there was (in principle) no pre-funded occupational or private pensions in the former GDR.

Described as a system 'on the verge of collapse',[95] as Schmähl[96] comments, it is not surprising that this should be a main focus for reform. Yet the overall source of late life income is complex; intra-family payments, limited income, health and long-term care insurance all play their part, and these interactions must be taken into consideration both at the macro and individual level.

There have been recent reforms of the basic state pension resulting in a move to a later retirement age of 65 for both sexes (while the legal age is already 65 for men, women have been allowed to retire at 60, and some men at 63). Although these reforms have also somewhat lowered the pension itself by linking it to net rather than gross earnings, this does not appear to have encouraged uptake of the voluntary supplementary schemes. It is this that is causing most concern. In the majority of cases the employer is not required either by law or by collective agreement to provide such schemes. Thus the amount spent on supplementary pensions, which remains at around 23 billion DM per year, is just a tenth of that spent on state pensions, 240 billion per year – there are 14 million state pensions and only 2 million supplementary pensions. However, Germany's unique social insurance system for family carers, is seen as another supplement to personal pensions. The 1994 new social care scheme introduced a new branch of social insurance paid by the insured workforce, and aimed at providing direct payments to those caring for older relatives. The 2001 reforms included a means-tested (social assistance like) transfer payment in case of insufficient income, and the introduction of a strictly regulated private pension component.

As Schmähl[97] has pointed out, the effects of demographic ageing on pay-as-you-go financed social insurance was the central topic in public debate that referred to a demographic crisis; a time bomb which will shake the fundament of the German economy, resulting in a generation conflict if there is no radical change. This was only really seen in a shift towards many more private pensions. The German debate was clearly framed towards this shift in the public–private mix. It is the declared objective of the government to compensate any reduction in public pensions by additional private pensions.[98] While there was no plan for extending occupational pensions, the original idea was to introduce a mandated private pension. Following strong opposition, based in part on concepts of intergenerational equity, those near to retirement age having no opportunity to fill the income gap, the government has left this as voluntary.

Greece

Currently, around 21 per cent of the population in Greece is over the age of 65, forecast to reach 27 per cent by 2020, and 33 per cent by 2050.[99] Social security is the responsibility of a large number of funds under the jurisdiction of the Ministry of Health and Social Security. The country operates a system of basic state pension, supplemented by compulsory occupational supplementary pensions, covering around 80 per cent of the employed population. Voluntary private schemes are limited. Recent reforms have tightened both contributions and pension payments, in recognition of the rapid maturing of many of these schemes over the very near future. While it has been described as a complex, inefficient and costly form of administration, reflecting the unplanned historical process that gave rise to it,[100] given the fragmented system that operated under military rule, and the fact that under half the population was covered, the system has been brought up to date considerably in the past 20 years.[101] Most private employees belong to the main Social Security Fund, IKA; public employees have a separate fund, and OGA covers farmers, fishermen and those with no pension provision, and everyone else is covered by special interest funds – such as those for bankers, lawyers, etc. The system is financed by earnings-related contributions, which vary considerably in relation to employee, employer contributions, and state subsidy. Throughout the 1990s, the government has attempted to streamline these funds, in an attempt to address the burgeoning pension spending, which doubled in the 1980s.[102] The replacement ratio for an average industrial worker on maximum benefits has been estimated at 107 per cent of average earnings, though clearly in a low wage economy pensions have to have high replacement ratios to provide even a basic income. The Greek pension is around 50 per cent of the EU average.

Italy

The Italian social security system must also be seen in the context of the general welfare system, which was seriously attacked in the 1970s and 1980s for its corruption and patronage.[103] The reforms of the 1980s were seen as restricted and restrictive, and driven by financial concerns, and it was not until the 1990s that the guiding principles of Italian welfare provision were seriously addressed.[104] This has been compounded by the demands of demographic change. Italy's population aged 60 and over currently stands at 22 per cent. It is forecast to rise to 29 per cent by 2020, and 37 per cent by 2050.[105] In addition, the dependency ratio will increase overall by a third, with the ratio related to elderly dependants doubling in this time. Indeed, the heavy increase in social security expenditure during the 1980s was due especially to the high number and level of retirement and invalidity pensions for workers; unemployment and family allowances increased only slightly or even decreased during this time.[106] The pensions system was thoroughly revised in 1992, with the intention of reducing both the impact on public expenditure and the general fragmentation of the system.[107] Recent reforms of the basic state pension have introduced flexible retirement between the ages of 57 and 65, and a move from a defined benefits to defined contributions system. The scheme favours in particular those who start their career early, and maintain a steady career progression until retirement age with no breaks in service. This has led to a move by others with different life work paths, in particular management and professionals, and those with high late life earning capacity, to turn towards supplementary pensions to compensate for predicted loss in pension income.

The Italian pension system has been, and remains, very generous in comparison with other EU countries.[108] During the 1980s, for example, replacement rates for an Italian pensioner in manufacturing were nearly twice those of an equivalent British pensioner. Given that current pensioners still enjoy, on average, an 89 per cent replacement of average earnings there is still only a small incentive for the mass population to turn to these supplementary schemes, with only 5 per cent of the population currently doing so.[109] Government figures suggest that under 30 per cent of the workforce is expected to take up a supplementary pension over the next ten years, predicting a sixfold increase in state pension spending over the next decade.[110]

Luxembourg

Luxembourg has the third youngest profile in the EU, with 19 per cent of its population aged 60 years or over. However, as with the other currently relatively young countries, Ireland, the Netherlands and Finland, it will experience a dramatic rate of increase over the next two decades, of around 60 per cent. The statutory pension scheme in

Luxembourg provides a high level of provision for most pensioners, with all beneficiaries granted a pension of up to the maximum rate of 80 per cent of their last wage. Supplementary schemes are not well developed and the government is currently undertaking a major review of all forms of pension provision in the country.[111]

Portugal

Portugal currently stands at just under 20 per cent of its population aged 60 or above, and over the next two decades it will experience the slowest rate of old age increase of all EU countries, at less than 30 per cent. Thus predictions suggest that it will be the youngest country in the European Union in 2020, with 24 per cent of its population aged 60 or above, rising to around 30 per cent by 2050. Currently, all citizens are entitled to social security, and coverage is compulsory for employees and most self-employed. It is a contributory programme; those who have not contributed receive a means-tested benefit at times of need. There is no provision for the creation of compulsory supplementary pension schemes. These are either at the initiative of the employer, or through the taking out of individual insurance. Yet, the economic and political uncertainty in Portugal is not conducive to the implementation of new provision, and neither the government nor the employed population appear willing to expand this sector at present.[112] However, Portugal's social security programme is currently undergoing review, with the likelihood that supplementary pensions will be recommended for expansion. Replacement value of the pension is 94 per cent, which in terms of the income provided is only 37 per cent of the EU average.

Spain

Currently, 22 per cent of Spain's population is aged 60 or over, forecast to rise to 26 per cent by 2020 and 32 per cent by 2050.[113] Combined with this increasing demographic pressure is a labour market which produces high rates of employment, thus encouraging early withdrawal by older workers.[114] Since 1984, unemployment benefit has been available to those over age 55, extended at age 52 from 1989, until they reach the statutory pensionable age.[115] Between 1980 and 1992, the number of pensioners rose by 1.7 million, though this was also inflated by a rapid expansion of disability pensioners, accounted for in part by fraud.[116] In addition, the level of poverty among older people remains one of the highest in the EU,[117] although this is alleviated to an extent by the high percentage of older people living with their kin, some 90 per cent.[118] In 1990, the contributory state pensions scheme was universalised, with the creation of a category of means-tested non-contributory benefits. In 1994 the Congress of Deputies appointed a reporting group within the Committee of Budgets to analyse the structure of the social security system, and make recommendations which would guarantee the viability of the state pension system. This report stressed the need to strengthen the state pension system, maintain pensioners' purchasing power through linking this to the consumer price index, and retain pensionable age at 65, but facilitate the remaining in employment after this age for those who wished it.[119] In the same year, the main political parties signed the Toleda Pact, which committed them to sustaining the existing social security system. Compulsory social insurance was to remain the mainstay of welfare policy, supported by non-contributory means-tested assistance financed from general taxation. A second voluntary tier of private-funded pensions was to be permitted.[120] However, while the recommendations suggested that the supplementary pension system be updated and improved, these are seen as so general as to have little influence on the low provision or uptake of supplemental pensions, which currently stands at less than 2 per cent of Spanish pensions.[121] Replacement value of the pension is 97 per cent, which in terms of income provided stands at 60 per cent of the average EU pension.

Reforms in the United States

As Achenbaum[122] has pointed out, social security was introduced later in the USA than in many European countries. He argues that this is directly related to the American ethos which values private over public responsibility. Those who have contributed through work are seen as deserving, the elderly workers for example, while those who are reliant on long-term public assistance are more likely to be branded undeserving. The self-financing and contributory elements of the US social security system thereby entitle recipients to earned benefits. As discussed earlier, within the continental European model social solidarity remains a key factor underpinning many European welfare states, with social security providing the largest part of retirement income, but in the Anglo-American model national social security provides only a base level income, intended to be supplemented by employer-based pension funds and individual savings.

In comparison with many other western countries, the USA faces a manageable financial challenge because the projected ageing of the population is less pronounced than elsewhere, and its Social Security programme is somewhat modest in comparison with some European countries.[123] However, as Schieber points out:

> . . . virtually every aspect of the US retirement income security system is underfunded in some regard. Social Security is facing substantial financial shortfalls as the baby boom generation moves into its retirement years. The employer-based pension system will require substantially higher future contributions to deliver benefits promised currently. Workers themselves have reduced their personal savings rates in recent years. . . . If we do not change direction soon, baby boomers will have to work much later into their lives than prior generations, or they will live out their retirement at standards of living well below those prior generations have enjoyed.[124]

As in the UK, US pension security comprises a three-tiered system, of which the pay-as-you-go Social Security is the first tier. Employer-provided pensions comprise the second tier, and individual schemes the third. Almost all workers are covered under the first tier, which provides, on average, half all non-earned income for those aged 65 and over. Half of the workforce are also covered by employer-based schemes, providing, on average, one quarter of such income, with the final quarter being provided from individual schemes. Social Security accounts for nearly all non-earned income among the lower income groups, while second and third tier income provides the majority for the higher earners. In relation to other countries, the replacement rate of Social Security, that is the ratio of benefits to pre-retirement earnings, is relatively low at just over 40 per cent.

In her exploration of the future of pay-as-you-go Social Security in the USA, Munnell[125] addresses two key questions: the extent to which the demographic, financial and political pressures will redraw the boundaries between public and private responsibilities; and how workers and markets will be affected by any such reforms. She points out that while current payroll taxes will adequately cover Social Security benefits until 2016, from then on the government can only meet the benefit commitments by drawing on the trust fund assets until the fund is exhausted in 2038. On current figures, the fund would then continue to provide 70 per cent of required benefits only. A raise of 2 per cent in payroll tax would enable the fund to continue with the current range of benefits until 2075. Furthermore, the US underfunded liability for Social Security over this period is less than one quarter, one of the smallest financing short-falls in the OECD. Schieber,[126] however, issues a warning over any complacency, pointing out that much of the programme's costs over the next 25 years is already built into benefits currently being paid, and that the underfunding liability may be an underestimation.

There was a move in late 2001 to cut back on the existing programme and replace a portion with private accounts, whereby individuals would contribute part of their income to these accounts which would be invested in private sector assets. Munnell, however, concludes that the forces behind moving pension income from the public to the private sector emerged not so much from demographic pressures, but from the political climate and the 1990 stock market boom. Furthermore:

> The important considerations are not public versus private but rather the amount of money going into and out of the program, how these monies are invested and whether pensions are provided under a defined benefit or defined contribution arrangement. The introduction of private accounts without additional funding will not improve the programs' finances or raise returns on individuals' payroll tax contributions.[127]

In addition, Munnell suggests that the move to a widespread use of private accounts not only shifts the financial risk of the basic pension to the individual but also contains the seeds for unravelling the entire US social insurance system:

The current Social Security pension is a defined benefit based on lifetime earnings, paid out as a lifetime annuity, and fully adjusted for inflation after retirement. Private accounts are defined contribution plans where benefits depend on contributions and investment returns, The change in the benefit commitment shifts substantial risks to the individuals and makes the benefits unpredictable.[128]

This, Munnell argues, is inconsistent with the goals of Social Security, which aims to provide workers with a predictable base income, which can then be supplemented by them from a variety of other sources. She points to the fact that the employer-provided second tier pensions are for the most part fully funded, with a remarkable growth in assets, so that by 2001 pension assets at $8.9 trillion stood only just behind the $11.6 trillion market value of all household-owned real estate, due in part to the pension reserves reflecting the large contributions made on behalf of the baby boom generation. Others, however, do not share her optimism.[129] Public service pensions cover some 13 million US employees.[130] They are still predominantly defined benefit plans. The second tier pension in the private sector has seen a large shift in recent years from defined benefit to defined contribution plans, and in particular towards 401(k) pension plans.[131] 401(k) plans allow employees to make additional pre-tax contributions and determine how and where these pension contributions will be invested. There has, however, been concern over the general uptake of 401(k) plans, with evidence that mandating these could increase the pension protection for those mobile workers in the bottom half of the pension income scale by up to 25 per cent.[132]

The final scenario is working longer and saving more:

> If the working-age population in today's society cannot be convinced to give up some of their current consumption levels, they will be left with the prospect of either working much later in their lives than most workers currently do or submitting to retirement standards of living significantly reduced from those they have achieved during their working years.[133]

However, the US savings record does not indicate that this will be an easy policy option to promote, even with preferential tax encouragement. Indeed, current calculations show that mid-life cohorts in the USA are only saving one-third of that required to accumulate sufficient assets to maintain the household's pre-retirement standard of living.[134] Even with the general decline in consumption seen in later years, this is a large shortfall. In addition, US personal savings rates consistently fell over the last two decades of the century.[135] However, analysis of savings patterns by younger cohorts[136] indicates there has been an increase in savings behaviour favouring personal retirement accounts, such as 401(k)s, which has not displaced other financial asset saving.[137] Consequently, the real personal financial assets of younger cohorts are substantially larger than those of their predecessors, with a predicted two-thirds increase in personal family assets at age 76 by 2015.

Adopting the Anglo-American model? Implications for the intergenerational contract

It is clear that, despite the above concerns over the ability of the USA to cope with its social security commitments, European nations are increasingly turning to a modified Anglo-American model of a publicly provided low level pension, supplemented by employer-based defined contribution pensions and individual savings. As Clark has noted, in the 1990s a booming US economy stood in contrast to the stultified European one:

> The solution to European woes was assumed to lie in the adoption of American labour market practices and the acceptance of neoliberal orthodoxies requiring labour market deregulation and workforce policy strategies . . . pension fund capitalism allowed old age security to be married to investment finance for restructuring, economic innovation and development.[138]

In addition, as touched upon earlier, from a European Union stance, the current national-based pensions schemes are seen as limiting freedom of movement of both labour and finance. Privatisation of pension provision is thus a key factor in opening up both of these.[139]

A note of realism is sounded, however, by Hoskins of the International Social Security Association, who reminds us that whether the mode of pension financing is public or private, retirement income must be paid for in some form by workers.[140]

Governments throughout the Western world are thus responding to the rising burden on social security programmes by increasing the funded component, and encouraging older workers to remain in economic activity for longer and to increase their personal savings across their lifetime. There are clearly concerns over the first element due to the volatility of market investment. In addition, measures to increase working life may fail, at least in the short term, due to the increasing affluence of those cohorts in late midlife, whose financial and political power is growing and will continue to grow.[141] Finally, as many commentators have pointed out, encouraging individuals to save at any stage of the life course is proving problematic. Nevertheless, as we saw in the previous chapter, current retirement rates are unsustainable over the long term, particularly given increasing longevity, and it is likely that an increasing proportion of older people will remain within the labour market. Yet, despite an increase in those reliant on their own economic activity or personal savings to support themselves in later ages, there will still be a need for a growth in public programmes. This will be required both to provide health and service care for those with increasing frailty and disability, and to provide economic support to those who are unable to provide for themselves. This will still require the maintenance of a strong intergenerational sense of responsibility, and a stable and committed intergenerational contract.

Notes

1 Munnell, 2002, p. 1.
1 ibid., p. 1.
2 Silverstein et al., 2001.
3 Myles, 1995.
4 Kinston and Williams, 1993.
5 Achenbaum, 1986.
6 With the exception, perhaps, of Aid to Families with Dependent Children (AFDC).
7 Binstock, 1983.
8 Thomson, 1989; Thomson, 1993.
9 Binstock, 1983.
10 Silverstein et al., 2000.
11 Peterson, 1999.
12 Tanner and Pinera, 1995.
13 Preston, 1984.
14 Hudson, 1997.
15 Silverstein et al., 2000, p. 281.
16 ibid., p. 282.
17 Clark and Whiteside, 2003.
18 Most publicly invested retirement pensions have an age bar preventing early take-up.
19 Clark and Whiteside, 2003.
20 Disney and Emmerson, 2002.
21 Mesa-Lago, 1991.
22 Schieber and Shoven, 1997.
23 Clark, 2003.
24 Schmähl, 2002.
25 Munnell, 2003.
26 Poterba et al., 1995.
27 Munnell, 2002.
28 Arnold et al., 1998; Diamond et al., 1996.
29 CBI, 2004.
30 OECD, 2004.
31 Disney, 1996.
32 Arnold et al., 1998.
33 Disney, 1998.
34 Department for Work and Pensions, 2004.
35 Bernheim, 1993.
36 Munnell, 2002.
37 Disney et al., 2004.
38 Andrietti, 2001.
39 Disney and Emmerson, 2002.
40 Ginn et al., 2001.
41 Thane, 2000, p. 235.
42 ibid.
43 Johnson and Falkingham, 1992.
44 Johnson and Falkingham, 1988.
45 Thane, 2000, p. 246.
46 Hannah, 1986.
47 Dawson and Evans, 1987.
48 Thane, 2000, p. 236.
49 Pochet, 2003.
50 ibid., p. 45 (author's emphasis).
51 ibid. (author's emphasis).
52 ibid.
53 Ibid., p. 59.
54 ibid.
55 European Commission, 1998; European Commission, 1997a; European Commission, 1996; European Commission, 1995b; European Commission, 1997b. This published material was updated and clarified through personal communication with members of the European Commission and Eurolink Age.
56 General contextual material was provided by Teague, 1998; Gillion, 1991.
57 This has been adapted from that proposed by Moira Denham, Eurolink age.
58 Eurostat, 1998.
59 Anderson, 1993; Ginn and Arber, 1992.
60 Ostrup, 1997.
61 Anderson, 1993.
62 Tanskanen, 1997.
63 European Commission, 1995a.
64 Mangan, 1997.
65 ibid.
66 Eurostat, 1998.
67 Bos, 1994.
68 Kapteyn and de Vos, 1998.
69 van Reil et al., 2002.
70 ibid.
71 Lutjens, 1997.
72 ibid.
73 Gould, 1996.
74 OECD, 2003.
75 Wadensjo, 1997.
76 Palme, 2003.
77 Emmerson, 2002.
78 Until the full equalisation of pensionable age is reached, women have a lower requirement to accrue 90 per cent, currently 39 years;.
79 Banks and Emmerson, 2000.
80 Emmerson, 2002.
81 Disney et al., 2001.
82 Tamburi, 1997.
83 Eurostat, 1998.
84 Prieler, 1997.
85 Eurostat 1998.
86 Pestieau, 1997.
87 ibid.
88 Ambler, 1991.
89 Palier, 2002.
90 ibid.
91 ibid.
92 ibid.
93 Lawson, 1996.

94 Schmähl, 2002.
95 Boersch-Supan and Schnabel, 1998.
96 Schmähl, 2002.
97 Schmähl, 2003.
98 ibid.
99 Eurostat, 1998.
100 Petmesidou, 1991.
101 Stathopoulos, 1996.
102 Petridou, 1997.
103 Saraceno and Negri, 1994.
104 ibid.
105 Eurostat, 1998.
106 Franco, 1993.
107 Niero, 1996.
108 ibid.
109 Corbello, 1997.
110 ibid.
111 Schroeder, 1997.
112 Ferreira, 1997.
113 Eurostat, 1998.
114 Gonzales-Catala, 1997.
115 Almeda and Sarasa, 1996.
116 ibid.
117 Aylaya, 1994.
118 Almeda and Sarasa, 1996.
119 Gonzales-Catala, 1997.
120 Almeda and Sarasa, 1996.
121 Gonzales-Catala, 1997.
122 Achenbaum, 1979; Achenbaum, 1986.
123 Munnell, 2003.
124 Schieber, 1997.
125 Munnell, 2002.
126 Schieber, 1997.
127 Munnell, 2002, p. 2.
128 ibid., p. 20.
129 Schieber, 1997.
130 Hsin and Mitchell, 1997.
131 Papke et al., 1996.
132 Samwick, 1997.
133 Schieber, 1997, p. 310.
134 Bernheim, 1993.
135 Schieber, 1997.
136 Venti and Wise, 1997.
137 Poterba et al., 1995.
138 Clark and Whiteside, 2003.
139 Pochet, 2003.
140 Hoskins, 2002.
141 Disney, 1998.

6
Changing families

As previously discussed, both the factors encouraging falling fertility and mortality and increasing longevity, thus leading to demographic ageing, are also directly influencing other areas of society. In addition, demographic ageing *per se* is also influencing behaviour. This can be clearly seen in relation to the intergenerational relationships and the family. We shall here discuss in more detail the actual changes experienced by contemporary western-style families, and the impact of these demographic forces on family structures and resultant kin roles and relationships.

Demographic change and families

As discussed in Chapter 1, the role of the family as a mode of social organisation has been significantly reduced by a combination of economic, social and ideological developments over the past century. In addition, the emergence of new family forms has raised questions over the roles and responsibilities of kin members. Reconstituted or recombinant stepfamilies, single parent families and cohabiting couples now comprise around 25 per cent of Western European families, for example, together with a growing number of ethnic minority families, whose kinship roles and relationships differ from the majority white populations. Also, demographic ageing combined with the ageing of individual life transitions is also impacting upon family structures, roles and relationships. The shift from a high-mortality/high-fertility society to a low-mortality/low-fertility society, results in an increase in the number of living generations, and a decrease in the number of living relatives within these generations. Increased longevity may increase the duration spent in certain kinship roles, such as spouse, parent of non-dependent child, or sibling. A decrease in fertility may reduce the duration of others, such as parent of dependent child, or even the opportunity for some roles, such as sibling.

At the level of the individual, a combination of forces is resulting in the ageing of some life transitions,[1] with all western-style ageing societies displaying an increase of age at first marriage and at remarriage, at leaving the parental home, at first childbirth. While public and legal institutions may be lowering the age threshold into full legal adulthood (the age of thresholds for inheritance, suffrage, jury service, alcohol and cigarette purchase and licensed driving having all fallen in many societies over the last half century), individuals themselves are choosing to delay many of those transitions which demonstrate a commitment to full adulthood – full economic independence from parents, formal adult union through marriage or committed long-term cohabitation and parenting. The ageing of youth transitions leads to later transition delay for both the individual and other kin members. Delaying the birth of the first child, for example, may lead to long intergenerational spacings, and a transition to both parenthood and grandparenthood at a later age than has been the recent historical norm. Similarly, extended economic dependence on parents not only delays the individual's full transition to independent adulthood, but also the experience for the parents of losing the last child from the family home – the empty nest syndrome.

Changing patterns of adult union

All western-style societies are currently experiencing rapidly changing trends in marriage. Cohabitation is increasing at all adult ages with individuals marrying later, facing a greater possibility of divorce, and being increasingly less likely to remarry following divorce. Table 6.1 illustrates the development in *crude marriage rates*[2] from 1960 to the year 2003 in the European Union. In terms of a European pattern in the development of marriage rates, the overall trend has been one of declining rates for most of the period. It is interesting to note that in 1960, Germany had the highest EU15 crude marriage rate standing at 9.5 per 1000, with Ireland having the lowest at 5.5 per 1000. By the turn of the twenty-first century, Denmark had the highest rate at 6.5 per 1000, with Belgium having the lowest at 4.03 per 1000. By comparison, in the year 2003, Germany's rate had fallen to 4.64 per 1000 while Ireland's was almost back at its 1960 level. For those countries experiencing a modest upturn in rates, the rates levelled off in the mid-1990s for all countries except Denmark where the lowest level had been in 1980. In the UK, crude marriage rates have been falling since the early 1970s and fell by 3–4 per cent per annum during this period,[3] with a fall from 330,000 first marriages in 1961, to 200,000 in 1997.

The crude marriage rate of both Canada and New Zealand fell to 5.3 per 1000 by 1997/8, Australia's to 5.9 by 1998. A similar fall also occurred in the USA, although at 8.8 per 1000 in 1996, it remains the highest in the western industrialised world. Even so, 40 per cent of US adults are unmarried.[4] We should also note significant ethnic differences in US marital rates. A comparison of men and women in midlife, when those who were likely to marry for reproduction and child rearing have already done so, reveals that white men and women are significantly more likely to have been married at midlife than black men and women. Indeed, currently over half of black men and women are unmarried, compared with a third of white men and women.[5]

Crude marriage rates are, of course, strongly affected by the demographics of the population in question. A measure of marriage which avoids these problems is the so-called total first marriage rate, which expresses the probability of first marriage for a person if that person passes through his/her life conforming to the age-specific first

Table 6.1 *Trends in crude marriage rates in the EU15 and selected OECD countries, 1960–2003*

	1960	1970	1980	1990	1995	2000	2003
Austria	8.3	7.1	6.2	5.8	5.3	4.8	4.58
Belgium	7.1	7.6	6.7	6.5	5.1	4.4	4.03
Denmark	7.8	7.4	5.2	6.1	6.6	7.2	6.50
Finland	7.4	8.8	6.1	5.0	4.6	5.1	4.95
France	7.0	7.8	6.2	5.1	4.4	5.2	4.57
Germany	9.5	7.4	6.3	6.5	5.3	5.1	4.64
Greece	7.0	7.7	6.5	5.8	6.1	4.3	5.13
Ireland	5.5	7.0	6.4	5.1	4.3	5.1	5.08
Italy	7.7	7.3	5.7	5.6	5.1	4.6	4.54
Luxembourg	7.1	6.4	5.9	6.1	5.1	4.9	4.45
Netherlands	7.8	9.5	6.4	6.4	5.3	5.5	5.00
Portugal	7.8	9.4	7.4	7.2	6.6	6.3	5.14
Spain	7.1	7.3	5.9	5.7	5.1	5.3	4.85
Sweden	6.7	5.4	4.5	4.7	3.8	4.5	4.36
United Kingdom	7.5	8.5	7.4	6.5	5.5	5.1	5.00

Note: For Spain 1965 and for the United Kingdom 1999.
Source: Council of Europe, 2001.

	1970–74	1995–98
Australia	7.2 (1978)	5.9
New Zealand	9.2	5.3
Canada	7.0 (1988)	5.3
USA		8.8

Sources: Australian Bureau of Statistics, 1998;
Annual Demographic Statistics, Canada, 1998; New
Zealand, Demographic Trends, 1999.

marriage rates of a given year. The rate refers to a synthetic cohort and is the sum of the age-specific first marriage rates in a particular year (generally up to age 49), and can therefore exceed 1.0 in years of strong progression of the number of marriages. The rate takes no account of the fact that a person can contract more than one marriage. Total female first marriage rates for the period 1960–2000 are shown in Table 6.2.

It is interesting and reassuring to note that the trend over the period for the development in the total female first marriage rates is similar to that seen for the crude marriage rates in Table 6.1, with declining rates for all countries (with a little variation across

Table 6.2 Total female first marriage rates in the European Union and selected OECD countries, 1960–2000

	1960	1970	1980	1990	1995	2000
Austria	1.03	0.91	0.68	0.58	0.56	0.54
Belgium	1.05	0.98	0.77	0.72	0.57	0.52
Denmark	1.01	0.82	0.53	0.60	0.65	0.73
Finland	0.96	0.94	0.67	0.58	0.57	0.62
France	1.03	0.92	0.71	0.56	0.50	0.62
Germany	1.06	0.98	0.69	0.64	0.56	0.58
Greece	0.79	1.05	0.87	0.73	0.75	0.52
Ireland	0.93	1.10	0.84	0.70	0.59	0.59
Italy	0.98	1.01	0.78	0.69	0.63	0.62
Luxembourg	–	0.88	0.66	0.64	0.56	0.55
Netherlands	1.05	1.06	0.68	0.66	0.53	0.59
Portugal	0.94	1.21	0.89	0.88	0.77	0.73
Spain	0.99	1.01	0.76	0.69	0.60	0.61
Sweden	0.95	0.62	0.53	0.55	0.44	0.53
United Kingdom	1.04	1.04	0.76	0.63	0.54	0.53

Note: For Spain 1965, Ireland 1998, Italy 1999 and for the United Kingdom 1999.

Source: Council of Europe, 2001.

	1975	1988–98	Reference year
	%	%	
Australia	75.4	60.2	1998
Canada	81.2	55.2	1994
New Zealand	95.4	40.3	1996
USA	80.4	59.5	1988

Note: For New Zealand calculated from age-specific first marriage rates.

Sources: Australian Bureau of Statistics, 1998; New Zealand, Demographic Trends, 1999. Canadian Statistics, 1994.

countries in the onset of the decline) and with a modest upturn at the end of the century for some countries.

If we now consider the remarriage rates for males and females, the downward trend in the period is even more dramatic. The UK remarriage rates fell severely during the period in question, with the remarriage rate for divorced men falling by 75 per cent between 1971 and 1995. We should, however, note that due to the increase in divorce (the vast majority of all remarriages during this period involving divorced people), there

Table 6.3 *The percentage of couples living in a consensual union by age group in the European Union, 1994*

	Total 16+	16–29	30–44	45–64	65+
Belgium	10	27	11	6	3
Denmark	25	72	28	8	6
France	14	46	14	4	3
Germany	9	30	8	4	4
Greece	2	9	1	1	1
Ireland	3	11	2	1	0
Italy	2	6	2	1	1
Luxembourg	10	28	10	5	2
Netherlands	13	54	15	4	3
Portugal	3	10	2	1	2
Spain	3	14	4	1	1
United Kingdom	11	38	12	3	1

Source: Eurostat, 1998.

was an increase in the number of remarriages throughout the EU, with the number of remarriages in the UK rising from 50,000 in 1961 to 120,000 by 1997.

Falling marriage rates are partly accounted for by a growth in pre-marriage cohabitation by both never married and formerly married couples. As Kiernan pointed out, prior to 1970 cohabitation was not new but largely statistically and socially invisible.[6] Yet by the turn of the century, around 10 per cent of all couples living in the European Union were cohabiting (Table 6.3), these couples being drawn from across the socio-economic spectrum. However, the proportion of cohabiting couples ranged from 25 per cent in Denmark to less than 3 per cent in southern Europe and Ireland, and from nearly one-third of European couples under 30 years of age to around 3 per cent of couples over 45 years of age. Standing at each extreme were the 72 per cent of Danish couples under 30 years of age who were cohabiting, compared with apparently no cohabiting couples over 65 years of age in Ireland. While we do not as yet have sufficient evidence, it is likely that these figures reflect variation in both cohort as well as age-related behaviour. The pattern is clear, however: despite cultural and cohort/age differences, there is a trend throughout Europe for couples of all ages and in all countries to undertake a period of cohabitation before, between or after legal marriage.[7] Whether all European countries will eventually follow the Scandinavian model[8] or be restricted by social, cultural and religious norms is still unclear.

Using national data from the UK, we can explore this phenomenon in more detail. Accurate longitudinal data on cohabitation is rare, but some indications of general trends can be gained from the UK General Household Survey (GHS), and British Household

Panel Survey (BHPS). The General Household Survey, for example, estimates a fivefold increase in cohabitation between 1979 and 1995. This is supported by data from BHPS suggesting that by the turn of the century, 70 per cent of all newly formed couple relationships were cohabitations,[9] with 20 per cent of all births being registered to cohabiting couples.[10] As with the European-wide figures, the UK indications are that younger people are more likely to cohabit. For example, in 1995, 25 per cent of never married women living in the UK were cohabiting, accounting for nearly one-fifth of all women aged 20–29 years. Mid-life and older women are less affected by this trend with under 10 per cent of 30 and 40 years olds cohabiting, this being partly due to a cohort effect and partly due to the fact that cohabitation still generally ends in marriage.[11] As we have already noted, however, this is less likely to be the case for formerly married couples, with remarriage rates following both death and divorce having fallen sharply since the 1970s. Indeed, while cohabitation is generally still seen as a transient state, the average length of cohabitation is increasing, with data from the General Household Survey suggesting that the average length of cohabitation rose by 70 per cent in the 1980s and 1990s, reaching 34 months by 1995.[12] A similar trend is found in the USA, which saw a sixfold rise in cohabitating couples between 1960 and 1993.[13] Only 7 per cent of women born in the late 1940s cohabited before age 25, by which time nearly three-quarters had married, compared with 55 per cent of those women born in the late 1960s.[14] Both Australia and New Zealand show similar trends, with around one quarter of men and women between the ages of 15 and 44 in partnerships cohabiting in New Zealand, rising to around two thirds of those in their early twenties. In Australia, 67 per cent of marriages in 1998 were preceded by a period of cohabitation.[15]

Divorce

In most western countries, divorce rates have risen steadily since the 1960s (Table 6.4) with some countries showing signs of a decline towards the end of the century, Belgium, for example, although this may simply be due to the use of period measures. The factors associated with this are complex, and include both demographic and social trends. Divorce appears more likely, for example, in those marriages with no children,[16] those preceded by more than one cohabitation,[17] those established when at least one partner was very young[18] and those which contain at least one previously divorced partner[19] – all trends which have increased over the past 30 years. Part of a deceleration in rates may be accounted for by social and legal factors[20] and by the increasing age at first marriage, with younger people, especially teenagers, being vulnerable to marital break-up.[21] This latter set of factors can be illustrated by the many countries which initiated a relaxation of divorce laws in the 1970s, allowing a backlog of divorces to travel through the system, creating a temporary upsurge.

It is difficult to talk of a European pattern of divorce in as much as individual countries varied significantly in their propensity to divorce in the period covered, and this

Table 6.4 *Crude divorce rates in the European Union, 1960–2000*

	1960	1970	1980	1990	1995	2000
Austria	1.2	1.4	1.8	2.1	2.3	2.4
Belgium	0.5	0.7	1.5	2.0	3.5	2.6
Denmark	1.5	1.9	2.7	2.7	2.5	2.7
Finland	0.8	1.3	2.0	2.6	2.7	2.7
France	0.7	0.8	1.5	1.9	2.1	2.0
Germany	1.0	1.3	1.8	1.9	2.1	2.3
Greece	0.3	0.4	0.7	0.6	1.1	0.9
Ireland						
Italy		0.2	0.2	0.5	0.5	0.6
Luxembourg	0.5	0.6	1.6	2.0	1.8	2.3
Netherlands	0.5	0.8	1.8	1.9	2.2	2.2
Portugal	0.1	0.1	0.6	0.9	1.2	1.9
Spain			0.5	0.6	0.8	0.9
Sweden	1.2	1.6	2.4	2.3	2.6	2.4
United Kingdom	0.5	1.1	2.8	2.9	2.9	2.6

Note: For France 1999, Germany 1999, Italy 1975 and Spain 1985/1999. No data for Ireland.
Source: Council of Europe, 2001.

variation has in some ways increased by the end of the century. In 1960, there was a clear north–south divide in relation to divorce with the northern countries of Sweden and Denmark, Austria and Germany having dramatically higher crude divorce rates than the southern countries (0.1 per 1000 population in Portugal and 1.5 in Denmark). By the year 2000, there is still a north–south divide but the majority of countries in the Union have crude divorce rates of 2 or more per 1000 population, while only Greece, Italy and Spain continue with rates below 1 per 1000. While acknowledging this north–south divide (which probably includes Ireland in the Southern European group), it should be noted that all countries of the European Union have experienced significant increases in the crude divorce rates in the period 1960–2000, with most countries experiencing between two and fivefold increases. At current rates, just under 50 per cent of all US marriages will end in divorce,[22] compared with around 30 per cent of all EU marriages, ranging from less than 10 per cent of Italian marriages, to 40 per cent of marriages in the UK. The annual number of divorces in the UK, for example, rose from 74,000 in 1961 to 145,000 in 1997,[23] resulting in the current dissolution of around 40 per cent of marriages in the UK.

However, while families in all industrialised nations have faced an increase in marital divorce over the past century, they have also faced a reduction in marital disruption due to death, so the figures for marital dissolution as a whole (death and divorce) reveal that the total dissolution level has remained remarkably constant, for example, at an annual rate of around 40 per 1000 US marriages over the last 150 years.

While marriage rates still remain high over a person's lifetime, and indeed an individual's chance of having been married increased steadily throughout the twentieth century, more marriages in the Western world now end in divorce than ever before. This has led to a bipolar situation. On the one hand, the lengths of many marriages are similar to those of earlier centuries. While historically marriages ended due to the early death of the wife, usually related to childbirth or reproductive complications, twenty-first-century marriages are likely to be cut short by divorce. On the other hand, those marriages which do not end in divorce are likely to be longer than at any other historical time as a result of increasing life expectancy for both men and women. The chances of an individual being never married or widowed are, therefore, falling. The chances of being, or having been, in a marital or cohabiting relationship are increasing. Before examining these trends in more detail, we must also recognise that they are modified by a variety of other factors. In particular, different class, ethnic and religious groupings and cohorts display varying trends, though these are generally matters of degree rather than kind. While acknowledging these diversities, for the purposes of this discussion we shall use national trends, only on occasion indicating specific group variation.

Ageing of life transitions

As we indicated earlier, a combination of forces is resulting in the ageing of some life transitions, with all western-style ageing societies displaying an increase of age at first marriage and at remarriage, at leaving the parental home, at first childbirth. Individuals are choosing to delay many of those transitions which demonstrate a commitment to full adulthood – full economic independence from parents, formal adult union through marriage or committed long-term cohabitation, and parenting. This is in contrast to public and legal institutions which are generally lowering the age threshold into full legal adulthood. While there are clearly a variety of forces operating, it can also be argued that an awareness of ever lengthening lifespans has given individuals at all ages the time and the liberty to delay certain transitions as they progress through adulthood. This can most clearly be recognised in the general delayed commitment to long-term adult partnerships and childbearing.

Marriage and remarriage

Concurrent with the fall in crude marriage rates and total first marriage rates, there has been an increase in the mean age of females at first marriage (Table 6.5). This is also reflected in the median age at first marriage (Table 6.6). For most countries of the European Union this began around 1970. In 1960, Ireland had the highest female mean age at first marriage (26.9 years) while Belgium and Denmark had the lowest mean age

Table 6.5 *Mean age of females at first marriage in the European Union, 1960–2000*

	1960	1970	1980	1990	1995	2000
Austria	24.0	22.9	23.2	24.9	26.1	27.2
Belgium	22.8	22.4	22.2	24.2	25.4	26.1
Denmark	22.8	22.8	24.6	27.6	29.0	29.5
Finland	23.8	23.3	24.3	26.0	27.0	28.0
France	23.0	22.6	23.0	25.6	26.9	27.8
Germany	23.5	22.5	22.9	25.2	26.4	27.2
Greece	25.1	24.0	23.3	24.8	25.6	26.6
Ireland	26.9	24.8	24.6	26.6	27.9	
Italy	24.8	23.9	23.8	25.5	26.6	
Luxembourg		22.8	23.0	25.3	26.6	27.1
Netherlands	24.2	22.9	23.2	25.9	27.1	27.8
Portugal	24.8	24.2	23.2	23.9	24.7	25.2
Spain			23.4	25.3	26.8	27.7
Sweden	24.0	23.9	26.0	27.5	28.7	30.2
United Kingdom	23.3	22.4	23.0	25.1	26.4	27.3

Note: For Belgium 1999, France 1999, Germany 1999, Greece 1999, Spain 1965, Ireland 1998, Italy 1999 and for the United Kingdom 1999.

Source: Council of Europe, 2001.

Table 6.6 *Median[24] age of males and females at first marriage in selected OECD countries, 1970–98*

	1970–74		1995–98		
	Women	**Men**	**Women**	**Men**	**Reference year**
Australia	20.9	23.3	25.9	27.8	1997
Canada			26.5	28.5	1998
European Union*	*23.0	*26.0	26.0	29.0	1995
New Zealand	20.8	23.0	26.7	28.7	1998
UK	21.4	23.4	26.0	27.9	1995

*Note: *Average age at marriage in 1980 and 1995*

Sources: Australian Social Trends, 1997; Eurobarometer, 1993; New Zealand, Demographic Trends, 1999; ONS, 1997; Statistics Canada, 1998.

(22.8 years). By the year 2000, Denmark had the second highest mean age at 29.5 years with Sweden having the highest of all the EU countries (30.2 years) while Portugal (previously with the 2nd highest mean age) has the lowest (25.2 years). A similar picture emerges for the USA. While 71 per cent of women born in the early 1950s had married by 25, this had fallen to 54 per cent of those born in the late 1960s.[25] As well as the cross-national differences pointed out above, there are also differences within countries. Those registered in lower socio-economic groups generally marry earlier than those in professional and managerial occupations. Similarly, there is variation across ethnic groups. In the USA by 1990, the median age of marriage rose to over 26 for white men and over 24 for white women, and nearly 29 for black men and over 27 for black women.[26]

One of the wider implications of these trends is a fall in teen marriages, the UK for example, seeing female teen marriages drop from one-third to 5 per cent between 1970 and 1995. Another is an increase in the proportion of single never married people within a country. Data from the USA reveal that in 1970, 16 per cent of US adults were single never married. This had risen to nearly one quarter by 1996. Age at remarriage is also increasing. The age at which people remarry is dependent on the age at which they first marry, the length of that marriage, and the time interval between marriages. Australia provides a clear example of this. The length of marriage prior to divorce and the length of time after divorce and prior to remarriage remained on average the same between 1977 and 1997. The increase in mean age at first marriage thus led to an increase in the mean age of remarriage, from 32 years for females and 36 years for males in 1977 to 38 years for females and 42 years for males by 1997.[27] However, the largest factor to account for the ageing of remarriage in Australia appears to be the increase in cohabitation, particularly among previously married people – 78 per cent of all remarriages of partners who had both been divorced involve a period of prior cohabitation.

The demographic trends then are striking. Mean age at first marriage and mean age at remarriage both increased whilst crude marriage rate, first marriage rate and remarriage rate decreased over the last quarter of the twentieth century.

Leaving the parental home

Within most countries of the European Union and the United States, young people are leaving home at a later age. The proportion of young adults who live with their parents has increased in the USA, for example, since the 1970s.[28] In 1997, 15 per cent of men and 8 per cent of women aged 25–34 lived at home with their parents, an increase since 1970 of 10 per cent and 7 per cent respectively. Furthermore, many of those children who choose to spend a protracted period of time outside the parental home before setting up their own, remain economically dependent on their parents through, for example, subsidised boarding and rental expenses, assistance with home buying and prolonged and expensive investment in education.

Within Europe, every EU member state, with the exception of Denmark and the Netherlands, saw an increase between 1987 and 1996 in those aged 20–29 years continuing to live with their parents. The most striking picture emerged from the Southern European countries with a 50 per cent increase in this same period for those in their late twenties. In 1996, more than 80 per cent of Spanish, Portuguese and Italian men and women aged 20–24 years lived in the parental home, and over 50 per cent of 25–29 year olds. This increase in age at leaving home also increases the age at which parents experience the so-called empty nest syndrome, the extended post-parental period following the departure from the family home of the child/children. In some societies, this is associated with a period of apparent grieving, especially for mothers. A range of factors is associated with this ageing of flying from the nest, including staying in education, financial uncertainty, peer example and, probably of most significance, delayed marriage.[29]

First childbirth

Regardless of the structural manifestation and location of household residence, younger cohorts in most western societies are now able to enjoy a lengthening of what Ryder describes as the period of 'horizontal' freedom between the 'vertical' structure of the family of orientation, and vertical structure of the family of procreation.[30] Delayed marriage is still associated with delayed first childbirth, as most children are still born within marriage, the frequency of marriage being a proximate determinant of fertility. Maternal age for first births rose throughout the second half of the twentieth century with both the mean age of women at birth of first child (Table 6.7) and the mean age of women at childbearing (Table 6.8) rising throughout the European Union, and this had a significant impact on falling fertility rates (Table 6. 8).

As it appears from Table 6.7, the mean age of women at birth of first child has almost everywhere increased, from around 1970, with no sign of a downturn by the end of the century. There is only limited variation in this mean age across the countries of the European Union and with no real change in the absolute variation from 1960 to the year 2000. In the UK, for example, the mean age of women at birth of first child rose by almost two years in the course of the last ten years of the century from 27.3 years in 1990 to 29.1 years in the year 2000, giving the UK the highest (available) mean age at the turn of the century.

As far as the mean age of women at childbearing is concerned, Table 6.8 reveals a similar increasing trend after an initial period of continued decline but with mean ages, of course, substantially higher than the mean age at birth of first child. By the year 2003, the low levels of fertility across Europe, as illustrated in Table 6.9, mean that the mean age at birth of first child and mean age at childbearing are converging almost everywhere. From the perspective of kin intergenerational relationships, delaying the birth of the first child affects the timing of subsequent life transitions, such as the empty nest syndrome and grandparenthood, and has clear implications for the availability of support in later life. Of more significance, however, is the decline in the total number of children being born in the Western world.

As we discussed in Chapter 2, there is a strong association between delaying childbearing and fertility decline. While there was a steady decline in total fertility levels in

Table 6.7 *Mean age of women at birth of first child in the EU15, 1960–2000*

	1960	**1970**	**1980**	**1990**	**1995**	**2000**
Austria			24.3	25.0	25.6	26.3
Belgium	24.8	24.3	24.7	26.4		
Denmark	23.1	23.8	24.6	26.4	27.4	
Finland	24.7	24.4	25.6	26.5	27.2	27.4
France	24.8	24.4	25.0	27.0	28.1	28.7
Germany	25.0	24.0	25.0	26.6	27.5	28.0
Greece		24.5	24.1	25.5	26.6	27.3
Ireland		25.5	25.5	26.6	27.3	27.8
Italy	25.7	25.0	25.0	26.9	28.0	
Luxembourg					27.4	28.4
Netherlands	25.7	24.8	25.7	27.6	28.4	28.6
Portugal			24.0	24.9	25.8	26.4
Spain		25.1	25.0	26.8	28.4	29.0
Sweden	25.5	25.9	25.3	26.3	27.2	27.9
United Kingdom				27.3	28.3	29.1

Note: For Austria 1985, France 1999, Germany 1999, Greece 1999, Spain 1975/1999 and for Ireland 1975.

Source: Council of Europe, 2001.

Table 6.8 *Mean age of women at first childbearing in the EU15, 1960–2000*

	1960	**1970**	**1980**	**1990**	**1995**	**2000**
Austria	27.6	26.7	26.3	27.2	27.7	28.2
Belgium	28.0	27.2	26.6	27.9	28.5	
Denmark	26.9	26.7	26.8	28.5	29.2	29.7
Finland	28.3	27.1	27.7	28.9	29.3	29.6
France	27.6	27.2	26.8	28.3	29.0	29.4
Germany	27.5	26.6	26.4	27.6	28.3	28.7
Greece		26.8	26.1	27.2	28.2	28.9
Ireland	31.5	30.4	29.7	29.9	30.2	30.6
Italy	29.2	28.3	27.4	28.9	29.7	
Luxembourg		27.2	27.5	28.4	29.0	29.3
Netherlands	29.8	28.2	27.7	29.3	30.0	30.3
Portugal	29.6	29.0	27.2	27.3	28.1	28.7
Spain	30.0	29.6	28.2	28.9	30.0	30.7
Sweden	27.5	27.0	27.6	28.6	29.2	29.9
United Kingdom	27.8	26.3	26.9	27.6	28.2	28.5

Note: For Germany 1999, Greece 1975/1999 and for Spain 1999.

Source: Council of Europe, 2001.

Table 6.9 *Total fertility rate in the European Union, 1960–2003*

	1960	1970	1980	1990	1995	2000	2003
Austria	2.70	2.29	1.65	1.45	1.40	1.34	1.39
Belgium	2.56	2.25	1.68	1.62	1.55	1.66	1.61
Denmark	2.57	1.95	1.55	1.67	1.80	1.77	1.76
Finland	2.72	1.83	1.63	1.78	1.81	1.73	1.76
France	2.73	2.47	1.95	1.78	1.71	1.89	1.89
Germany	2.37	2.03	1.56	1.45	1.25	1.36	1.34
Greece	2.22	2.40	2.22	1.39	1.32	1.29	1.27
Ireland	3.76	3.87	3.24	2.11	1.84	1.89	1.98
Italy	2.41	2.43	1.64	1.33	1.20	1.23	1.29
Luxembourg	2.37	1.97	1.49	1.60	1.68	1.79	1.63
Netherlands	3.12	2.57	1.60	1.62	1.53	1.72	1.75
Portugal	3.16	3.01	2.25	1.57	1.40	1.52	1.44
Spain	2.86	2.88	2.20	1.36	1.18	1.24	1.29
Sweden	2.20	1.92	1.68	2.13	1.73	1.54	1.71
United Kingdom	2.71	2.43	1.89	1.83	1.71	1.65	1.71

Note: The total fertility rate is the average number of children that would be born alive to a woman during her lifetime if she were to pass through and survive her childbearing years conforming to the age-specific fertility rates of a given year.

Source: Council of Europe, 2001, Eurostat 2003.

the period 1960–2000 throughout the EU, by the end of the century uncertainty as to the direction of these trends had risen. Some of this uncertainty is due to the use of period measures. Still, however, fertility remains below reproduction level. Of additional interest is the reversal in the general north–south relationship. In 1960, Ireland and the southern European countries had the highest levels of fertility (with the Netherlands also experiencing a high level of 3.12 but Greece having a low level), with Ireland easily having the highest level of 3.76, while the northern countries had lower levels (Sweden at 2.20 being the lowest). By 2000, the roles were reversed. Italy now had the lowest level of only 1.23 – much lower than the levels experienced by the northern countries in their own baby bust periods – while Denmark was among the highest at 1.77, although Ireland maintained its status as the EU country with the highest level of fertility.

Against this backdrop of declining fertility, out-of-wedlock births have increased with fertility outside marriage increasing for all European countries towards the end of the century, though still remaining well below that for married women. For example, nearly one quarter of children were born outside marriage in 1995. The highest figures were, as to be expected, in the Scandinavian countries and the UK, with around half of all births in Sweden and Denmark, and over a third in Finland and the UK born outside legal marriage. In the UK, at least, the majority of these are to cohabiting couples, some 20 per cent of all births in 1996.[31] It is interesting to note that a similar picture is emerging in the USA, with an almost tenfold increase in out-of-wedlock births in the last half of the century, standing at 32 per cent in 1996, with 44 per cent of all first births outside marriage,[32] though again just under half were registered to cohabiting couples.[33]

Explanations and trends

These figures need, however, to be placed in the context of historical marriage patterns and in relation to the various propositions which have arisen to explain these. It then becomes clear that the early marriage trends of the mid-twentieth century were themselves historically unusual following a longer felt pattern within Western Europe for late marriage and low marriage rates, the delay of marriage probably being until a man could establish an independent livelihood adequate to support a family. The dominant thesis concerning the Western European Marriage Pattern was expounded by Hajnal[34] in 1965, and while subject in later years to a critical reassessment[35] and an acknowledgement of regional and subgroup variation,[36] the basic descriptives remain sound. Hanjal maintained that there existed two dominant marriage patterns within Europe – in Western Europe marital age was high and rates of marriage low, resulting in a high proportion of people who never married, and this had been the pattern since at least the sixteenth century. Prior to this, Western Europe followed the Eastern European Pattern, as did non-European and traditional societies, with high marital rates and low age of marriage. Following the ideas of Malthus, whereby delays in marital union performed a check on unbridled reproduction and overpopulation, Hanjal argued that the nuclear family system, in existence since at least medieval times, required the delay of marriage until a man could establish an independent livelihood adequate to support a family Alternatively, in societies with extended or joint families, newly married couples could be incorporated into the existing economic unit. In addition, there is evidence from throughout Europe that other economic[37] and demographic constraints, such as gender imbalances and differential labour participation,[38] also restricted partner availability at certain times.

By the early twentieth century in Western Europe,[39] nuptiality started to increase and both men and women began to marry earlier; explanations for this include the growing economic prosperity and the introduction of contraceptive practice within marriage. These trends were encouraged throughout Western Europe after the Second World War, due to the post-war marriage boom. However, by the 1960s 95 per cent of people in Western Europe were or had been married, perhaps the heyday of marital life. By the 1970s the rates had fallen to those of 1900 and, as we saw, have declined ever since. As Harper has argued, new behaviour has to be both culturally and socially acceptable as well as economically advantageous,[40] and thus ideas based on increased productivity or intergenerational wealth transference, must also be placed in a social context. As the economic constraints to marriage were dismantled in the nineteenth century, so it became socially and culturally acceptable to reject the concept of a period of celibacy in early adulthood. By the 1970s, at least in Western Europe, the social and cultural constraints to sexual relations outside marriage had also been removed and so cohabitation began to supplement, and then replace, marriage. The fall of the final barrier, that of childbirth outside wedlock, has led to the recent dramatic falls in marital union, particularly in the Scandinavian countries.

While it was argued for some time that within colonial USA strong economic opportunities for young men allowed marriage at early ages,[41] a recent reanalysis[42] of the limited data suggests a broad similarity between the USA and Western Europe during this time. By 1890, marriage ages had reached a peak of 22 for women and 26 for men although there were some regional variations. Explanations for this include the low availability of men following the losses of the Civil War[43] and the declining availability of land at this time.[44] The rapid growth of well-paid wage labour stimulated by urban industrial growth was probably associated with the fall in first marriage ages, for white men at least, in the late nineteenth and early decades of the twentieth centuries, with another economic boost to lower ages occurring again in the 1960s, when median marriage ages hit 22 for white men and 20 for white women. As we saw, these have been rising ever since, at around one year per decade, and by 1999 the marriage age had returned to overtake that a century before. The picture for blacks reveals even more contrast between the decades. From 1870 to 1940 the trends in age of marriage between blacks closely followed that for whites, but at around two years younger.[45] This, it has been suggested, may be due to a lack of incentives to delay marriage until economic success was achieved as the black population had far lower expectations about economic opportunities and possible occupational mobility.[46] However, after 1970 there was a divergence in ages and by 1990 black men were marrying around two years later than white men, and with a three-year difference between black and white women.[47]

While economic theories have dominated the explanations for these changing marriage ages, there seems far less understanding of the sudden rise in marriage age in the Western world in the last decades of the twentieth century. Fitch and Ruggles[48] suggest that, in the USA, a growth in low-income employment for young white males after 1970, leading to an overall reduction in wages for this group, may have encouraged a delay in marriage. It seems, however, that the income-related arguments that seemed to provide some historical understanding, may need to be revisited in the light of changing late twentieth-century social norms and employment patterns. In particular, as Waite has pointed out for the USA, we need to include the gender dimension as a dynamic variable in the equation. Drawing on the independence theory of marriage, which postulates that women will delay marriage if other more attractive alternatives are present,[49] she suggests that the growth of female occupational structure had a significant influence on marriage ages and rates. The growth of female educational and employment opportunities since

1970 has substantially decreased women's economic dependence on a spouse. This has been substantiated by more recent work, drawing on longitudinal analysis, which showed that the rise in female employment and an increase in female wages, allowed women the possibility of delaying marriage.[50]

However, to these theories we need to add the general ageing of life transitions notion, which occurs as individuals recognise the general lengthening of their own life-spans and those of their peers. This turns the relationship between fertility and marriage around, and postulates, that for women in particular, ever lengthening lifespans have also allowed them the liberty to delay childbirth, and that the strong association which still remains between marriage and childbearing in most western societies, is also contributing to an increased age, or delay, in marriage. However, because marital unions now have the potential to last far longer than historically has been the norm, this has certainly placed strains on such relationships, often resulting in marital break-up, divorce and reconstituted families. Alternatively, it can be argued that because infant mortality has fallen and because early death through disease, war, famine and (for women) reproduction is no longer the common experience, individuals feel more comfortable about establishing marital unions later in life, bearing children later and having fewer children.

We shall now turn to the impact of these main demographic trends for individuals and families.

Changing family roles and relationships as societies age

As we discussed in Chapter 1, there are pervasive myths concerning the disintegration of the family, and the impact that this will have on caring for the increasing number of older people a society has to support. Particular concern focuses on loose vertical families with long spacing between the generations, increasing voluntary childlessness and the potential of cohabitating, divorced and reconstituted families to provide the stability required for family care.

Loose vertical families and increasing voluntary childlessness

The increasing delay of the birth of the first child, highlighted above, has indeed the potential to create a loose vertical family structure with long intergenerational spacings. Three concerns have recently been raised.[51] First, that parents and grandparents who enter their roles much later in life may not experience these roles for as long a period of time as younger people. Second, that the longer age spacings may well create difficulties in the development of bonds across the life course, especially as this may result in simultaneous demands from adolescent children and ageing parents. However, as we discussed above, many individuals are currently experiencing both parental and grandparental roles for far longer than has been historically the norm,[52] and indeed it is the simultaneous demands that women are now facing as grandmothers that may be of most importance. Finally, the later an individual has a child, the fewer children that individual has, with significant implications for that individual's care and support in later life. However, as Uhlenberg has pointed out:

> [t]he most critical distinction in number of children for the elderly is between any or none, and the second most important contrast is between one and two or more. To the extent that family declines are associated with movement from large- to moderate-sized families, the changes are not overly consequential for parent-child relationships in later life.[53]

Furthermore, a variety of US studies indicate that concerns over the increasingly short supply of children for dependent older persons may be misplaced. Indeed, in both the USA and the UK, the highest percentage last century of very old women without children or with just one child occurred in the 1990s among cohorts born at the turn of the nineteenth and twentieth centuries. One quarter of these women had no children, and a further quarter had just one child. The proportion of women over 85 years of age with two or more surviving children will actually increase over the coming decades, from less than 50 per cent in 1995 to almost 75 per cent by 2015.[54] However, even though this will be followed by an increasing proportion of women with just one or no children, it will not return to the levels of the 1990s, according to current predictions which run to 2050. Also worth noting is the fact that increasing childlessness in cohorts born after 1960 means that fewer adult children will have simultaneous commitments to an older parent and children. So childlessness in today's younger cohorts paradoxically could lead to more time available for caregiving to older relatives.[55] Given that today's trends towards a healthy life expectancy continue, it will be another 40 years before the impact of this increased childlessness on family provided care is realised. Furthermore, as we shall discuss in Chapter 7, the provision of care and support to frail elders is complex and not a simple question of reliance on children.

Cohabitation

Concern has also focused on the increase in cohabitation. It is now recognised that there are different types of cohabitation, including a series of short-term, frequently dissolved, temporary relationships, single pre-marriage cohabitation, and long-term stable marital-type unions. Many of the existing and future consensual unions may well support the long-term vertical and lateral kin relationships developed through marriage. However, most studies do not distinguish between the different forms of cohabitation.[56] While demographically most people still end up in a marital union at some time of their lives, and most cohabitations will end up as marriages, we still know little about the impact of a period of cohabitation on later life nor on wider family relationships.[57] Indeed, our general understanding of cohabitation, particularly outside the Scandinavian countries, is limited, and the debate as to the processes behind its growth continues to be polarised between those who see it is a protest against conventional living and those regarding it as a practical living arrangement for a turn-of-the-century industrialised society.[58]

There is discussion, for example, as to whether marital union between existing cohabiting partners is in some sense different from other marriages, in as much as, in the former case, the existing union is transformed without any actual change in living arrangements. It is thus unclear whether such transition to marriage necessitates an alteration in the norms and expectations of the relationship or whether marriage following cohabitation is primarily a confirmation of the relationship, which has been already established.[59] There is evidence, however, from both the USA and the UK that people who cohabit prior to marriage have a higher propensity to divorce, regardless of whether they marry their initial cohabiting partner,[60] although this may not apply to cohabitations when both partners are never-married.[61] Life Table calculations from Sweden, one of the few countries with reliable data on non-marital unions, reveal that while every third Swedish marriage ends in divorce, every second consensual union ends in separation. In addition, most of the consensual unions which are not dissolved, evolve into marriages with high levels of dissolution risk. Indeed, if couple formation and dissolution rates remain constant, only 10 per cent of all consensual unions, compared with 70 per cent of all marriages, would last until death.

Perhaps the potentially biggest impact is from the growth of cohabitations in later life, particularly following divorce, as these are less likely to end in marriage. By 1998 around 15 per cent of all cohabitations in Australia, for example, were among the 40–59 year age group.[62] It may be that such late life alliances do not provide the stability for the extensive cross-kin interactions and relationships supported within marriage-based families or stepfamilies. This may be particularly important in terms of reciprocal care in late life. However, the assertion that these relationships are less stable is based primarily on evidence from younger cohabiting couples. As older adults move to this form of mid and late-life union, the picture may be very different.

Divorce

Moving from cohabitation to divorce, there is a range of cross-cultural evidence which indicates that, in comparison with non-married people, married people have an advantage which may be measured across both health and socio-economic variables.[63] As Waite has pointed out, the marital status of a person is a dimension of family structure, which deeply affects their living arrangements, support systems and individual well-being. Intact husband–wife families provide a multiple support system for a spouse in terms of emotional, financial and social exchanges, and married people tend to enjoy higher levels of health and survival, social participation and life satisfaction than persons who are not married.[64] Not only do married people appear to have an advantage in terms of both health and longevity, but this mortality differential between the married and non-married population appears to have increased over the past decades. Among the non-married category at all ages, most studies find the divorced have the highest mortality rate, followed by the widowed and then the never married. Divorced men are at an extra disadvantage in relation to widowed men, however, in that they frequently also lose social support networks, which appear more likely to be retained by both widowed men, and widowed and divorced women. Given that women generally have stronger and more multifaceted networks than men, they are often able to retain stronger social support following divorce.

The marital status distribution of a cohort at any particular time period is determined by its past experience with marriage, divorce and remarriage, as well as by differential survival by marital status. Dissolution in younger life often leads to remarriage or cohabitation by one or both partners, introducing a variety of complex reconstituted family structures, which impact upon both reciprocal family care and intergenerational transmission. Dissolution in later life can also lead to loneliness, lack of support and care, and loss of roles.

Cohorts entering old age early last century are different from those currently entering old age, and those who will enter over the next several decades. For example, each successive US cohort entering old age in the twentieth century experienced lower mortality rates and higher divorce rates over its lifetime.[65] Similarly, current dynamics of marriage and family forms among younger US cohorts will result in larger proportions of non-married older persons in the second quarter of this century. The differential implications of widowhood versus divorce are clearly at their most acute in late life. Among these older age groups we see a general pattern of decreasing widowhood and increasing experience of divorce. Older people thus seem to be following general trends although at a much lower rate of increase, with subsequently smaller numbers involved.

Between 1980 and 1996, the percentage of divorced people aged over 65 in the USA almost doubled from 3.5 per cent to 6.4 per cent;[66] these figures emerge from a complex interaction of an increased divorce rate in mid and late life, as well as a fall for all age groups in the rates of remarriage following divorce. At the beginning of the last century, the number of US men aged 55–64 who were widowed outnumbered those who were divorced by 20 to 1. By the mid-1970s, divorced men outnumbered widowed men, reaching three times as many by 2000, and by the 1990s there were more divorced US women aged 55–64 than widowed. Given declining mortality for men, and lack of remarriage generally and particularly among older ages, this trend will continue into old age for the next few decades at least. In addition, the trend for increased divorce and lack of remarriage seems to have stabilised since the mid-1980s and it is, therefore, likely that those currently in midlife will also experience high rates of divorce in later life.

Given the still low rate of divorce among older people, there is a paucity of data pertaining to this group. The limited evidence we do have suggests that divorced older men fare worse than their younger counterparts. Among older age groups, for example, mortality among divorced men is particularly high in comparison to married men.[67] In addition, interaction between fathers and their children tends to decline significantly following divorce. In fact, 80–90 per cent of all children live with their mothers after divorce, with one US study suggesting that half of adolescents living with their mothers after divorce had no contact with their fathers.[68] While older divorced women are as likely as widowed women to co-reside with a child, and supportive intergenerational relationships are likely to continue for widowed, divorced and married older women, data from the US National Survey of Families and Households suggests a contrasting picture for men. Among nationally representative divorced men aged 50–79 years, only half of the fathers saw or communicated with at least one child weekly, only 11 per cent maintained contact with more than one child, and one-third had no contact at all with their children. This suggests that these men are less likely to have adult children available for them in time of need. Yet, mother–child relations for older divorced women remain quite similar to those of women who do not divorce, with, if anything, an intensification of mother–child relationships among divorced women. Thus there is some evidence that maternal attachment by children increases after divorce, and women often intensify their kin relationships following divorce.[69]

Most studies exploring the impact of divorce on well-being and standard of living have indicated that immediately after divorce younger cohorts appear to experience a general improvement in the economic situation for men and a significant decline for women.[70] However, the interruption of savings and destruction of assets associated with divorce are likely to depress the economic well-being of both men and women divorced in later life. Indeed, the rather limited empirical evidence we have suggests that divorce is associated with lower economic well-being among all older people. Thus, US data on both income and wealth indicate that older persons who are married enjoy much higher standards of living than non-married older persons, with the highest rates of poverty being experienced by those who are divorced – as much as three or four times the married rate.[71] Uhlenberg's work on older divorced women, for example, which controlled for both race and educational attainment, found that these women were more likely to continue to work in later life and to reduce living expenses by sharing their homes. In addition, compared with those who were married, never married or widowed, divorced men and women both reported higher levels of dissatisfaction with their economic condition.[72] In summary, while older divorced men and women both experience the highest poverty rates of any unmarried group, divorced men experience the highest mortality rates, have weaker social support networks, and have less contact with their children.[73]

Marital dissolution clearly also has implications beyond those for the couple themselves. For example, there is considerable evidence that individuals whose parents divorce are at a greater risk of experiencing divorce themselves.[74] This is also substantiated by family systems theory, which suggests that individuals who have experienced conflict in their family of origin are likely to re-enact these patterns in their family of choice.

The relationship between divorce and widowhood is complex. As was indicated earlier, due to the reduction in early widowhood through death, the rate of marital dissolution has remained remarkably constant, with divorce replacing death as the primary cause of marital break-up. In the eighteenth century, for example, the average length of an American marriage was 12 years, and well over half of all children spent a part of their childhood in a single parent family or stepfamily. The decline in death rates has made divorce more likely, or even more essential, and the relaxation of religious and social control has made divorce more possible. The picture has the additional complexity that widowhood is predominantly a late life experience, while divorce has been a young and mid-life phenomenon, but, as we have discussed, is becoming increasingly more common in older age groups.

Research looking at the differing impact of divorce and widowhood on family and intergenerational relationships has suggested that there are significant gender differences in the experience of these. Women face economic decline through both widowhood and divorce, but are able to maintain strong family and other relationships, while men are cut off from personal relationships through divorce to a far greater degree than through widowhood.[75] In addition:

> the recombination of new kin relationships following divorce is far more complex than it is following death. In the latter, while new combinations are formed, and have been historically so, there is but one family line to follow. Marriages cut short by death have only to integrate biographies from the past on remarriage, while those ended by divorce have also to include the new kin narratives, which develop parallel with their own new family lines.[76]

In summary, last century saw a shift in the cause of marital dissolution from death to divorce. Historically, men and women have both experienced high levels of widowhood, including multiple widowhood. Now men and women in early late life are more likely to be divorced than widowed. Divorce, especially divorce which is not followed by remarriage – an increasingly common experience particularly among this age group – has negative consequences for both men and women, especially in their old age. However, we must also remember that there is as much heterogeneity among those who are divorced as among any other marital group, and as divorce becomes the common experience of many more older people, the effects of being divorced in later life may be very different in the future. Regardless of this, with a rising incidence of divorce and declining propensity to remarry, it is likely that more older people will live alone in future than before. The rise will be greatest for men, who formerly have escaped being alone in old age due to their greater likelihood of dying before their spouse. Now the rising incidence of divorce for all ages, means that men will be more likely to find themselves living alone. In addition, under a regime of low fertility, both men and women will have fewer children and in all western industrialised countries geographical mobility increasingly results in separation from children. Given that children currently have a higher propensity to remain with the mother after a marital divorce or cohabitation split, an increasing number of men may find themselves without child support in later life. However, of these future older men, many may well have experienced periods of independent living throughout their lives, and thus be better adapted to cope with this.

Reconstituted families – linked beanpole families

Second marriages and subsequent birth of children often have to be assimilated into the ongoing relationship between a former husband and wife, in addition to the assimilation of a former spouse's latest offspring, and the inclusion of step and half-siblings from current and previous marriages. The new family forms emerging this century include the linking of *multi-beanpole families* (vertical families with few horizontal relations), thereby creating the horizontal or extended stepfamily. It is not yet clear within these new families at what point affinity ends within modern kin relationships. As we lose birth cousins, nephews and nieces, will we acknowledge step-cousins, step-nephews and step-nieces as part of our new extended families? We also do not fully understand the process by which family members set about rewriting their new roles and relationships, becoming in essence new kin to each other. Indeed, while the downward generations are often considered, few have explored this question in relation to antecedent generations – how modern families incorporate grandparents, step-grandparents and grandparents-in-law into the complex network of modern western kinship.

In terms of the myriad complexities of new families, there is one key difference between families reconstituted through divorce and those reconstituted through death. In the latter, while new combinations are formed, and have been historically so, there is only one family line to follow; the dead spouse does not form his or her own new descendant kin line, bringing a second stepfamily into the family. Those who say that death has been replaced by divorce are neglecting this fact. Following the dissolution of a marriage with children, new relationships pivoting around those children must be sustained and recreated, including maintaining extended family relationships, which though cast off by the parents are blood-linked to the children. Among the most viable of these are grandparents. One family today may well have several lateral tiers of grandparents, each with a biological link to one or more children of a reconstituted family. However, even this is not historically unprecedented. Divorce was legally practised and remarriage was encouraged in Augustan Rome as a way of building family ties, leading to numbers of complex families, during a time of apparent growth of individualism within the society.[77] However, this society did not have to cope with the lengthening of generations of current times, nor with the upwards as well as downward complexities.

There has been limited British research on the role of reconstituted or stepfamilies in caring for older adults.[78] The broad conclusions from all these studies are that the complexities of the ensuing relationships do not lend themselves to any particular pattern or structure of care. However, the dominant care relationship of blood-related daughter for mother, found within non-reconstituted families, seems to remain central. As an extensive qualitative study by Dimmock and colleagues on the role of stepfamilies in later life relationships concludes, while there is a growing awareness of the possibilities of looser-knit, divorce extended families, when it comes to 'the crunch' the availability of care will usually depend on access to close 'blood ties'.[79] Clearly we need more research in this area to quantify this assertion.[80] As Elder[81] has noted, the lives of parents and children are intimately linked both in the present and the future, and the crises of one generation become the self-defining deficits of another.

While we have shown that much of the fear underlying the myth of the collapsing family and its future inability to care for dependent kin is not based on empirical evidence, it is also clear that there are uncertainties surrounding new family forms and the impact of marital dissolution in later life. What then are the trends for which we do have some understanding? In particular, we are seeing a lengthening of adult unions and parent-child relationships, and a growth in the experience of multigenerational families.

Lengthening adult unions and parent–child relationships

Directly related to longer life expectancy, the average length of marriages has increased,[82] with WHO data suggesting that, by the turn of the century, the great majority of those marriages not terminated by divorce would exceed 40 years.[83] This is in contrast to figures which reveal that the common experience of marriage at the beginning of the twentieth century in the USA, for example, was likely to be under 25 years for a white couple, or as low as 10 years for an African-American couple.[84] Awareness of some of the implications of long-lived marriages was apparent by the middle of the twentieth century. Commentating on the UK's Royal Commission on Marriage and Divorce 1956, which, like the Royal Commission on Population (1949) before it, laid out a pessimistic future, Titmuss[85] pointed out that marriage had never been so popular as in the immediate post-war years. He argued that the fall in family size, concentration of childbearing in the early years, falling average age of marriage and increasing life expectancy, especially of women, were leading to long-lived marriages and long years of companionship without the demands of young children. He also considered that those marriages which did survive reflected the high level of marital commitment still present in society, particularly as early reproduction combined with increased longevity was leading many mid-life women to question their roles for the following 30 or 40 years after-reproductive activity. A theme that was to be taken up in subsequent decades by the explosion of feminist writings on the patriarchal family.[86]

In his thesis on the emergence of the modern life cycle in Britain, Anderson[87] also highlights a distinctive emerging modern life pattern for most in the late twentieth century which already included many of the factors we have been discussing: most will experience old age, most marry at least once, most will have children, most will have a married child by the time they are in their fifties, and most will have a grandchild before they are 60. More recently for the USA, Bengtson and others have studied such long-lived marriages in more detail. They report that for these long-lived marriages marital satisfaction tends to rise in later life to levels expressed by younger married people, after a typical dip in midlife.[88] There is of course a survivor effect here, with many of the dissatisfied mid-life marriages ending in dissolution. In addition, the dimensions which make early and late life marriage happy and successful differ, with elements such as physical attraction and passion, being replaced by familiarity and loyalty.[89]

Second, despite the delaying of child birth, the rate of increasing longevity now means that most parent–child relationships will be lived out as predominantly non-dependent adult dyads. As Riley[90] predicted in the early 1980s, the common experience for many parents and children would soon be around 60 years of joint life, of which under one-third would be spent in the traditional parent/dependent child relationship. Recent analysis of US/UK data[91] suggests that we have reached this point. Around one quarter of UK women and nearly 40 per cent of US women aged 55–63 still have a surviving parent. These women have thus spent around 60 years a child, some 40 of them in an adult relationship with a living parent. This relies on re-bonding in adulthood, sometimes also referred to as 'reverse bonding'.[92]

As Harper describes elsewhere, the association between marital and parental roles will loosen:

> As the common experience of parenthood moves to more than 50 years of shared life, parents and children are adjusting to spending most of their relationship as independent adults. Similarly husbands and wives are spending fewer of their joint lives as parents of young children . . . Relationships which have been historically based on a hierarchy which existed in part to support successful reproduction must move to greater equality, both child-parent, and husband-wife, as traditional roles based on parenthood give way to companionate relationships.[93]

However, not only will parents and children spend longer in non-dependent relationships, but the time spent as a child with dependent parents is also increasing. Within the USA, for example, the time spent as the daughter of a parent aged over 65 now exceeds the time spent as the mother of a child aged under 18. This must, however, include the caveat that, while for much of the last two centuries, a high proportion of those over the age of 65 would be in varying degrees of dependency on others for some aspect of their daily living, this is now no longer the case. Indeed, given that it is now not until after age 80 that the crucial stage for relying on children for assistance is reached,[94] we should perhaps be comparing age over 80 with under 18. What is then apparent, is that adult US women now spend more time without a dependant – albeit a dependent child or potentially dependent parent – than with one.

This has important implications for our understanding of the sandwich generation, or women in the middle phenomenon[95] whereby women, in particular, are faced with coping with simultaneous demands from dependent parents and children. As we shall see later, however, the apparently growing significance and length of grandparenthood are placing further demands on the roles and relationships of adult women.[96] It is not that unusual for a mid-life woman to be an active grandmother with child care responsibilities, mother of a new parent, and daughter of an increasingly frail elderly mother. We shall return to this in Chapter 10.

Verticalisation of the family structure

The *verticalisation* of western family structures leading to *beanpole families* has been identified in both the USA and the UK.[97] Recent mortality and fertility trends have resulted in the reduction of horizontal ties or *intergenerational contraction*, that is a decrease in the number of members within each generation, and an increase in vertical ties or *intergenerational extension*, that is a rise in the number of living generations.[98] These generations will typically have longer gaps between them.[99] In addition, family members are spending more time in intergenerational family roles than before: more time as parents and children, more time as grandchildren, and more time as great-grandchildren/great-grandparents even. In two recent US national surveys, the Health and Retirement Survey[100] and the AARP Intergenerational Linkages Survey, more than half of the respondents reported being members of four-generation families.[101] In both cases, however, the respondents were aged over 50, something we shall return to later. One US study indicated that a fifth of all women surviving to beyond age 80 years will spend some time in a five-generation family as great-great-grandmothers.[102] Similarly, work in the UK confirms that as mortality rates continue to decline, more children will have surviving grandparents and more people in late middle age and early old age will have both upward and downward generational ties,[103] with 75 per cent of a recent British survey reporting to be part of a three-, four- or even five-generation family group.[104]

Harper describes the changing linkages in the family:

> Individuals will thus grow older having more vertical than horizontal linkages in the family. For example, vertically, a four-generation family structure has three tiers of parent-child relationships, two sets of grandparent-grandchild ties and one great grandparent-grandchild linkage. Within generations of this same family, horizontally, ageing individuals will have fewer brothers and sisters. In addition, at the level of extended kin, family members will have fewer cousins, aunts, uncles, nieces and nephews. However, while the number of living generations will increase, the absolute number of living relatives will decrease.[105]

As Harper continues, however, we must be careful not to assume that the multi-generational family will be the norm for most families throughout an individual's life. Analysis of cross-sectional data from the International Social Survey Program[106] (ISSP), covering the USA, Australia, Austria, West Germany, Great Britain, Hungary and Italy, revealed that, at least at the end of the 1980s, a very small percentage of individuals

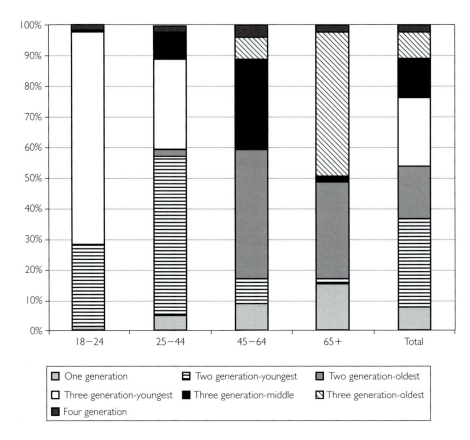

Figure 6.1 *Multigenerational families.*
Source: International Social Survey Programme (ISSP) covering the USA, Australia, Austria, West Germany, Great Britain, Hungary and Italy; adapted from Farkas and Hogan, 1995.

were living in a complex multigenerational family. Just under half of the 10,000 respondents lived in a two-generation family, 43 per cent had three living generations, but under 3 per cent were part of a four-generation family (see Fig. 6.1 and Table 6.10).

We should also note the difference between the USA and Europe. An individual in the USA was more likely to have both a surviving child and a surviving parent than in any of the European countries. While cross-sectional data have limitations in that they do not allow comment on the process of change within these families, such findings do place the verticalisation debate in perspective. As Harper concludes:

> While it is likely that during an individual's lifetime, he or she will experience a period of complex, possibly four or even five generational living, even if for only a short portion of the life course, at any one time the percentage of such long chain multigenerational families within a society is still low, though likely to increase over the coming decades.[107]

Table 6.10 *Multigenerational families by age*

	18–24	25–44	45–64	65+	Total
	%	%	%	%	%
One generation	0.6	5.6	9.3	15.9	7.4
Two generation – Youngest	27.4	52.1	8.3	1.2	29.1
Two generation – Oldest	0.1	2.6	41.9	31.7	17.4
Three generation – Youngest	69.7	28.5	0.3	0.1	22.3
Three generation – Middle	0.6	9.4	29.1	1.9	12.7
Three generation – Oldest	0.0	0.1	7.3	46.8	8.7
Four generation	1.6	1.8	3.7	2.4	2.4

Absolute number of respondents 10,131

Source: International Social Survey Program (ISSP) covering the USA, Australia, Austria, West Germany, Great Britain, Hungary and Italy; adapted from Farkas and Hogan, 1995.

In conclusion

We have long recognised that historically the extended family and the household were not the same,[108] and it is unlikely, in western industrial societies at least, that the increase in the number of living generations will result in a return to the multigenerational households seen early last century. We now also need to acknowledge that the nuclear family and the household are increasingly disjointed units. There are a growing number of family/household combinations, and the life course experience of any individual is fragmented into many possible combinations.

As Harper has described elsewhere,[109] the common experience for an individual born in the first half of the twentieth century was to be born into a marital union and to reside with those married parents within the one household until the individual's own marriage or birth of first child. Living alongside numerous siblings, cousins, uncles and aunts, many births and many infant deaths would be experienced. As the parents aged or died, an independent household comprising married partner and children would be established, and this remained an intact unit until the death of a partner, or the marriage and parenthood of children. The marriage would be most likely to end in midlife due to the death of the spouse.

An individual born now or late last century has the expectation of a variety of family and household forms. He or she may be born into a consensual union, which then becomes a marital union, which ends in divorce, resulting in a single parent – probably female-led – household. This then becomes a reconstituted family with cohabiting adults, then married adults with a combination of step-siblings within the one household. The individual may well leave the household on reaching adulthood forming an independent household for several years before entering into a consensual union, with a subsequent out-of-wedlock birth, followed by a marital household, and on divorce heading either a single person household again or forming a lone parent household, thus repeating the pattern of his or her parents. The union may indeed be childless (one-third of women in their mid-thirties are yet to have their first child) or with only one or two children, though these children are likely to survive to adulthood. He or she is unlikely to have many siblings, or indeed cousins, and will increasingly face caring for a broad set of dependent parents, with whom he or she has had a long adult relationship. His or her own marriage or union will be one of companionship for most of its existence, rather than one formed mainly to look after young children, and he or she may experience many different forms of union, which fit into the demands of an ever lengthening life-span and the various stages of that lifespan.

Notes

1 Harper, 2004a.
2 Crude marriage rate is the number of marriages per 1000 estimated mean population.
3 Murphy and Wang, 1999.
4 Raley, 2000.
5 Waite, 1995.
6 Kiernan, 1999.
7 Kiernan, 2000.
8 Lesthaeghe, 2001.
9 Buck and Scott, 1994.
10 Rowlands et al., 1997.
11 Buck and Scott, 1994.
12 Murphy and Wang, 1999.
13 Farley, 1996.
14 Raley, 2000.
15 Australian Bureau of Statistics, 1998.
16 Waite and Lillard, 1991.
17 Lillard et al., 1991; Kiernan and Mueller, 1999.
18 Murphy and Wang, 1999.
19 Australian Bureau of Statistics, 1997; Kiernan and Mueller, 1999; Haskey, 1983.
20 For example, Australian Family Law Act, 1975 and Belgium Reform Act, 1995.
21 Murphy and Wang, 1999.
22 Cherlin, 1992.
23 FPSC, 2000.
24 Raley, 2000.
25 Fitch and Ruggles, 2000.
26 Australian Bureau of Statistics, 1999.
27 Median age at marriage is the age at which there are as many marrying above that age as are marrying below.
28 Goldscheider and Goldscheider, 1994.
29 Though of course the factors behind remaining in the parental home are also those associated with delaying marriage.
30 Ryder, 1965.
31 Rowlands et al., 1997.
32 Ventura et al., 1998.
33 Waite and Bachrach, 2000.
34 Hajnal, 1965.
35 Lundh, 1999.
36 ibid.
37 van Poppel and Nelissen, 1999.
38 Wall, 1996.
39 Harper, 2004b.
40 ibid.
41 Landale, 1989.
42 Fitch and Ruggles, 2000.
43 ibid.
44 Easterlin, 1976; Landale, 1989.
45 Fitch and Ruggles, 2000.
46 Landale and Tolnay, 1991.
47 Fitch and Ruggles, 2000.
48 ibid.
49 Waite and Spitze, 1981.
50 McLanahan and Casper, 1995.
51 Bengtson et al., 1990.
52 Harper, 2004a.
53 Uhlenberg, 1995.
54 ibid.
55 Henretta, 1998.
56 Lesthaege, 1992; Lewin, 1992.
57 Haskey, 1992.
58 Lesthaege, 1992.
59 Lewin, 1982.
60 DeMaris and Rao, 1992; Popenoe, 1993.
61 Kiernan and Mueller, 1999.
62 Australian Bureau of Statistics, 1998.
63 Waite, 1995; Waite and Bachrach, 2000.
64 Waite and Bachrach, 2000.
65 Uhlenberg, 1994.

66 US Bureau of the Census, 1997.
67 Uhlenberg, 1995.
68 Cherlin, 1992; Bornat et al., 1998.
69 Hagestad, 1985.
70 Waite and Bachrach, 2000.
71 ibid.
72 Uhlenberg, 1995.
73 Waite, 1995; Fox and Kelly, 1995.
74 Amato, 1994; Bumpass et al., 1991.
75 Hughes and Waite, 2004.
76 Harper, 2004a, pp. 25-6.
77 Saller, 1991.
78 Finch and Wallis, 1994; Finch, 2004; Bornat et al., 1998; Bornat et al., 1999; Dimmock et al., 2004; Haskey, 1998.
79 Dimmock et al., 2004.
80 Though there is US evidence that this is the case in relation to the bequest motive.
81 Elder, 1994.
82 Myers, 1990.
83 ibid.
84 Morgan and Kunkel, 1998.
85 Titmuss, 1958.
86 Friedman and Sarah, 1982.
87 Anderson, 1985.
88 Bengtson et al., 1990.
89 Reiss, 1960; Brehm, 1992.
90 Riley, 1983.
91 Grundy, 1999.
92 Harper, 2004a.
93 Harper, 2004c.
94 Uhlenberg, 1995.
95 Rossi, 1987.
96 Zeilig and Harper, 2000.
97 Bengtson et al., 1990; Hagestad, 1986; Goldman, 1986; Grundy, 1999; Harper, 2004c.
98 Bengtson et al., 1990.
99 Hagestad, 1988; Shanas, 1980.
100 The Health and Retirement Survey is a prospective panel survey of persons born 1931-1941.
101 Soldo and Hill, 1995; Bengtson and Harootyan, 1994; Bengtson, 1995.
102 Hagestad, 1988.
103 Grundy, 1999.
104 Dench et al., 1999.
105 Harper, 2004c.
106 Farkas and Hogan, 1995.
107 Harper, 2004c.
108 Laslett and Wall, 1972.
109 Harper, 2004c.

7
Intergenerational relationships and family care

The provision of informal kin-based care for older people has become an important component of care provision in most western societies. The key issue, already identified in Chapter 1, is to understand the current and future health and social care needs of our ageing populations, how dependent these will be on the provision of family and other informal care, and whether families will be able to sustain any increased demand due to changing individual life course trajectories and dispersed kin networks. In order to fully address the above, we need an understanding of the following: whether there will be an increase in demand for family care; whether there will be a decline in actual availability of kin care; and whether there is any evidence of a change in kin attitudes towards providing care. In addition, we need to address the broader health and social care context. Namely, whether there will be an increase in need and demand for late life care and support in general, and what alternative resources exist beyond the family.

Increasing long-term disability

As populations age, so we shall see an increase in non-communicable adult diseases which tend to result in non-fatal outcomes, such as long-term disability. In general, these require an increase in health and social care which can be provided in the community, rather than medical care which requires hospital and specialised medical treatment. A useful measure of this is disability-adjusted life years, or DALYs, which combine years of life lost (YLLs) through premature death, with years lived with disability (YLDs). One DALY is equivalent to one lost year of healthy life, with the measured disease burden being the gap between a population's health status and that of a normative global reference population with high life expectancy lived in full health.

As we can see from Fig. 7.1, just over half the lost years of healthy life in the developed world in 2002 were as a result of disease and or injury in adults aged between 15 and 59 years, and one-third in adults aged over 60.

We can also examine this in more detail through national longitudinal studies. The current US picture of disability, for example, can be ascertained from the two large longitudinal studies AHEAD and HRS which both include measures of health conditions, level of physical functional ability, cognitive functioning, and use of health care services.[1] AHEAD also includes six measures of activities of daily living: getting help or having diffi-

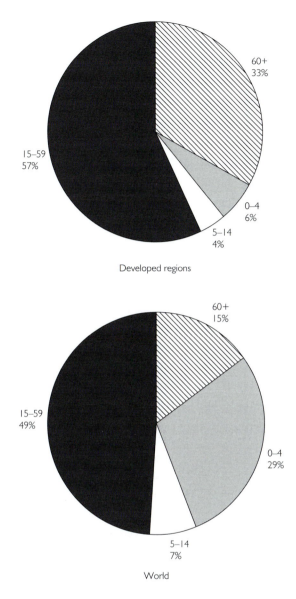

Figure 7.1 *Distribution of disease burden (DALYs) by age group and region, 2002.*
Source: WHO, 2003.

culty with walking, dressing, bathing, eating, getting out of bed, and using a toilet, these all being good measures for assessing increased need for informal care. The proportion of women having difficulty with at least one activity of daily living increases from one-third of those in their seventies to half of those aged 80 or over. For men, the percentage increases from one-fifth to one quarter respectively. This substantiates other research indicating that women have both increased longevity and higher rates of morbidity in industrialised countries.[2] It also reveals that two-thirds of women and four-fifths of men in their seventies had no difficulty with activities of daily living. Even among the older age groups, half of women and three quarters of men reported no difficulties. However, there are significant relationships between health, wealth and income, so that the average income of individuals in excellent health is more than three times as high as the average income of individuals in poor health, and their average wealth accumulation more than five times as high.[3]

Similar findings emerge from the English Longitudinal Study of Ageing. Here there is a significant health difference between the socio-economic groups. This is reflected in activities of daily living. Thus less than 15 per cent of professional and managerial men and women aged 60–74 had difficulties with these activities, rising to nearly one quarter of routine and manual workers. Among those aged 75 and over these figures had risen to just under one-third of the professional and managerial group, and half the routine and manual group. However, taken as a whole, nearly three-quarters of those in their seventies (75 per cent of men and 72 per cent of women) had no difficulty with activities of daily living, and neither had over half of those in their eighties (62 per cent of men and 56 per cent of women).[4]

Furthermore, as we saw in Chapter 1, there is growing evidence, particularly from the USA, of a compression of morbidity. That is, the lengthening of healthy life is being accompanied by an actual shortening of the period of disability prior to death. Work by Manton on the US National Long Term Care Survey reveals an increasing reduction in the prevalence of chronic ill health among older Americans.[5] The total number of those in the USA aged 65 and over rose by 30 per cent between 1982 and 1999, but the percentage of those who were significantly disabled fell from 26.2 per cent to 19.7 per cent during that time, with the rate of decline doubling during the period. In addition, Manton argues that each successive cohort is becoming healthier, and that this effect is likely to last through to old age (Fig. 7.2).

This evidence of declining disability at advanced ages[6] is consistent with the possibility of an age-specific decline in the use of US health and social care resources. We do not have comparable data for Europe. However, in the UK, ONS 1999 reported an increase in healthy active life, particularly for men in their seventies, and the General Household Survey reveals that the proportion of those over age 85 who were capable of living independently rose from 68 per cent to 81 per cent between 1980 and 1991.

An alternative scenario, however, is not to examine the total amount of disability in the older population, but to assess the amount of care which will be required at any one time period. Given that the need for care often increases dramatically as an individual approaches death, we can examine the long-term changes in the number of elderly persons who need care by comparing over time the proportion of the population that is in the final year of life. Using census data on the size of the American population by age,

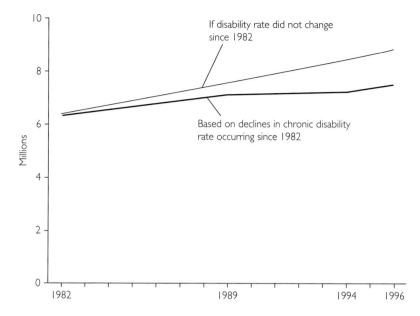

Figure 7.2 *Number of chronically disabled people aged 65 and over in the USA, 1982–96. Source: Manton, 2000.*

and vital statistics data on the probability of death by age, in 1960 and 1997,[7] Johnson and Lo Sasso computed the number of Americans aged 65 and older in the last year of life, per 10,000 persons in the total population. The rate increased from 53 per 10,000 in 1960 to 64 per 10,000 in 1997. This does indicate that while there is currently no predicted increase in demand for family care through increasing disability alone, there may be a period effect as the demographic bulge, combined with a delaying of the onset of morbidity, sweeps though the population.

It is also important to build into our analysis the economic effects of health and disability. As Johnson[8] has pointed out, good health causes individuals to accumulate different levels of resources, poor health to use up these resources as they address health problems. Similarly, the better health at younger ages of recent older cohorts might possibly lead to a higher level of accumulated resources.[9] This is linked to a higher overall income of future western older populations and the ability of themselves and their families to buy in substitute services rather than rely on informal kin provision, particularly in the USA. What is unclear, however, is the increase in demand which will arise as successive cohorts arrive in later life with a higher standard of education and general awareness of health care possibilities. This is encouraged by the vast array of public information now freely available via the internet and media in general. Evidence from both the USA and the UK,[10] for example, suggests that mid-life cohorts are now far more demanding in their health care needs, and this may include informal care.

Spectrum of formal and informal care resources

The second determining set of factors comprises alternative resources beyond the family. These clearly vary widely from country to country, and are heavily dependent on government policies and funding.

United Kingdom

The United Kingdom provides publicly funded services and resources which encourage the integration of kin into the care package. The General Household Survey reports that around 4 per cent of adults care for an adult in their own home, and a further 8 per cent look after someone living elsewhere, accounting for nearly five and a half million carers. The majority of this care is for those aged over 65;[11] of these, 58 per cent are women. Half of these have been caring for more than five years, one quarter for more than ten years. Given the relatively low level of assets of most older people in the UK, private care is not accessible. As Harper and Leeson[12] point out, current UK government policy for older and disabled people aims to promote health and independence, through providing person-centred services to meet individual needs, help people remain in the community, and support carers. Such policies are very heavily reliant on the availability of unpaid, informal, typically family, care from within the community[13] and indeed current models for service distribution specifically factor in available family care.[14]

The establishment of community-based care as the pivotal leg of government policy occurred in 1989 when the White Paper on Community Care emphasised the need for older people to stay at home for as long as possible.[15] The resultant 1990 NHS and Community Care Act laid down the development of community care provision, enabling older people to remain at home. Behind the rhetoric lay one simple premise, care *in* the community meant care *by* the community meant care *by* families. This was formalised in 1995 with the Carers (Recognition of Services) Act and the subsequent National Strategy for Carers in 1998. This aims to provide information and support to carers, particularly to enable them to combine employment and caregiving, and provide care for carers in the form of relief and respite services.

In 2001, the National Service Framework for Older People (NSF) became the main policy instrument for the modernisation of health and social care services for older people.[16] The goals of the NSF include promoting independence and person-centred care. In July 2000, the government announced in the NHS Plan[17] the development of services for older people. Intermediate care services between hospital and home were to be introduced to prevent loss of independence. By placing the focus on policies that enable older people to stay in their own homes while receiving care, the NHS Plan places independence as central. A major stated objective is to ensure that older people can secure and sustain their independence in a home appropriate to their circumstance.

The Better Care, Higher Standards initiative is a joint measure from the Department of Health (DoH) and the Department of the Environment, Transport and the Regions (DETR). Local authority strategies have shifted the focus to adapting older people's properties, so that ongoing home maintenance will help older people to plan their housing future as they grow older. Extra government funding for Home Improvement Agencies (HIA) has enabled many older people to stay in their own homes for longer periods. The Supporting People Programme provides information services,[18] and the Pension Service and Third Age Services (TAS) form an integrated gateway to access pensions, benefits, health, housing and social care.

Other EU countries

A similar emphasis on independence, community care and integration of family-based care and support can be seen throughout Europe.[19]

France

France has provided domestic services *(aide menagère),* such as house cleaning, shopping, etc. for its older needy population since post-war times. This has been supplemented since 1978 by home health care services *(services de soins infirmiers à domicile),* covering bathing and feeding, etc. although it is currently estimated that less than 1 per cent of older persons living at home are reached by this latter service. However, the French also have a long history of legally requiring citizens to fulfil a maintenance obligation to the family.[20] Children and children-in-law have a maintenance obligation to their parents, grandparents and in-laws, spouses to each other. The debate, today, focuses around whether increasing the socialisation of former family obligations towards older relatives will hasten the already perceived decline of family solidarity.[21] As Chwalow describes:

> By not allowing for a complete socialisation of the maintenance obligation, the State is caught acting in the name of national solidarity while not being reimbursed by the family, and requiring the family to reimburse the money provided to the older person in need. The law is therefore highly criticized for its negative effects, as it authorises the State to recover from descendants, or even from an inherited estate, some or all of the social aid payments made to older people in need.[22]

Currently, the state recovers less than half (around 40–45 per cent) of the money it spends on social aid for older people. This financial obligation, however, is being increasingly supplemented by informal family-based care and services, with 90 per cent of old dependent adults living at home receiving informal care, the majority from family members.[23]

Germany

A variety of support services are offered to German elders – information and counselling, recreation, mobile services, domestic care – however, these are provided by different agencies and result in an uncoordinated typically inefficient community care package.[24] Payment for these is generally in the hands of the recipients through the provision of benefits, partially state and partially insurance funded. The majority of German adults are insured, including since 1995 long-term insurance which covers, among other things, home-based care. German data reveal that 80 per cent of long-term care benefits are received by those over age 65, two-thirds over age 75. Despite the range of professional services, the majority of home-based care is provided by family members, three-quarters of whom are female, divided more or less equally between daughters and spouses. Around 40 per cent of carers for those aged 65–79 are wives, falling to 12 per cent among those caring for someone aged 80 and older. One quarter of those providing care to elders aged between 65–79 are daughters, rising to 44 per cent of the carers for those aged 80 and over. Furthermore, three-quarters of these carers stated that they were available to care 24 hours a day. These carers are eligible for payments from benefits, though only half of family carers appear to take such payments from their kin.[25] As Dohner and Kofahl state, these figures demonstrate that, despite the high demands of German working lives, the family remains the mainstay of care for older people in the home.

Italy

The strong presence of mid-life women is also apparent in other European countries. Formal care for older people in Italy is supported by the transfer of money from the state to supplement the income of the older person and enable them to purchase private services as well as to take up local public services.[26] Italy currently has a range of home care services, coordinated by the Provinces and guided by the Regions. These tend to be *ad hoc* and rather uncoordinated, covering domestic care such as housework, bathing, feeding and recreational activities. As a result, the family still provides the majority of home-based care. Estimates from Italy suggest that 80 per cent of family carers are female, divided between spouses and daughters, with one study reporting over half of all women aged 54–65 having provided parental care or support in the past 12 months.[27] There is concern in Italy that the dramatically falling fertility rate will only compound these pressures, contributing to future much smaller familial networks on which older persons can call. Furthermore:

> a woman often has to combine her caring tasks nowadays with her role as a grandmother, a figure which today is more and more involved in looking after the children of daughters and daughter-in-laws, who often have just become mothers due to the increased mean age at first birth and are involved in external working activities themselves. This plurality of roles – daughter, wife, mother, grandmother, working woman – is certainly a contributory factor to the fact that middle-aged women, especially if full-time carers, are subject to a relatively high risk of depression and stress.[28]

In recognition of this, the Italian government has started a process which should result in the future adoption of policies 'of support to families with elderly people in need of home care . . . with a view to safeguarding the health of women who are, in most cases, the main [person] responsible for the assistance'.[29]

Poland

Of particular interest are the European countries in transition, as socialist systems move to introduce private and voluntary-based components. Within Poland a modernising social service programme sits alongside the former health care structures. Older people who remain in their homes are entitled by law to social support, though provision does not always cover demand.[30] Of particular interest is the provision of formal care services, as these are provided in the older person's own home only where the family is unable to provide this kind of help or the person concerned does not have a family.[31]

Polish law also requires children to make maintenance payments to needy parents, though in practice the law is rarely evoked. Regular financial assistance from children is received by less than 13 per cent of older people, but 80 per cent of needy elderly report receiving regular care from their children.

This emphasis on the family as the primary caregiver is fundamental to the Polish system of elder care:

> The fundamental role of the family in providing care for older people is mainly the result of the traditional model in which multigenerational families have lived together, which is not always the practice of choice, but is very often the only alternative because of the housing shortage which has existed since the war. It has often been shown that the type of care offered by a family to the older person is, in general terms, equivalent to what the older person offers the family in return for care (use of housing, care of grandchildren, financial assistance). In recent years, it is even possible to observe an increase in the financial assistance offered to children by their elderly parents, in return for the expected care offered by children during times of illness and disability. This testifies to the closeness of the family and mutual obligations of one generation to another.[32]

The limited research in this area, reports that two-thirds of needy elderly rely on children and grandchildren, and only 25 per cent on spouses. This relatively low rate of spousal care relative to the EU15 countries is a reflection of the still high level of widowhood among these elderly cohorts. When this is factored in, the majority of those with a living spouse report the spouse as the primary caregiver.

Portugal

A similar picture emerges from across Europe: a basic home care system being provided by the government, but reliant on a spectrum of supplementation from family members. Thus Portugal has very limited pubic provision, reliant on the fact that:

the family is considered the centre of the tradition of collective responsibility to provide care . . . indeed [within] the image of family solidarity, including its oldest members, caring for them within the family circle is deeply rooted in Portuguese society's cultural values.[33]

While there has been limited debate on this issue, there is growing recognition that a social policy on old age is required, one which supports families in their attempt to combine informal care with public programmes and professional services, thus making the demands of modern life compatible with family responsibilities to older relatives.[34]

Greece

Probably at the farthest end of the continuum in Europe is Greece. Here parents transfer significant capital resources to their children enabling the establishment of their own families, in return for a tacit understanding that care in dependent old age will be forthcoming. Given a very slim form of public welfare provision, such family obligation and reciprocity is still vital.[35] However:

despite reciprocity and a greater ease in social relations between generations, this does not mean that fulfilling care obligations is easy . . . small urban flats quickly become overcrowded when an older person needs to move in to receive care and where the family's income is not enough to allow additional space to be rented or purchased.[36]

Yet, the traditional roles adopted by older and rural Greek generations still negates against acceptance of welfare services. The provision of professional assistance in the work of family care is seen as an enigma and an unacceptable wedge within a personal intimate relationship.

Sweden and Denmark

However, even at the other end of the welfare spectrum, in both Sweden and Denmark, with their extensive provision of home health and social care services and strong emphasis on the rights of older people to choose their way of life and maintain independence within the community, the family still plays an integral role. Indeed, with the continued reduction in institutional beds, the family is seen as a crucial component of the community care package. Policy developments are thus focused on supporting caregivers, including programmes to provide financial support, psychosocial support and respite care and relief.[37]

United States

Successive UK and European governments have, therefore, integrated informal family care into their health and social care policy for older adults, while seeking to empower older people themselves. The United States presents a different picture however. Such care is overseen at the State level and thus varies widely across the nation. The role of private-based home care services is key here, and given the relatively high income of many, particularly white Americans, provides an integral part of elder care. Johnson and Sasso, for example, highlight a shift toward paid and away from family caregivers over the past two decades. Between 1982 and 1994, the proportion of elderly persons with disabilities who relied only on informal helpers declined from 74 per cent to 64 per cent, while the proportion with paid helpers increased.[38] They also stress the role that adult children may play in helping their frail parents finance the costs of formal home care. This is particularly since third parties, such as Medicare, Medicaid and private insurance, often do not cover home health care services. Furthermore, there is evidence that many disabled elderly persons who receive formal home care pay their caregivers themselves.[39] Paid caregivers thus provide up to 40 per cent of all long-term home-based assistance, with one-third of heavily dependent elderly relying completely on formal care. However, despite this, it is still estimated that 80 per cent of all home care and support is provided informally, by family, neighbours and volunteers. Elderly men are most likely to receive such care from spouses, elderly women from daughters.

In conclusion, from the evidence available for Europe and the USA, we can see that the extension of active healthy life will increase the demand on families for non-care services, but at the same time allow spousal care to increase as there will be a reduction in widowhood and an increase in the health and activity of potential carers. There are a range of alternative public and private services available for supporting older people in the community. These all, however, rely on input from families and most governments are encouraging and formalising these. It appears that, currently, only within the USA will there be a significant use of privately purchased services by family members in substitution for practical care and support. This, however, may change, as future cohorts of European elderly people themselves become wealthier and may wish to purchase services rather than rely on kin care. There will, though, be a hidden intergenerational transfer here, as resources which might have been passed onto younger generations either through direct transfers or through inheritance, will instead be used by elderly parents to pay for long-term support and social care services. Notably, there is a range of European evidence[40] that payment for family-based service does not influence willingness to provide such care, and family members are generally reluctant to receive financial payment for kin-based care.

Changing availability of kin care

It is, therefore, recognised that despite modern dispersed living arrangements,[41] families still play an important role in late life. With the increasing number and proportion of the population in later life, these contacts and relationships will increase in significance over the next few decades. Despite the growth in individual household living and individualistic values,[42] there remains a consistent body of evidence that many families remain committed to care and support their kin both in terms of expressed attitudes and behaviour. Families, including step and reconstituted family members,[43] thus provide both reciprocal care[44] and social support.[45] Increasing life expectancy at later ages implies that more members of successive cohorts will reach the age at which help with activities of daily living may be required, and family members are a likely source of at least some of this help.

Intergenerational transfers of care and services are both age- and gender-related. While these generally flow from older to younger generations, they gradually decline during the life course, and those from the younger to older generations increase and dominate.[46] From a peak of parent to child transfers when the parents are in their early sixties, and/or the children are young adults, this declines rapidly, so that as the parent reaches their mid-seventies child to parent transfers begin to dominate.[47] While there exist no formal mechanisms to ensure family care in late life, it is possible within most western societies to identify a series of determinants of support criteria used by individuals to select kin caregivers. In most western societies, those defined as closest to the care recipient are most likely to provide maximum support, typically spouse or child, in the latter case most likely daughter.[48] Data from the USA, for example, suggest that 57 per cent of primary caregivers for impaired elders over 70 living in the community, are either the spouses or adult children of the care recipients.[49] For those without a spouse, due to widowhood, divorce or being never married, adult children account for 42 per cent of all caregivers. Data from the Eurobarometer[50] suggest that two-thirds of the care provided to older people within the EU as a whole comes from within the family. In the UK, in particular, spouses and children supplement formal care for elderly people by up to 80 per cent of required community-based care.[51] In addition, while most care and support is provided by female carers, there is growing recognition of the role that elderly male spouses are now playing.

These care relationships, however, are clearly heavily dependent on the health and economic resources, commitments and life stage of the individuals, their family structures and networks, including complex patterns of biological and step-relationships.[52] While acknowledging that demographic complexities affecting contemporary families limit future predictions,[53] it is also important to try to gain a broad understanding of the ways in which contemporary factors are currently influencing and may in future influence kin relationships. As we have discussed earlier, given the rapidly changing demography of the family, and the impact this is having on kin roles and relationships, there are concerns that families will be unable to sustain the increasing elder care which will be required. As we discussed in Chapter 6, declining fertility implies a reduction in the number of kin available to provide care; changing family structures and age transitions influence the availability and willingness of younger generations to care; and changing female activity across the life course, in particular, reduces the availability and willingness of women to care.[54] In addition, the increase in the number of step and reconstituted – so-called 'blended' – families suggests kin networks will increasingly comprise family members with highly diverse levels of connectedness and commitment to each other.[55]

The evidence, however, is at times contradictory. For example, on the one hand, the apparent growth in current voluntary childlessness is seen as affecting the future supply of children available for informal care. On the other hand, it is also argued that increasing childlessness in cohorts born after 1946[56] means that currently fewer adult children will have simultaneous commitments to both children and parents, thus increasing caregiving time. However, increasing levels of female employment suggest that women are less likely to provide full-time care than in the past.[57] While the delaying of life transitions, in particular those associated with union and child birth, leads to longer intergenerational spacings, and possible demand conflicts, particularly for mid-life women.

One particular concern is that consensual unions will not provide stable extensive cross-kin relationships. However, this is based on evidence from younger cohabiting couples, and as older adults move to this form of mid- and late-life union, the picture may be very different. Many of the existing and future consensual unions may well support the long-term vertical and lateral kin relationships developed through marriage. In addition, while divorce may be replacing death in long marriages, those marriages which do survive appear to provide a strong base for elder care, particularly by the spouse. There is some valid concern, however, over the rise in divorce and the impact this has on men. Interaction between fathers and their children tends to decline significantly following divorce, indicating that these men are less likely to have adult children available for them in time of need. As we saw in Chapter 6, while most people will at some time experience living within a multigenerational family, this is likely to be specific to the early and late life course. Four-generational beanpole families may well increase but will probably not be the majority family form in the West. In addition, there is evidence that we shall see the emergence of the extended stepfamily as a more common form, with several vertical families being linked together by marital and consensual unions, and providing an extended kin network. Finally, as Soldo and Hill[58] remind us, while numbers of children are an important aspect of kin availability, the characteristics of the children, individual parent–child relationships, whether biological or stepchildren, employment, and geographical dispersion will also affect who is available and willing to provide care. Let us now review evidence from the USA which examines these factors (briefly considered in Chapter 6) in more detail.

The availability of children to provide elder care in the USA

The childbearing years for the AHEAD cohorts who were born pre-1923 included the low fertility years of the 1930s, while many of the HRS cohort were in their childbearing years during the post-war baby boom of the 1950s. As Henretta's evaluation[59] of these cohorts indicates, there is a large difference in the levels of fertility and childlessness so that the 1931–41 birth cohort has larger family size and lower levels of childlessness than pre-1923 cohorts, particularly those born before 1914. These differences between cohorts are magnified by two further factors. First, more of the children of the earlier birth cohorts have died, thereby reducing the number of children who potentially are available to provide help. Second, the younger HRS respondents are more likely to have stepchildren who therefore have a larger effect on family size. Thus current mid-life adults are less likely to be childless and more likely to have three or more living children or stepchildren compared to the very old. These results reflect three distinct processes: cohort differences in fertility, the effect of ageing on (children's) mortality, and changing period levels of remarriage. As Henretta stresses, however, while availability of children appears greater in the younger cohorts examined here, this pattern will not be continued in subsequent US cohorts as more recent birth cohorts have had lower fertility, and the number of children and stepchildren of the older population will begin dropping around 2005.[60] We must, however, be careful about extrapolating such data to other populations, for there are not only differences among cohorts, but also among the same cohorts living in different countries. For example, persons aged 53–63 have more living parents and more living children in the USA than in the UK.[61] The availability of children who may be able to provide help is thus highly variable between countries and over time within one country.

The increase in divorce for each successive cohort has led to the continuous growth of reconstituted families consisting of both children and stepchildren.[62] Therefore the availability of child support is also predicated on whether stepchildren are likely to play the same role in caregiving as biological children:

> The category of stepchildren is very heterogeneous, including persons who were raised by the respondent as well as some who were adults when the respondent became a stepparent. Heterogeneity among individuals in this group is likely to mean that stepchildren will, on average, have less commitment to care for the stepparent. On the other hand, a larger family network does increase the probability that at least one child or stepchild will serve as an emotional confidant or provide help. This role is likely to be particularly important for the small percentage of these cohorts who have only stepchildren.[63]

The availability of children to provide care also depends on the characteristics of each child, in addition to their numbers. The child's employment, geographic distance from parent, and presence of own children affect the caregiving network by raising or lowering that child's availability.[64] For example, Henretta reports for the USA that having one's own children or having more education reduce the probability of providing elder care.[65] Alternatively, children who have received earlier financial help from a parent are more likely to provide care for that parent later.[66]

Another factor which is causing concern is that increasing levels of mid-life employment among women in the USA mean that daughters are less available to provide full-time care than in the past. The percentage of women aged between 45 and 65 in the US labour market has risen since 1960 from one- to two-thirds.[67] Johnson notes:

> . . . ongoing demographic and socioeconomic trends are increasing time pressures for women with frail parents who attempt to fulfill both their traditional caregiving responsibilities and their emerging responsibilities in the workplace. Over the past generation, women have assumed a much larger role in the labor market, limiting the amount of time they are able to devote to other responsibilities, including caring for their frail parents. The increased work responsibilities of women, who have historically been the primary caregivers for the frail elderly, may become incompatible with their caregiving responsibilities.[68]

Various studies in the USA have examined this relationship between female caring and labour market responsibilities,[69] addressing both the impact of caring on labour market supply and of paid labour on caregiving. The results indicate the complexity of the relationship underlying the bold assertions that caregiving by women is being reduced by increased labour market participation. What is clear, however, is that the demands on these women are increasing, including the necessity to juggle time and energy commitments. Johnson and Lo Sasso's recent review of these studies[70] indicates the complexity, with there being a negative, but rather small, effect on both hours worked and amount of caregiving provided. Their own work on women aged 53 to 63, using HRS data, explores this relationship in the US context in more detail, suggesting that as more women assume important roles in the labor market, providing time-intensive personal care assistance will become increasingly more difficult. In particular, the findings from their study suggest that devoting time to the informal care of elderly parents may be incompatible with full-time paid employment at midlife. Women aged 53 to 63 who helped their parents with personal care activities cut back their hours of paid, on average, work by 751 hours per year or by about 70 per cent. Although additional research is needed to determine whether these reductions in labour supply come about through early retirement or reduced weekly hours of work, the results suggest that special work arrangements, including flexible work schedules and part-time work, may be necessary if people with frail family members are to balance their work and caregiving responsibilities successfully.

Johnson thus suggests for the USA that, given the growth in women's employment rates and the difficulties that working women encounter when they provide hands-on personal care, formal home health care is likely to become an increasingly important option for frail elderly persons in the near future: 'Women with high earnings capacity may choose to focus their efforts in the workplace and help their elderly parents financially, rather than divert time from their paid work to provide personal care assistance to their parents.'

Of equal importance, however, the study revealed the low level of care actually given by mid-life women to parents. Less than half these women had living parents, and only one quarter of these gave help to their parents, more specifically, only about 11 per cent of women at midlife devoted more than 100 hours per year to assisting their parents. For these women who do care, however, the personal cost is high. The average loss in working hours was 751 hours per year, accounting for $12,750 in pre-tax wages. Those who cut back their labour supply to care for frail family members also lose retirement savings because they accumulate fewer credits toward future Social Security and private pension benefits. Others may lose health insurance benefits if they drop out of the labour force before they become eligible for Medicare benefits.

Working carers in Europe

A range of research has also been undertaken in Europe.[71] As Anderson highlights, not only is the average age of the European workforce increasing, but also patterns of labour force participation, of entry and exit, have changed markedly over the last two decades. In particular, the female employment rate increased from 44 per cent in 1975 to over 50 per cent by the end of the century, and this appears to have counted for most of the growth in employment during this time. Women now account for some 42 per cent of the European workforce, though remaining below 40 per cent in Spain, Greece, Italy and Luxembourg.[72] While the proportion of men aged 55–64 participating in the EU workforce fell by 6 per cent, between 1986 and 1997, it rose by 4 per cent for women.[73] Anderson also notes, as a point of interest, that while only 6 per cent of men are employed part-time, one third of women work part-time. However, this varies across the European Union, with particularly high rates in the Netherlands (67 per cent of female employment) and in the UK (44 per cent) but with very low rates of part-time female workers in Greece (8 per cent), Italy and Portugal (both 12 per cent).[74] As Anderson points out, this employment picture has complex links to the demands of family care. Just under half of UK carers are working full-time or part-time,[75] and there does seem to be an association between working and caregiving. The British Household Panel Survey[76] reports that, whereas 77 per cent of all men in the age group 16–64 are economically employed, this falls to 62 per cent of male caregivers. The figures for women are 60 per cent and 43 per cent respectively. They report that carers are less likely to be in employment than non-carers and are more likely to work part-time. Interestingly, a recent UK survey[77] of men and women aged 50–69, reported that the number of carers who were fully retired was slightly less than non-carers, 37 per cent to 41 per cent. However, of those carers who had retired, 14 per cent said caregiving had influenced their decision to retire, and 10 per cent reported that they had lost or given up their job. There is clearly a complex relationship here between the demands of caring and the necessity of working to provide an income, particularly in cases where the carer is the only income earner.

The other factor for consideration is co-residence. This is much more prevalent in the Southern European countries than it is in Northern Europe, the UK or the USA. As

Anderson makes clear, the extent of home-based care depends significantly upon the composition of the household. Families in Spain, Italy and Greece are more likely to share the same household as the dependent older person, and therefore to provide care within the household. As a result, there is much lower non-resident caregiving in these southern countries, only around 4 per cent of children give such care as compared to 20 per cent of children in Finland, and 12 per cent in Denmark, Sweden, the Netherlands and Ireland. In terms of hours spent caregiving, one-third of co-resident carers spent at least 50 hours a week on caring while more than half of non-resident carers devoted less than 5 hours a week to these activities. Anderson concludes, that while there is no necessary conflict between working and caregiving, carers often experience reduced opportunities in employment and may, particularly where their care responsibilities are heavy, leave economic employment altogether. For example, two-thirds of German carers of working age were in employment when caring began with over a quarter subsequently giving up work and a quarter reducing working hours;[78] in a British survey twice as many carers gave up work or reduced hours as non-carers;[79] and a study in Spain reported that a quarter of carers had left employment or reduced hours.[80] This is substantiated by a pan-European survey which found that one quarter of the women and 15 per cent of the men felt that providing care to a dependent adult limited their employment opportunities. As in the USA, European carers reported lower incomes and reduced occupational and personal pensions.

Anderson[81] provides a clear summary of the contrasting context in both the USA and the UK to elder care and employment, arguing that, unlike the EU, corporate America has woken up to the pressures that its (valued) employees face in caring for elderly relatives:

> To retain skilled employees and to maintain productivity, it does appear that a growing number of US companies, albeit mainly the bigger household names (e.g. AT&T, IBM, Hewlett Packard, Bank of Boston), are providing support. These developments are usually characterized as: policies – for work organization and working time, particularly for different forms of flexible working hours and flexible location, such as homeworking; services – typically for information, advice and referral, but also including support to develop community services, transport for dependent relatives, and some workplace-based care provision; and benefits – such as preferential rates for long-term care insurance that covers the older person, or cash compensation for time taken off to care.

However, as Anderson points out, the United States and the European Union present different contexts and prospects for the reconciliation of working and caring:

> In general, Europeans have more extensive support through social protection schemes and related community and care services – accepting that these are highly variable and may not be directed to the support of carers. Some of the private company initiatives from the USA may be neither necessary nor appropriate in the European context . . . In Europe, the emphasis has been upon working time and organization, good communication and explicit management support, rather than the development of special eldercare initiatives.

Financial transfers

Finally, there has been extensive work in the USA concerning financial transfers to older parents, as part of and as a substitution for actual physical care. As we described earlier, there is generally a higher acceptance of such transfers as part of kin caregiving in the USA, than in Europe. As Smith[82] has recently suggested, the increase in better health at younger ages might possibly lead to a higher level of accumulated resources which can then be used to offset late life health changes. Similarly, Henretta reports recent analysis of AHEAD data[83] which shows how economic resources combine with kin resources and individual health to affect receipt of support. Having available informal help – measured by living with a spouse or others, or having children – increases the likelihood of receiving informal help and decreases the likelihood of receiving formal help (which would generally require payment or public programme use). Higher income is associated with a lower probability of receiving informal help but has no effect on formal help. Individual financial resources can facilitate the purchase of housing and personal services in assisted living facilities or the purchase of services in the community such as transportation or housekeeping. Indeed, while poverty among those aged 64 and under has increased slightly since the early 1970s, the poverty rate among the elderly population has declined because of the large real increases in Social Security during the 1970s,[84] the creation of a need-based Supplemental Security Income programme for the elderly, and the growing adequacy of occupational pensions and higher lifetime income streams.[85] In addition, the children of this older cohort have also benefited from increases in wealth and income. Henretta points out that lifetime incomes have risen in successive cohorts in the USA, peaking among the early baby boom cohort born before the mid-1950s.

Family caregivers

Throughout Europe and the USA, older people are increasingly looking to retain the status of independent adults, in control of their own resources. This is key to our understanding of the role of family, for as we shall now explore, we must move away from the stereotypical view of children as the primary caregivers for older adults, and begin to recognise that increasingly it is spouses who care for each other in later life. First, it is important not to confuse household with family. As Table 7.1 reveals for the UK, while there has been a steady decline, since the 1960s, in the percentages of elderly people in co-residence with their children, contact between parents and children who are not living in the parental household remains high.

However, it is not only children who provide care and support. Data from the Berlin Ageing Study (BASE), for example, has stressed the importance of extended kin in providing support for older generations. In particular, extended relatives may take over specific functions when central family relationships have dropped out from the older adult's

Table 7.1 *Percentage of parents aged 65 and over having contact with child*

Date	% of those aged over 65 with a living child, who are living with a child in UK	% of those aged over 65 with a living child, who are not living with a child in UK, seeing a child weekly in UK
1962 (Shanas)	42	77
1986 (ISSP)	13	69
1995 (British SA)	16	61
2002 (60+) ELSA	10	60

Source: Adapted from Murphy, 2004; ELSA, 2002.

Table 7.2 *Percentage giving care to older persons in England by age of carer*

Looked after	50–54	55–59	60–64	65–69	70–74	75–79	80+	Total
Men								
Spouse	3.4	4.7	5.8	5.8	9.3	10.8	10.6	6.4
Children/grandchildren	4.5	4.0	5.4	4.8	4.2	1.4	0.5	3.9
Parent/parent-in-law	6.5	4.9	3.1	3.2	0.8	0.7	0.0	3.4
Other relative or friend	2.3	0.9	2.1	3.3	2.5	3.1	1.0	2.1
Women								
Spouse	4.8	5.7	7.5	8.0	8.0	8.3	4.2	6.5
Children/grandchildren	7.8	8.8	11.0	9.0	4.7	3.1	1.1	6.8
Parent/parent-in-law	11.2	11.1	6.9	3.4	1.0	0.0	0.1	5.5
Other relative or friend	3.2	2.3	4.3	5.1	3.6	4.8	3.2	3.7

Source: ELSA, 2002.

personal network.[86] Lang's analysis[87] suggested that such relatives needed a stimulus to engage, and the degree of interaction was closely dependent on the stimuli – widowhood resulting in closer support from extended kin than loss of a sibling, for example. The extended kinship ties of older people:

> seem to entail a reserve potential of diverse functional transactions that can be activated in case of enhanced needs in later life due to social loss or owed to lifelong patterns of family structure. Findings are therefore also relevant to the understanding of future perspectives on the family, for example, with respect to possible increases of single households in some European countries.[88]

However, perhaps of most importance is the role that spouses play in providing informal care to each other. As Table 7.2 and Table 7.3 reveal for England and Germany respectively, spouses provide a large percentage of care to each other. In particular, over a quarter of men in the German study were giving care to a spouse, and 10 per cent of men in their eighties

Table 7.3 *Percentage giving care to older persons in Germany by age of older person and relationship to carer*

| | Persons in need of care | |
Relationship	65–79	80+
Spouse (female)	39	12
Spouse (male)	22	5
Daughter	24	44
Son	2	6
Daughter-in-law	6	17
Son-in-law	0	0
Other relatives	6	9
Friends/neighbours	2	7

Note: Three-quarters of these carers stated that they were available to care 24 hours a day.
Source: Dohner, H. and Kofahl, 2001.

Table 7.4 *Hours spent caregiving by male and female carers in England by age*

Hours spent caring (% caring in last week)	50–54	55–59	60–64	65–69	70–74	75–79	80+	Total
Men								
Up to 19 hours	65.6	57.9	55.2	51.0	47.2	36.5	23.6	52.5
20–49 hours	15.5	18.8	16.2	16.7	18.9	15.2	11.3	16.5
50–167 hours	4.2	5.4	4.7	2.2	3.9	5.2	6.0	4.4
168 hours (constant)	14.7	18.0	23.9	30.1	30.0	43.1	59.1	26.6
Women								
Up to 19 hours	56.1	51.6	51.2	51.6	40.1	47.1	44.1	50.7
20–49 hours	20.1	17.0	18.3	19.5	19.5	14.2	14.7	18.2
50–167 hours	4.1	6.5	5.4	3.9	9.4	5.3	5.9	5.5
168 hours (constant)	19.8	24.8	25.0	25.0	31.0	33.3	35.3	25.6

Source: ELSA, 2002.

in England are primary caregivers for their wives. Furthermore, as is clear from Table 7.4, of those men who were caring for more than 19 hours, 60 per cent were caring full-time.

Is there any evidence of a change in kin attitudes towards providing care?

There has long been strong theoretical support for the notion of declining kin willingness to provide care for older relatives, particularly in association with modernisation theory.[89] The work of Goode[90] was particularly influential here, with his thesis that while the extended family encouraged respect and prestige for elders, the conjugal or nuclear family not only lacked the resources to provide care and support for elderly dependants, but also its very encouragement of independent living left older dependent adults in an ambiguous position. Such ideas were furthered by historical research which revealed the apparent transition in developed countries from familism to individualism. Hareven's detailed analysis of nineteenth-century New England families, for example, suggested that individuals subordinated their own needs to those of the family out of a sense of responsibility, affection and obligation, rather than with the expectation of eventual gain. This sense of obligation towards kin was a manifestation of family culture, and took priority over individual needs and personal happiness.[91]

Hareven's key study, based on life history interviews with two cohorts of New England children who were born between 1910–19 and 1920–29 reveals how both these cohorts were, to some degree, transitional between a milieu of deep involvement with extended kin, reinforced by strong family-orientated values, and the more individualistic ways of life and values that emerged after the Second World War. Yet neither cohort was free from the complexities of caring for elderly parents: the older cohort accepted their lot with resignation, the younger cohort with guilt. This work clearly highlights the complexity of decisions regarding the needs of family members. These are not only set obligations and responsibilities defined by cultural norms, but are also based on individual judgements which take into account both personal needs and resources, as well as those of other family members. In addition, Harevan provides a method of understanding how inter- and intra-generational mutual support develops over a person's lifetime, and how such support is shaped by historical circumstances.

However, Harevan's work[92] also highlights the considerable diversity in cultural obligations to family members, and how these family obligations change over time. Following a life course and historical perspective, she argues that we need to unravel the three connected times in an individual life: *historical time* – historical circumstances such as migration, war, social and cultural change, economic collapse or boom; *individual time* – an individual's timetable of life transitions such as marriage, childbearing, retirement; and *family time* – the manner in which the individual timetables of family members are woven together to optimise family circumstances. Exploration of experiences across the life course thus enables us to consider patterns of support achieved in old age in the light of the social, economic and cultural conditions that the respective cohorts encountered over their lives.[93]

Contrastingly, McFarlane's[94] work on the origins of English individualism, concludes that the English family has from at least medieval times operated primarily on individual rather than collective principles. However, there is evidence that within contemporary Britain family responsibilities towards older parents are confused. As Finch's Family Obligations Survey[95] revealed, there is little normative agreement in Britain on the obligations and responsibilities of adults towards other adult kin. In addition, norms relating to care obligations also vary between cohorts, each cohort carrying not only its own demography, but also its own life history.

Regardless of cultural origins, in both the USA and the UK, as in other western societies, by the late twentieth century the concept of full personhood was closely tied to the ability to live alone.[96] Thus the ideal of the nuclear family household makes living in an independent household an indicator of full adult status, something which young people strive for and older people resist giving up. This results in problematic re-entry into an extended family household following widowhood or increasing frailty.

There has also been extensive debate concerning the role of political and legal structures in transforming national patterns of kinship ties and obligations. The traditional framework for understanding welfare regimes comes from Esping-Anderson's analysis,[97] which identified liberal, social democratic and conservative states. Liberal welfare states rely on full employment and market mechanisms and institutions to support the welfare of its populations. Such countries have means-tested assistance, modest universal transfers and modest social insurance plans, for example, Canada, Australia and the USA. Social democratic welfare states, such as the Scandinavian countries, use high levels of taxation and generous universal services and benefits to promote a high level of social equality. Conservative states institutionalise the family as the primary welfare provider. These include the southern European countries, such as Italy and Spain. However, these definitions have come under criticism, most notably for failing to recognise the transference of policy between countries, thereby blurring such rigid distinctions.[98]

More recent work has identified subtle differences in family responsibilities. While Segalen[99] perceives an increasing blurring of family patterns within the EU, Reher's[100] work on family contact, still identifies a clear distinction between the 'weak-family' societies of northern Europe and North America, and the 'strong-family' Mediterranean societies. Murphy's[101] analysis of family contact, using ISSP data, supports many of Reher's[102] propositions, though he stresses the fluidity and rapid change of such kin contact. This analysis closely supports Millar's[103] research into how family obligations are defined in law and policy in the 15 EU countries and Norway. Within the EU as a whole, there appears to be a spectrum of responsibility, defined at the national level. At either end stand the Scandinavians, whose intergenerational contract has allowed the development of policy focused on individual entitlements and citizenship rights for all, those in need expecting to receive state rather than family assistance, and the southern Europeans who expect to rely almost exclusively upon the extended family. The obligations of those in the UK and Eire are nuclear family-based, and mixed.

Alongside this, runs the empirical evidence discussed in Chapter 1, which highlighted that, regardless of theoretical notions of norms and normative behaviour, the family still acts in a supportive manner towards its kin, in times of need. Thus Scandinavian research has highlighted the importance of kinship within a modern welfare state and indicated both increased contact with family members and a significant move towards a more positive view of the family as a supportive institution.[104] Data from northern Europe suggests that the vast majority of mid-life adult children would provide for their parents in a variety of practical ways. Southern European societies still support strong imperatives to care for needy relatives, and even US families continue to reveal a strong sense of obligation held between the generations.[105]

In conclusion

Households and family networks are becoming smaller; adult unions are changing and life course changes, particularly for women, are reducing opportunities for caregiving. However, family ties are remaining strong both in terms of contact and attitude and older adults are providing, and will continue to provide, major sources of elder care in particular as their healthy life expectancy increases. Such care will increasingly come from spouses rather than children as the life trajectory and demands across the life course change, particularly for women. In addition, increasing healthy life expectancy not only delays morbidity, but also increases the number of healthy late life carers. Families are also providing support through reciprocal financial transfers. The indications are that families will continue to care, but that older people themselves will also become increasingly independent in their care and support needs.

Notes

1 The AHEAD Study is a prospective panel survey of the US population born in 1923. The Health and Retirement Study (HRS) is a parallel study of a younger cohort – persons born between 1931 and 1941. In relation to the above question, these data provide insight into the number of children available to provide care in successive cohorts. The English Longitudinal Study of Ageing (ELSA) is closely based on HRS, and is a survey of people born before March 1952.
2 Kinsella and Gist, 1998.
3 Smith et al., 1999.
4 Marmot et al., 2003.
5 Liu et al., 2000; Manton and Land, 2000; Manton, 2000.
6 Manton et al., 1993; Manton et al., 1997; Crimmins et al., 1997; Fogel and Costa, 1997; Costa, 1998.
7 Johnson and Lo Sasso, 2004.
8 ibid.
9 Smith and Kington, 1997.
10 Leeson, 2004.

11 Lothian et al., 2001.
12 Harper and Leeson, 2002; Harper and Leeson, 2003.
13 Harper and Leeson, 2002.
14 Harper and Leeson, 2003.
15 Department of Health and Department of Social Security, 1989.
16 Department of Health, 2001.
17 Department of Health, 2000.
18 DETR, 2001.
19 Philp, 2001.
20 Jani-Le Bris, 1993.
21 ibid.
22 Chwalow et al., 2001.
23 ibid.
24 Dohner and Kofahl, 2001.
25 ibid.
26 Lamura et al., 2001.
27 ibid.
28 Lamura et al., 2001, p. 115.
29 Reported in Lamura et al., 2001.
30 Bein et al., 2001.
31 ibid., p. 173.

32 Bein et al., 2001, p. 176.
33 Figueiro and Sousa, 2001, p. 200.
34 ibid.
35 Triantafillou and Mestheneos, 2001.
36 ibid., p. 84.
37 Hassle, 2001.
38 Liu et al., 2000.
39 ibid.
40 Adam and Hutton, 2001; Dohner and Kofahl, 2001.
41 Grundy, 1987; Grundy and Harrop, 1992.
42 Scott et al., 1999.
43 Bornat et al., 1999; Dimmock et al., 2004.
44 Askham, 1998; Wenger, 1992; Finch, 1989; Harper, 1987; Cicirelli, 1983; Ettner, 1996; Mui, 1995; Silverstein and Waite, 1993; Sloan et al., 1997; Spitze and Logan, 1989; Spitze and Logan, 1990; Spitze and Logan, 1992; Stern, 1995; Wolf and Soldo, 1994.
45 McGlone et al., 1999; Wenger, 1984; Allan, 1985; Townsend, 1957; Murphy, 2001.
46 HRS, 2004.
47 This scenario has been questioned as to whether there is sufficient recognition of the full extent of services provided by parents to their children, even in extreme old age.
48 Harper and Lund, 1990; Ikels (2004) for example, suggests that family structure, including number and proximity of children, and cultural values, which determine the kin relationship, gender, or numerical positioning of the selected child, are primary variables in many societies, followed by family history and personal influences.
49 McGarry, 1998.
50 Anderson, 2004.
51 Arber and Ginn, 1992; Twigg, 1992; Askham, 1998.
52 Harper, 2004.
53 Haskey, 1998.
54 Wolf and Soldo, 1994.
55 Wachter, 1997.
56 Grundy, 1999.
57 Anderson, 2001.
58 Soldo and Hill, 1995.
59 Henretta, 1998.
60 Wachter, 1997.
61 Henretta et al., 2001.
62 Schoen and Weinick, 1993.
63 Henretta, 1998.
64 ibid.
65 Wolf et al., 1997.
66 Henretta et al., 1997.
67 US Bureau of the Census, 1998.
68 Johnson and Lo Sasso, 2004.
69 Wolf and Soldo, 1994.
70 National Survey of Families and Households (NSFH); Survey of Income and Program Participation (SIPP); National Longitudinal Survey of Mature Women; National Long Term Care Survey (NLTCS) and its companion Informal Caregivers Survey.
71 Anderson, 2004.
72 European Commission, 2000a.
73 European Commission, 2000b.
74 European Commission, 1999.
75 Department for Education and Employment, 2000.
76 Corti and Dex, 1995.
77 Humphrey et al., 2003.
78 Schneekloth and Potthoff, 1993.
79 Corti and Dex, 1995.
80 Larizgoitia-Jauregi, 2001.
81 Anderson, 2004.
82 Smith and Kington, 1997.
83 Norgard and Rodgers, 1997.
84 Ippolito, 1990.
85 Burkhauser et al., 1988.
86 Litwak, 1985.
87 Lang et al., 1998; Lang, 2000; Lang, 2004.
88 Lang, 2004.
89 Cowgill and Holmes, 1972.
90 Goode, 1964.
91 Hareven, 1982; Hareven, 1996.
92 Hareven, 1978; Hareven, 1982; Hareven, 1986; Hareven, 1996.
93 See also Elder, 1978.
94 MacFarlane, 1978.
95 Finch, 1989.
96 Keith et al., 1994, p. 20.
97 Esping-Andersen, 1990.
98 Salais, 2003.
99 Segalen, 1997.
100 Reher, 1998.
101 Murphy, 2001.
102 Reher, 1998.
103 Millar, 1998.
104 Leeson, 2005.
105 Bengtson et al., 2002.

8
Late life economic security in developing countries

For the past fifty years, older people have been all but invisible in international development policy and practice . . . development policy has been focused on achieving economic growth and increased productivity. Older people, typically characterized as economically unproductive, dependent and passive, have been considered at best as irrelevant to development and at worst a threat to the prospects for increased productivity. As a result, development policy in the post-war era has excluded and marginalized people purely on the basis of their age.[1]

The effects of population ageing on the developing world

As we noted in Chapter 1, there are actual benefits from population ageing in the developed world – more age balance, mature less volatile societies, with an emphasis on age integration. The issues will be very different elsewhere and here lies a fourth myth – that the developing world will escape from demographic ageing. Instead, the massive size of ageing facing these countries is potentially devastating with estimates of 1 billion older people within 30 years. Perhaps most significant of all is the speed at which these countries are ageing. As Figure 1.1 in Chapter 1 illustrates, while it took around 50 years for most of the countries in the developed world to move from 7 per cent to 14 per cent of their population over age 65, in the case of Sweden 85 years, and France 115 years, many developing countries will achieve this in half the time.

Not only is such ageing occurring at a far greater pace than we have seen in Western nations, but few, if any, developing countries have the economic development and infrastructure necessary to provide widespread public pensions and health care to these growing elderly populations. Around one quarter of the world's older population live in absolute poverty, the majority in developing countries. For many of these, late life poverty is but the end of a lifetime of poverty.

The poverty and lack of basic needs of these people are clear from the Human Development Indicators.[2] Table 8.1, for example, shows the contrasting access to basic sanitation and clean water.

Nearly half the population of much of *Asia* live in poverty, most of whom have no access to basic sanitation.[3] Significant proportions of the population in some of these countries, such as Afghanistan (75 per cent),[4] Bangladesh (55 per cent) and Pakistan (45 per cent), have no access to health services, 88 per cent of Afghans, and 59 per cent of Nepalese have no access to safe drinking water. Bangladesh has 45 million illiterate

Table 8.1 *Access to sanitation and water*

	% population using adequate sanitation facilities	% population using improved water facilities
OECD	100	100
Developing countries	52	78
Arab States	81	86
East Asia/Pacific	48	75
Latin America/Caribbean	78	85
South Asia	39	89
Sub-Saharan Africa	55	54
Central/Eastern Europe/CIS	N/A	N/A

Source: Human Development Report, 2002.

adults, Pakistan 48 million, and India 300 million. Child mortality in the region runs at 8 per cent. In *Africa*, between one-third and one half of the population of Sub-Saharan Africa have no access to basic sanitation, safe drinking water, or health services, rising to nearly three-quarters of the population of countries such as Chad, Zaire and Somalia. One-third of the adults in Egypt, Ethiopia and Morocco and half in Niger are illiterate. Infant mortality runs at 17 per cent. While the people of *South America* fare slightly better, nearly two-thirds of the population of El Salvador and Guatemala have no access to health services, and 40 per cent no access to safe drinking water, while 45 per cent of people in Bolivia have access to neither safe drinking water nor sanitation, rising to 75 per cent for both in Haiti.

For these societies trying to tackle the issues of old age then, this forms just one component of providing for the many who cannot provide for themselves – through childhood, sickness, disability or old age. Faced with such extremes, issues around old age have not been a major concern for the governments of developing countries.

Schulz[5] has recently highlighted four main reasons for this. First, as discussed in Chapter 2, in developing countries older people currently remain a small proportion of the total population. Older people may be among the most vulnerable populations in the world, yet faced with such massive problems of poverty and deprivation, their needs are seen by many governments as but a small part of national want. Indeed, among the most vulnerable groups – children, women, those with disabilities and elderly people – it is elderly people that governments appear most frequently to place last. However, it is not only individual governments who have taken this stance, the world development agenda must also bear responsibility.

Second, given the predominately rural nature of these societies, most of the population are outside the formal wage economy, involved in informal labour and thus able to keep active, until disability or extreme frailty occurs. In these societies, families remain the predominant providers, supporters and caregivers of older people when such need arises. Indeed, more than half the world's old people depend on families[6] and so the material security of older adults is intimately meshed with that of their extended families. Older people are often systematically excluded from access to basic services and support, these actions justified by arguments concerning the need not to jeopardise the traditional family and community support networks of older people.[7] Third, national developmental priorities favour investing in the long-term potential of younger people. Finally, older people are considered to be resistant to change, less adaptable and thus an impediment to development.

Yet, older adults are susceptible to a range of factors which make them particularly vulnerable and should thus move them up the development agenda. These include: poor health and frailty, compounded by inadequate or inaccessible health services; lack of family or community support and/or large numbers of dependants; landlessness, limited skills or limited capital to invest in productive activity; and low status.[8]

The 40 million Africans who are over age 60 already comprise 7 per cent of Africa's population, forecast to rise to 102 million by the mid-century, of whom 22 million will be over 80 years of age.[9] As Darkwa and Muzibuko[10] point out, this elderly population is very unevenly distributed across the continent. While the majority reside in rural areas, the percentage in urban areas is projected to reach just under half, 42 per cent, by 2015. Currently, the Southern African region has the highest percentage of its population aged 60 or over, with around 7 per cent of South Africa aged 60 or over, 6.7 per cent of Lesotho, and 5.4 per cent of Botswana. The Northern African region has around 5.9 per cent, with just under 5 per cent for Eastern and Western Africa. Most of these older people have no access to a regular income or pension, while those few, mainly private sector workers, who do have access to pensions, receive low benefits which are continually eroded by inflation. These are also often difficult to collect because of complex bureaucracy or limitations of access due, for example, to residential isolation. In Kenya, for example, it can take up to ten years after eligibility, for a pension to be processed.[11] There is also low access to formal health care services and high incidences of malnutrition. Alongside this is an alarming rise in vulnerability to abuse, due in part to a breakdown in traditional values, which in some cultures protected elders, but also due to new myths such as that sexual intercourse with an old person can cure HIV/AIDS. Older Africans are also increasingly carrying the burden of coping with the African HIV/AIDS crisis, supporting and caring for their children as they die of the disease, taking on primary economic and social responsibility for their orphaned grandchildren, as well as finding themselves increasingly vulnerable to the disease itself.

The Asian/Pacific region, home to 600 million older people, is the most rapidly ageing world region, with 20 per cent of the projected population in 2050 over the age of 60, accounting for two-thirds of the world's 2 billion elders.[12] Despite the tremendous diversity in the region, older people throughout Asia are consistently and disproportionately among those living in greatest poverty.[13] The level of literacy and education is particularly low among these older Asians, many of whom find themselves isolated in rural areas or impoverished urban communities. Over half the Asian elderly population live in India and the People's Republic of China. Of India's 70 million elders, aged over 65, 80 per cent live in rural areas, 40 per cent live below the poverty line, with a further third just above.[14] Levels of poverty and dependency are related to social class and caste[15] but around half of all older people are fully dependent on others, with a further 20 per cent stating that they are partially so.[16] The majority live with their families, and are thus reliant on family economic success, and at times of crisis, and when the family is under stress, priority is generally given to the well-being of younger dependants.[17] Indian older women are particularly vulnerable. They are likely to be widowed, dependent, and have limited income or control over assets.[18]

Around 70 million older people live in the *Central and Eastern Europe* region, some 15 per cent of the total population, forecast to rise to 122 million within the next 50 years. A recent Help the Aged report gives a stark description of their lives:

> Older people in the region have seen the disintegration of systems that they helped to build, and that they expected to provide for them in old age. They have seen their children migrate; they have seen their opportunities to support themselves independently fall away as unemployment and inflation have taken their toll[19] . . . Disillusionment, powerlessness and bewilderment characterize many of this older population.[20]

Many of these older people are the generation who were displaced during the Second World War, victims of Stalin's mass deportations, and who lived through the upheaval of the post-war conflicts within the former Soviet Union. Most striking is the rapid fall in life expectancy. Male life expectancy fell during the early 1990s, for example, by some five years in Russia and the Ukraine, and four years in the Baltic countries. This seems to be exacerbated by the stress of the transition,[21] leading to excessive alcohol consumption, increased violence and accidental death, and an upsurge in cardiovascular and circulatory disease. It may also be related to general environmental deterioration and pollution in the years preceding transition. In addition, the once sound guarantee of strong pension benefits after retirement has disappeared as the soviet-style non-indexed pensions have plummeted in value following post-communist inflation.

Seven per cent of the world's older population live in Latin America and the Caribbean, some 41 million in 2002. By 2050 the number of those aged over 60, is forecast to quadruple to 181 million, of whom 37 million will be over the age of 80. While there will be more young people than old in the world until 2050, the crossover will occur earlier in Latin America, and by 2030 those over 60 will outnumber those under 15. The problems experienced by elderly people in this region mirror those in the rest of the developing world. They experience high levels of poverty and low pension coverage, with two-thirds of older people having no guaranteed income, inadequate social protection, deteriorating family support structures, and low levels of government interest or investment in their needs.[22] Older women are particularly vulnerable in this respect, as they are more likely to have had little or no education, and to have worked in the informal and domestic sector with no eligibility for pensions, and few savings. The massive rural migration of younger people into the cities during the past few decades, has had a significant impact on older populations in many of these countries. For example, while less than half of Bolivia's total population are now rural, nearly two thirds of the older population live in rural areas. Many of the region's rural inhabitants are older women, who find themselves isolated in abandoned rural communities, unable to understand the complex paperwork required in many South American countries in order to access age-related benefits and services.[23] In addition, recent environmental degradation and poor farming techniques in this region have left these rural populations to survive on unproductive land, further compounding their problems. These difficulties are particularly acute among the older indigenous populations who make up large proportions of the central American states, the Amazon basin, Bolivia and Columbia. A recent study suggested, for example, that three-quarters of those over age 60 in Bolivia had a native first language.[24]

At the turn of the twenty-first century, however, as the global ageing revolution is at last gaining recognition, and with its major impact in developing countries beginning to be acknowledged, the needs and capacities of older people are starting to appear on the development agenda. It is also now widely, though not exclusively, accepted that far from being an obstacle to economic progress, social security in its broadest sense encourages such progress as people are relieved of the anxiety of poverty.[25]

Broadening social security

There has long been interest in the appropriateness and possible development of social security for the developing countries. In the 1960s, debate was divided between those who believed that social security programmes had their own inbuilt momentum which would eventually lead to universal coverage,[26] and those who argued that this would not occur until a certain level of economic and political development had been reached.[27] It is now generally accepted that with improved health and welfare of the population economic production can improve and social security will also aid in the much-needed reduction in fertility and rapid population growth. The provision of social security for the older population is seen as twofold. First, older people will benefit from the broad population-based initiatives to provide basic food, sanitation, drinking water and health services. Second, specific targeted systems will provide support and care for frail older people per se. The challenge here is how to combine state-based and community family-based systems. We shall draw both on the literature on general social security and old age pensions, in particular, as many of the debates are linked.

Social security

The concept of social security is to use social means to prevent deprivation, and vulnerability to deprivation.[28] This has been extended over the twentieth century from notions of providing relief, compensation and pension rights to those unable to earn a living, to cover a spectrum of now accepted social rights. Sitting alongside the right to work lies the right to acceptable housing and environment, standard minimum income, and access to health and social services, including education. However, key here is the definition of deprivation. The traditional *utilitarian notion*, underlying much of welfare economics, is to define this in terms of a subjective acceptance of one's state.[29] An individual may be objectively materially deprived in relation to others but apparently satisfied with their state. As Sen points out, this has been used by governments over the world to justify non-intervention on the ground of non-demand. A second definition has been the relationship of income or lack of income to the quality of life. This has been developed into the *basic needs approach*, which lays down the minimal amounts of necessary goods (housing, food, etc.) required to avoid deprivation. This again is problematic, as the conversion of such commodities into quality of life will vary between individuals, societies and economies. A third stance identified by Sen is the *living standards and capabilities approach*. This identifies certain basic activities and assesses the capability of individuals to perform these chosen functions. This approach of addressing capabilities and functions can be used to evaluate poverty and deprivation, focusing on, for example, capabilities to be adequately nourished, to be comfortably clothed, to avoid escapable morbidity and preventable mortality:

> Seeing poverty as a capability failure may, at first sight, appear quite a departure from the traditional idea of poverty, which is typically associated with a shortage of income . . . however, the . . . ultimate concern of poverty analysis has to be with the deprivation of living conditions, for example the lack of nourishment (rather than of the income to buy nutrients), exposure to preventable diseases (rather than the inability to buy medicine), and so on.[30]

Moving from the conceptual to the stance of public policy, the provision of economic security in late life has been caught up in the broader debate concerning welfare provision in the developing countries. This questions whether countries require separate and directed welfare policies rather than expecting that such provision will be taken care of through general economic growth and expansion.[31] While this question is clearly the focus of debate in development economics, the arguments of Dreze and Sen are forcefully put. They point out that there are considerable dangers in relying on economic growth *per se*:

> Any reliance on GDP per head either as a means of protection or as a vehicle of promotion, can be extremely treacherous, partly because of distributional inequalities, but also because of the limitations of private markets in generating good living conditions.[32]

There is also significant evidence that rich countries did not overcome their historical deprivation by economic growth alone; rather, conscious public efforts to enhance living conditions have played a substantial part in that achievement.

A commonly held counter-argument to this, however, is that developing countries cannot afford to develop their own welfare systems. However, while it may be true that complex and expensive programmes such as those developed in western-style countries, might be difficult to replicate, these are by no means the only possible models, or indeed the only suitable welfare models for new developing economies. Indeed, as Atkinson and Hills[33] point out, the government supported, comprehensive programmes of industrialised nations, based on poverty lines and safety nets, are inappropriate for the developing world. Here resource constraints, the low level of institutional development and the relative powerlessness of the needy require provision with different structures and forms.

Indeed, the very factors that make the provision of widespread public welfare programmes essential – high incidence and severity of deprivation, limited development of formal social security systems, limited or inappropriate coverage of public support, resource constraints, low levels of institutional development and the relative powerlessness of much of the population due to poverty – are the same factors that make their implementation problematic.[34] Furthermore, Burgess and Stern[35] argue that such western models instate programmes which redistribute resources to the better off, away from the poorer sections of the community. They call for programmes with a wide perspective which take into account the complex relationships between kin, household and family support, and their interactions with state provision.

Burgess and Stern then attempt to theorise an appropriate pattern of welfare provision for developing countries. Their starting point is the successful prevention by social means of very low standards of living, irrespective of whether these are the result of chronic deprivation or temporary adversity. These social means include direct interventions, alterations to market functioning, and redistributive policies, and focus on the role of public action at the state, community and family level. In other words, this is a broader concept than that typically understood in the developed world, with its emphasis on specific public programmes involving social assistance and social insurance, and indeed as currently being implemented in many developing countries. Burgess and Stern thus move the debate beyond action enacted or imposed by governments to include household and community contributions, diversification of economic activity and improvement of market functioning, and also include the role of public pressure: 'The definition of social security suggested here includes public action at the household, community and state level to remove or reduce deprivation and vulnerability.'

Who then, ask Burgess and Stern, should supply such social security – the family, extended or nuclear, the village, the social or religious group, the employer, the city, the government, a private organisation? Efficiency, obligations and incentives all contribute to the answer. For example, inter- and intra-household transfers already provide significant forms of social security in developing countries. Transfers between related or proximate individuals, for example, mitigate the risks associated with loss of income in old age and with disability and unemployment.[36] However, insurance is best provided by those outside the family or even community, as adverse factors may well affect not only the family members in distress, but also those within the community or family who might be providing the insurance.

It is, therefore, clear that a multifaceted approach to the issue is required; one that combines individual contribution, via work or saving, some form of pension-style provision, and family and community support. The possibility of saving for late life is so limited for the vast majority of these populations as to currently have a negligible input. The contribution of older workers, both to their own economic security and to the collective economy, remains high.

Late life work and the economic contribution of older workers

Major difficulties in fully understanding the economic contribution of older people in developing countries arise due to limited theoretical development and lack of sound empirical evidence. While we have a growing source of small-scale, high quality, qualitative studies, and a large mass of anecdotal cases, we still lack large-scale rigorous quantitative data sets at the local, national and regional level, though these are now being developed and collected. The technical difficulties of this data collection, however, which can influence its reliability are still an issue. However, it is clear that high rates of economic participation by older men and women are common to most, though not all, developing countries (Fig. 8.1). This, combined with far lower life expectancy, means that the period of lengthy retirement found in OECD countries is not a typical experience in these developing countries. Though data are scarce, estimates[37] suggest that half of the population in developing countries is economically active throughout their sixties, a third in their early seventies and around 20 per cent of those over age 75. As is clear from Fig. 8.1, while there has been some decline in late life economic activity in these countries, labour force participation for both men and women over age 65 remains relatively high. Though rates for women remain considerably lower, they are increasing.

This leads to a significant impact by older workers, far in excess of the relative national impact in developed countries. In addition, there is the contribution older people make to the informal economy. Older people are frequently responsible for such tasks as cooking, childcare, water collection and, throughout the developing world, often assuming full responsibility for the home thereby releasing the younger adults for economic employment. As HelpAge International have recently stated:

> Indeed despite chronic poverty, the majority of older people in the developing world
> support themselves and contribute to their families and communities. The growing
> number of older people, particularly older women, who are responsible for raising

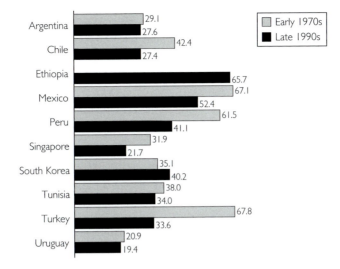

Argentina — 29.1 / 27.6
Chile — 42.4 / 27.4
Ethiopia — 65.7
Mexico — 67.1 / 52.4
Peru — 61.5 / 41.1
Singapore — 31.9 / 21.7
South Korea — 35.1 / 40.2
Tunisia — 38.0 / 34.0
Turkey — 67.8 / 33.6
Uruguay — 20.9 / 19.4

☐ Early 1970s
■ Late 1990s

Note: Data for Ethiopia in the early 1970s are not available.

Figure 8.1 *Labour market participation rates in less developed world, men aged 65+ in selected countries.*
Source: Kinsella and Velkoff, 2001.

children in communities afflicted by disease, conflict and migration, requires policy changes to help this age group contribute as much as they can for as long as they are able.[38]

There is, however, considerable variation between countries. So, while the Asian countries of Indonesia, Pakistan, Thailand and the Philippines maintain participation rates of over 50 per cent for men into their late sixties, countries in the Latin American region such as Argentina and Chile fall to below a third. Similarly, the contrast between rural and urban areas is striking. In India, for example, 90 per cent of Indian workers remain in the agricultural sector, where there is no retirement age,[39] and there is thus a high level of economic activity in later life. Consequently, while nearly half of urban elderly men receive a pension, this falls to less than one fifth in rural areas.[40] In addition, only the 10 per cent of the working population employed in the organised sector, comprising mainly government employees, are subject to mandatory retirement, at age 60 for national government positions and age 55–60 for state government employees.[41] Despite this, there is a long religious and cultural notion of retirement. Two of the four *ashramas* of the lifespan cover old age – *vanaprastha*, the age of retirement, typically 60–80, and *sanya*, the time of renunciation, 80–100.

Various theories have been put forward to explain these trends,[42] including labour market opportunities and demands, variation in pension coverage, health status and family factors. At one level there is evidence that many of the patterns observed in developed countries are replicated in developing countries. In the 1980s, for example, a World Health Organisation survey[43] of labour force participation of those over age 60 in the Western Pacific, covering Fiji, Korea, Malaysia and the Philippines, identified the factors of greater household wealth, being in a skilled or white-collar job, and health limitations as all encouraging withdrawal from the labour force.[44]

Others have highlighted the role of modern urban development in rendering older people's skills outdated.[45] In particular, modern market incentives, which promote efficiency, innovation and growth, also cause labour dislocation, unemployment, social disruption and inequality, with older people being particularly vulnerable to these factors. In the People's Republic of China, for example, the introduction of an open system of labour market mobility and job choice has removed the guarantee of lifetime employment. Even in rural areas, new agricultural practices now compete against the traditional, and as communal land plots are removed, entire families dependent on these find their livelihood declining, leaving little surplus for those not able to support themselves.[46]

However, there are large cultural as well as social and economic factors behind retirement decisions in these countries. As McCallum[47] points out, using evidence from the same WHO study, within the Pacific Asian region alone, there are complex interactions of ethnicity, socio-economic status, gender, rural/urban residence, cultural norms, family wealth and available sources of income. Thus within Fiji, Malaysia, the Philippines and Korea, older migrants and ethnic minorities are more likely than others to be working after age 60. This preference for work is partly explained by the increased work ethic of those trying to establish themselves in a new country, but also due to exclusions from certain labour market sectors, in particular the public sector, which typically carries the best pension provision. The exception is the Chinese Malaysians who are more likely to be reliant on families, due to the cultural Chinese norm regarding the family, whereby older Chinese reach an age when they expect to be taken care of, regardless of their level of functional health.[48] Family support is also strong among the Melanesian populations, and in rural Fiji and Malaysia. The Chinese Malaysians, Indians and Fijians all prefer work to pensions, except for the Indian Malaysians, large numbers of whom work for the Railway and Public Works Department and are thus covered by good pension provision. In urban Fiji and Malaysia, provident funds provide good pensions to urban public workers but not rural workers, and only low level pensions to urban private sector workers. Throughout the region, wealthy families wish to avoid the 'shame' associated with their elders having to work, and so family support among these elite groups takes priority over other forms of income. Cultural norms and lack of pension coverage for women mean that they are more likely than older men to be working, often surviving on informal employment activities and remittances from children.

Similar examples come from Africa. Retirement is not widespread in Kenya, for example. Rural Kenyans do not retire from domestic or farm work,[49] but continue within a system that still relies heavily on the children and older people to sustain the household economy.[50] Women, in particular, continue with a heavy burden throughout their lives as they undertake the bulk of agricultural and domestic labour as well as caregiving.[51] Many male urban workers, who may have spent their lives in the formal sector, will return to their family homes in rural areas on old age, and take up a rural working pattern.[52]

While health allows, the !Kung hunter-gatherers of Botswana[53] remain active both as hunter-gatherers and in their newer roles as workers for their settled neighbouring Bantu pastoralists. However, from midlife onwards, as their physical prowess, strength and eyesight start to decline, male hunters increasingly choose to rely on the abilities of the younger !Kung to provide. Similarly, older frailer men find the physically demanding stock keeping work such as cattle driving difficult to undertake. However, neither the foraging nor settled older !Kung are able to amass the material basis required to control the services of young people, and so, with the onset of frailty dependence on kin becomes the norm. Successful ageing is thus seen as a balance between two factors – maintaining good health and physical stamina in order to provide for oneself, and maintaining close relationships with adult children so that they will provide when one is too frail. The concept of old age being associated with a period of leisure does not exist. !Kung life with its minimal division of labour, absence of a hierarchy whereby older people can obligate younger people to work for them, and scarcity of material resources ensures contributory activity until extreme frailty occurs. Furthermore, not only is there no occupational retirement, there is no social retirement or spatial retirement, in that older people cannot choose to withdraw from the public arena – they are not shielded by money or private housing from other members of the community.

> Consequently they are immersed in the everyday wear and tear of living. These experiences are undoubtedly psychologically and physically exhausting at times . . . On the other hand, the high rates of compulsory participation keep old people socially motivated and challenged by frequent novel events.[54]

Clearly, we need to take heed of detailed ethnographic studies to remind us of the dangers of formulating overarching strategies and schemes for material security in late life, based on national or even regional criteria, without taking into account the extreme complexity of existing provision, needs and capacities.

There are also conflicting views on the merits of encouraging or discouraging late life employment. Many view the economic independence that employment brings to older people as an essential component of the three pillars of security in old age: family, work and pension.[55] Others, however, have discussed the concept in similar terms to those used in developed countries. The argument here is that increases in worker longevity, combined with only slow falls in fertility and thus large cohorts of new workers, when put together with slow economic growth, are stretching the capacity of many economies in developing countries to absorb these additional workers. Measures such as lowering ages of retirement are thus mooted as a method of solving youth unemployment.[56]

Public programmes

As we discussed in Chapter 1, most people in developing countries have no prospect of a secure and sustainable income in their old age. Few of working age are covered by public programmes, less than 20 per cent of workers in many Latin American countries, less than 10 per cent in south-east Asia, and under 5 per cent in parts of Sub-Saharan Africa.[57] Such benefits are often limited to a few urban-based occupational groups, typically retired government staff or public enterprises. Such workers make up only a small percentage of the overall labour force and in most countries those in the informal sector – farm workers, day labourers, the self-employed and family workers – are excluded.[58] In addition, beyond the covered elite sector, there is no redistributive element. Indeed those who are uncovered may partially pay for those who are covered through higher prices of consumer goods, leading to even further inequity.

Public programmes in practice

Schulz[59] has classified the variety of current public programmes into ten broad categories. Most countries have legislated for *national social insurance pension schemes*, though coverage is minimal, and tends to favour the more affluent workers in urban-based regular employment. *Social allowances* or universal programmes provide benefits to all elderly residents or citizens regardless of means, while *social assistance programmes* provide benefits under means test of income and/or assets. *Social service programmes* operate similarly but through the provision of actual services. Both *employer liability programmes*, which legally require employers to provide benefits to their employees and/or dependants, and *occupational pension schemes*, usually requiring a joint employer/worker contribution, place emphasis on the employers. These in particular tend to be based in a limited number of typically urban or industrial occupations. Then there are a series of employer/worker savings schemes: *mandated defined contribution programmes*, requiring workers and/or employers to contribute to retirement accounts which are then invested on their behalf by a private institution, and *provident funds*, a similar scheme for workers, invested in the public sector. *Savings incentive programmes* encourage private savings for retirement, sometimes in tax beneficial retirement accounts which cannot be touched until a specified age. All these savings encouragement programmes are affected by the inherent difficulty of providing adequate late life benefits from compulsory savings. Finally, *mutual benefit societies* occupational groupings of members organised under the principles of mutual aid, provide benefits through collective decisions and member contributions. One of the oldest forms of old age provision in the developing countries, there is a large and growing number of these mutual aid societies, which are particularly appropriate to a predominantly rural agricultural-based society.

The role of colonial rule has significantly influenced formal social security pension development in the developing world. In particular, the provident funds, established in most British colonial countries, were developed with the expatriate workers in mind. Similarly, the mutual benefit societies, which were modelled on the friendly societies of France, Belgium and Great Britain.[60] As with the OECD countries discussed in Chapter 4, the complexity of the systems can be illustrated by looking at the variety of programmes in existence at our baseline year of 2000.

Africa

A recent review[61] identifies six distinct patterns of social security pension programmes in the continent. The proximity of North Africa to Europe encouraged the earliest and most comprehensive systems, based on social insurance principles, which have operated in Algeria, Egypt, Libya, Morocco and Tunisia since the 1950s. The West African Retirement Pensions Fund, a voluntary plan introduced during the French colonial period, was adopted in many French-speaking West African countries. Compulsory, mainly defined benefit programmes were introduced in the early 1960s following independence, benefits being determined by length of service and average earnings, with early retirement benefits from age 50. Provident funds were established in the British colonies of Gambia, Ghana, Kenya, Nigeria, Seychelles, Swaziland, Tanzania, Uganda and Zambia. Most of these have subsequently been converted to defined benefit programmes. Several countries in Southern Africa have only recently established social security pensions, for example, Lesotho, Malawi, Namibia, Botswana and Zimbabwe, the latter two as late as the 1990s, while others are yet to establish a social security programme for private workers. Armed conflicts have delayed progress or even destroyed elementary schemes, as in Sierra Leone, Eritrea, Ethiopia, Somalia, Democratic Republic of Congo and Liberia. Botswana, Namibia, Mauritius and the Seychelles have established universal flat rate pensions, while South Africa has recently introduced a means-tested pension. However, while pension and insurance programmes do exist in many African countries, based on European models and encouraged by international agencies, their provision almost exclusively covers the urban-based, formally employed old and thus only around 10 per cent of all workers are covered.

Asia and the Pacific

As already discussed, population ageing will affect Asia more than any other world region, with a predicted two-thirds of the world's older population resident here by the middle of the century. In those countries with strong Confucian values, the emphasis on family responsibility for older relatives has slowed the pace of social security pension programmes.[62] However, falling fertility and the disruption of extended families through urbanisation and consequent rural migration have led to smaller, dispersed family units, and recent years have seen the development of national pension provision, under the heading of supplementing traditional family support, such as those in South Korea in

1988 and Thailand in 1998.[63] However, many Asian countries have no mandatory social insurance programmes. These include the former British colonies mentioned earlier who provide old age benefits via provident funds. Others, such as South Korea, Pakistan, the Philippines and Vietnam have introduced social insurance pension programmes for employees. However, small enterprises, below ten workers, and the self-employed are typically excluded, and this is increasingly being recognised as a problem which must be addressed. Thus Malaysia has now extended its coverage to all employees, regardless of the size of the firm, South Korea now obliges rural workers and the self-employed to contribute to their scheme, and the Philippines has also extended coverage to the self-employed.

Despite extensive coverage of most urban workers in the early years of the People's Republic of China, economic changes since the Cultural Revolution, and particularly during the 1990s, have significantly reduced social security pensions coverage. Only state sector workers are covered, and since the height of central planning in the middle of the century, when around 90 per cent of all urban workers were in the state sector, this has fallen to around one half.

The Middle East

This region is unique in having relatively advanced economic development and, in some cases, very high wealth, and yet still retaining high fertility. Mortality is falling in line with the developed world, and male and female longevity is increasing. As a consequence, this region is facing population growth and an absolute ageing of its population, but not a relative ageing. Most countries are thus producing large numbers of young workers for their economies. All the countries of this region have now established similar traditional social insurance programmes, which is not surprising given their strong cultural similarities. All have been established since 1950, and all have adequate funding to pay current benefits. The first social security pension programme was established in Iraq, which converted its 1956 provident fund into a social security pension plan in 1964. Yemen and Oman were the last to follow, implementing programmes in 1991. Coverage rates are higher in this region than in Africa or Asia, but do not cover all workers, and generally exclude foreign workers, who make up a large percentage of the regions' labour market. Jordan is the exception to this, covering migrant workers on the same basis as its own citizens.

A striking feature of this region is the young ages at which pensions may be drawn down. This is indicative of the unusual features of the Middle Eastern labour market. Unlike other economically advanced nations, these are able to draw on a continuous source of internal young labour, and also currently on widely available young foreign workers. The debates concerning the retention of older workers have not surfaced here. While male retirement pension ages in Saudi Arabia, Bahrain and Iraq are 60, other countries have far lower ages, especially for women. Jordan has age 46 for both sexes, Yemen has age 45, Kuwait age 40 (but only for women) and the Lebanon has any age, so long as 20 years' contributions have been paid. Indeed in Bahrain, so long as 20 years' contributions have been paid, the pension can start to be drawn down, regardless of whether or not the worker has ceased working. In most systems, while both employee and employer contribute, the weighting is heaviest on the employer. In the wealthier countries income replacements are high. Kuwait, in particular, has generous pension benefits, so that a worker with 30 years service could expect to receive a replacement rate of up to 95 per cent of his last month's earnings, and this could be taken as early as age 50. Not unsurprisingly, the outlier here is Israel, which provides a flat rate defined benefit programme, benefits varying by marital status and number of children, with workers earning below half the average wage paying lower contributions.

Central and Eastern Europe

The social security pension programmes of these countries inherited systems designed to suit their former planned economies, programmes which provided nearly universal coverage, typically comprising pensions, benefits and health care. As a result, the region still bears the highest tax burden related to pension provision, at some 20 per cent.[64] These systems are currently in the process of adapting to more market orientated activities. While coverage was high during the former time of high public sector employment and collectivised agriculture, there was no automatic system for indexing benefits, as inflation was low and there was a presumption that wage differentials would be low. Universal coverage has now been significantly reduced as the private sector has entered the economy, and the impact of persistent inflation during the 1990s has been initially resolved through fixed amount increases. Lack of indexing to inflation with automatic adjustment, has led to a significant reduction in the once generous replacement levels. Indeed, in both Latvia and Lithuania, the effect of flat rate adjustments has converted earnings related pension schemes into flat rated ones, with workers receiving more or less the same pension regardless of previous earnings. While in the former Soviet Union countries, replacement has fallen to around 40 per cent. It is now widely recognised that the pension systems can no longer meet the needs of the retired population which is in itself growing rapidly, partly as a result of labour market changes encouraged by the development of the private sector. In many of these countries, disability benefits are being increasingly used as a means of supporting early retirement, with those on disability pension benefit now comprising around 40 per cent of all pensioners in Poland, and over 20 per cent in Croatia, Hungary, Macedonia and Slovakia.

Comprehensive reforms are, therefore, being implemented in Croatia, the Czech Republic, Hungary, Latvia and Poland. Some are adopting defined contribution programmes, and voluntary employer provided pensions are supplementing state pensions in the Czech Republic and Hungary. Croatia has introduced a mandatory fully funded tier, and Poland and Latvia have established notional plans – mandatory pay-as-you-go defined contribution plans. In Poland all new workers have to participate in a national account system and a fully funded account system, while in Latvia the worker's individual account balance is credited with a rate of return equal to the growth of the national taxable wage base. Hungary has established an individual account system to lie alongside their defined benefit scheme.

Latin America

The countries of South America have all had social security pension programmes for at least 50 years. Chile (1924), Uruguay (1928) and Brazil (1934) led the way, with the Caribbean countries finally achieving coverage in the 1970s – Trinidad and Tobago in 1971 and Antigua and Barbuda in 1972. The past 20 years have seen a revolution in South American pension provision, closely watched by the rest of the world. Chile was the pioneer with its move in 1981 from a government-controlled traditional social security pension system to an individual account-defined contribution programme, managed by private sector pension fund managers, with the benefits received dependent on the investment returns to the workers' accounts. Other countries have also now reformed including Peru (1992), Columbia and Argentina (1993), Uruguay (1995), Mexico (1996), Bolivia (1997), El Salvador (1998) and Nicaragua (2001). While most countries have retained their traditional social security pension programme in some form,[65] Chile, Bolivia, El Salvador and Mexico have closed theirs to all new entrants. Argentina and Uruguay have a mixed system, while low income workers in Uruguay only participate in the state-run programme; Columbia and Peru have competing programmes with workers able to select one.

Portuguese-speaking Brazil retains a traditional unfunded social security pension programme, administered by the federal government's Institute for National Social Security, to which about half the labour force of 60 million contribute with some 19 million beneficiaries. This provides generous benefits based on the final three years of those with 35 (men) or 30 (women) years' contributions. Alongside this there is a pension regime for government workers – contributors and recipients both number around 3 million – and a further 3 million workers are covered by funded pension plans to supplement the national system, currently with around 1.5 million recipients. However, despite the extensive provision of programmes over many years, due to the large informal sector in this region many workers are still not covered by social security pensions. This is either because their type of employment is not covered, or because their employers evade making contributions despite being obliged to by law. Furthermore, a recent World Bank study[66] concluded that Brazil's social security system faces problems of unsustainable fiscal deficits, inequalities and actuarial imbalances and lack of diversification due to low coverage of funded schemes.

As a recent World Bank report has commented:

> Latin America is the right place to study pension reform. The longest and most varied experience with the *multi-pillar approach* is in Latin America. Starting with Chile in 1981, twelve countries in the region have adopted multi-pillar arrangements, best distinguished from earlier systems by the prominence of a mandatory funded component, administered by purpose-built and dedicated private providers.[67] (Author's emphasis)

As the report continues, when judged against the objectives of the reform, the multi-pillar approach can be credited with some success. The fiscal burden of pensions has been reduced with total pension debt-to-GDP ratios falling in most of these countries. The reforms also appear to have improved the incentives to contribute to the formal system, and increased equity. The report concludes, however, that these successes should be qualified. In particular, two key issues cause concern: *coverage* has remained limited and, despite incentives, the general *savings* rate has been low:

> In Colombia, Peru and Argentina, the option given to new workers to choose between the old and new systems creates uncertainty regarding the fiscal liability of government. In Colombia, where workers can change their choice every three years, this problem is particularly dangerous and severely weakens the reformed system. Chile is increasingly concerned about the rising costs of the minimum pension guarantee, driven in part by falling numbers of active contributors in the labor force. And pensions of government workers continue to exercise a serious fiscal burden in countries such as Peru, Argentina and Mexico. . . . Coverage ratios—after rising modestly due to the reforms—have stalled at levels of about half of the labor force in those countries where workers' participation is highest.[68]

In addition:

> many workers cease to contribute to the pension system after completing the minimum contribution requirement, preferring other long-term savings instruments to those offered by dedicated pension providers, and even more importantly revealing a preference for government schemes for pooling resources to insure against old age poverty, compared with government-mandated savings instruments.[69]

Furthermore:

> The ability of the multi-pillar model in isolating the pension system from abuse by governments may also have been oversold by reformers. It is now clear that unsustainable fiscal and monetary policies can jeopardize even well-implemented funded schemes.

India

The elderly population of India is growing rapidly. Numbering 57 million in 1991, 77 million in 2000, those aged over 60 years are predicted to reach 141 million by 2020, by then accounting for nearly 10 per cent of the population.[70] India provides an example of the historical development of pensions. The protection of those in the organised government services dates back to the colonial period, when the British introduced the concept of retirement benefits. In 1881 the Royal Commission on Civil Establishment created a pension system for all government employees, British and Indian. Following independence in 1944, this was retained, and in a series of Five Year Plans provisions were introduced over the next 20 years to provide pension and welfare benefits for all central and state government employees, and large basic industries. Currently some 10 per cent of the population are thus covered. Those receiving the most comprehensive package are civil service employees. They are covered by a non-contributory programme which covers up to 50 per cent of their final salary after 33 years of service, and is funded from Government of India general revenues. They are also eligible for a range of further benefits including, for central government employees, free medical care for themselves and their dependants. In addition, these employees are eligible for a variety of contributory schemes. These middle and upper income groups are thus able to save and plan for a comfortable retirement.[71] Non-civil servants working in the organised sector, such as those employed in the large industries and services, are covered by similar, though not as comprehensive, schemes.

Of current concern, then, is the 90 per cent of the workforce who are not covered, mainly agricultural workers. Their entire working life is spent with little job protection or security and low wages; indeed, two-thirds of this population, some 97 million workers, are engaged in temporary or casual employment.[72] Until the 1980s, the only forms of late life security available to these workers beyond the family were insurance-based schemes – life insurance and savings-linked insurance – both of which had a very low take-up. During the last 20 years of the century, however, state-based pension schemes were developed in all states. These provide an average pension of $50 a year (though this varied from $18 in Assam to over $80 in Rajasthan and West Bengal), less than 10 per cent of the average per capita income of $440, but seen as sufficient for basic existence.[73] Different restriction and eligibility criteria operate in different states, and many of the basic difficulties in administration and delivery reported elsewhere – cumbersome application processes, inappropriate eligibility criteria, delays and irregular payments – (see below) are also common in India.[74]

The 1990s saw a series of new initiatives for older people: the National Social Assistance Scheme, incorporating the National Old Age Pension Scheme for the elderly destitute, and the Annapurna Programme. In 1999 the Government of India announced a National Policy for Older Persons.[75] This states that all older persons below the poverty line will be beneficiaries under the Old Age Pension Scheme. The National Old Age Pension Scheme is for those over age 65 who have little or no regular means of subsistence. The monthly payment is around $1.75, less than half the average state provided pension. The scheme has been particularly vulnerable to administrative error, with regular misidentification of recipients and incorrect dispersal of payments.[76] In addition, despite the fact that this was not meant to interfere with existing state pension benefits, many states are now choosing to disburse only the national benefits, and channel their own resources to other programmes.[77] Alongside the National Old Age Pension Scheme runs the Annapurna Programme. This is primarily a food dispersal programme run by the Ministries of Rural Development and of Food and Civil Supplies. Around 6 million elderly destitutes are given monthly donations of grain, although again, distribution processes have been less than adequate. Furthermore, as Irudaya Rajan[78] points out, the combined government budget allocation for the National Old Age Pension Scheme and the Annapurna Programme is but a tenth of that spent by the government on its own employees!

There has been considerable recent debate over India's social security programme. Few of the rural workers are covered under any plan, and the destitute who are eligible often fall foul of the poor bureaucratic and administrative procedures. Furthermore, pensions for urban-based retirees have been falling in real terms, and the real returns on the contributory schemes are lower than are available on other forms of investment.[79]

Current debates

Public versus private funding

There is an active ongoing debate over the respective merits of publicly funded programmes versus private provision in later life, described by Augusztinovics as the 'great controversy'.[80] The International Labour Office (ILO) has consistently advocated a universal, state-provided social security system, on the grounds that economic activity in old age is falling in most parts of the world, and socio-economic change is reducing the ability and willingness of children to care for their parents.[81] During the 1980s and 1990s this approach was increasingly questioned by the World Bank[82] who queried the value of public schemes on the grounds of low rates of returns, inadequate protection from inflation, and the incentive to evade the consequent taxes required.[83] In particular, the World Bank opposed the ILO's argument that increased social welfare was required to compensate for decreasing family support, arguing instead that pensions and other public social welfare programmes caused reduced support by children for elderly parents.

Augusztinovics refers to the World Bank's milestone report 'Averting the Old Age Crisis',[84] saying it:

> may be considered the best-known exemplification of what has become the 'new pension orthodoxy'. The report presents a universal strategy of pension privatization. The Bank's leading pension expert makes it clear that the multi-pillar model should be introduced mainly because of efficiency and growth considerations, referring to a better provision of old-age security as a mere 'secondary argument'.[85]

In opposition:

> The International Labour Office and the International Social Security Association are the new pension orthodoxy's *most prominent opponents* (original emphasis), defending the Bismarckian-Beveridgean welfare state tradition against neoliberal individualism. Among other arguments, opponents point out that an old-age security system mainly based on private pension funds . . . boils down to a risky strategy for the insured since the investment risk has to be borne by the individual.[86]

There is general agreement by both sides, however, that some form of three-pillar structure is appropriate, combining a publicly funded minimum income guarantee for the very poor (first pillar), a combination insurance-based scheme (second pillar), and encouragement of voluntary saving (third pillar). Indeed, as Augusztinovics points out, the former Chief Economist of the World Bank, Stiglitz, has argued that a privately managed second pillar is not always optimal and the debate over pension form should include a more expansive view of the optimal second pillar incorporating the option of a public defined pension plan.

However, as Gorman notes,[87] the World Bank's approach, with its argument for the primacy of the market in the production of pensions, its assumption that most people are able to save for their own old age, and its belief that a key determinant of older people's welfare is the performance of the whole economy, has had a powerful influence on governments. A number of countries are now looking to reform their state social security pension programmes in line with World Bank recommendations.

Universal non-contributory pensions

An equally contentious issue is that of universal non-contributory pensions. There is still a widespread assumption that universal non-contributory pension schemes are unaffordable in developing countries.[88] Indeed, the ILO standard is a contributory pension scheme. However, most citizens in the developing countries are unable to make full and necessary contributions to such schemes. Furthermore, it is also being increasingly recognised that universality is a feasible option for low-income countries so long as the annual pension transfer rate is below 1 per cent of GDP, with successful achievements even in impoverished countries such as Botswana and Namibia.[89]

In particular, these schemes are protected from costs associated with population ageing and variable economic performance.[90] Moreover, traditionally vulnerable groups, such as women and those in the unpaid informal sector, are covered, and there is evidence that older people are investing such pension income in their families, paying for education and investing in family economic ventures.[91] Overall these schemes can play an important role in poverty reduction. Indeed as McCallum[92] has long pointed out, the requirement of material support in old age is related to poverty alleviation and income maintenance. Combining non-contributory means-tested pensions to alleviate poverty, with occupational contributory pensions to maintain income addresses both these issues.

There is also growing evidence that many employers view pensions as supplementary salaries[93] and even if pensions and benefits have a low real value, many households hold these benefits as their most reliable income.[94] Work in South Africa,[95] for example, has found that pensions to poor elderly raise the standard of living and provide security for entire households. The reliability of pensions means that the income can be used strategically and it allows households to obtain credit that they would otherwise not be eligible for.[96] Rather than pensions 'crowding out' familial support,[97] there are wider positive benefits:

> Some worry about the potential of this public spending [i.e. pensions] to 'crowd out' individual savings, and to reduce transfers between generations. A growing body of research shows, on the contrary, that it 'crowds in' care, the status of the elderly, the health status of children, the creation of local markets, and micro-enterprise formation.[98]

The need for reform

Beyond the major debates, there are also many aspects of current schemes which require reform. Schulz,[99] for example, suggests that there are key weaknesses in the availability, adequacy and equity of public programmes in many developing countries. In addition, most administrative and implementation structures are expensive, poorly regulated and cumbersome. The administrative costs can be a major expense, reaching 18 per cent in Mexico,[100] for example, thus influencing the amounts of benefits ultimately paid out. Similarly, the requirement for trained and specialised personnel is rarely given priority. There is also a high level of non-compliance by both governments and employers. All these factors contribute to, and further compound, the often generally low return on investment portfolios. Finally, the growing introduction of competition and privatisation is leading, in some regions, to unaffordable or even unavailable products and services for large segments of the population.

There is therefore a need, Schulz argues, to unbundle the many different benefits and services offered by social security institutions into those that could be extended to the poor and those that are affordable only by middle and upper income groups. *Rural and poor populations*, for example, could be targeted through specialised programmes more appropriate to their situation such as crop insurance programmes or guaranteed income programmes. Examples of these include the IMSS Solidaridad in Mexico, peasant insurance in Ecuador, the indigent programme of social insurance in Costa Rica, the agricultural workers pension scheme in Keral, the Social Assistance Programme in Maharashtra, and the Social Guarantee Programme in Gabon. Similar priority for these populations could also be given to primary and preventative health care, disability protection, and assistance for widows and old persons without access to family support.

Urban and formally employed populations may also be eligible for a variety of programmes. Eligibility or benefit determination under one programme is sometimes related to benefits received from another programme. This can lead to too high or too low benefits being paid.[101] In addition, high inflation erodes the real value of benefits where pensions are not indexed[102] and there is a need to provide better protection against the excessive levels of inflation operating in many of these countries.

Another important consideration is the extent to which a pension scheme is designed to redistribute income within the relevant population. For example, in plans that redistribute major amounts of income there is often a weak link between a worker's personal contributions and the benefits the worker actually receives. Yet the link between pay in and benefits received is often one major criteria for judging pension equity. There may also be unintentional redistribution arising, for example, from changes over time in the provision or performance of different schemes.

There is, therefore, confusion over the increasing complexities of the growing number of schemes, and public confidence in such programmes is falling. While this can be rectified to an extent through education and the simplification of the programmes, this is also compounded by administrative corruption, inflation, benefits not materialising as described and governments falling behind with payments. As Schulz concludes: '. . . pensions should be available, adequate, fair and understood. Unfortunately, social insurance programmes in most developing countries today can be criticized with regard to their success in achieving all four goals'.[103]

Several commentators[104] are calling for a complete rethink of public programmes. New structures involving family and community input need to be implemented, and the cost of current programmes needs to be cut through administration improvements and consolidation. Savings thus achieved could then be used to provide more universal benefits, alongside specific targeted programmes for those in special need. The challenge, however, is how to begin to implement such reforms in a climate which places older people and their needs last in a long list of poverty and want.

Notes

1 Gorman, 1999, pp. 3-4.
2 UNDP, 2002.
3 UNDP, 1996.
4 Pre-the US incursions following September 11th 2001.
5 Schulz, 1999.
6 World Bank, 1994.
7 Gorman, 1999.
8 ibid.
9 HAI, 2002.
10 Darkwa and Muzibuko, 2002.
11 HAI, 2002.
12 ibid.
13 ibid.
14 NSSO, 1998.
15 Sharma and Dak, 1987.
16 NSSO, 1998.
17 Vijaya Kumar, 1990.
18 Irudaya Rajan, 1999; Irudaya Rajan et al., 1999; NSSO, 1998.
19 HAI, 2002, p. 52.
20 ibid.
21 World Bank, 2000.
22 HAI, 2002.
23 ibid.
24 ibid.
25 Hoskins, 2002.
26 Perrin, 1969.
27 Cutright, 1965.
28 Dreze and Sen, 1991.
29 Sen, 1985.
30 Dreze and Sen, 1991, pp. 8-9.

31 Dreze and Sen, 1991.
32 Dreze and Sen, 1991, p. 31.
33 Atkinson and Hills, 1991.
34 Burgess and Stern, 1991.
35 ibid.
36 Burgess and Stern, 1991; Platteau, 1999.
37 HAI, 1999.
38 HAI, 2001.
39 Irudaya Rajan et al., 1999.
40 Vijaya Kumar, 2003.
41 ibid.
42 Hermalin and Chan, 2000; Raymo and Cornman, 1999.
43 Andrews et al., 1986.
44 Agree and Clark, 1991.
45 HAI, 1999.
46 Ibid.
47 McCallum, 1990.
48 Malaysian Chinese Association, 1987 quoted in McCallum, 1990.
49 Cattell, 2002.
50 Halperin, 1987.
51 Cattell, 2002.
52 Cattell, 2001.
53 Keith et al., 1994.
54 ibid.
55 HAI, 1999.
56 Agree and Clark, 1991.
57 World Bank, 1994.
58 Schulz, 1999; see also ISSA, 1980.
59 Schulz, 1999.
60 ibid.
61 I am indebted to the e-pensions list for this excellent review of pensions plans from which much of the following material is derived.
62 SSA, 1999. There have been some excellent overviews and analysis of Asian social security programmes. See on China: Feldstein, 1998; Friedman et al., 1996; James, 2000; James, 2001; Liu and MacKellar, 2001; Ma and Zhai, 2001; McCarthy and Zheng, 1996; Wakabayashi and MacKellar, 1999. On other Asian countries: Asher, 1998; Asher, 2000; Bui et al., 2000; Holzmann et al., 2000; Hu et al., 2000; Prescott, 1997; Yang, 2001.
63 ILO, 1997.
64 Palacios and Pallarès-Miralles, 2000.
65 Mesa-Lago, 1997; Gill et al., 2005a; Gill et al., 2005b.
66 World Bank, 2001.
67 Gill et al., 2005b.
68 ibid.
69 ibid; see also Packard, 2002.
70 Raju, 2002.
71 Vijaya Kumar, 2003.
72 ibid.
73 Irudaya Rajan, 1999.
74 Vijaya Kumar, 2003.
75 Raju, 2002.
76 Irudaya Rajan, 1999.
77 Vijaya Kumar, 2003.
78 Irudaya Rajan, 1999.
79 Liebig and Rajan, 2003.
80 Augusztinovics, 2002.
81 Gorman, 1999.
82 World Bank, 1994.
83 Gorman, 1999.
84 World Bank, 1994.
85 Augusztinovics, 2002, p. 25.
86 ibid., pp. 25-26.
87 Gorman, 1999, p. 6.
88 HAI, 1999.
89 Willmore, 2001.
90 OECD, 1988.
91 HAI, 1999.
92 McCallum, 1990.
93 Harper, 1994.
94 ibid.
95 Lund, 2002; Schroeder-Butterfill, 2003; Case and Deaton, 1998.
96 Schroeder-Butterfill, 2003.
97 Cox and Jimenez, 1990; Treas and Logue, 1986.
98 Lund 2002, p. 682.
99 Schulz, 1999.
100 Mesa-Lago, 1989.
101 Schulz, 1999; see also Leavitt and Schulz, 1983.
102 Vitas, 1999.
103 Schulz, 1999, p. 90.
104 Schulz, 1999; Gorman, 1999.

9

Supporting families and elder care in developing countries

While a baby girl born in Japan today can expect to live for about 85 years, a girl born at the same moment in Sierra Leone has a life expectancy of 36 years. The Japanese child will receive vaccinations, adequate nutrition and good schooling. If she becomes a mother she will benefit from high-quality maternity care. Growing older, she may eventually develop chronic diseases, but excellent treatment and rehabilitation services will be available; she can expect to receive, on average, medications worth about US $550 per year and much more if needed.

Meanwhile, the girl in Sierra Leone has little chance of receiving immunizations and a high probability of being underweight throughout childhood. She will probably marry in adolescence and go on to give birth to six or more children without the assistance of a trained birth attendant. One or more of her babies will die in infancy, and she herself will be at high risk of death in childbirth. If she falls ill, she can expect, on average, medicines worth about US $3 per year. If she survives to middle age she, too, will develop chronic diseases but, without access to adequate treatment, she will die prematurely.[1]

Health and social care needs

As we saw in Chapter 8, the demographic revolution will have a major impact on developing countries. However, while income security and health care in later life are now central to policy developments in all countries in the developed world, they are only just beginning to become part of mainstream policy in some parts of the developing world. It is the rapidity of the demographic transition which will be of significance over the next couple of decades. In particular, as acute infectious diseases are conquered and populations survive into later ages, so the rate of chronic non-communicable disease will grow. The recent example of the reduction of polio at the end of the twentieth century illustrates the potential rapidity of successful health initiatives (Fig. 9.1).

As a result of such success stories, the numbers of adults surviving to experience chronic disease and disability are increasing. The prevalence of such chronic diseases and disability in later life can be significantly reduced though health measures in early life, yet few governments currently see this as a priority when put alongside such needs as child and maternal welfare.

As described in Chapter 7, a useful measure of the level of chronic disease is disability-adjusted life years, or DALYs, which combine years of life lost (YLLs) through premature death, with years lived with disability (YLDs). One DALY is equivalent to one lost year of healthy life, with the measured disease burden being the gap between

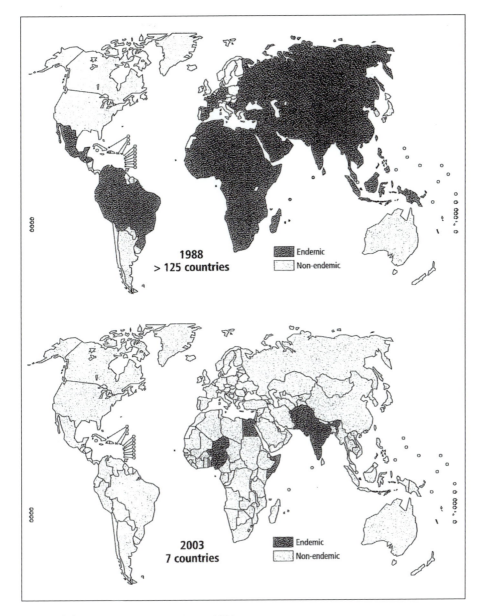

Figure 9.1 *Endemic polio in 1988 and 2003.*
Source: WHO 2003.

a population's health status and that of a normative global reference population with high life expectancy lived in full health.

As is clear from Fig. 9.2, the disease burden in much of the developing world is concentrated in children and younger adults. Indeed, nearly 50 per cent is accounted for in high-mortality developing regions by those aged under 15 years. What is also striking,

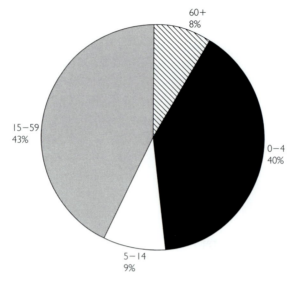

High-mortality developing regions

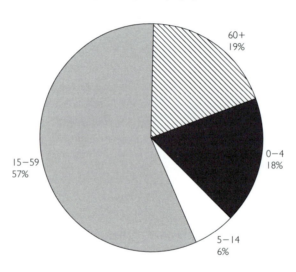

Low mortality regions

Figure 9.2 *Distribution of disease burden (DALYs) by age group and region, 2002.*
Source: WHO, 2003.

however, is that as mortality rates fall, so the burden of disease moves up the age structure, so that in low-mortality developing regions, 57 per cent is accounted for by adults
aged 15–59, the same percentage as in the developed world. Indeed, a comparison
between the last two regions reveals that if these low-mortality developing regions
progress in a similar manner, the disease burden over the next few years will shift from

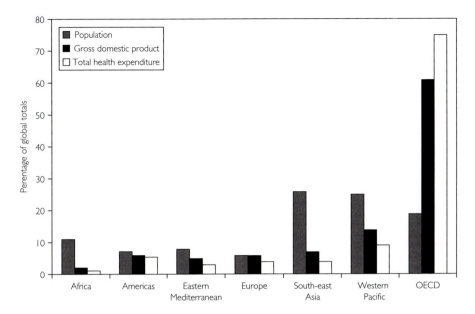

Figure 9.3 *Inequality in health spending and incomes by region, 2001.*
Source: WHO, 2003.

those under age 15, currently 24 per cent, to those over age 60, currently 19 per cent, eventually mirroring the proportions found in the developed world of 10 per cent and 33 per cent respectively. This is in contrast to the situation found in the high-mortality developing regions where the respective proportions are 49 per cent for those under age 15 and only 8 per cent for those over age 60. Clearly the developing world faces a massive increase in demand for care and support of older adults with chronic noncommunicable disease and disability. Indeed, the disease burden among all adults, over age 15, by broad cause shows a striking spectrum across developed, low-mortality developing and high-mortality developing regions. Nearly 95 per cent of the total disease burden in the developed world arises from non-communicable disease. Infectious diseases rise to account for 20 per cent of the disease burden in the low-mortality developing world, such as South-east Asia, and over 60 per cent in high mortality regions such as Africa. As the cause of death shifts from infectious to non-communicable disease, so countries require a shift in resources from acute infectious disease treatment to long-term care.

Health expenditure varies considerably between regions (Fig. 9.3). Thus the OECD countries with less than 20 per cent of the world's population account for 75 per cent of the global health expenditure, while South-east Asia, with 25 per cent of the population, accounts for less than 5 per cent of the expenditure. Similarly, while some 155 countries have now developed public health care systems for older people, these are primarily in the developed world, and cover only one-third of the world's older population.[2]

In order to provide a balanced approach to health and social care in late life in these developing regions, an integrated system needs to be developed which emphasises preventative and primary care, promotes the inclusion of families and elders themselves in developing and supporting mutual aid programmes, and encourages the re-evaluation of cultural traditions, thereby preserving beneficial practices and eliminating harmful ones.[3] The emphasis on community involvement is now also a priority for WHO[4] and governments are beginning to recognise that priority must be given to primary and preventative health care, including specific programmes for older women, if they are to address the forthcoming ageing of their populations. Currently, however, both medical and health care provision varies widely. In addition, this provision is currently focused on maternal and child welfare and infectious diseases. Non-communicable disease, long-term care and the basic health and social support required by people as they grow frailer with old age are still very limited in many parts of the world. Nevertheless, rapid economic growth over the past three decades has enabled some middle-income countries to develop or enhance the provision of public health and social services to older people,[5] and in some of the more affluent nations, wealthier older people are able to afford private personal social services. Generally, however, there are negligible public services to support older people in developing countries, and these are concentrated in urban areas.[6] Such facilities are often overcrowded, unevenly distributed and overstretched due to lack of funding and qualified workers. Thus we have, for example, the stark contrast between Singapore, with its spectrum of good quality public services available to all older people, and Bangladesh where few older people have access to any public service care at all.

The delivery of basic health care to most older people occurs informally within the community. Many countries have developed, and are continuing to develop, a mixed care system for their elderly dependants, the combination depending on the particular social, economic and religious factors extant within that society. In many Muslim countries it is religious groups who provide health and economic security; in the People's Republic of China the commune and firm played a large role until recently; in Israel trade unions provide health services and pensions.[7] However, throughout the developing world, it is the family which bears the highest responsibility for the provision of health and social care and support, as well as material security. Indeed, as a recent World Bank report points out, more than half the world's old people depend on families[8] and the health and social care and material security of older adults are intimately meshed with that of their extended families. This is emphasised by the UNFPA[9] who identify the promotion of the role of families and other informal support providers as key in addressing the issue of population ageing.

Alongside the psychological support role that kin generally play, families in developing countries serve two fundamental roles. They provide economic security and basic health and social care. This chapter will consider the continuing role of the family, and the pressures exerted on such kin support, arising from demographic change, economic development and long-term crises such as poverty, famine and HIV/AIDS.

Family-based transfers

Intra-household and inter-household transfers between related or proximate individuals constitute a basic form of social security in developing countries. To a large extent the family or community serves many of the roles carried out by formal institutions in developed countries. . . . Transfers between related or proximate individuals have been shown to serve the purpose of risk mitigation, insurance against income shortfalls, support for the elderly in retirement, help during illness, unemployment insurance, educational loans and financing of rural-urban migration. These transfers represent an important component of household income and expenditure both in traditional village and rural households as well as urban households.[10]

It is also apparent that informal family-based transfers are able to overcome many of the difficulties faced in establishing general social security programmes. As Burgess and Stern go on to discuss, it may be that kinship ties and common backgrounds mitigate the general problems of information and communication found in more impersonal market settings; the sanctions of social opprobrium which may arise from fraud can be strong within a family or community, and these together may overcome the problems of false or over claiming. On a more negative note, all members of a household or community may be affected at the same time by adverse phenomena, such as famine, war or environmental crisis, placing severe constraints on the family's ability to provide at times of greatest need. Indeed, endemic poverty remains a significant intergenerational risk factor. If a family is trapped in poverty, the capacity of younger adults to assist older relatives may be significantly impaired. This may be overcome by developing a public service framework which can supplement family and community informal support, and even replace it at times of crisis or sudden acute need.

Such intergenerational support is commonly perceived as being assisted by strong norms of behaviour.[11] These underpin family-based support systems, and enhance the ability of families to inculcate altruism and to enforce social norms.[12] While there are many examples of such reciprocal behaviour,[13] the interpretation of intergenerational relations is problematic, and the relationship between norms and behaviour complex.

The heterogeneity of families

The previous chapter revealed the diversity of family and intergenerational relationships within western countries resulting from varied demographic, economic, social, cultural and historical factors. There is even more diversity between and within regions in the developing world. However, some broad themes can be identified which are now occurring to greater or lesser extents in most if not all developing countries. The increase in the older populations, both in absolute and relative terms, is being accompanied by various international social and economic changes: industrialisation and urbanisation are increasing; geographic mobility is increasing; female participation in the economic labour force is increasing and, undoubtedly linked to this, family size is reducing, with a general shift from extended families – in their many and varied forms – to a more nuclear pattern; and perceptions of family norms and obligations are changing.

The region of Asia provides a good example of how diverse family forms and roles are playing out against these broad international processes. East and South-east Asian families are generally characterised by falling fertility and dominant, though declining, multigenerational patriarchal family systems. Within this generality, however, lies a multitude of family and household forms, roles and relationships.

Korea, Taiwan, Singapore and Hong Kong, for example, have a typical stem family system, whereby elderly parents live with a married child. This is culturally supported by Confucian beliefs – historically common to all four societies. These beliefs emphasise the vertical child–parent relationship over the lateral husband–wife relationship. Filial piety (ko) towards parents demands co-residence and continual attention to their needs.[14] However, while three-generational households remain the most common form of living for older persons in all four societies, the average household size has fallen significantly over the past 50 years, with a concurrent rise in single person and nuclear family-based households, and a fall in multigenerational households.

Indonesia's population is ageing rapidly with limited formal financial support, health care or institutional care for older people.[15] Interestingly, given the general stereotype of families in this region, many family systems in Indonesia are not traditionally extended, but nuclear family types with bilateral kinship reckoning, and high levels of divorce.[16] Strains in the economy have resulted in rapid return migration from the urban areas by young rural migrants, many of whom now find themselves dependent on their rural ageing parents.[17]

There has been a strong family tradition in the People's Republic of China, with a norm of co-residence between elderly parents and adult son plus wife and children.[18] Despite a concerted attack by the Communist Party on patriarchal power and arranged marriages, it made little attempt to change the expectation that elderly parents should live with an adult, typically male, child. However, in recent years such norms have been changing, especially in the urban areas. As Davis-Friedmann has noted, while in rural areas the multigenerational household is viewed as the culmination of years of preparation for old age, in urban areas this has long been seen as a necessity rather than a choice.[19] So much so, that, as China transforms its economy, the necessity of state promotion of the tradition of family support for older relatives is now being acknowledged.[20]

As Schulz[21] points out, given the complexity of evolving family structures in developing countries, a great deal of caution is required in stating what the family can and should do in support of elderly people. However, the one virtual constant facing families at the turn of the century is that they are being expected to cope with the challenge of ageing at precisely the time when the family as an institution is under severe pressure to change.[22]

Kreager's work on *age structural transition*[23] has relevance here:

> The compound effects of larger cohorts reaching old age . . . are likely to create demands on several younger cohorts over two differing durations. Where there is a great density of major life course events (say, where young people experience marriage, procreation, and take-up of new jobs in a short space of time), then the support available to older age groups may in those intervals be seriously constrained. Wider social adjustments to population ageing, like increased immigration, may become part of, and accentuate, uncertainties for some or all groups. Different provinces, and different ethnic, religious or other groups within them, may be affected to a greater or lesser degree.[24]

So, alongside the diversity of individual, family and community situations we must also place the impact of differential demands on cohorts due to their demographic positions.

The vulnerability of families

Throughout the developing world there is a growing awareness of the vulnerability of the family, in particular given the scale of the demand which will arise as these populations age:

> There is a strong consensus on the importance of the family as a basic component of the social structure, and a key role assigned to families is that of providers of care at every stage of life. Care in old age is still perceived as a special responsibility, particularly in the absence of alternatives in the form of public support structures. However, the rapid demographic transition of recent decades accompanied by other changes such as migration, urbanization and the increasing numbers of women entering formal workforces have called into question the continuing capacity of the family to provide effective care in old age.[25]

There are numerous studies revealing how the availability of family support is being disrupted and eroded by demographic, social, cultural, economic and political change. Wars, civil unrest and environmental disasters are displacing families throughout Africa;[26] three-generation families in Latin America are in decline so the percentage of older adults living alone in this region now accounts for one-fifth of all over 55 year olds;[27] urbanisation and changing female labour force participation are threatening the assumed role of the family in providing elder care in Asia.[28] Similarly, fertility decline is seen as contributing to the spread of the nuclear family, and to a consequent perceived reduction in potential carers.[29] Data from Korea,[30] for example, predict a doubling of those older widows without a surviving son, estimated to reach nearly one-third by 2025, though this will be partly compensated for by an increase in surviving male spouses during this time.

Much of this evidence feeds into the debate discussed earlier (Chapter 6) about the role of the extended and nuclear family, with the generally accepted view being that fertility decline and Westernisation/industrialisation would inevitably lead to the collapse of the extended family, along with its extensive supportive roles. This view is now being questioned, in particular in relation to the validity, reliability and replicablity of supporting empirical evidence from the developing world.[31] For example, fertility decline, though rapid in some areas, such as Asia, is currently predicted to settle at around two to three children per family, sufficient to allow continued non-resident or co-resident support, particularly in those regions where there is no sex preference for the co-residency.[32] Similarly, even though younger couples may be shifting towards a preference for independent rather than co-resident living, this does not necessarily preclude reciprocal exchanges of support and care,[33] though these may shift in kind. Evidence from Sri Lanka,[34] for example, suggests that reciprocal care is more likely to occur between co-residents than non-co-residents, the latter being more likely to exchange money or goods. Even in those regions where extended familial co-residence has not been the norm, or has declined, co-residence in later life is still likely to occur,[35] suggesting that a distinction is made between the norm of nuclear household formation, and the allowance of extended family co-resident living in times of need, such as frailty in old age. Indeed, as Hermalin[36] has stressed, it is important:

> . . . to distinguish form from function in terms of family structure and relationships. With increasing incomes and supply of housing, elderly parents and children may choose to live apart to gain more space and privacy, but this may not imply any diminution in levels of material or emotional support.[37]

In addition, measures of household composition and co-residency between the generations are poor indicators of intergenerational flows which comprise exchanges both within and beyond households.[38] Indeed, elderly people living alone are not necessarily childless or vulnerable; lone residence may be a temporary stage of the family life cycle, or even reflect preferences as in East Java,[39] and evidence from Thailand and the Philippines shows that those living in households with their children are not necessarily secure.[40]

Finally, there is a prevalent view that all elderly people are, on the whole, in need of support.[41] Most research focuses on the support provided by adult children to elderly parents,[42] while failing to recognise the continuation of downward transfers from parent to child even in old age.[43] This stereotype, that all older people are a dependent drain on younger households, is now being widely questioned.[44] There are frequent examples of younger households co-residing successfully with older adults even in times of extreme poverty and strife, suggesting that the older relatives may indeed be positively contributing to the household and enabling its survival through crisis.[45] Indeed, intergenerational support is typically reciprocal in nature. There are examples from across the developing world of older people taking primary caregiving responsibility for children and grandchildren, and providing the main income for the household.[46] There are also examples where adult children take more in support than they contribute.[47] Even quite frail older people are not passive recipients of care but may also be active contributors to household economies through cash transfers or in-kind contributions such as childminding or domestic chores.

We must also remember, however, that there are large numbers of elderly people who do not have family resources: around half of all older people in the developing world do not have a spouse,[48] and an estimated 10–25 per cent are childless.[49] This is compounded by migration which leads to young people moving to cities, some sending back remittances but others unable or unwilling to do so. There has been extensive consideration of childlessness in Asia,[50] and the following in-depth study provides an excellent illustration of the issues:

> Pathological sterility may curtail the fertility of many women. Divorce and remarriage may effectively separate parents from their children. Children may have left the community and be out of contact. Or they may be present, yet enmity, incapacity, or other commitments prevent them from providing any help. Thus around a numerical core of couples actually childless on conventional demographic grounds (primary and pathological sterility plus child mortality), we need to consider a broader band of de facto childless: those whose children, present or absent, are unwilling or unable to take a caring role.[51]

The authors also highlight the direct relationship between poverty and childlessness. Poverty impacts directly on fertility due to its relationship with health; it also affects exposure to, and treatment of, sexually transmitted diseases. Poorer people are more likely to be widowed and lose children in childhood and infancy. Also, wealthier individuals and couples are in a better position to provide material security to a potential adoptee, and are thus more likely to be given a child to raise. By being able to offer a good inheritance or other benefits to their children, rich adoptive parents are able to cement their ties to adoptive children, making it less likely that the child will return to its biological parents. Many childless elderly access this support from offspring who are not their biological children through informal adoption or *anak angkat*, which is prevalent in South-east Asia. (Though the authors caution that only half the adoptions among the childless resulted in long-term support in later life.) Other methods of quasi-child support resulted from acquiring children via marriage or remarriage. A paradoxical example is patronage, whereby older people provide services to wealthier members of the community, in return for support when they are old. Finally, the wealthier members of the communities studied were able to buy in services, provided elsewhere by children.

In summary, then, we can conclude that family support is a *necessary* but *not sufficient* guarantee of old age security. Thus, while there is considerable concern over the pressures faced by many family systems in developing countries as a result of social, economic, political and environmental forces, there is widespread evidence that family support systems continue to exist and to provide effective care and security for elderly relatives throughout much of the developing world, and that older people in return provide economic and social support to younger people. Indeed, many governments are now integrating family and informal care directly into their policies for older people, an increasing number explicitly relying on co-residence and kin support as the mainstay of care for their older population. The Indian government relies on the co-residence of older people and their married sons, a norm that is commonly followed.[52] Families are given full responsibility for their elderly members in the Philippines; in wealthier Singapore, the government supports only those without children.[53] Hungary relies on co-residence of older people with their married children to solve problems of old age care.[54] It is also clear, however, that formal health, social and financial support provision is needed to take the place of large families, which in return will also encourage the acceptance of smaller, healthier and better educated families.

Finally, Apt[55] makes the important comment that public policy often involves the identification of target groups, without necessarily considering the knock-on effect for other groups of a particular intervention. For example, introducing institutional day care for young children, may not only reduce resources for other target groups, but also remove an important social and economic role from older people, who have traditionally provided such day care. Far better, she argues, is to integrate the older people into the new institutional arrangements, thereby satisfying the needs of young and old alike.

While, as we saw earlier, Africa still has low proportions of its population over age 60, the region is of key importance in understanding the impact of demographic ageing on the family, as over the next couple of decades the current pressures of economic and cultural change will here closely combine with population ageing. The evolution of family structures in many parts of Africa is thus closely associated with changing patterns and demands for reciprocal family care between older and younger members of the family. In this way, it provides a relevant illustration of the processes at work as populations begin to age.

Changing family structures in Africa

> The hand of the child cannot reach the shelf nor can the hand of the elder get through the neck of the gourd on the shelf. Akan Proverb[56]

Thus, the elder lifts the child to the shelf, so that the child may share with the elder the fruits of the gourd. While there is clearly considerable diversity in family patterns between counties, regions and ethnic groups, some basic features can be identified.[57] As Tengan[58] notes, the African social system is traditionally formed through an extension of family into extended family into social organisation, and it is sometimes difficult to note where kinship ends and social organisation begins.

The African family is typically a collective entity in which marriage is viewed primarily as an alliance between two kinship groups rather than between two individuals. In addition, procreation is the primary objective of marriage and infertility provides grounds for dissolution. The transaction of marriage thus places reciprocal rights and obligations on kinship groups, which continue after the death of the individuals. From this arises such practices as *levirate* or *widow inheritance*, whereby it is expected that a member of the deceased husband's kinsmen will take in the widow and cohabit with her. Similarly, the practice of the *sororate*, which imposes upon the kinsmen of a deceased or barren wife an obligation to provide another woman from their kin group. In many African societies, marriage is potentially polygamous, in that there is no legal impediment to the husband contracting subsequent marriages before widowhood or divorce. The African household is typically multigenerational.

The extended family in Ghana, as described by Apt,[59] provides an example of these kin structures. This kin group is an ancestral family of either maternal or paternal blood relations, which can extend over three or four generations in a direct line, taking in siblings and their children. Members of the extended family are obliged to help each other and, even when geographically separated, are expected to continue to provide emotional and financial support. Traditionally, the parent–child bond does not weaken on the child's marriage, and it is this which provides security in old age. In addition, on their death or migration, children, grandchildren and siblings can be replaced by substitutes. Among many ethnic groups in Ghana, the aged enjoy high status as mediators and experts on social problems, folklore and tradition, holding official positions in family councils and ceremonies. Apt suggests that Ghanaian responsibilities to elderly relatives are supported by three principles:

- *Social recognition* is achieved by conforming to cultural expectations of assistance to parents or other elderly relatives.

- *Reciprocal duties* between children and elders are linked. In the Ga patrilineal system, for example, the son is trained to take up the father's job for the economic stability of the group.

- *Family solidarity* is maintained through conformity to authority, with an individual's sense of emotional security defined by acquiescence to the authority of the family.

In a practical sense also, the large extended family is able to satisfy the interests of the dependent elderly. Thus the large number of young able-bodied members enables more avenues of economic employment to be accessed, and in addition they have more personal resources available for caring for frail elderly dependants.[60]

However, as with other regions, economic and political factors are severely testing African traditional family structures.[61] Families are being separated and displaced by the frequent wars and civil strife, and increasing environmental disasters such as floods and droughts, which lead to famine and homelessness. Economic hardships are making it diffi-cult for families to ensure the surplus required to provide care and support for depen-dants, including older people. Education, urbanisation and industrialisation are having a steady impact on kinship roles and relationships. Similarly, encroaching western cultural values, and the shift from traditional to state leadership, are perceived to be undermining traditional values, including respect for older people.[62] For example, throughout Africa there is evidence that western-style formal education encourages income-earning employment for the young, and diminishes the authority and knowledge-based status of the older population.[63] Finally is the issue of childlessness. The most likely cause, sexually transmitted diseases leading to infertility, is facilitated by many marriage customs, including the social acceptance of pre-marital and extra-marital relationships, polygamous marriage and other plural marriage forms. Polygamy increases the sense of security in old age due to the presence of many children and young wives, though there is some evidence that the cost of educating children is now beginning to count against this.[64] It has been esti-mated that in Sub-Saharan Africa, for example, around one-fifth of women are childless.[65] This may be compensated for through fostering which is widespread in Sub-Saharan Africa – the stated rationale for fostering is 'to provide support for childless elderly individuals'.[66]

Ghana

Apt's extensive studies of Ghana[67] identify those factors which are currently undermin-ing the traditional West African family. The context to this change is the significant decline in living standards for the majority of Ghanaians at the end of the last century. Unemployment, underemployment, inflation and the rising cost of living have severely impacted upon younger adults who have to support not only themselves and their chil-dren, but also their elderly parents and others within the extended family. Rural–urban migration which causes the physical separation of younger members from the family is also having an increasing impact. It has long been recognised that migration to urban areas results in the isolation of older people in rural areas.[68] While, in theory, the tradi-tional support of rural elderly people through personal services by kin is replaced by cash payments sent by the now urban-based younger kin, the small formal employment sector, low wages and job insecurity mediate against young Ghanaians being able to ful-fill these obligations to their elderly parents.[69] Similarly, return visits by these younger urban migrants to their older rural-based relatives are limited.[70]

For older people who also migrate to urban areas, with illiteracy at 80 per cent among this group, few have the education or training necessary for salaried urban employment. Similarly, urban housing arrangements are not conducive to extended family co-residence. In rural Ghana the widespread availability of land and suitable build-ing materials, ensures that additional dwellings may be added to existing structures as and when required to support extended family co-residency. In urban areas, however, not only is there little or no space for the erection of further dwellings, but existing accommodation is often subject to strict landlord control, limiting, either by regulation or by rent increase, the number of family members able to reside together. This forces families to subdivide into smaller residential units, affecting not only the psychological cohesion of the extended family, but also the shared economic and personal care arrangements. Previous reciprocal services thus become impossible even when kin reside within the same geographical area of the city.[71] Many older people subsequently find themselves both unemployed, or in very menial work, and increasingly excluded from a traditional extended family co-residency, which carries the benefits of shared money and personal resources.

Finally, as Apt describes, western ideals of individualisation and romantic love are increasingly forming the basis for marriage rather than the traditional concept of uniting clans. There has been growing evidence for some time of the prevalence of nuclear family forms in Ghana's cities,[72] an increasing number of women in the labour force, and a growing tendency for monogamous marriages. Such developments are also being encouraged by changes in Ghanaian law. For example, in 1985 the Ghana government introduced the Interstate Succession Laws, which identified spouses and children as the sole benefactors of inheritance, excluding other kin.[73] The increasing legal settlements of property rights, outside the traditional jurisdiction of the family, only mirrors the social and cultural changes which are occurring within. In conclusion, Apt and Grieco identify three forces working against the Ghanaian extended family as an intact support system for elderly dependants. First, the departure of able-bodied young members of the family through migration, second, the departure of female caregivers through education and employment opportunities, and third, the inability of the remaining able-bodied members to earn income due to increasing unemployment, underemployment and low salary levels.[74]

Aboderin[75] has recently extended this analysis to suggest that declining family support for older people in urban Ghana may be explained at the dynamic interface of two competing theories – political economy and modernisation – either of which alone satisfactorily address the question. Thus she argues that at the very time that economic change is putting tremendous stress on contemporary Ghanaian families through increased costs, in particular for health care and education, and increased demands, especially for consumption goods, so, due to trends identified within modernisation, norms of obligation are shifting to favour the needs of younger people over old. Families faced with increasing and competing demands will prioritise the perceived needs of their children over their parents. This partly arises because the traditional sanctions against those neglecting older relatives are breaking down.

Botswana

A contrast is provided by a small ethnography of the Herero people of Botswana.[76] Despite considerable environmental and economic pressure, these peoples are seen as a traditional and prosperous group – self-consciously ethnic and endogamous, while fully participating in the developing economy of Botswana. Traditionally cattle keepers, older Herero have control of resources, in particular the cattle. Sons stay on the father's land until his death, when the land is redistributed, and even then older women retain control of some of the cattle which they use to ensure care and resources from younger kin. For example, they allow younger kin to milk their cattle and give them the milk, in return for the promise of the inheritance of the animals following the older person's death. Children are especially important resources for older people because they act as caregivers for the elderly. In many ways, the presence of children, who perform daily tasks such as fetching water, fetching firewood, and cooking is the key to successful ageing among the Herero. Because there is a very large proportion of (pathological) childlessness in the cohort of people now around 70 years of age, fosterage is an important feature of Herero society from the point of view of care for the elderly. It is also a further instance of the Herero perception of family relations, for it is children who are seen as more interchangeable and the elderly who are viewed as the individualised focus of family responsibility, and of pride in fulfilment of that responsibility. Caregiving for elderly relatives is here a given, there being little commentary on whether care should be given, rather who will be able to boast that they are the caregivers.

HIV/AIDS

Finally, it is not possible to discuss the family in an African context, without discussing the devastating impact of HIV/AIDS.

The scourge of HIV/AIDS in Sub-Saharan Africa is clear from Table 9.1. Some 15 million adults and 2.6 million children are infected with the disease, accounting for around 80 per cent of world adult infection and 90 per cent of world child infection. Nine per cent of Sub-Saharan Africa's adult population under the age of 50 is infected. As is clear from Table 9.2, however, while Africa accounts for 70 per cent of the global AIDS epidemic, less than 1 per cent of the adult population with HIV/AIDS are receiving antiretroviral therapy.

There is, however, limited data on the infection rate of HIV/AIDS in the over 50 age group. As can be seen from Table 9.1, UNAIDS does not collect data on infection rates beyond the age of 49, and despite the massive epidemiological studies sponsored in Africa by the UK's Medical Research Council (MRC), it is only now that they are collecting large-scale epidemiological data on the over-fifties. Even in Uganda, Africa's success story on the reduction of new infections of the HIV virus, from 18.5 per cent in 1995 to 6.1 per cent in 2000, there are few data on HIV infection in the over-fifties. The data which are available suggest that less than 1 per cent of people over the age of 50 are infected with the virus, likely to be a significant under-representation of the infection.

Table 9.1 *People living with HIV/AIDS*

	Adults (% 15–49)	Women (15–49)	Children (0–14)
OECD	0.28	360000	19000
Developing countries	1.32	18000000	2900000
Arab States	0.35	250000	35000
East Asia/Pacific	0.20	600000	40000
Latin America/Caribbean	0.61	640000	60000
South Asia	0.55	1500000	170000
Sub-Saharan Africa	9.00	15000000	2600000
Central/Eastern Europe/CIS	0.48	270000	15000

Source: Human Development Report, 2002.

Table 9.2 *Coverage of adults in developing countries with antiretroviral therapy, by WHO region, December 2002*

Region	Number of people	Estimated need	Coverage (%)
Africa	50000	4100000	1
Americas	196000	370000	53
Europe	700	80000	9
Eastern Mediterranean	3000	9000	29
South-east Asia and Western Pacific	43000	1000000	4
All WHO regions	300000	5500000	5

Source: WHO, 2003.

Indeed in parts of Africa there exists the belief that sex with an older person can cure AIDS, which leaves many older women, in particular, vulnerable to traumatic abuse. In addition, as improved treatment prolongs the life of AIDS patients, more people are ageing with the disease and moving into this age group. Furthermore, the full rate of infection among people over the age of 50 through sexual activity is unrecorded and the risk and rate of infection through exposure in caring roles are poorly understood. In fact, older people are repeatedly ignored and excluded from both educational campaigns on the spread of HIV/AIDS, and programme interventions dealing with the epidemic.

However, it is the devastating impact HIV/AIDS has on communities through the decimation of entire adult generations which most affects older people. For although older people do not figure highly in infection rates, they are the most severely affected in terms of the economic, social and psychological burden of caring for their sick children and the orphaned grandchildren left behind. By the end of the twentieth century, it was estimated that 16 million children under 15 had lost either one or both parents to

HIV/AIDS, and that another 40 million would be orphaned by 2010.[77] More than half the orphaned children in Zimbabwe live with their grandparents, and in South Africa and Uganda 40 per cent do.[78] The physical and mental stress of caring for children, grand-children and others with HIV/AIDS increases the vulnerability to disease, with the older carer becoming more susceptible to infections of tuberculosis and other AIDS-related illnesses. Support is therefore needed for these older carers to protect their own health and that of their families, while enabling them to care adequately and safely for their dying children. Economic support is also required for the increased costs associated with HIV/AIDS in terms of treatment and funeral expenses for the sick, and school fees, food, clothes and shelter for the children left behind.

It is being internationally recognised that it is important to develop strategies at local, national and regional level to address the issue of HIV/AIDS for older people. The African Union's draft Policy Framework and Plan of Action on Ageing recommends the need to include older people's issues in policies relating to HIV/AIDS, recognises that older people are at risk from infection, that they are major providers of care, that they require community support, and that they are both educators and learners relating to HIV/AIDS awareness. Similarly, the 2001 United Nations General Assembly Special Session signed a Declaration of Commitment (Articles 65 and 68) which commits member states to implement, by 2005, national policies to provide a supportive envir-onment for children infected with or affected by HIV/AIDS, and to review the social and economic impact of the disease on women and elderly people, particularly in their role as caregivers.

As the WHO[79] stated in 2000:

> Throughout sub-Saharan Africa older people, particularly older women, carry the burden of HIV/AIDS in the community. At the household level, they provide care and support for those who are sick and dying. Across the continent many who are sick return home when they can no longer cope. It is their older parents who become the main carers – providing physical, emotional and economic support. In many cases, older people exhaust their savings by buying drugs or turning to traditional healers in search of a cure. Older people face the trauma of losing several of their children to the AIDS pandemic as many families suffer multiple losses and their household security is destroyed.[80]

The real impact of HIV/AIDS on older people is graphically illustrated by cases such as that of Sophie, a Zimbabwean grandmother:

> Sophie is 82 years old and a resident of a Zimbabwean township. Here she lives with her granddaughter Thoko, who has chronic learning disabilities, suffers from epilepsy and is orphaned after the untimely but expected death of her parents from AIDS.
> There are just two rooms in Sophie's home: a kitchen, which is probably 2 square metres, and a second room, which is probably 9 square metres, where they both sleep. In this room there is one bed, two small cupboards and no chairs. I sit on one of the massive rocks pushed up against the back wall, while Sophie sits on the bed, constantly

wringing her wiry hands, and Thoko sits on the floor next to her, looking admiringly, one assumes, up at her grandmother, never taking her eyes away from this tiny old woman, who is the only source of her own life and survival.

Thoko is tied to the bed with a lead, two metres long attached to her left ankle. Sophie explains that this is because the neighbours have begun to complain about Thoko wandering around and into their houses, mainly to beg for picture books and magazines, and she herself is just not quick enough on her feet to catch Thoko if she does wander off.

So Thoko spends most of her time just lying on the concrete floor paging through books and magazines, time and time again. Not reading them, simply smiling at the photos and pictures.

For Sophie, old age is the constant worry about what will happen to her granddaughter when Sophie dies.[81]

In conclusion

A recent UNFPA report[82] on older people concludes that:

> In a large number of developing societies, family has traditionally been the primary source of care, often in the form of co-residence with adult children. However, although care is more easily and willingly provided to older people within households than outside them, elements of social modernisation suggest that in developing countries the retention and support of older persons within the home is becoming increasingly unsustainable.[83]

As the report continues, even where co-residence persists, the extended family structure does not necessarily imply a family supportive of older people.

It is clear that sustaining a family-only care and support approach for elderly people is becoming increasingly less effective, and most governments now recognise the need for a limited public programme to act as a safety net. However, the provision of public formal support in later life will never completely replace informal support by kin, and the indications are that even in the most economically and politically advanced nations there is at present no general desire for this. Rather, the aim of public policy should be: to sustain the independent status of adulthood, however culturally defined, for as long as possible in old age; to provide good quality health and medical care to the frail and dependent elderly population; to supplement rather than substitute support and simple instrumental care by kin; and to support families in their caring role.

Notes

1 WHO, 2003, p. 5.
2 UNFPA, 1999.
3 UNFPA, 1999; Periago, 2005.
4 WHO, 2003.
5 Gorman, 1999.
6 UNFPA, 2002.
7 Burgess and Stern, 1991.
8 World Bank, 1994.
9 UNFPA, 1999.
10 Burgess and Stern, 1991, p. 59.

11 Chye, 2000; Caffrey, 1992; Lopez, 1991; Lamb, 2000.
12 Bhaumik and Nugent, 2000; Schroeder-Butterfill, 2003.
13 Harper, 1992.
14 Kono, 1994.
15 Hugo, 2000; Asher, 1998.
16 Hetler, 1990; Schroeder-Butterfill, 2003.
17 Breman, 2001; Schroeder-Butterfill, 2003.
18 Harper, 1992; Davis-Friedmann, 1991.
19 Davis-Friedmann, 1991.
20 UNFPA, 1999.
21 Schulz, 1992.
22 Chawla, 1988 quoted in Schulz, 1992.
23 Kreager and Schroeder-Butterfill, 2003.
24 ibid.
25 Gorman, 1999, p. 52.
26 HAI, 2002; Apt, 2002.
27 HAI, 1999.
28 Martin, 1988; Martin, 1990.
29 Mason, 1992.
30 Lee and Palloni, 1992.
31 Knodel and Saengtienchai, 1996.
32 Knodel et al., 1992.
33 Knodel et al., 1996; Uhlenberg, 1996.
34 Uhlenberg, 1996.
35 Andrews et al., 1986.
36 Hermalin, 2000.
37 Hermalin, 1999, p. 104.
38 Natividad and Cruz, 1997.
39 Schroeder-Butterfill, 2003.
40 Knodel and Saengtienchai, 1999; Knodel and Debavalya, 1997; Domingo et al., 1993.
41 Clay and Vander Haar, 1993; Nugent, 1985; Caldwell, 1976.
42 Knodel and Chayovan, 1997; Martin, 1989; Hermalin, 2000.
43 Schroeder-Butterfill, 2003.
44 HAI, 1999; 2002.
45 Rosenzweig, 1994.
46 Hermalin et al., 1998.
47 Kreager and Schroeder-Butterfill, 2003.
48 ILO 1997.
49 Kreager and Schroeder-Butterfill, 2003.
50 Myers, 1992; Hermalin et al., 1992; Martin and Kinsella, 1994; Kreager and Schroeder-Butterfill, 2003.
51 Kreager and Schroeder-Butterfill, 2003, p. 4.
52 Vatuk, 1982.
53 Treas and Logue, 1986.
54 Mogey et al., 1990.
55 Apt, 2002.
56 Quoted in Apt, 1992.
57 Mair, 1969.
58 Tengan, 2002.
59 Apt, 1992.
60 Apt and Grieco, 1994.
61 Apt, 2002.
62 HAI, 2002.
63 Apt, 1992; Khasiani, 1994.
64 Moller and Welch, 1990.
65 Frank, 1983.
66 Keith et al., 1994.
67 Apt, 1992; Apt, 1993; Apt and Grieco, 1994; Apt, 1971; Apt, 1972; Apt, 1991 quoted in Apt and Grieco, 1994; Apt, 1980; Apt, 1986; Apt, 1987 quoted in Apt, 1992; Apt, 1996; Apt, 1997.
68 Ominde and Ejiogu, 1972.
69 Okraku, 1985.
70 Apt, 1992.
71 Apt, 1993.
72 Caldwell, 1969; ONS, 1997.
73 Apt, 1992.
74 Apt and Grieco, 1994.
75 Aboderin, 2003; Aboderin, 2004.
76 Keith, 1994.
77 UNAIDS et al., 2002.
78 Ainsworth and Filmer, 2002.
79 WHO, 2001.
80 Quoted in HAI, 2002, p. 36.
81 Leeson, 2005.
82 UNFPA, 2002.
83 ibid., p. 5.

10
Equal treatment, equal rights: ending age discrimination

Ageist prejudice is deeply entrenched and widely pervasive. . . . It is treated as in some way 'natural', even by many older people. Whatever their political rhetoric, governments exploit ageism to subsidise the affluence of more favoured social classes. Ageism is, however, as great an affront to the supposed values of our society as is sexism or racism.[1]

Age discrimination and ageism

Age discrimination can be direct, which occurs when a person is treated less favourably because of their age. It can also occur indirectly, when older people are disproportionately affected and disadvantaged by a particular policy or practice. Of equal concern is ageism which pervades western society, and is found in the attitudes and behaviours of individuals and institutions. Indeed 'age discrimination results from ageism which is a form of prejudice'.[2] Harding[3] identifies direct age discrimination in the UK – in employment practices, such as age restrictions to applications for jobs and mandatory retirement ages; in health, such as age limits for cancer screening programmes and the former explicit exclusion of people over the age of 70 in clinical trials; and in benefits, such as longer waiting times for disability benefits for older people than for younger people. She also identifies implicit age barriers which have become unquestioned practice, such as lower local authority fee contributions to residential care for older people than for younger, and GPs referring fewer older people for specialist care in response to perceived, though not openly stated, age limits for some treatments. Indirect discrimination, she argues, operates in subtle and unconscious ways, often as a failure to include older people, rather than a deliberate policy to exclude them. So, for example, tolerating behaviour and attitudes towards older people in institutional care which would not be acceptable for younger adults, or designing social services for older people which cater for minimum needs, rather than promote active community and citizen involvement as is the case with services for younger adults. It is worth stressing that discrimination is not necessarily unfair; indeed, positive discrimination is a well-established mechanism for addressing inequalities in health. Discrimination on the basis of a stereotype, however, cannot be defended. Ageism is as pervasive and disempowering as racism and sexism:

The basic ethical foundation upon which measures to combat unfair discrimination rest is that although human beings may be unequal in their skill, intelligence, strength or virtue, it is 'their common humanity that constitutes their equality'. . . . All of us share a common humanity and are entitled to be treated equally on the basis of individual merit rather than on the basis of group stereotypes or assumptions. This applies as much to older people as it does to women or to people of different sexual orientation, skin colour or ethnic origin.[4]

Age discrimination, however, is apparent across society – in financial services, in housing allocation, in education and training, in health and social care. A recent UK report identified six areas where age discrimination was occurring: work, health care, social care, education, transport and social security.[5] In addition, discrimination in financial service provision has also been highlighted.[6] In terms of education and lifelong learning, for example, while older people are being encouraged by the UK government to lead full and active lives, fulfilling roles as responsible citizens, there are ageist stumbling blocks in both further and higher education for older people. Thus, those wishing to undertake non-vocational training in further education are finding that such non-accredited learning courses are being cut, while those over the age of 50 wishing to undertake higher education are denied any financial support unless they are in a position to re-enter the labour market.[7] This apparently arbitrary age cut off at 50 is contrary to the large amount of evidence which shows that education increases the ability to lead active independent lives, helps alleviate some of the problems of social isolation, and increases both mental and physical health. Yet in the UK active citizenship is often discouraged. Age 70 is the cut-off for undertaking jury service, for example, though this will prove an interesting test of the criteria that a random and thus hopefully representative group of citizens are called to assess their peers when it excludes some 20 to 25 per cent of these citizens. Highlighting the inherent ageism of British society even further was the 2001 UK Census which excluded individuals over the age of 75 from indicating their economic or voluntary contribution to the country, and requested that they did not give their educational achievements.

Age discrimination and health care

Perhaps of most concern, is age discrimination in health care and in employment. Let us take the UK NHS provision as an example of the first. The British NHS provides a comprehensive range of services covering prevention and screening, diagnosis, treatment, therapy and palliative care. Yet as the recent report by the Kings Fund stated:

Despite the fact that the majority of older people describe themselves as being in good health (less than 1 per cent of the older population is in hospital at any one time), older people tend to be stereotyped as a homogenous group characterised by passivity, failing physical and mental health and dependency. Such views are observable in society generally but also among health and social care professionals, who may have more frequent contact with older users with complex health needs.[8]

As the report continues, the fact that adult NHS and social care services are utilised by older people suggests that services are responding at some general level to an ageing population. However, it does not necessarily follow that services are designed with older people's needs in mind or that age discrimination is rare. The UK Secretary of State for Health, in fact, recently announced the development of new standards to outlaw age discrimination in the NHS. The report goes on to highlight key areas where age discrimination is to be found. So, while the General Medical Council's guidelines for doctors include the following: 'a patient's lifestyle, culture, beliefs, race, colour, gender, sexuality, age, social status, or perceived economic worth [should not] prejudice the treatment you provide or arrange',[9] some services still apply explicit age restrictions.

The age limits on breast screening, for example, have caused controversy. In the UK, women aged between 50 and 64 are currently called every three years for breast screening, extended in 2004 to all women up to the age of 70. However, as the Kings Fund report points out, some commentators have argued there was sufficient evidence to do this earlier and questioned whether the time taken to review the upper age limit was related to resource constraints[10] or, perhaps, ageist assumptions about the benefits of screening older women.[11] Furthermore, Age Concern has argued that a further 1500 lives could be saved annually if the programme was extended to all older women in the UK[12] regardless of age. They point out that physiological health and life expectancy vary enormously between individuals and many women may wish to take advantage of breast screening into very old age. Currently, self-referrals among older women remain low, partially due to a general lack of information available to older women, but also because the very existence of an upper age limit of 65/70 may be restricting older women from putting themselves forward.

A second, very different example, highlighted by the report, concerns the *Over 75 Health Check*, whereby all registered patients over the age of 75 are offered an annual primary care health check. While there is some evidence that these result in increased referrals and uncover unmet need, they are generally unpopular with general practitioners, who argue that the additional workload they generate is not justified[13] and distracts from providing health care services to those in real need.

Of more concern are the discretionary age limits which the report highlights. Drawing on recent Age Concern research, for example, the report highlights a range of services which have upper age limits which may not be openly publicised, including heart bypass operations, knee replacements and kidney dialysis.[14] For example, 20 per cent of UK cardiac care units in 1991 operated upper age limits and 40 per cent had an explicit age related policy for thrombolysis despite the fact that research suggests that older people may derive the most benefit from this treatment.[15] Similarly, a recent review suggested that 40 per cent of new cardiac rehabilitation programmes operated with upper age limits.[16] However, the report concludes that in the particular case of cardiac care, such age limits may become less common, as the UK National Service Framework for coronary heart disease is implemented, as this stresses that effective cardiac care should be available to all patients able to benefit.

Other areas where older people are offered different or less aggressive treatment to the younger populations include renal failure and cancer treatment. For example, the report found that within the UK older patients are less likely to be accepted for treatment for end stage renal failure. Similarly, older people may not always be offered the best treatment available for their cancer, with such decisions resting on a lack of available evidence of the effectiveness of cancer treatment in older people – partly due to the omission of older people in the past from clinical trials. This has now improved in the UK with the funders now requiring justifications for age-based exclusions from trials. There is also a lack of information, combined with stereotypical conceptions, about older people's preferences for end-of-life treatment. For example, studies of patient preferences in the USA highlighted the preference of older patients for aggressive treatment if this improved survival and revealed that older patients coped better psychologically with a cancer diagnosis than other age groups.[17] This view has to be countered, to an extent, by the lack of alternative palliative care available generally in the USA compared with the UK.

The use of age criteria for delivering health care, and in particular for screening, is clearly complex, because, in some cases at the national level, age is statistically associated with clinical ability to benefit. However, what is of concern is that this may deter people of all ages from requesting health services which are of benefit to them as individuals. The relationship between age and need is complex. As Harris argues:

> To define need . . . in terms of capacity to benefit and then to argue that the greater number of life years deliverable by health care, the greater the need for treatment . . . is just to beg the crucial question of how to characterise need or benefit . . . the principle of (health care delivery) should be to offer beneficial health care on the basis of individual need, so that each has an equal chance of flourishing to the extent that their personal health status permits.[18]

Furthermore, the age discrimination debate has become caught up in the wider debate concerning health care rationing in a tight resource system. For example, proponents of explicit rationing mechanisms tend to advocate a general utilitarian approach in order to maximise the health benefits for a given population. However:

> This tends to discriminate against older people because of the way in which health benefits tend to be measured – in terms of 'quality adjusted life years' (QALYs). There are several ways in which QALYs discriminate against older people. Firstly, because older people have lower life expectancies, health interventions in older age groups generate fewer 'life years' than interventions in younger age groups. Secondly, years lived in disability are given lower weight than years lived in full health. This discriminates against people with chronic disabilities and illness (many of whom will be older people). Finally, QALYs do not capture the breadth of outcomes that may be especially important to older people, such as independence, or the impact of an intervention on carers and family.[19]

Age discrimination within a tight resource environment such as the provision of health care is thus a complex and potentially contentious issue. In particular, advocates who suggest that all older people are automatically discriminated against because of their disempowered status may unintentionally act against the interests of older people. There will always be competition for scarce resources, and what may be in the interests of one group may deny another. Indirect age discrimination is the most complex of all, particularly in those areas where older people make up the majority of the recipients of a service, such as social and long-term care for example. Several issues remain key however. To use age *per se* as the sole discriminatory variable can rarely be justified, especially in relation to adults at the older end of the life course. Decisions should always be based on individual merit and not on the basis of stereotypical age-based assumptions. Second, it should be recognised that indirect discrimination which affects predominantly one sector of the population, for example, people at the end of their lives, can lead to ageism, ageist attitudes and ageist behaviour. Thus a society which fails to provide acceptable pay conditions and training to those expected to care for older people, whose own needs and wishes are often undervalued or even ignored, is in danger of sending a strong message that it is ageist and that such ageism is acceptable in both attitudes and behaviour.

Age discrimination and employment

Overt, direct age discrimination is present in the area of employment. Most Western countries accept mandatory retirement ages, which allow individual companies, and indeed the state public services themselves, to require individuals to retire purely on a chronological age criteria.

> If I am told that I cannot work because I am not qualified, then I have the choice to get more qualifications or retrain or do nothing. If I am told I cannot work because I am too old, then there is nothing I can do about this. I am completely disempowered.[20]

Indeed, it is the very essence of age discrimination for an older employee to be fired because the employer believes that productivity and competence decline with old age.[21] This is even more disempowering than women facing the marriage bar. While a completely unacceptable position, women did have the choice to marry and quit work or not to marry and continue. A man reaching age 55 has no control at all over his future if he is faced by a blanket disallowance simply because he has lived through 55 birthdays.

Employment discrimination on grounds of age is particularly disempowering as within modern society we are increasingly defined by our employment status. Of particular interest, therefore, is the 2000 EU directive on age discrimination and employment. If European countries accept anti-discriminatory legislation on work then this may give a strong signal that age-based discrimination is unacceptable is all other areas of life.

EU Framework Directive on age discrimination and employment

On 27 November 2000, the Council of the European Union adopted Council Directive 2000/78/EC, whose purpose:

> is to lay down a general framework for combating discrimination on the grounds of religion or belief, disability, age or sexual orientation as regards employment and occupation, with a view to putting into effect in the Member States the principle of equal treatment.

The provisions of this directive, sometimes called the Framework Directive, which applies only to employment, are modelled on those of Council Directive 2000/43/EC adopted in June 2000 – which applies to racial and ethnic origin discrimination not only in employment, but also to such discrimination in the context of social protection, including social security and health care, social advantages, education, and access to and supply of goods and services which are available to the public, including housing. Article 18 contains an exception that allows an additional period of three years from 2 December 2003, or until 2 December 2006. Although implementation of the directive has so far been uneven at best and in many cases non-compliant,[22] of the 15 EU member states, only Belgium, Sweden and the United Kingdom have informed the European Commission, as required by Article 18, that they intend to take advantage of the extension. Germany, apparently, will also ask for the additional three years to implement the directive on the criteria of age.

In relation to age, the directive in principle establishes a general framework for equal treatment in employment and occupation, which applies to labour market activities and vocational training. It lays down minimum requirements of prohibiting discrimination by member states, without justifying any regression from current levels of protection. It applies to all persons in employment or seeking employment or training, private and public sector employers, providers of vocational guidance and training, workers' and employers' organisations, professional organisations and public bodies. The directive prohibits both direct and indirect discrimination, harassment, victimisation and instructions to discriminate. It has the potential to protect against age discrimination in access to employment, training, working conditions (including dismissal and pay), and membership of professional or worker organisations. However, there are numerous exemptions, including mandatory age-based retirement.

Osborne has recently drawn upon the American experience with the Age Discrimination in Employment Act (ADEA) in order to highlight potential issues which may arise as the EU Framework Directive as implemented. Enacted in 1967 and in effect since early 1968, the ADEA serves: to promote the employment of older persons based on their ability rather than age; to prohibit arbitrary age discrimination in employment; and to help employers and workers find ways of meeting problems arising from the impact of age on employment. Following the 1967 Act were two sets of amendments and an Age Discrimination Act each strengthening the original ADEA. In 1975 the Age Discrimination Act prohibited age discrimination in all programmes or activities receiving federal assistance; the 1978 ADEA amendment extended the age range for the protected group from 40 to 70, raising mandatory retirement age to 70 in the same process. This upper age limit was subsequently eliminated in the 1986 amendment, thus banning mandatory retirement, with some very limited exceptions.

As Osborne points out, while the most obvious and blatant forms of age discrimination impacting the work place at the time of the ADEA's enactment, such as mandatory age-based retirement and age limitations in hiring, have been largely eliminated, more subtle forms of age discrimination have evolved and remain entrenched in the work place. While the ADEA and the EU Directive are broadly similar in approach and scope, there are major implications in the exemptions the EU Directive allows. For example, Article 4 and Article 6 provide what he describes as a minor exception and a potentially major problem.

Article 4, Section 1 of the directive allows member states to 'except from the definition of discrimination a difference in treatment based on a characteristic related to one of the four grounds covered by Article 1 – religion or belief, disability, age or sexual orientation – where such a characteristic constitutes a genuine and determining occupational requirement, provided that the objective is legitimate and the requirement is proportionate.' This is roughly equivalent to the ADEA's exception for a 'bona fide occupational qualification reasonably necessary to the normal operation of the particular business.' As Osborne notes, the ADEA's exception has caused few problems because it has been interpreted narrowly. As a result, outside the pubic safety arena, the courts have not accepted it and, consequently, employers rarely attempt to invoke it. Non-safety cases that have been successful include, for example, where a producer of entertainment has a requirement for a young actor to play the part of a child, or where a clothing merchant recruits young models to advertise fashions for teenagers. In reality, however, the actual requirement in such circumstances is for applicants having the appearance of being a certain age rather than actually being of that age.

Article 6, which applies only to age and not the other three grounds covered by Article 1, is a very broad exception. Section 1 'allows Member States to exempt differences of treatment . . . if . . . they are objectively and reasonably justified by a legitimate aim, including legitimate employment policy, labour market and vocational training objectives, and if the means of achieving that aim are appropriate and necessary.' Section 1 also provides a non-exhaustive list of circumstances to which the exception applies, including: the setting of special conditions on access to employment and vocational training for young people and older workers; the fixing of minimum conditions of age, professional experience or seniority in service for access to employment; the fixing of a maximum age for retirement which is based on the training requirements of the position in question or the need for a reasonable period of employment before retirement.

As Osborne notes, all three of these conditions would violate the ADEA. Furthermore, paragraph (25) of the Preamble acknowledges that the purpose of Article 6 is to provide 'flexibility' depending on the differing circumstances in each of the member states. It is therefore essential to distinguish between differences in treatment which are justified, in particular by legitimate employment policy, labour market and vocational training objectives, and discrimination which must be prohibited. Yet crucially, how to make and enforce this critical distinction is left completely to the discretion of the member states.

Finally, Article 2, Section 5 of the directive provides an exception for national laws relating to public safety and health. This will then clearly provide many employers with a means for requesting that those who are no longer safe to carry out their working activities should withdraw. Hopefully, a process which will apply to all workers of all ages.

Osborne argues that the major strength of the directive is in its coverage, in that it requires all 15 current EU member states to implement prescribed minimum protections against discrimination on four grounds – religion or belief, disability, age and sexual orientation – with the objective of the creation within the Community of a level playing field as regards equality in employment and occupation. The ten additional countries that became member states in May 2004 will also have to comply with the directive. Thus, all the major European countries eventually should have laws prohibiting discrimination in employment by both public and private entities on the basis of age and the other three grounds. Unlike the ADEA, whose application is limited to people aged 40 and older, the directive specifies no age limits, so that member states may choose whether or not to establish age limits in the implementation/transposition process. Furthermore, the directive applies to both the *public and private* sectors, including public bodies. As originally enacted, the ADEA applied only to private entities. It was subsequently amended to apply to both federal and state government employers, except for US military personnel, but the Supreme Court has recently ruled that state governments are not liable to ADEA suits for damages by their employees. Thus, the coverage of the directive is broader than the ADEA both in terms of age and the entities and institutions to which it applies. Osborne also identifies a further major strength of the directive in that it applies to both direct and indirect discrimination, whereas the most significant weakness of the ADEA is that it does not state explicitly that it prohibits age discrimination arising from disparate impact – the US equivalent of indirect discrimination.

Weaknesses of the EU Framework Directive

In terms of weaknesses, the range of exemptions allowed under the directive, and the flexibility of member states to decide which to allow significantly undermines much of the directive's purpose. As Osborne states:

The most significant weakness of the Directive is, of course, Article 6, which applies only to the age ground. This provision, if adopted by the Member States in the transposition/ implementation process, will likely generate more controversy and litigation than all of the other Articles of the Directive combined.[23]

Furthermore, resolution of the questions of when an age-based employment action is objectively and reasonably justified by a legitimate aim and whether the means of achieving that aim are appropriate and necessary and which aims are legitimate and which are not is likely to take a long time and will undoubtedly vary widely among the member states. The result of this process may be several quite different bodies of law rather than a more or less uniform approach to the problem of age discrimination in employment. Osborne goes on to state that the flexibility inherent in Article 6 may jeopardise the achievement of the objective of the directive, namely the creation within the Community of a level playing field as regards equality in employment and occupation. Of most concern, however, is that the directive does not address national mandatory retirement laws, once again leaving it to each member state to decide what, if any, reforms to implement regarding the area in which differences in treatment based on age arguably have the most significant effect on national economies and, indirectly impact the economy of the EU as a whole.

Osborne thus concludes that unless the member states take a much more aggressive approach to implementation of the directive, it will provide much less protection against age discrimination in employment than workers in the EU have a right to expect from the promise of its provisions:

> In the Framework Directive, the European Council proposed a comprehensive approach to combating and eliminating employment discrimination on the grounds of religion or belief, disability, age and sexual orientation in the Member States. Given the long history of age-based employment policies across Europe, age discrimination will be the hardest of the four grounds covered by the Directive for the Member States to address effectively. The Framework Directive contains significant weaknesses that can be exploited by those states that lack the political will to act boldly to eliminate age discrimination. Given the uneven and disappointing record on implementation of both the Racial Equality Directive and the Framework Directive thus far, the prognosis for addressing effectively age discrimination in employment both by the current and new Member States any time soon is not encouraging.[24]

Even though the majority of the member states did not fully comply with the 2 December 2003 deadline, only the United Kingdom, Belgium and Sweden notified the Commission that they will take the allowed additional three years, until 2 December 2006, to implement the directive's provisions regarding age discrimination. Four member states, Austria, France, Italy and Ireland have reported full implementation, although questions remain regarding the effectiveness of the transposition in the first three. Denmark, the Netherlands, Greece, Finland, Luxembourg, Spain and Portugal are in various stages of achieving transposition although, again, questions remain regarding the effectiveness of the implementation proposals. Of all the member states, Ireland appears to have the most comprehensive approach to age discrimination as well as the political will to fully implement the Framework Directive's provisions on age, although, as we shall now see, there are major issues here.

In addition to what is perceived by many to be ineffective implementation of the directive by some member states, it is clear that the directive:

> while a laudable pan-European attempt at addressing age discrimination in employment that has been entrenched in the social fabric of the EU Member States since at least the end of World War II, contains broad exceptions to its prohibitions that unless specifically limited during transposition into national laws and/or subsequently interpreted quite narrowly by the courts of each Member State, have the potential to eviscerate its carefully crafted protections.[25]

The European fabric includes not only different employment and labour market traditions, but also different existing employment legislation which incorporates age discrimination. Thus Austria, Belgium, the Netherlands and Spain have primary legislation; Finland, France and Italy have an existing employment act, code or decree; there is no relevant legislation in Denmark, Sweden, Luxembourg, Germany or the UK, though the latter has a non-statutory code of practice; in Portugal age discrimination on grounds of age is prohibited in the constitution and in Greece at a minimum age only. Only Ireland has an existing Equal Status Act and Employment Equality Act which covers both employment and access to goods and services.

However, behind this lie some interesting commentaries on national attitudes and practices in relation to age discrimination. A comparison of Ireland and Sweden provides an interesting illustration of this. The Irish 1998 Employment Equality Act addresses age discrimination in the labour market, being extended in 2000 by the Equal Status Act which covers the provision of goods and services. A comprehensive Act similar in coverage and scope to the EU Directive, it is the implementation and in particular the exemptions which have attracted interest. While seen initially as a watershed in age discrimination legislation, the array of exemptions and justifications sound a cautious note for the carrying out of the EU-wide legislation. Thus existing retirement ages continue to apply and furthermore the employer may fix different retirement ages. Differences in pay and employment terms and conditions based on seniority are allowed, as are differences based on sound actuarial or other evidence that significantly increased costs would be incurred by the employer if discrimination were not allowed. Even ageism in recruitment is allowed, in that recruitment age limits may take into account the cost and time of training and allow for a reasonable period of employment prior to retirement.

Sweden takes a different stance, which emerges from the Scandinavian welfare model. The Swedish Constitution regulates public employment and requires that appointments are made on objective criteria. Age is not considered an objective criterion. Nor does the Swedish Employment Protection Act accept age as an objective criterion for dismissal. The overriding principle is that of good practice in employment, which is upheld by the courts, requiring that employees are treated in an acceptable and ethical manner. Age discrimination is not accepted as consistent with good practice.

As we saw in Chapter 4, Sweden has a far higher age of normal retirement and, as a result a lower level of unused productive capacity than any other EU country included in the Gruber and Wise study.[26] While, as we discussed, there are a variety of interacting forces behind the emergence of early retirement, the societal acceptance of compulsory redundancy at age 60 or 65, under the guise of retirement, has clearly had a strong impact in most European countries. The fact that three countries – USA, Sweden and Japan – the first two without mandatory retirement practices and Japan with a system that acts to guarantee job security up until age 60, have the lowest levels of withdrawal gives a clear indication that mandatory retirement practices based on age alone have had their impact.

However, the general strictness of employment protection for regular workers may also have an impact here. This varies widely between countries, with Australia, Canada, the UK and the USA having minimal levels of protection, while Japan, Germany, Italy, Sweden, the Netherlands and Portugal have high levels. There is conflicting evidence as to whether such protection increases or decreases the employment rates of older workers, as indicated, for example, by the dichotomous position of the USA versus Japan and Sweden. While restrictive employment legislation may protect workers who already have a job, this may be at the expense of workers without employment. Sweden has the additional factor of the *first-in-last-out rule*, which holds that employers must give priority of continued employment to those who have been employed longest; where the length of employment is equal, workers who are older have priority.[27] As the OECD report into employment and ageing in Sweden states:

> On the one hand, the high rate of employment in the age group 50–64 in Sweden may
> be explained by employment protection legislation that works in favour of older
> employees. When enterprises are forced to reduce staff, the principle of the first-in-last-
> out rule will hold since older workers have usually been employed longer, they face a
> lower risk of being made redundant than younger workers. On the other hand, it may
> reduce mobility of older workers . . . since an employee who switches to another job will
> lose the employment security they have built up on their tenure in their former job.[28]

However, as the report goes on to discuss, while the *first-in-last-out* rule still holds generally, agreements with unions, particularly in the state sector, are relaxing this rule partially to protect the rights of younger workers. The re-skilling and continual training and upgrading of all workers, including older workers, are increasingly seen as key to ensuring job protection.

Finally, the new member states will face a particular challenge in transposing anti-discrimination legislation. Age discrimination is a relatively unfamiliar concept in many of these countries, and employment rates of older workers are generally low, around 30 per cent. Older workers often find it difficult to access training and new employment opportunities, and the new anti-discrimination practices should play an important role as part of a broader approach to raising labour participation rates of older workers.[29]

UK Age Diversity Code of Practice

The UK Age Diversity Code of Practice[30] is often given as an example of good employment practice. The code covers good practice in six aspects of employment:

- *Recruitment* – recruit on the basis of skills and abilities to do the job.

- *Selection* – select on merit by focusing on skills, abilities and performance.

- *Promotion* – base on ability or potential to do the job.

- *Training and development* – encourage all employees to take advantage of relevant opportunities.

- *Redundancy* – base decisions on objective, job-rated criteria.

- *Retirement* – ensure that retirement schemes are fairly applied.

However, despite strong government support for following these guidelines, and their reiteration in the new Commission for Equality and Human Rights White Paper,[31] the entrenched ageist attitudes and behaviour within the UK labour market are all too apparent.

This can be seen, for example, in the response by a large UK employers' federation to the DTI's consultation paper *Equality and Diversity: Age Matters*.[32] While overtly claiming to support in principle that individuals should be judged on the basis of their ability and skills, and not on stereotypes related to their age, the response is littered with ageist and unfounded stereotypical assumptions. They assume that from age 50 onwards competence declines, absences increase, and potential for development decreases, all stereotypical fallacies which we corrected in Chapter 4. The federation also stated that it was preferable to recruit and train younger workers who were more likely to stay long enough to get a decent return on training investment. In fact, as we saw in Chapter 4, older workers, if not made redundant or compulsorily retired, are a far more loyal and stable workforce. The response was also very paternalistic and ageist in its views of older workers, as if most adults are not realistic about their capacity to continue. There was also confusion about the role of pension schemes, which are a form of saving whereby the employee saves and the employer contributes to this saving in the form of deferred income. The federation argued that after a particular age, if that was beyond the expected normal retirement age, employees should not be obliged to contribute their part of the package, thus negating the very basis of the deferred income relationship, and the fact that working later to increase retirement income will increasingly become one of the key drivers for many people. The federation argued for the DTI to introduce a fixed default retirement age of 65 as part of the 2006 age discrimination legislation.

Working and saving for retirement

A strong pragmatic reason for anti-age discrimination legislation is to ensure that individuals have access to employment for as long as they are able to contribute, in order that they are able to save enough to carry them through the increasingly long life expectancies they are now forecast to enjoy. The ageing of life transitions, which we discussed in Chapter 6, has significant implication for late life income. For example, the widening of access to higher education to eventually cover half the population, combined with an increasing necessity for individuals to pay for this, negates against early life saving while loans are paid back. The housing market has put extra demands on early life income, and the combination of later entry into the labour market and later commencement of parenting both delay the commencement of saving for post-employment. Work by the UK Pensions Policy Institute, for example, has calculated the proportion of earnings required to be saved on top of the Basic State Pension and the State Second Pension in order to achieve a gross replacement level of two thirds. As is clear from Fig. 10.1, an individual who is not able to start saving until he reaches age 40, would need to save 19 per cent of his annual income if he were to retire at age 65, but only 4 per cent if able to continue just five years longer until age 70.

Given this, the position of the employers' federation mentioned above, demanding a fixed mandatory default retirement age of 65, is completely unjustified in the new longevity climate. Of more concern, however, are the prevailing views of management consultants who continue to peddle the myth that graduates will be able to retire at age 50. Dismissing the notion that work–life balance is a possibility in the modern Anglo-American labour market, they argue that graduates should expect to work for 20 years and then aim to retire and do the 'life' bit.[33] This is an ingenuous portfolio of advice given the increase in longevity and downfall in pension provision these graduates will experience in their lifetimes. The UK Government's recent Green Paper was not called *Working and Saving for Retirement* for nothing.

The European situation does seem even more unacceptable when one considers that not only the USA, but also Australia (1996 ban on age discrimination; 1999 ban on compulsory retirement), Canada (1960s age discrimination legislation) and New Zealand (1993 Human Rights Act) have all introduced age discrimination legislation which appears, to some extent, to protect the rights of older workers. Yet, while sex

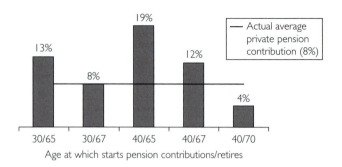

Figure 10.1 *Proportion of earnings needed to be saved on top of the basic state pension and the state second pension in order to achieve a gross replacement level of two-thirds, for an individual on median earnings reaching 65 in 2028.*
Source: Slide prepared by O'Connell, Pensions Policy Institute.

and race discrimination have been extensively evaluated, age discrimination has received less attention. In fact, US research which was carried out on the period when age discrimination legislation was introduced in the USA suggests that it boosted employment rates of those workers over age 60[34] and reduced retirement.[35] There is, however, also evidence that it does not affect the hiring of older workers, who still seem to be at a disadvantage, possibly due to their more expensive pension costs in defined benefit regimes.[36] As we saw in Chapter 5, most employers in the private sector at least are moving away from these to defined contribution schemes. Recruitment is also the biggest single cause of age discrimination complaints in Australia.[37] Other concerns are that this will lead to expensive age discrimination cases have not been borne out in other countries, with age discrimination cases in the USA and Australia running at less than 10 per cent of all discrimination cases each year. Finally, the arguments of neo-classical economists[38] that age discrimination legislation interferes unwarrantedly with the market mechanism and is unjustified as employers will not act against their own interests,[39] did not stand the test in the 1950s when large numbers of older workers were removed from the labour market, and replaced by immigrant labour, at the very time when these older workers were requesting to remain economically active, and would have proved a stable labour force.[40] As Encel notes, 'There is abundant evidence that employers and managers are influenced at least as much by popular stereotypes as by rational calculation'.[41]

We must also not forget that age discrimination acts at the lower as well as the upper end of the spectrum. Issues concerning youth wages, for example, have proved particularly contentious, although there is some agreement that these should be redefined as training wages and thus focus on the ability and qualifications rather than the age of the individual.[42]

In summary, we can see that there is a variety of evidence that many older people do not leave employment voluntarily, encounter greater difficulties in being hired, and that employers make stereotypical incorrect assumptions about individuals on the basis of their age alone. Age discrimination damages workers, business and the economy. It limits recruitment, training and promotion of able workers, and it damages economies by wasting an experienced, skilled workforce. The general conclusion of those countries who do have some form of anti-discrimination legislation is that it has a place in dealing with the pervasive problem of age discrimination. Indeed, in the USA it has been argued that:

> the predominant effect of age discrimination legislation has been to reduce the likelihood that firms renege on long-term commitments to older high-paid workers, and consequently to strengthen long-term relationships between workers and firms.[43]

However, this is the beginning of a long process of tackling institutionalised ageism inherent within most societies, a process which requires more than one approach:

> multiple approaches, including public awareness campaigns, greater exposure of the research findings and a more proactive approach to monitoring discrimination are necessary if discrimination in employment is to be significantly reduced.[44]

Age discrimination and the development agenda

It is not only in industrialised countries that issues of age discrimination need to be urgently addressed; older people in developing countries are also subject to discrimination on grounds of age at local, national and even international level:

> Ageing is both a universal and personal experience. The rights and principles we espouse and deny today are our rights, now and in the future. But millions of older people across the world face chronic poverty, untreated illness, homelessness or inadequate shelter, violence and abuse, lack of education, little or no access to the law, fear and isolation. . . . Age discrimination is our core concern. All societies discriminate against people on grounds of age. Ageism and stereotyping influence attitudes, which in turn affect the way decisions are taken and resources allocated at household, community, national and international level.[45]

HelpAge International – ten-point plan

Pointing out that the only specific provisions for older age – the UN Principles for Older Persons, calling for independence, dignity, care, self-fulfilment and participation – are not yet incorporated into international human rights law, HelpAge International (HAI) has recently identified a ten-point plan for ending age discrimination to ensure that older people across the world benefit from the full range of internationally accepted human rights[46] (Fig. 10.2).

> 1 Recognise the human rights of older people and the benefits of population ageing for human development.
> 2 Allocate older people their fair share of national and global resources.
> 3 Guarantee adequate social protection and minimum income in old age.
> 4 Provide accessible and free health care for older people.
> 5 Make credit, employment, training and education schemes available to people regardless of age.
> 6 Put an end to violence against older people.
> 7 Ensure policy makers listen to and act on the views of older people.
> 8 Include and consult older people in emergency aid and rehabilitation planning after disasters and humanitarian crises.
> 9 Establish international practice standards to govern public policy on ageing.
> 10 Support older people in their role as carers.

Figure 10.2   *Ten actions to end age discrimination*
Source: HelpAge International, 2001.

We shall now look at each of these suggested actions in more detail below.

1 Recognise the human rights of older people and the benefits of population ageing for human development

The context to this recommendation is that most older people wish to remain active members of their societies, working and living alongside their families and communities. They want to be involved in development programmes, to contribute their expertise and knowledge and learn new skills. One issue, however, is that both older and younger people need to be encouraged to value their contributions, as household and reproductive activities are not usually accorded economic value. Indeed:

> failure to record these diverse contributions – by official statistics, communities, individuals and older people themselves – reinforces stereotypes that stress older people's welfare *needs* over and above their social and economic *contributions* to society.[47] (Author's emphasis)

HAI recommends that the design and delivery of international development and resourcing initiatives, such as donor aid budgets, poverty reduction strategy papers and Heavily Indebted Poor Countries (HIPC)-related debt relief programmes, should give priority to growing older populations in resource-poor countries.

2 Allocate older people their fair share of national and global resources

This requires that national and international budget strategies take account of ageing populations. In particular, HAI suggests that national and international policy should assert the citizenship rights of older people to a proportionate share of available resources as a matter of equity, alongside supporting the development potential of older age groups in a systematic and targeted way. Data collection at national and international level should demonstrate the numbers of older people living in poverty and how they might escape from it, and age-based indicators should be adopted to measure progress in poverty reduction, including intergenerational benefits of investing in older age groups.

3 Guarantee adequate social protection and minimum income in old age

Pointing out that the primary concerns of older people in all countries are for material security and access to food and health care, HAI states that international and national initiatives designed to regulate social protection on an equitable basis are not responding to the requirements of ageing populations. Yet without the safety net of social protection, ageing brings with it reduced rights to food, health, transport, housing, sanitation and other basic services. They thus recommend that resource-poor countries should be supported financially and technically to deliver a range of social protection mechanisms, including minimum income, as an integral part of their development policies.

4 Provide accessible and free health care for older people

As HAI notes, older people should have the same access to health care as other age groups but, in fact, they often get less than their fair share. The specific health issues of older people should be included in strategies to improve overall health status, with particular attention given to the health risks presented by social isolation, self-neglect, poor nutrition, the effects of menopause and failing sight:

> Older women's health needs should be given special attention, especially as they often forego treatment and medication in favour of younger family members. Older men, in particular, suffer high levels of mental health problems, and receive little or no support from the health services.[48]

This, HAI suggests, needs input from the highest international level, ensuring, for example, that global initiatives on health, including the Global Health Fund, include older people and international investment in WHO includes funding for work on chronic disease and ageing.

5 Make credit, employment, training and education schemes available to people regardless of age

Most poor people work into very old age and therefore have the same requirements as other age groups for employment, credit, development assistance, education and training schemes. Yet, credit is often denied on grounds of age and there is an upper limit on most loan schemes. Furthermore, as we have already seen, as with other age groups, credit, education and training opportunities improve older people's prospects, and their capacity to support their families. In addition, many older people are educators themselves of future generations:

Lifelong access to education, training and development resources is a right and a necessity to tackle the discrimination older people face. Stereotypes that portray older people as unable to learn new skills, or being too wedded to past practices, need to be challenged. Too many older people are marginalized by lack of literacy and numeracy.[49]

Policy makers, development agencies, communities and older people need to confront practice and attitudes that effectively exclude people on grounds of age from education schemes. In particular, age-based limits to credit, employment and training should be illegal.

6 Put an end to violence against older people

HAI calls for the strongest possible statement condemning violence against older people, as an infringement of their most basic human rights:

The extent and nature of violence perpetrated against older men and women is only just becoming apparent. The issue is now being talked about, to a great extent because older people are daring to speak out, and are being asked about it more frequently. Older people are telling us that they view old age with anxiety and fear, not only because of worsening poverty, but due to increasing dependency on others and consequent vulnerability to physical, sexual and psychological abuse. Men and women suffer abuse at the hands of close family, community, government officers and other professionals.[50]

When ageing is associated with a decline in productive capacity, the result is often abandonment, the removal of assets such as property and inheritance rights, and lowered social status in the family and community. Older women may become vulnerable if they lose family protection when they become widows:

National and international legislation to protect people from violence is often not applied in cases of violence against older people. It is essential to confront attitudes and systems that allow violence against older people to go unchallenged, as well as to ensure that older men and women have equal access to the law at national and international level.[51]

It is recommended by HAI that governments should work towards a national and comprehensive strategy to stop violence against older people, encompassing a supportive legal framework, and public education and training for professional staff in the public sector to equip them to detect and act on abuse. In addition, it calls for the Office of the High Commission of Human Rights to appoint a special rapporteur on older people, to seek out and publish data on the violence experienced by older people on a regular basis.

7 Ensure policy makers listen to and act on the views of older people

Consultative processes linked to poverty reduction and human rights compliance at local, national and international level must include the perspective of older age groups. In particular, formal barriers to participation, such as age limits, need to be removed by law and in practice, and positive efforts should be made to reach out to and involve older people. This requires the active engagement of older people's organisations in national planning processes.

8 Include and consult older people in emergency aid and rehabilitation planning after disasters and humanitarian crises

Older people make up 10–20 per cent of refugees and internally displaced persons and undergo the same difficulties of finding food, shelter and security in the immediate aftermath of an emergency as other vulnerable groups, and suffer disproportionately from mobility constraints, long journeys, the cold and other adversities. In addition:

> Older people are often left behind in villages and farms, either to guard property or because they are physically unable to flee. Yet they also care for their children and grandchildren, and help to rebuild communities traumatised by war and loss. Against all odds they contribute to and even in some cases run emergency programmes and support rebuilding efforts within communities and families.[52]

Yet, despite all this, their needs are often marginalised in humanitarian relief. HAI believes that this is due to deep-rooted attitudes that regard older people as passive and as having less to contribute than other groups. It calls for the immediate implementation of UNHCR's policy on older refugees and the objectives outlined in the International Strategy for Action on Ageing, relating to older people in emergency situations.

9 Establish international practice standards to govern public policy on ageing

The UN Principles for Older Persons provide a global framework to govern practice on ageing. The five key themes, the right to independence, dignity, care, self-fulfilment and participation, respond well to the core concerns of older people, and can form the basis of policies and programmes that are inclusive, value-based and present sustainable models of development. Unfortunately, the Principles are not yet incorporated into international human rights law. In addition, as HAI notes, older people increasingly rely on goods and services from the private sector, where the lack of regulation leaves opportunities for bad practice. They thus recommend the establishment of regulatory mechanisms, based on human rights standards, for the delivery of services to older people and an incorporation of human rights principles into the training and education of health care providers. In particular, issues of ageing should be incorporated as a category in human rights treaties and conventions, and ensure that standards of government compliance are monitored and reported on, in the same way as other categories of vulnerable sectors of society.

10 Support older people in their role as carers

Finally, as we saw earlier, caregiving is a growing issue for older people. As HAI also highlights, older women tend to shoulder much of the responsibility of caring for both older and younger family members, yet receive little recognition or material support for their work, nor training or information to assist them. This is being compounded by conflict and natural disasters, HIV/AIDS and rural–urban migration. HAI recommends that regular programmes of support for older carers should be established at national and international level, including training as carers, respite care, literacy and education provision, material support and support for school fees.

Finally, we should note that this is not a cosmetic exercise. The agenda is wide, and potentially has significant ramifications for older people's material security, health and well-being. Only a change in social attitudes, including the attitudes and expectations of older people themselves, will reduce discrimination and exclusion of older people, and crucially result in the allocation of resources to meet their needs.[53]

Notes

1 Grimley-Evans, 2003, p. 20.
2 Roberts, 2000.
3 Help the Aged, 2002.
4 Lester, 2001.
5 Help the Aged, 2002.
6 Clark, 2002.
7 Soulsby, 2000.
8 Roberts, 2000, p. 1.
9 General Medical Council, 2001, paragraph 13.
10 Torgerson and Gosden, 1998.
11 Sutton, 1997.
12 Age Concern England, 2000b.
13 Bengtson and Harootyan, 1994.
14 Age Concern England, 2000a.
15 Dudley and Burns, 1992.
16 Whelan, 1998.
17 Turner et al., 1999.
18 Harris, 1997.
19 Roberts, 2000, p. 8.
20 Leeson, 2004.
21 Osborne, 2004.
22 ibid.
23 ibid., p. 17.
24 ibid., p. 27.
25 ibid., p. 2.
26 Gruber and Wise, 1999.
27 OECD, 2003a.
28 ibid., p. 85.

29 European Commission, 2004.
30 Age Positive, 2002.
31 Department of Trade and Industry, 2004.
32 Department of Trade and Industry, 2003.
33 This is reflected in a variety of modern management consultancy materials.
34 Adams, 2000; Neumark and Stock, 1999.
35 Adams 2000; Ashenfelter and Card, 2000.
36 Hirsch et al., 2000; Hutchens, 1988.
37 Encel, 2001; Steinberg et al., 1998.
38 Posner, 1985.
39 Encel, 2001.
40 Harper and Thane, 1989.
41 Encel, 2001, p. 17.
42 ibid.
43 Neumark, 2001.
44 Bennington and Wein, 2000, p. 32, quoted in Encel, 2001.
45 HAI, 2001, p. 1.
46 ibid.
47 ibid., p. 5.
48 ibid., p. 11.
49 ibid., p. 12.
50 ibid., p. 13.
51 ibid.
52 HAI, 2001, p. 17.
53 ibid.

11
Mature societies: planning for our future selves

We concluded Chapter 1 by suggesting that the reality of demographic ageing can be approached in different ways. Governments can introduce ameliorative policies and wait for a more age-symmetric population to arrive, they can attempt to manipulate population structures through increasing fertility or immigration, or they can actively explore the many advantages of a society with a mature population, adapt to take full advantage of these opportunities, and work towards creating the framework for an age symmetric society. As our discussion has now shown, much of the predicted change over the next two decades will arise through the particular dynamics of current cohorts, not only their specific demographic make-up but also their attitudes and behaviour. In Chapter 10, we examined the barriers caused by the inherent ageism and age discrimination, institutionalised in both the developed and developing world, at international, national and local levels. We now conclude by exploring how we can harness the experience, expertise and creativity of such an historically large number of older people, and create a mature age integrated society, in which chronological age becomes irrelevant, alongside a real appreciation of individual characteristics.

While there are a spectrum of issues to be considered, and more currently unseen, which will emerge over the next few decades, three appear to be pressing. First is the establishment of age integration; secondly the incorporation of older people and ageing into the wider development agenda; and thirdly individual and societal acceptance that the human condition is final and inevitable and includes death and a period of decline. We may be pushing back the boundaries of frailty, but we shall never replace the eventual finality of life.

Creating age-integrated societies

Age integration has been defined as breaking down structural barriers and bringing together people who differ in chronological age through the recognition that 'age criteria are flexible rather than fixed'.[1] The removal of structural age barriers, such as those to opportunities in work and education, allows the introduction of flexible age criteria so that access, entry, progress and exit are not constrained by chronological age. Age heterogeneity would then result from the aggregation of individuals of different ages within the same set of structures or roles. There is evidence that these processes may already be commencing. We shall consider this in relation to age integration in the work place and within families.

Age integration in the work place

As we saw earlier, one of the barriers to age-integrated workforces is the general reluctance of employers to hire older workers, even in those countries with anti-age discrimination legislation.[2] Yet 50 years ago, when they were last seen as a valuable component of the workforce, there was ample evidence that older workers made an active and valuable contribution to economic activity.[3] While there were changes in capacity with age, these could be overcome through retraining and adaptation of the work environment.[4] Furthermore an age-integrated workforce was perceived to be a versatile workforce.[5] Such evidence is all the more abundant today,[6] with the latest US research findings from the manufacturing sector (whose employers register the highest concern that their older workers will not be able to maintain productivity rates as they age) showing that as a group those aged 55 and older are as productive as those aged 35–54, and more productive than those aged under 35.[7]

In addition, we may already be seeing a downturn in early retirement rates, and a more composite transition from full-time economic activity to full-time retirement. This may include periods of unemployment, employment and 'retirement', and the increasing use of second career or 'bridge jobs' during this period. Evidence from the USA in particular, suggests a possible reversal in the trend towards early retirement, while government policies in Western Europe and Japan are now turning towards encouraging workers to remain within the labour market.

In the USA, following large decreases in employment after age 60 during the 1970s and early 1980s, the rate of decline for men slowed noticeably during the late 1980s.[8] During the 1990s there was virtually no change in the percentage of men aged 60–64 in the labour force, with the years 1992–97 seeing a slight increase from 55.3 per cent to 55.6 per cent. For those in their fifties, the rate of increase in early retirement withdrawal slowed during the 1990s, and may even have begun to reverse for this age group. Indeed, in the USA there are several studies which suggest that men aged 50–64 are increasing their economic activity and that men in their fifties are reversing their trend towards early retirement.[9] Recent participation rates from the US Bureau of Labor Statistics reveal a drop in younger worker rates by 0.7 per cent, the largest experienced in all recessions since 1960, accompanied by an unexpected increase by 2 per cent among workers over age 55. As Eschtruth and Gemus state, the magnitude of this rise in labour force participation during a period of recession is unprecedented in post-war US economic history.[10] They believe that this US trend is partially related to changes in pension provision, particularly the take-up in 401(k) plans, so that stock market declines are persuading some workers to postpone retirement, and even some recent retirees to rejoin the workforce. So, while some authors suggest that the long-term trend to early retirement will continue in the decades to come,[11] an increasing number are beginning to argue that we may indeed see a trend towards increasing US labour force participation among older workers.[12]

Similarly, in the UK there has been a slight increase in employment among the 50–64 age group, which fell from 77 per cent in 1984 to 71 per cent in 1995, increasing a little to 73 per cent by 2001.[13] For UK women, the higher level of mid-life employment is characteristic of more recent birth cohorts of women. During the 1970s and 1980s, the percentage of women aged 55–64 in the labour force increased slightly from 52 per cent to 57 per cent (1979–2002) (compared with a fall from 80 per cent to 62 per cent for men) reflecting the balance between the trend towards early retirement and trend towards mid-life labour force participation among successive birth cohorts. These trends continued during the 1990s, resulting in an increase in labour force participation from 37.1 per cent to 40.2 per cent by 1997.

Early retirement may be, for some, a transition between a first and second career. Analysis of 2 waves of ONS Retirement Survey[14] suggested, for example, that 8 per cent moved in and out of spells of employment, unemployment and retirement. Similarly, in the UK there is evidence from both the Labour Force Survey and ONS that the increased employment rate of both men and women in their fifties during the 1990s, was related to the growth in self-employment. This may reflect the increased levels of opportunities for self-employment due to the accumulation of social and economic capital at these later ages.[15] There is also evidence that this group are moving increasingly into small businesses, which may form the transitional bridge jobs between work and retirement. Quinn and Kozy's work with 1992 HRS suggests that by the end of the 1990s 28 per cent of men over 49 were in bridge jobs following retirement from their previous occupations.[16]

Future trends?

A key question is whether the experiences of current cohorts may reflect possible future trends. The context to this is provided by Henretta's overview of longer-term change in the USA. He first suggests that the declining unemployment and tight labour markets of the 1990s played a part in stabilising labour force participation levels. He then identifies three forces which may change the trend to earlier withdrawal: demographic, labour market and social security. By 2016 the cohort entering retirement age bands 60–64 will be almost as large as those in midlife today. The retirement effect will be significantly stronger, and employers will be losing a far larger percentage of trained employees than ever before. He further points out that, in the USA at least, the current cohort of 60 to 64 year olds still has a far lower level of schooling than those coming up behind it. While the retirement of this current cohort of older workers will raise the overall level of education of the workforce as a whole, this effect will be lost for subsequent cohorts. This effect will, however, be compounded by the increasing number of mid-life returns to education and lifelong learning programmes. Furthermore, the outdating of skills among the US workforce will be reduced as subsequent cohorts are better educated and thus find it easier to upgrade, something that Harper has highlighted for the UK population. Finally, better health and less disability have been predicted for successive US cohorts.[17] Fogel and Costa,[18] for example, have argued that improved health among current older adults may indicate trends affecting the whole population, thus younger cohorts as they age will enjoy even better health. Henretta[19] suggests that social and self-expectations for persons in their sixties and seventies may change with better health and vigour, as may their willingness to engage in economic employment. Here, both their health and their health-driven perception of the significance of being a certain age will be of importance. Employers may change their attitudes in line with the change in social expectations and be willing to create opportunities.

Henretta also predicts changes in the labour market which will encourage later and possibly more flexible withdrawal from economic employment. There now appears to be growing evidence[20] that the long-term trend of increasing institutional support for age-structured employment careers has halted. Younger people are less likely to spend their careers in jobs that offer increasing rewards and security in return for longer tenure. Increasingly, older workers will hold the expectation of far more variable patterns of career endings, plus the possibility that more non-career jobs will be available. This has in part been encouraged by changes in the US industrial structure towards the service sector. Here employers are more likely to have contingent and part-time employment arrangements. Similarly, more changes within firms are occurring. In order to cope with increasing competition and technological change, some employers are keeping a smaller proportion of employees in career employment, and more in contingent employment, which allows greater adaptability.

Henretta's final argument concerns changing government regulation concerning social security.[21] The birth cohort 1952 falls in the middle of these changes so that those individuals reaching age 65 in 2017 will have to wait a full year until they are age 66 to receive full social security benefit. At age 62 they can take the benefit at 75 per cent rather than the 80 per cent currently. These changes, and others undoubtedly to follow, mean that employers may manipulate their contributions to social security in order to persuade good workers to stay in the labour market. In addition, these reforms will lie alongside the increase in defined contribution pensions, replacing the traditional defined benefit plans. The benefit 'cliff' of defined benefit plans will be removed, and as contribution plans lack incentives to retire at a specific age, this strong incentive for early retirement will also be increasingly reduced.

Harper[22] has produced similar arguments for the UK, pointing out that the attitudes and experiences of older people today are not necessarily those of the future. Younger cohorts, currently in early and midlife, will have very different education, labour market and health experiences. They are already growing accustomed to a less rigid labour market[23] with greater access to part-time and flexible working patterns, and the need for continual skills updating and retraining. These individuals may have different aspirations in later life, and the financial incentives and disincentives for economic employment will undoubtedly have changed. Alongside this is growing evidence from the USA[24] that these cohorts will be healthier, and that this cohort effect is likely to continue into old age. The economic and social attitudes towards late life employment and retirement are thus likely to be different, possibly very different, for these younger cohorts who are approaching late life work and retirement decisions over the next three decades.

It may be argued that there are cyclical labour market trends which mirror demographic patterns. Thus in the immediate post-war period there was an emphasis on retaining older workers at a time of youth labour shortage.[25] This was replaced in the last quarter of the twentieth century by a negative view of older people as a younger labour force emerged. It may follow then that the predicted fall in the number of younger people entering the labour market over the next 20 years will in itself lead to the retention of older workers and a more integrated workforce. However, as we have seen, there are now considerable complexities in the system and attitudes are firmly entrenched in some sectors, both in relation to the perceived characteristics of older workers and the attractions of early retirement. It may need effective intervention by governments to counterbalance these. The policies against age discrimination discussed in Chapter 10 may be only part of the strategy required to integrate older people back into the workforce. Rather, governments may need to introduce more targeted schemes.

The Scandinavian transitional retirement schemes provide appropriate models. These were introduced in the four Nordic countries in the late 1980s and early 1990s as a means of enabling older workers to withdraw from full-time employment. Now they are being considered as a means not to *remove* older workers but to *retain* them by allowing a flexible withdrawal from full-time employment.

Denmark, for example, has recently reformed its scheme which allows transitional early retirement through raising the number of hours allowed to be worked, and the lifetime insurance contributions required to be paid in order to qualify for the scheme. This is an attempt to encourage more participation in the labour market.[26] The Finnish gradual retirement scheme was introduced in 1987 for public workers and in 1989 for private workers, partly to increase flexibility on retirement. It was also thought that employment would be created by the scheme. A part-time pension is thus available to workers between the ages of 55 and 64.[27] Norway has a traditional very high rate of late life work. In 1999 only 44 per cent of those aged 65–66 were in receipt of a pension, and only 33 per cent of 60–65 year olds. Since 1973 it has offered a part-time pension scheme to those aged 67–70. A similar scheme has been introduced for those aged over 62.[28] In many cases the worker remains with their employer, but on a part-time basis.[29]

Another policy option is to encourage employers to hire and retain older workers through the use of subsidies. The argument here is that the only way to break down ageist stereotypes and create conducive working environments and business structures for an integrated workforce, is for employers to see that such workforces provide good business practice. There already exist several such subsidy schemes in Europe. French companies hiring unemployed people aged 50 or above can take advantage of the *Contrat Initiative Emploi* (contract to promote employment), a subsidy which reduces the employer's social security contributions. It is paid indefinitely if the person is disabled or has been unemployed for more than one year. Germany has an integration subsidy, the *Eingliederungszuschusse*, which corresponds to 50 per cent of wages for those hiring long-term unemployed people over age 55. Sweden's Special Employment Subsidies Programme encourages employers to recruit persons above the age of 57 who have been unemployed for at least two years. However, as is clear, all these are targeted at long-term unemployed older people, rather than at older workers in general. Furthermore, of course, there is the possibility that such age-targeted programmes would be challenged under full age discrimination legislation.

The Norwegian model – a more inclusive work place

The Norwegian model is an example of a more holistic approach. In 2001, the government and social partners (employers and trade unions) in Norway signed a tripartite agreement on a more inclusive work place. By 2003, 50 per cent of all employers and 85 per cent of trade unions had joined. The objectives are not only to increase participation for older workers, but also to reduce sickness absences and assist those with disabilities. Practical measures include: early follow-up on employee sickness, combined with government reimbursement of employers' expenditures for purchasing health care services and rehabilitation; wage subsidies for those employing individuals with disabilities as well as subsidies for work place adaptation; and the introduction of the National Initiative for Senior Workers to improve the labour market prospects for older workers alongside a 4 per cent reduction in the social security contributions paid by employers for those over age 62. Of particular relevance to developing a longer-term strategy for a more inclusive work place are the obligations laid upon both employer and employee. The employer must set up systems to systematically address the problems of ill health and declining functions, and when an employee is unable to continue their job due to sickness or ill health, the employer is obliged, in collaboration with the authorities, to supply training so that the individual has the opportunity to qualify for another job in the company (clearly an easier task within large companies). In return, the employee must inform the employer about changing functional capacity, agree to a dialogue with the employer about necessary changes in work tasks, participate in whatever training is considered necessary, and cooperate with the employer on adapting the work place as necessary.

This is a limited model, geared as much to individuals with long-term sickness and disability, as to older workers in general, although clearly a small number of older workers will fall into this category towards the end of their working lives. However, it is important because it lays out the key elements of a long-term strategy for encouraging and facilitating an integrated workforce:

- Adapt the financial incentive and benefit system to encourage the retention of the older workforce.

- Adapt the work environment to create a more flexible inclusive work place, which will undoubtedly bring benefits to all workers across the life course.

- Provide training and education for all, including continual skills upgrading.

- Increase dialogue between employers and employees so that all workers are seen as individuals, and not numbers defined by their age, and enable all workers to plan and adapt for all life course transitions.

Let us now look at each of these elements in more detail.

Financial incentives and benefit system

One of the issues discussed in Chapter 5 was the increasing use over the past 25 years of disability and long-term sickness benefits to fund early retirement. There is considerable variation within European countries as to the percentage of retired who moved onto sickness or disability benefit as a form of early retirement, from nearly 30 per cent in Switzerland, to less than 3 per cent in neighbouring Austria. Many countries are now tackling this to ensure that such benefits support the permanently disabled and sick, but that those who can return to work, at any age, are encouraged to do so. This also entails a change in societal attitudes as most individuals who leave economic employment due to sickness or disability in their fifties do not return. Other reforms which we addressed earlier concerned replacement rates which are very high in some European countries, and state pension age.

There is a general move in many OECD countries to raise the state pension age. The USA is committed to raising its Social Security age to 67, although this will not become fully effective until 2027, and there are calls in the UK to raise the state pension age to 70 over the next two decades,[30] although the UK government is currently resisting these. There are, however, strong arguments for retaining the state pension age at 65, while providing significant incentives for workers to remain economically active beyond this age. Or, it has been suggested, state pension age should be abolished and actuarial methods applied to calculate entitlements. This has two main strands. First, while the majority population will, under current predictions, increase its healthy life expectancy and, given appropriate policies to provide an inclusive non-discriminatory working environment, will gradually extend the accepted age, or spectrum of ages, of retirement, there will always remain within the population a tail of those who will need, for mental and physical reasons, to withdraw earlier. These people are also likely to have lower educational and training attainments, and thus lower levels of life earnings. If the state pension age is raised, this group will inevitably end up on state benefits for a few years before they are able to draw the state pension. Second, there is a strong argument for removing the retirement precipice, and allowing gradual withdrawal from economic activity.

Even with the most optimistic health predictions, it is unlikely that the majority of the population will, within 20 years, be willing and able to work at full capacity beyond the age of 75. Age 70 will simply become the new precipice.

A model which would provide a fair and more affordable system would be to reinstate the state pension as Beveridge first intended it, as a provision of late life income to be drawn upon when individuals can no longer economically support themselves. This would result in a spectrum of retirement ages with individuals negotiating with their employers the best time to withdraw. The new Swedish pension reforms described in Chapter 5 provide such a flexible model. From age 61 onwards, it is possible to work and draw a pension at the same time. The earnings-related (defined contribution) pension can be drawn at 100 per cent or partially in steps at 75 per cent, 50 per cent or 25 per cent and combined with full or part-time work. Since there is no longer a stipulated retirement age, pension entitlements can be earned for an indefinite period. Alongside this is a minimum guaranteed pension which cannot be drawn before the age of 65. The UK Pensions Policy Institute[31] has suggested an alternative model of a *citizens' pension* to be drawn at age 70 at a financial level to ensure a good standard of living for all citizens. This could lie alongside a means-tested pension for those unable to continue to support themselves until this age.

Or a completely novel model could be introduced which bases statuary entitlement not on age but on life contribution, with allowances for care responsibilities, etc. Thus, those entering economic contribution on leaving school at 16 would be able to draw their state-provided pension after, say, 45 years from age 60 onwards. Those taking advantage of higher education and entering up to ten years later at 25 would have to continue for a similar 45 years until, in this case, age 70. This would also satisfy those who have concerns that workers with lower educational qualifications and typically engaged in more physically demanding occupations have lower health status in later life.

Flexible inclusive work place

The past 20 years have seen increasing recognition within OECD countries of the need to improve both physical and psycho-social work environments. This has been particularly the case in the Scandinavian countries. While the move from manufacturing to services has reduced the physical demands of many working environments, the health and social care sector still retains many physically taxing jobs. Given that this is where the increased demand will be over the upcoming decades, this will remain as a key work place issue. Similarly, the psycho-social work environment has worsened in many sectors, particularly due to a perceived increase in stress. Interestingly, however, recent surveys have indicated that older workers are generally less dissatisfied with their working environment than young people. The Third European Survey on Working Conditions 2000, found, for example, that only 33 per cent of workers over the age of 50 reported unpleasant working conditions, compared with 40 per cent of those aged 25–49.[32] It may be that those older workers who found conditions unpleasant retired, and thus left a biased sample. However, the Norwegian Labour Force Survey, 2001 found that less than 3 per cent of older workers reported unpleasant working conditions as a reason for switching jobs.

A recent OECD report provides a template for developing inclusive age integrated working environments based on flexibility and individualisation.[33] The working environment should be adapted through work rotation, reorganisation of work tasks, and ergonomic improvements, and employees should feel they have control over their own work situation wherever possible. In particular, all workers should have flexibility in their working-time arrangements, including the possibility of part-time work at times of life course need: 'More emphasis needs to be placed on adapting workload and working time to individual needs . . . the right balance needs to be found between each worker's individual capacity and workload'.[34]

Training and education

As we have already seen, the evidence from many OECD countries is that the educational qualifications of future older workers will increase, in some cases significantly, and this should have an important impact on productivity and improve employment prospects for older workers.[35] Furthermore, the inherent training component of new technological labour means that future cohorts of older workers will have experience of continual training and skills updating. Supplemented by vocational and lifelong learning, and adult education and training, this will significantly enhance the employability of older people[36] and address upcoming national skills shortages, particularly in the health and social care sectors. Some European countries already operate study leave schemes allowing employees to return to full or part-time education or training.[37] It is important that such education and training is targeted, builds on previous experiences and skills, and is properly evaluated. Far more research and evaluation of the effectiveness of different types of lifelong learning and training is required from a business stance. However, the general impact of education at all ages on health and well-being should not be underestimated.

Dialogue: planning for late life work

This element may well – in the long term – prove to be the most crucial. One of the key areas of concern expressed by European employers in relation to age discrimination is managing the departure of older workers. Whether this is a convenient front behind which to hide, a real business issue, or symptomatic of the tremendous change in attitudes towards late life work and older people which has occurred over the past 25 years, is unclear:

> The adverse human impact on the individual employee and the rest of the workforce in dismissing an older worker, particularly after a long and successful career, on competence grounds, should not be underestimated and many companies will undoubtedly baulk at having to take such a step.[38]

The key here is dialogue between employer and employee. One of the drivers discussed earlier for the introduction of mass retirement at a fixed age was the increasing bureau-cratisation and administration of the work place. Faced with these complex procedures, employers found the ability to remove pre-known numbers of workers each year, and thus replace and train new workers a convenient administrative tool. This, however, was before the development of highly sophisticated and competent human resource tools, teams and departments. Indeed, the professional body of this group are committed to the removal of age discrimination in employment because it is seen to be wasteful of talent and harmful to both individuals and organisations.[39] It is not by coincidence that the occupational sector with the lowest record of age discrimination complaints in the USA is the human resource sector! Key here is early intervention, so that across the life course employees are given the opportunity to discuss and plan their job profiles and expectations. This is becoming routine in many large organisations. Given the tremen-dous success, highlighted earlier, of early and pre-retirement training courses in per-suading an entire cohort that retirement was a positive step, particularly given the extremely negative environment described in Chapter 4 against which they were intro-duced, similar Planning for Late Life Work courses and training programmes aimed at highlighting the benefits, necessity and potential for the individual of late life work will also play a crucial role here, and should form a key component of government strate-gies. Furthermore, the concern that employees whose performance declines toward the end of their career will be subjected to the indignity of performance/capability proce-dures, will disappear when such performance/capability procedures are routine for all employees across the life course.

The OECD highlights, for example, the case of the Norwegian transport firm, Linjegods. In the context of competition from other companies for scarce workers and faced with an average retirement age of 58, the company instigated a scheme whereby all employees meet with the human resource division at age 55 to discuss needs and wishes; this is followed up two years later and the practical possibility of employees reducing working time and hours allowed for those over age 62. Those working to between age 65 and age 67 receive a bonus on departure.[40] Clearly such transitional schemes need to be adapted in the light of the changing workforce and labour market over the next couple of decades, and ageist elements reduced and or removed, but the framework of individual dialogue plus appropriate financial and practical measures is a valuable one, particularly if a stronger element of training is introduced. Of equal signif-icance from the aspect of ageing societies, was that the company responded to the demands of the labour market, and increasing competition for scarce workers inherent within ageing societies, not only as a business procedure but also in line with the con-cept of an inclusive age-integrated workforce.

Age integration in the family

As we saw in Chapter 6, one of the developments of mature societies is the opportunity for greater age integration within families due to the increase in multigenerational relationships. The emergence of the vertical or beanpole family has increased the likelihood that an individual will become a grandparent or grandchild, and remain in this role for several years. It is estimated in the USA, for example, that three-quarters of all adults will become grandparents,[41] and that currently half of those aged over 55 are members of a four-generation family.[42] Almost one-third of grandparents will go on to experience great-grandparenthood,[43] and one estimate reports that a fifth of all women who die after 80, will spend some time in a five-generation family as great-great-grandmothers[44] A similar picture may be found in the UK. Here estimates indicate that 29 per cent of the adult population of Great Britain are grandparents,[45] with approximately 10 per cent of all adults under 56 years being grandparents, 66 per cent of those aged 56 to 65 years, and over three-quarters of those over 66 years of age. Other estimates suggest that three-quarters of the population will eventually attain grandparenthood.[46] This represents a considerable historical change, for as Uhlenberg[47] notes for the USA, whereas nearly one-fifth of all children born in 1900 would be orphaned before reaching 18, more than two-thirds of those born in 2000 will still have both sets of grandparents alive when they reach 18. Similarly, by the age of 30 one-fifth of the 1900 cohort had a living grandparent, compared with three-quarters of those born in 2000.

Reciprocal support – the role of grandparents in age-integrated families

Not only are families now more likely to span multiple generations, but as a result of earlier demographic trends, when people married earlier and had more closely spaced children, individuals are currently experiencing the transition to grandparenthood at younger ages.[48] They are therefore likely to occupy the position for a longer proportion of their lives, indeed it has been estimated that the average length of grandparenthood currently in Western Europe and the USA is 25 years, with the result that some people may be grandparents for over half their lifetime.[49] In addition, the lengthening of healthy active old age is enabling grandparents to build a relationship with their grandchildren into their own adulthood.[50] This mirrors the re-bonding[51] between adult parents and children referred to in Chapter 6.

The nature of the grandparent relationship varies widely across a spectrum from sharing occasional interests and leisure activities to providing regular intimate personal care. Interestingly, despite the increase of residential mobility, most surveys report a relatively high degree of contact between grandparents and grandchildren, with average physical contact occurring at least once a month supplemented by other forms of communication.[52] The strength and type of these relationships are also related to the gender, age, health, residential proximity and family line of the kin, with research from both the UK and the USA suggesting that grandmothers, particularly of the maternal line, have a more involved relationship with their grandchildren.[53] One obvious reason for this is that child rearing has been a culturally encouraged area of competence for women throughout their life course, thus grandmothers are most often drawn into caring for their grandchildren. This is connected with the familiar notion of women as 'kin-keepers', who as 'ministers of the interior'[54] place a lot of emphasis on maintaining interpersonal and family ties. There is also evidence that maternal grandparents are more likely to have frequent contact with grandchildren[55] and that grandchildren tend to have a stronger bond with maternal grandparents.[56] This supports the notion that familial continuity is most likely to persist through women.[57] Maternal grandmothers are also considered more influential than paternal grandparents in terms of promoting 'closeness' and a 'sense of security'.[58]

Various roles of grandparenthood have been identified. Bengtson,[59] for example, identifies what he refers to as five separate symbolic functions of grandparents: being there; grandparents as national guard; family watchdog; arbiters who perform negotiations between members; and participants in the social construction of family history. Harper et al.'s study of grandmothers[60] identifies grandmothers as carers, replacement partners (confidante, guide and facilitator), replacement parents (listener, teacher and disciplinarian) and as family anchors (transferring values, attitudes and history). Grandparents can also provide important role models for children[61] and transfer economic resources to younger generations.[62]

Grandparents as custodians and family mediators

Finally, it should be noted that grandparents are also playing an important role in relation to the rising incidence of divorce, and the emergence of complex reconstituted families. Within close supportive relationships grandparents can provide considerable stability and emotional and practical support to their children and grandchildren.[63] Alternatively, a prior disjointed grandparent–parent relationship may be unable to sustain the subsequent disruption of parental divorce, leading to a complete breakdown in grandparent-grandchild interaction.[64] Given the strength of the maternal grandmother link with the grandchildren relative to the paternal line and grandfather relationships, and that custody in many countries is usually with the mother, paternal grandparents are at higher risk of losing contact with their grandchildren. Work on single parent and reconstituted families in the UK and the USA[65] reports strong contact following divorce through the maternal grandmother line, and limited contact via the paternal grandparent line.

There is also extensive work in the USA highlighting the role of grandparents as custodial parents. This is particularly the case within African American families where maternal grandmothers in particular can play a key caregiving role. There is evidence that this is also the case among UK Afro-Caribbean families.[66] The limited work on the role of the grandparent within reconstituted or stepfamilies[67] serves to illustrate the complexity and range of such new family forms, which range from long-term marital-based unions, where the step-parent (and thus step-grandparents) have been in these roles since the grand-children were very young, to brief cohabiting unions in which the grandparents have little opportunity to establish a relationship with new step-grandchildren.

Sandwich men and women

This growth of age-integrated families has important implications for our understanding of the sandwich generation, or women in the middle phenomenon,[68] whereby women, in particular, are faced with coping with simultaneous demands from dependent parents and children. The apparently growing significance and length of grandparenthood are placing further demands on the roles and relationships of adult women.[69] It is not that unusual for a mid-life woman to be an active grandmother with childcare responsibili-ties, the mother of a new parent, and daughter of an increasingly frail elderly mother. Increased longevity, especially of women, and the continued emphasis of children remaining with their mothers after marital separation, are giving increased significance to the grandmother role. While data on the role of grandfathers are limited,[70] it will be interesting to see the roles and relationships developed by the new grandfather gener-ations. The first generation of men to be present at and in some cases play an active role in their children's birth are now becoming grandfathers. There is evidence that they were more active in the upbringing of their children and more involved in their children's lives. It will be interesting to note the role they will now play in the lives of the children of their children.

The age-integrated family

The age-integrated family, with members stretching from birth to well into their eight-ies and nineties, and experiencing high levels of contact, appears to be a growing phe-nomenon in many western societies, and most individuals will experience it at some point during their lifetime. Indeed, Bengtson has recently gone so far as to propose that 'for many Americans, multigenerational bonds are becoming more important than nuclear family ties for well being and support over the course of their lives'.[71]

He goes on to argue that the longer years of 'shared living' created by demographic ageing have resulted in increased opportunities and needs for interaction, support and mutual influence across more than just two generations. In addition, such multigenera-tional relationships also encourage continuity and stability across time,[72] providing a latent network of kin[73] which can be activated in time of need.

Policy implications of age-integrated families

Despite considerable public rhetoric, the expected age wars between the generations have not erupted. In other words, younger cohorts have not risen up to protest against policies which benefit older adults, policies which may seem to operate against the interests of younger and mid-life people. Foner[74] suggests two reasons why people of working age in the USA favour programmes which benefit older people. First, younger people have a stake in protecting public programmes for older adults because these programmes relieve them of financial responsibility for elderly people in their own families. Second, younger adults wish to protect these programmes for their own old age.

It can be argued, however, that of more importance is the relationship of the micro and macro experience of such social relations, and in particular how they are mediated within kinship roles and relationships. Thus, while public programmes operate at the national level most people actually experience them at the individual, family or community level. First, people experience intergenerational relationships at the micro-level. Through this intimate kin-based relationship with older relatives, older people are no longer the 'other,' but individuals younger people have contact with and knowledge of. Opportunities for such contact and knowledge across the generations obviously increase within age integrated families. Second, individuals see their own families benefit from macro-level policies even if they themselves are not benefiting. This is rewarding due to affective intergenerational ties. Third, there are the mutual economic interests of these programmes as younger people may well receive direct or indirect benefits/exchanges from these programmes Thus while entitlements for older adults are financed and dispensed at the macro-level, a different process is at work in the age integrated family at the micro-level. At this level there are intra-family exchanges that often result in a circulation of benefits from older to younger family members. The relative financial security afforded the old by public programmes permits them to contribute to their offspring and grandchildren. So, rather than parents becoming rich at the expense of the young, the young benefit both directly and indirectly from the public funds received by older adults.

The possibility for increased interaction between successive generations which arises from societal ageing, therefore impacts not only within families but also has repercussions in the wider public and policy arena.

Ageing and the development agenda

As we saw in earlier chapters, older people are among the poorest in every developing country. They have the lowest levels of income, education and literacy, they lack savings and assets, have only limited access to work, and even in times of crisis are usually the last to be cared for under emergency aid programmes. Perhaps of most concern is health care, for as acute diseases are conquered we are going to see a rapid increase in chronic illness and disability, but with no long-term care programmes or facilities to tackle this. As a recent UNFPA report commented, 'improving health, financial security and comfort in later life will become a higher priority as populations grow older, issues that should be assessed as an integral part of the formulation of social development policy, programmes and strategies'.[75]

Ageing has recently started to figure on the development agenda at national and global levels. Beyond specific policy initiatives, the wider question of development and ageing has been addressed from two stances. First, what is the impact of economic development on sustaining and supporting the growing older population in these countries? Second, and more intellectually challenging, how will population ageing affect development? As a recent UNRISD report declared:

> Neoliberal globalization generates a number of well-known problems. It leaves behind poor economies and weaker strata in strong economies. With few exceptions, this has fuelled a rise in income inequality both across and within countries, thus making a reduction in poverty difficult to achieve. It increases the volatility of most economies, their vulnerability to external shocks and the risk of global recessions. This growing exposure to global economic forces requires stronger 'shock absorbers'. The development of social insurance mechanisms and increased government spending can be viewed as performing such an insulating function.[76]

Paradoxically, at the very time that integration into the world economy requires the development of adequate social insurance mechanisms, the competition triggered by globalisation generates the opposite effects, eroding social norms and national regulations by encouraging downward bidding by developing countries in an attempt to attract foreign investment. This reduces tax revenues, social insurance and other social expenditures and erodes labour market standards.

Alongside this:

> A combination of forces – the World Trade Organization thrust towards the privatization of social services, the Organization for Economic Co-operation and Development emphasis on basic social provisioning and the NGO substitution for government provisioning – is unraveling the social contract in societies that used this to cement the welfare state.[77]

concluding that international agreements are therefore needed to establish minimum global standards and regulate those services.

In addition, as Lloyd-Sherlock[78] has noted, the well-being and quality of life of older people are strongly conditioned by their capacity to manage opportunities and risks associated with rapid and complex change, such as is now occurring in many developing countries, and this requires a combination of global and national strategies combined with locally generated community level initiatives.[79]

Crucial to both of the questions identified earlier, the impact of economic development on sustaining and supporting the growing older population in these countries and how population ageing will affect development, is the role of intergenerational relationships, both in providing immediate mutual support to each other, and the longer-term impact that population ageing is having on these relationships. For example, given the accepted role that children are still perceived to play in providing old age security, the provision of a secure income in later life is not only important to alleviate late life poverty, but is also fundamental to the issue of reducing fertility and expanding populations, and thus lies at the centre of economic and social development in these regions. However, as Apt points out in the African context:

> As yet, national governments . . . have not tackled the issues of how to develop an appropriate social welfare policy for their rapidly ageing populations. Social welfare has typically had a low priority, while the contribution of the family to social welfare has been largely neglected. As a consequence, policy thinking on how better to harness the energies and resources of the family and the community in resolving the social needs of individuals and groups has barely commenced.[80]

In order to develop sound policy it is important to take account of the changes over the life course.[81] The well-being of older people is partially a function of their characteristics and earlier behaviours as well as their familial and social networks. This means that programmes can seek to affect well-being through interventions at various stages of the life course. As in the developed world, future cohorts of older people are likely to be very different in their characteristics compared with current cohorts, due to demographic and socio-economic changes. They will be better educated, more urban, have smaller families and better overall health. Social protection, both formal and informal, can play a key role in mediating these relationships.

However, despite the integration of ageing into development agendas:

> The facts about population ageing have yet to induce policy makers to redirect global and national resources to the growing numbers of older poor, especially in resource-poor countries. Social development thinking is beginning to define, measure and act on poverty in a multi-dimensional way, paying attention to principles of empowerment and participation, and to the promotion and realization of the full range of economic, social, cultural and civil, human rights for all people. But the International Development Targets and the Millennium Goals do not reflect the impact of population ageing. As long as older people fail to benefit from contemporary development policies and practices and experience chronic poverty, progress towards international poverty eradication goals will be compromised.

The Second World Assembly on Ageing, held in Madrid in 2002, attempted to tackle this. While addressing the needs of old people throughout the world, its communiqué has special relevance to those living in developing countries. The context to the Second World Assembly on Ageing, was placed firmly in a general historical framework of social development and human rights,[82] including the adoption of commitments and guiding principles of major United Nations conferences and summits.[83] The International Plan of

Action on Ageing, adopted at the First World Assembly on Ageing in Vienna, was asserted to have guided action on ageing over the past 20 years. Issues of human rights for older persons were taken up in 1991 in the formulation of the United Nations Principles for Older Persons, which provided guidance in the areas of independence, participation, care, self-fulfilment and dignity. They were highlighted again in 1995 in General Comment No. 6 of the Committee on Economic, Social and Cultural Rights, on the implementation of the International Covenant on Economic, Social and Cultural Rights, which asserted the entitlement of older persons to the full range of rights recognised in the Covenant. The concept of a society for all ages, which was developed as the theme for the 1999 International Year of Older Persons, contained four dimensions: individual lifelong development; multigenerational relationships; the interrelationship between population ageing and development; and the situation of older persons. A strong human rights framework has been established.

The International Strategy for Action on Ageing

A human rights based approach to development in general and societal ageing in particular is essential for the creation of an inclusive society for all ages, in which older persons participate fully. Age discrimination must be eradicated in all of its insidious forms and the achievements and dignity of older persons afforded the respect they command. At the same time, in the spirit of a society for all ages, the rights of older persons should not be incompatible with those of other age groups and the reciprocal relationships between the generations must be nurtured and encouraged.[84]

The International Strategy for Action on Ageing identified nine central themes, each involving detailed recommendations for action at the national level (Fig. 11.1).

The recommendations for action are organised according to three priority directions: development for an ageing world; advancing health and well-being into old age; and ensuring enabling and supportive environments. The Plan is divided into issues, objectives and actions. These include: the active participation of older people in society and development; the recognition of the social and economic contribution of older people and their active participation in decision making; the enhancement of employment opportunities, and access to knowledge, education and training; the strengthening of intergenerational solidarity; the reduction of poverty among older people by 50 per cent by 2015, and ensuring sufficient minimum income for all older persons; the improvement of housing, transport and the living environment; the protection of older people from abuse; and enhancing the public recognition of older people.

In the light of concerns raised in Chapters 1 and 9 concerning health care, priority direction II: Advancing health and well-being into old age is of particular interest. Health promotion and well-being throughout the life course, and universal and equitable access to health care services are identified as the broad key issues. The objectives of each are laid out in Fig. 11.2.

1 The achievement of secure ageing, which involves reaffirming the goal of eradicating poverty in old age and building on the United Nations Principles for Older Persons.
2 Empowerment of older persons to fully and effectively participate in the social, economic and political lives of their societies, including through income-generating and voluntary work.
3 Provision of opportunities for individual development, self-fulfilment and well-being throughout life as well as in late life, through, for example, access to lifelong learning.
4 Guaranteeing the economic, social and cultural rights of older persons as well as their civil and political rights, including the elimination of all forms of discrimination on the basis of age.
5 Commitment to gender equality in older persons through elimination of gender-based discrimination, as well as all other forms of discrimination.
6 Recognition of the crucial importance of intergenerational interdependence, solidarity and reciprocity for social development.
7 Provision of health care and support for older people, as needed.
8 Facilitating partnership between all levels of government, civil society, the private sector and older persons themselves in translating the International Strategy into practical action.
9 Harnessing of scientific research and expertise to focus on the individual, social and health implications of ageing, in particular within developing countries.

Figure 11.1 *International Strategy for Action on Ageing.*

Issue 1: Health promotion and well-being throughout the life course
Objective 1: Promotion and protection of health and well-being throughout life and reduction of the cumulative effects of factors that increase the risk of disease in older age.
Actions
(a) Give priority to poverty eradication policies to improve the health status of poor and marginalized population groups;
(b) Set gender-specific targets to improve the health status of older people and reduce disability and mortality;
(c) Identify the main socio-economic factors that contribute to the onset of disease in later life and address them through health, economic, social and legal means;
(d) Focus first on the major known risks, arising from unhealthy diet, physical inactivity and other unhealthy behaviours, such as smoking and alcohol consumption in health promotion, health education, prevention policies and information campaigns;
(e) Implement measures to curb the marketing and use of potentially harmful products. In particular, take comprehensive action to control the marketing and use of tobacco products and provide help to stop smoking at all ages;

Figure 11.2 *Advancing health and well-being in old age..*

(f) Minimize exposure to pollution from childhood and throughout life;

(g) Ensure that the misuse of prescription drugs is minimized, through regulatory and education measures.

Objective 2: Development of policies to prevent ill-health among older persons.

Actions

(a) Design early interventions to prevent or delay the onset of disease and disability;

(b) Ensure that gender-specific primary prevention and screening programmes are available and affordable at older ages;

(c) Provide training and incentives for health and social service professionals to counsel and guide people reaching old age on healthy lifestyles and self-care;

(d) Pay attention to the danger arising from social isolation and reduce its risk to the health of older people by supporting community empowerment and mutual aid groups, including peer outreach and neighbourhood visiting programmes;

(e) Rigorously apply and reinforce occupational safety standards that prevent injuries at all ages;

(f) Prevent injuries by measures safeguarding pedestrians, implementing fall prevention programmes, minimizing hazards in the home and providing safety advice.

Objective 3: Access to adequate nutrition for all older persons.

Actions

(a) Guarantee equitable access to clean water and safe food for older people;

(b) Promote lifelong healthy nutrition from childhood, with particular attention to ensuring adequate nutrition in women during their reproductive years;

(c) Prepare national dietary goals aimed at encouraging a balanced diet to provide adequate energy and prevent micronutrient deficiency, preferably based on local foods;

(d) Pay particular attention to nutritional deficiency and associated diseases in the design and implementation of health promotion and prevention programmes for older persons;

(e) Educate older persons and the general public, particularly informal caregivers, about specific nutritional needs of older persons, including adequate intake of water, calories, protein, vitamins and minerals;

(f) Provide dental services to prevent and treat disorders that can impede eating and cause malnutrition;

(g) Include specific nutritional needs of older persons into curricula of training programmes for all health and care professionals.

Issue 2: Universal and equitable access to health-care services

Objective 1: Elimination of age- and gender-based inequalities to ensure that older persons have equitable access to health care.

Actions

(a) Seek equity in the distribution of health resources to older persons; in particular reduce unequal access to care for older people who are poor by the reduction or elimination of user fees, provision of insurance schemes and affordable access to essential medications;

Figure 11.2 *(continued)*

(b) Aim at negotiating bilateral and multilateral agreements on compulsory licensing and parallel exports of life-saving drugs to meet the essential need for medications;

(c) Educate and empower older persons in the effective use and selection of health services;

(d) Apply and enforce existing conventions to protect the rights of older persons to primary health care and to eliminate discrimination in health care based on age;

(e) Utilize technology such as telemedicine to reduce geographical and logistical inequalities in access to health care in rural areas.

Objective 2: Development and strengthening of primary health-care services to meet the needs of older persons and ensure their inclusion in the process.

Actions

(a) Give highest priority to access to primary health care and the establishment of community health programmes for older persons;

(b) Implement the commitment of the twenty-fourth special session of the General Assembly to attain the goal of universal and equitable access to primary health care, with particular efforts to rectify inequalities, inter alia, those related to age;

(c) Support local communities in providing health support services to older persons;

(d) Include traditional medicine in primary health-care programmes where appropriate and beneficial;

(e) Train primary health-care workers and social workers in basic gerontology and geriatrics.

Objective 3: A continuum of health care to meet the needs of older persons.

Actions

(a) Develop regulatory mechanisms to set appropriate standards of health care for older persons;

(b) Implement community development strategies that determine a systematic needs assessment baseline for the planning, execution and evaluation of locally based health programmes. The baseline should include contributions from older persons;

(c) Improve the coordination of primary health care and social services;

(d) Train health and social service workers in models of primary health care that include the contributions of older people;

(e) Encourage the use of traditional health-care providers where they are considered to be safe and effective;

(f) Enable people whenever possible to die with dignity in a place in which they themselves decide, in the company of people of their own choosing and as free from distress and pain as possible.

Figure 11.2   *(continued)*

National Governments have the primary responsibility for implementing the broad recommendations of the International Strategy for Action. A necessary first step in successful implementation of the Strategy is to mainstream ageing and the concerns of older persons into national development frameworks and poverty eradication processes. Programme innovation, mobilization of financial resources and development of necessary human resources will be undertaken simultaneously. Accordingly, progress in the implementation of the Strategy will be contingent upon effective partnership between Government, all parts of civil society and the private sector.[85]

One of the key concerns following the World Assembly has been the urgent necessity of moving the priority statements onto the international and national development agendas. Many of the goals for health and well-being laid out above, however, lie comfortably alongside the priorities of the WHO.[86] In particular, the need for an integrated systems approach to delivering health care, which emphasises both acute infectious disease and chronic long-term conditions, primary and preventative care, and increased training of the health and social care workforce. While there is concern in many quarters at the progress in establishing ageing as a key development priority, it is also clear that as the numbers and proportion of older people rise in many developing regions, so the priorities of development generally and that of the community advocating on behalf of older people will start to naturally converge.

Reclaim old age

The *ageing and society paradigm*,[87] is a conceptual framework for designing and interpreting studies of ageing and illuminating the place of age in both individual lives and the surrounding social structure. It suggests that in response to social change, individuals within a particular cohort may begin to develop certain patterns of behaviour. These are then perceived as being age-typical patterns and are then defined as age-appropriate norms, expectations and rules, which become institutionalised within social structures. In turn, these structural changes redirect the behaviour of future cohorts. The emergence and consolidation of retirement as an expected right of healthy later life may be seen as such a process. It is clear that during the last quarter of the twentieth century, the withdrawal of healthy active adults in their fifties and early sixties from economic activity had profound implications for society's preconceptions and definition of men and women in their fifties and sixties. The emergence of early retirement created the association of 'retired' and 'old' from age 50 onwards. Indeed, the notion of the Third Age which Laslett conceived of as commencing during an individual's sixties as they retired from full-time economic employment, is now being defined as beginning at age 50.[88] Or even as the Third Age Foundation boldly assert in a recent UK report, 'Older people is the term used for the purposes of this report to refer to those aged 40+'. Given that many of these individuals at age 40 have a life expectancy of a further 50 years – are we really to believe that some two-thirds of the adult population are now defined as older people? Yet across the Western world, financial and other services are now defining the older consumer group as the over-50s; housing is being built for those over age 50; in many countries individuals can draw their pensions from age 50. At least one UK local authority now allocates 'old peoples'' social services to those aged 50 or above, on the grounds that this is 'politically correct'; and many in the sales sector consider that identifying a late life product as one 'for those in their 50s' is a good sales technique since the older consumer will be more likely to purchase a product apparently targeted at those some 20 years younger. However, the social, cultural and economic dynamics driving this are not necessarily those focused on the well-being of the individual.

This is not to deny the original rationale for claiming age 50 as a transition. The female menopause occurs at around age 50, and the often associated, though crucially never *causally* associated, change of roles and relationships which were perceived to occur around then gave impetus for the inclusion of men in this transition. It is now becoming clear that the economic rationale for encouraging early retirement was in fact one of the key drivers behind this. However, with the ageing of life transitions, whereby leaving full-time education, forming stable adult unions and becoming a parent are all being delayed, most individuals in their fifties are still active parents and partners and full contributors to community and economic life, as they were when they were in their thirties and forties. Indeed, given the multiplicity of roles, and diversity of life course experiences, most individuals will spend much of their adulthood moving back and forth between a spectrum of responsibilities with no sense of an abrupt transition at 50. What is key is the acknowledgement of continuous change across the life course with no predetermined chronological junctures which transition us from one state to another. The author recently interviewed a women in her fifties who was simultaneously a granddaughter, grandmother, parent and child, worker and carer, and wife, and she seamlessly shifted between these roles not only daily but also across her life course.

In our eagerness to claim later life we have created something which starts at age 50, and may continue for nearly half a lifetime. As a result, however, the reality of old age, the likelihood of increasing frailty and the inevitability of approaching death that will come to the very old, are in danger of being marginalised. The recognition of this rejection of the reality of true late old age has an established history within the literature, though it has been compounded in recent years by the steady march of the definition of old age back through the age spectrum.[89]

As both Achenbaum[90] and Cole[91] have so vividly shown, historical and cultural contexts have critically impacted upon societal preconceptions and individual experiences of old age. Tracing the North American understanding of ageing, Cole argues that early American settlers, inspired by their faith and vision of life as a spiritual journey, found strength and personal development in the 'acceptance of decline and decay in old age'. Hope and triumph were linked dialectically to tragedy and death. However, this acceptance of the human condition was swept away as:

> [the] rise of liberal individualism and of a moral code relying heavily on physical self-control marked the end of the American culture's ability to hold opposites in creative tension, to accept the ambiguity, contingency, intractability, and unmanageability of human life.[92]

Initiated in North America by the Protestant anti-bellum revivalists, a similar code of industry, self-denial and restraint can be identified among the British Victorian male swept forth by liberal capitalism. Thus the former existential integrity of the progress of life:

> was virtually lost in a liberal culture that found it necessary to separate strength and frailty, growth and decay, hope and death. A society overwhelmingly committed to material progress and the conquest of death abandoned many of the spiritual resources needed to redeem human finitude.[93]

Driven by their belief in the power of the individual will, Victorian moralists rationalised experience in order to control it. Ideological and psychological pressures to master rather than accept old age generated a dichotomous tension in the perception of old age, one that retains power, albeit with different groups, today.

> Rather than acknowledge ambiguity and contingency in ageing, Victorians split old age into: sin, decay and dependence on the one hand and virtue, self-reliance and health on the other. . . . anyone who lived a life of hard work, faith and self-discipline could preserve health and independence into a ripe old age; only the shiftless, faithless, and promiscuous were doomed to premature death or a miserable old age.[94]

Thus acceptance of finality as a natural part of the human condition, which could enrich and inform all life, was slowly replaced throughout the late nineteenth century by a view that 'physical decline was "one of life's problems to be solved through will power, aided by science, technology and expertise"'.[95]

By the middle of the twentieth century the personal responsibility part of the continuum had been almost completely replaced by scientific responsibility. Modern science had clearly documented the physical decline in later life. But rather than returning to an acceptance of this decline, and the rebuilding of an ethos which fully acknowledged this as part of the human experience, modern science having discovered the 'problem' of old age resolved to solve it: 'Unable to infuse decay, dependence and death with moral and spiritual significance, our culture dreams of abolishing biological ageing'.[96]

Within Anglo-American society and subsequently across many other cultures acceptance of finality is thus replaced with the cultural construct of human frailty: a notion that death and decline can be reversed, cured, somehow transcended by science, based around cultural constructs of how the body should be rather than around human experience. By not seeing infirmity as a common experience of all human life, and one that is expanded in later life, the opportunity to address infirmity at all ages is lost, and the frailty of older people is simply seen as setting them apart from younger persons.

As societies age it is important that the full potential length of active adulthood is recognised, enabling most individuals to remain fully active and contributory while they are able. However, it is equally important that we then allow that there will be for most of us a period, brief or long, of morbidity and disability at the end of our lives – that is the reality of old age. Then societies can refocus resources to those elders in real need, ensuring targeted accommodation, financial, social and health care services for frail disabled older people regardless of their chronological age. This is the reality – old age as a integral part of adulthood.

Developing a framework for understanding the dynamics of mature societies

We must be careful as we develop more mature societies, that we do not overplay the role of age and of old age. Our argument is that age-integrated mature societies will display certain characteristics due to their demographic profile. However, as we have consistently argued, there is nothing inherent in chronological age and we must be wary of confounding age with cohort and life course, and implying that societies with large numbers and proportions of those in later life consistently act in certain ways owing to their age profile *per se*. Rather there are the complexities of cohort and period effects, and we need to acknowledge that each cohort brings with it specific life dimensions, dynamics and life histories, and each time period introduces particular institutional and structural contexts. There are three main themes to consider.

First, what are the implications, if any, of a society including large numbers of older adults? Second, are attitudes and behaviour associated with specific age ranges or are any identifiable trends related to cohort behaviour? Third, and I believe most significantly, what are the implications of having for the first time an age integrated society, whereby large numbers of successive cohorts and generations have the opportunity to live alongside one another for a period of time and learn from each others' experiences? Let us take two examples – the impact of ageing societies on the environment and politics – and explore these questions.

The impact of ageing societies on the environment

A recent excellent review by Wright and Lund[97] points out that while experts in many fields are beginning to consider the profound effects of ageing society on various institutional, economic, political and social aspects, the environment has been a missing part of the public policy debate concerning the implications of an ageing society. Drawing on our framework, we can here identify three broad questions. First, how will rapidly ageing societies impact upon the natural environment at the local, national and global level? Will older people continue to consume less, or will future cohorts continue their expensive resource consumption into later life? And are there specific things associated with large numbers of mature and older adults that can specifically impact upon the environment? In the short term we are already seeing an impact in certain parts of the developed world. In the UK, for example, increased housing demand and pressure on car ownership have all been partly blamed on the ageing of the population.

Second, is the question of the relationship of environmental attitudes to age and cohort. Do these vary significantly as we grow older, or do we carry cohort experiences with us through life in defining our views? Either way we must explore whether attitudes towards the environment change over the next few years because we have either a mature society or because this particular group of older adults were all influenced by specific environmental awareness factors at specific times. Third, is the intergenerational argument – that a mature society is a society that is even more aware of the passing of generations because individuals within this society will increasingly live to see the birth and growth to adulthood of an increasing number of new generations. As Page[98] has noted, we cannot neglect the stewardship and sustainability of natural resources if we want to ensure the quality of life for our future generations, many of whom will now be born before we die.

First, how will rapidly ageing societies impact upon the *natural environment* at the local, national and global level? This question was debated over a decade ago by AARP,[99] with the conclusion that at that stage there were only speculations, and these were both negative and positive.[100] However, the relationship between patterns of consumption and age[101] and the impact of this has recently been discussed in the light of the environmental debate.[102] Currently older adults consume less than younger ones, particularly from their seventies onwards. This is partially explained by age, in particular decreasing activity due to physical decline, but also to the life course, with younger and mid-life adults committed to high levels of consumption based on establishing a home and rearing children. The cohort effect has been somewhat neglected. There is, however, debate now in the USA over whether the high consumption of the currently mid-life baby boomers will be continued on into late life, with significant resource and environmental implications.[103]

Second, is the question of the relationship between *environmental attitudes* to age and cohort. Here not only is the evidence again limited, but we also have to deal with the question concerning the confounding relationship between cohort and age. For example, a survey of US adults aged 25 and over reported[104] that the oldest (65+) and the youngest (25–49) shared the greatest concern for environmental well-being, and the strongest sense of environmental stewardship. Those over age 65 also had a strong propensity to act in an environmentally friendly manner, and to change their behaviour in line with environmental values. The finding that they were less likely to be actively involved in environmental protests or action groups is well supported by the literature on age and political activism, and may be explained more by the theory of selective withdrawal[105] from physically demanding activities with increasing age, than by any direct relationship with environmental issues *per se*. Dietz *et al.*[106] also report similar pro-environmental behaviour by older age groups in the USA in relation to consumption. Other studies, however, have not identified these relationships or indeed suggested a negative correlation.[107] What is, however, clear is that we are addressing a complex analytical question requiring a high level of sophistication in its measurement, and that far more detailed recognition of the role of local influences and socio-economic factors[108] needs to be measured alongside the complex interactions of age, cohort and life cycle.

Third, is the *intergenerational argument* – that increased verticalisation of age groups within an ageing society results in greater intergenerational contact and awareness, in particular at the intimate or family level. Members of such societies will be more aware of the stewardship obligations towards our planet, as they have already met those who will benefit or suffer from the actions of their generation. In the US survey reported above,[109] the oldest (65+) and the youngest (25–49) age groups shared the strongest sense of environmental stewardship. These two groups both had a clear sense of intergenerational responsibility, each placing strong emphasis on the importance of leaving a clean environment for their children and grandchildren. Given that these are the two age groups who, as parents and grandparents of young children, will have greatest personal contact with subsequent generations, we may here be picking up a life course factor rather than age *per se*. We should also be questioning the impact of increasing environmental education on their parents and grandparents in the USA and other developed countries, as this is leading to a strong sense of environmental values among children.[110]

In conclusion, as Wright and Lund[111] propose, an ageing society may wish to consider developing an environmental ethic for the benefit of future generations, reminding us in the words of the environmentalist Thiele,[112] that 'we borrow the earth from our children and grandchildren because we have inherited the earth as a trust from parents and grandparents'.

The impact of ageing societies on politics

We can apply the same framework and questions to the field of political attitudes and behaviour. A current public fear is that the large numbers of older adults will result in the emergence of a massive grey vote in western countries, one which blocks any forward thinking radical change that may not be in their own self-interest. Again this is partially driven by yet another myth or stereotype about ageing societies and older people themselves. For another public perception is that older people are more conservative and more likely to vote for grey issues.[113] Ageing societies are thus seen as politically stagnating, conservative societies. However, the evidence for this is in fact limited or even negligible, and this highlights again the common mistake of confounding age with cohort and with period or historical effects.

For example, the comprehensive review by Binstock and Day on ageing and politics in the USA concluded that:

> As is the case with ideology and partisanship, policy priorities and opinions on political issues vary little across age groups. Much more striking are the cleavages that cut across cohorts, such as gender, educational, racial and ethnic, gender and partisan divisions. When asked to identify the national and community problems of greatest concern, adults

of all ages offer similar replies. Changes over time in people's primary concerns – shifting priorities between foreign affairs and the domestic economy, for example – *reflect period effects much more than inherent differences between older and younger people.*[114] (Author's emphasis)

Indeed, the only age-related factor that seems to have been consistently verified is that older people tend to vote at a higher rate than younger people, with some fall-off, presumably due to increase in frailty, among the very old.[115] Research in the USA also indicates that this is reflected in older people reporting the highest level of interest in political campaigns and public affairs.[116] However, on closer examination, even this observation hides complex interactions. For example, repeated empirical studies have shown that both European and American voting turnout increases from its lowest rate in early adulthood to rise rapidly until age 35–45, and then more slowly until age 70, only declining slightly after this.[117] As a consequence, the percentage of the total vote cast by older voters is higher than their proportionate representation in the voting population.[118] In the 1996 US election, for example, older voters aged 65 and over comprised 16.5 per cent of the electorate, but cast 20.3 per cent of the vote.

The pressing question is whether this and other related observed patterns are driven by age or cohort factors. Binstock's analysis of participation rates between 1972 and 1996 suggests that birth cohort replacement is the driver, as each age cohort coming through has a lower participation rate than the previous one at that age. Thus a particularly active voting cohort has moved through the elections, interacting and compensating for any effects arising from chronological age. However, as Binstock and Quadagno point out, a European study carried out over the same time period, also came up with similar age group differences in Swedish and German turnout. Given that these three cohorts would have experienced a series of very different political events during their lives, they conclude that perhaps it is life cycle events that hold the key. However, we should also bear in mind that these particular cohorts also grew up in an era of mass communication and growing transnational cultural influence. It is highly likely that the sense of political activism which erupted in the 1960s may well have had similar impacts upon the three birth cohorts in their three different countries.

More pragmatic factors may also be contributing. A study of US electoral registration[119] highlighted the relationship between age, voter registration and turnout. The association here is moderated by length of residence in one's home, which is age related, younger people being far more residentially mobile. Binstock and Quadrango also examine the relationship between knowledge and interest in current affairs, and motivation to register and vote.[120] Several studies have suggested that interest in and knowledge about politics,[121] news[122] and current affairs,[123] increases with age, declining only slightly with advanced age. However, again the relationship between age, cohort and life cycle in this process is unclear.

Then there is strong evidence in the general political literature that those with high levels of political party identification have a stronger commitment to vote,[124] with data from the USA showing that current older adults have a stronger identification with the major political parties. While there is evidence that length of political attachment (which can be clearly related to the age of the individual concerned) strengthens that attachment, Binstock and Quadagno stress the influence of cohort factors here. Drawing on the work of Alwin,[125] they highlight the fact that the strong partisan attachment found among the older US age groups over past decades, may not be replicated in future years, as the baby boomer and post-baby boomer generations have continuously revealed less identification with particular political parties than the cohorts which have preceded them.

In conclusion, we can note that current cohorts of older people are committed voters and show keen interest in current and public affairs. However, this may not be replicated in future generations as it may be a cohort effect. Furthermore, beyond this increased political commitment, which has been seen to be related to current older populations having more time for such activity and thus may not be consistent as the lifestyle and commitments of older generations change, there is little firm evidence of other significant associations. Indeed, even the commonly held perception that older people are more conservative is not substantiated by cross-national research. Rather, political affiliation tends to be fixed in early life and generally maintained, at least for current cohorts.

Finally, despite the rhetoric, there is little evidence of intergenerational conflict in political affiliations:

> People of all ages are deeply divided in their ideological and partisan orientations; but these do not pit older and younger people against each other. Although older people are commonly thought to be more conservative than younger people, most of the evidence . . . in the United States refutes the notion that people become more conservative as they age. Similarly, cross-national studies of social and political values generally conclude that generational differences in value orientations – degree of materialism, individualism, secularism, and devotion to authority, for example – are due primarily to cultural and social conditions effecting a cohorts' socialization, and not to universal life-course changes.[126]

Thus while there has traditionally been broad-based support in many western countries for maintaining public pensions,[127] this has also clearly reflected political partisan rather than cohort or age lines.[128]

Those who hide behind the rhetoric of public popularity and voter power, should also familiarise themselves with the evidence from studies of different cohorts, which indicates that both those younger cohorts who will arrive in dependency at the tail end of, or just after, the main demographic bulge, and older mid-life cohorts, are generally realistic about future public commitments, and, if anything, support a shift towards a public system which prioritises need over age. Paradoxically, US research suggests that those mid-life cohorts about to benefit from public programmes for older people are the most positive towards allocating public revenues on criteria of need rather than age.[129]

What is of most significance, then, for our understanding of key issues within mature societies, is to recognise that while age- and cohort-related behaviours should be added into future equations, these are not fixed and will change over a cohort's lifetime, as well as within and between cohorts. Alternatively, however, the role of age integration and intergenerational relationships has a pervasive dynamic, which we noted as significant in averting age wars in the light of public programme costs, and again as potentially important in public pro-environmental behaviour. In relation to public programmes, younger people were content to contribute to the wider good because they saw this as including kin members of an older generation; in relation to environmental behaviour, older people were content to contribute to the wider good because they saw this as including kin members of a younger generation. It is this aspect of mature societies, the possibility of increased interaction between successive cohorts and generations, which may prove to be the consistent and stable force within all societies as they mature.

In conclusion

During the twentieth century, within most developed countries populations changed – from 1 old to every 10 young as the century began, to 1 old to every 2 young by the late 1980s, to 1:1 by the early years of the twenty-first century. Developing countries saw a dramatic increase in absolute numbers of older people, moving from a few million to nearly 1 billion in that time. During the same period, three months of life expectancy was added at birth every year in Europe. The speed and magnitude of these changes are historically unprecedented, their full implications difficult to grasp. Laslett talked of '*cultural lag*' in which wider society has not yet caught up with the current facts of old age. Riley talks of '*structural lag*' whereby institutions need to adapt. It is clear that there is also '*individual lag*', whereby people need to re-address their life course activities in full recognition of their potentially significantly increased longevity.

From the middle of the century, we can expect balanced age profiles as the large bulge of older adults moves through and dies. Ageing societies will have become fully mature age-symmetric societies. The mature societies which will emerge over the next few decades in most developed countries and some developing countries in transition, will be historically unique in both their demographic profile and the long and healthy active lives they potentially promise for many individuals. Many of the perceived characteristics of both these societies are not due to their demography, but to a combination of this with the experiences, attitudes and behaviours of current cohorts. There are, however, some factors which will be unique, in particular the possibility of age integration throughout society, and of increased interaction between successive cohorts. This is likely to prove to be a consistent and a relatively stable force within all societies as they mature. The significant benefits which may arise from a society which harnesses life experiences and capabilities from such a large spectrum of cohorts, with their very different life course characteristics, are unprecedented. However, this will only occur if those controlling our government and economy today turn from fearing such a future, and work towards creating the framework for tomorrow's mature societies. This includes removing age discriminatory practices, encouraging age-integrated behaviour and creating a space for the full recognition of the eventual frailty, and finality, of old age.

Notes

1 Riley, 1976.
2 Ashenfelter et al., 1973; Kohli et al., 1991; AARP, 1995; Bennington and Wein, 2000.
3 Harper and Thane, 1989.
4 Welford, 1958; Meier and Kerr, 1976; Fleischer and Kaplan, 1980.
5 Belbin, 1958 and Le Gros Clark, 1959.
6 Warr, 1994; Hellerstein et al., 1999.
7 Hellerstein et al., 1999.
8 Henretta, 1994.
9 Herz, 1995; Burtless and Quinn, 2000.
10 Eschtruth and Gemus, 2001.
11 Williamson and McNamara, 2001; Costa, 1998.
12 Henretta, 2000; Burtless and Quinn, 2000; Steuerle and Carasso, 2001.
13 Barham, 2002, p. 6.
14 Disney et al., 1997.
15 Harper and Vlachantoni, 2004.
16 Quinn and Kozy, 1996.
17 Manton et al., 1993; Manton et al., 1997.
18 Fogel and Costa, 1997.
19 Henretta, 2000.
20 Loscocco, 2000; Henretta 1994.
21 Social Security Administration, 1997.
22 Harper and Laslett, 2005.
23 Gallie, 1998.
24 Manton, 2000.
25 Harper, 1989.
26 Jensen, 1999.
27 In 2000.
28 Gould and Solem, 2000.
29 OECD, 2004.
30 CBI, 2004.
31 Pensions Policy Institute, 2004.
32 Paoli and Merllie, 2001.
33 OECD, 2003a.
34 ibid., p. 106.
35 Bassanini and Scarpetta, 2001.
36 OECD, 2001.
37 OECD, 2003b.

38 Response by an UK employers federation to the government consultation on implementing age discrimination legislation.
39 CIPD, 2004.
40 OECD, 2004.
41 Giarrusso et al., 1996.
42 Soldo and Hill, 1994; Bengtson and Harootyan, 1994 ; Bengtson, 1995.
43 Szinovacz, 1998.
44 Hagestad, 1988.
45 Meadows, 2004.
46 Tunaley, 1998; Dench et al., 1999.
47 Uhlenberg, 1996.
48 Jerrome, 1993.
49 Kornhaber, 1996.
50 Hagestad, 1988.
51 Harper, 2004a.
52 Cherlin and Furstenberg, 1986; Sticker, 1991; Hodgson, 1992; Ponzetti, 1992; Creasey, 1993; Dench et al., 1999; Harper, 2005.
53 Cherlin and Furstenberg, 1985; Tinsley and Parke, 1988; Uhlenberg and Hammill, 1998; Roberto and Stroes, 1995; Cunningham-Burley, 1986; Thompson et al., 1990.
54 Hagestad, 1985, 1986.
55 Uhlenberg and Hamill,1998.
56 Chan and Elder, 2000.
57 Harper, 2005.
58 Hyde and Gibbs, 1993.
59 Bengtson, 1985.
60 Harper et al., 2003.
61 King and Elder, 1997.
62 Bengtson and Harootyan, 1994.
63 Kornhaber and Woodward, 1981; Aldous, 1985; Johnson, 1988; Kennedy, 1990; Kennedy and Kennedy, 1993.
64 Rossi and Rossi, 1990; Kruk, 1995.
65 Hilton and Macari, 1997; Bornat et al., 1999; Harper et al., 2003.
66 Harper et al., 2003.
67 Bornat et al., 1999; Dimmock et al., 2004.

68 Rossi, 1987.
69 Zeilig and Harper, 2000.
70 Leeson, 2004b.
71 Bengtson, 2001, p. 5.
72 Silverstein *et al.*, 1998.
73 Riley and Riley, 1993.
74 Foner, 2000.
75 UNFPA, 1999.
76 Mkandawire, 2001.
77 Ibid.
78 Lloyd-Sherlock, 2001.
79 Moser, 2001.
80 Apt, 2002, p. 44.
81 Hermalin, 1999.
82 United Nations, 2001.
83 The Committee for Social Development identifies the following adoption of commitments and guiding principles of major United Nations conferences and summits as having also played a significant role in advancing the framework for policies on ageing, including: Health for All in the Twenty-First Century and the Alma-Ata Declaration 1978; Vienna Declaration and Programme of Action of the World Conference on Human Rights, 1993; Programme of Action of the International Conference on Population and Development, 1994; Copenhagen Declaration and Programme of Action of the World Summit for Social Development, 1995; Beijing Declaration and the Platform for Action of the Fourth World Conference on Women, 1995; the Habitat Agenda and the Istanbul Declaration on Human Settlements of the Second United Nations Conference on Human Settlements (Habitat II), 1996; Dakar Framework for Action of the World Education Forum, 2000; the Further Initiatives for Social Development of the twenty-fourth special session of the General Assembly 2000; and the United Nations Millennium Declaration of the United Nations Millennium Summit, 2000.
84 United Nations, 2001, paragraph 14.
85 ibid. paragraph 150.
86 WHO, 2003.
87 Riley *et al.*, 1999.
88 UK ERSC New Dynamics of Ageing Programme.
89 Harper, 1987.
90 Achenbaum, 1979.
91 Cole, 1992.
92 Cole and Gadow, 1986.
93 ibid.
94 ibid.
95 Cole, 1992.
96 Cole and Gadow, 1986.
97 Wright and Lund, 2000.
98 Page, 1997.
99 Wright and Lund, 2000 quoting the 1989 Environmental Resources and Ageing Society workshop sponsored by AARP and Resources for the Future.
100 Harootyan and Takeuchi, 1993.
101 OIA, 2002.
102 Pebley, 1998.
103 ibid.
104 AARP SCAN, 1992.
105 Jennings and Markus, 1988.
106 Dietz *et al.*, 1998.
107 Mohai and Twight, 1987.
108 Guagnano and Markee, 1995; Dietz *et al.*, 1998.
109 AARP SCAN, 1992.
110 Coates, 1998.
111 Wright and Lund, 2000.
112 Thiele, 1999.
113 It was reported in August, 2004, for example, that the UK political parties were identifying key issues with which they could target the growing number of ageing baby boomers.
114 Binstock and Day, 1996.
115 Myers and Agree, 1993.
116 Jennings and Markus, 1988.
117 Myers and Agree, 1993.
118 Binstock and Quadagno, 2001.
119 Timpone, 1998.
120 Flanigan and Zingale, 2002.
121 Strate *et al.*, 1989.
122 MacManus, 1995.
123 Jennings and Markus, 1988.
124 Flanigan and Zingale, 2002.
125 Alwin, 1998.
126 Binstock and Day, 1996.
127 Ponza *et al.*, 1988.
128 Ponza *et al.*, 1988; Rhodebeck, 1993.
129 Silverstein *et al.*, 2000.

Bibliography

AARP (1995) *American Business and Older Workers*, American Association of Retired Persons, Washington, DC.

AARP SCAN (1992) Environmental Issues and an Aging Population, *1*, American Association of Retired Persons, Forecasting and Environmental Scanning Department, Washington, DC.

Aboderin, I. (2003) Modernisation and Economic Strain: The Impact of Social Change on Family Support for Older People in Ghana, in Bengtson, V. L. and Lowenstein, A. (eds) *Global Aging and Its Challenge to Families*, Aldine de Gruyter, New York, pp. 284–302.

Aboderin, I. (2004) Modernisation and Ageing Theory Revisited: Current Explanations of Recent Developing World and Historical Western Shifts in Material Family Support for Older People, *Ageing and Society*, **24**(1), pp. 29–50.

Abrams, P. (1970) Rites de Passage, *Journal of Contemporary History*, **5**(1), pp. 175–9.

Achenbaum, W. A. (1979) *Old Age in the New Land: The American Experience since 1790*, Johns Hopkins University Press, Baltimore, MD.

Achenbaum, W. A. (1986) *Social Security: Visions and Revisions*, Cambridge University Press, Cambridge.

Achenbaum, W. A. (1995) *Crossing Frontiers: Gerontology Emerges as a Science*, Cambridge University Press, Cambridge.

Achenbaum, W. A. (1998) Toward a Psycho-History of Late-Life Emotionality, in Stearns, P. N. and Lewis, J. (eds) *An Emotional History of the United States*, New York University Press, New York, pp. 417–30.

Acton Society Trust (1960) *Retirement: A Study of Current Attitudes and Practices*, AST, London.

Adam, S. and Hutton, J. (2001) The Netherlands, in Philp, I. (ed.) *Family Care of Older People in Europe*, IOS Press, Amsterdam, pp. 135–60.

Adams, S. J. (2000) Three Essays on the Economics of Ageing, PhD thesis, Dept. of Economics, Michigan State University, Ann Arbor, MI.

Age Concern England (2000a) New Survey of GPs Confirms Ageism in the NHS, *Press Release 17 May, 2000*, Age Concern England, London.

Age Concern England (2000b) Older Women Unaware of Breast Cancer Risk ACE, *Press release 11 October, 2000*, Age Concern England, London.

Age Positive (2002) *Being Positive about Age Diversity at Work: A Practical Guide for Business*, Department for Work and Pensions, London.

Agree, E. and Clark, R. (1991) Labour Force Participation at Older Ages in the Western Pacific, *Journal of Cross Cultural Gerontology*, **6**, pp. 413–29.

Ainsworth, M. and Filmer, D. (2002) *Poverty, Children, Schooling and HIV/AIDS: A Targeting Dilemma*, World Bank, Washington, DC.

Aldous, J. (1985) Parent–Adult Child Relations as Affected by the Grandparent Status, in Bengston, V. L. and Robertson, J. F. (eds) *Grandparenthood*, Sage, Beverly Hills, CA, pp. 97–116.

Alewyn, R. (1929) *Das Generationsproblem in der Geschichte, Zeitschrift für deutsche Bildung*.

Allan, G. A. (1985) *Family Life: Domestic Roles and Social Organization*, Basil Blackwell, Oxford.

Almagor, U. (1978a) The Ethos of Equality among Dassanetch Age-Peers, in Baxter, P. T. W. and Almagor, U. (eds) *Age, Generation and Time: Some Features of East African Age Organisations*, C. Hurst, London.

Almagor, U. (1978b) *Pastoral Partners: Affinity and Bond Partnership among the Dassanetch of South-West Ethiopia*, Manchester University Press, Manchester.

Almeda, E. and Sarasa, S. (1996) Spain: Growth to Diversity, in George, V. and Taylor-Gooby, P. (eds) *European Welfare Policy: Squaring the Welfare Circle*, Macmillan, Basingstoke, pp. 155–76.

Altmann, J. (1980) *Baboon Mothers and Infants*, Harvard University Press, Cambridge, MA.

Alwin, D. F. (1998) The Political Impact of the Baby Boom: Are There Persistent Generational Differences in Political Beliefs and Behavior?, *Generations*, **22**(46–54).

Amato, P. R. (1994) Life-Span Adjustment of Children to Their Parents' Divorce, *Future Child*, **4**(1), pp. 143–64.

Ambler, J. S. (1991) *The French Welfare State: Surviving Social and Ideological Change*, New York University Press, New York.

Anderson, B. (1993) The Nordic Welfare State under Pressure: The Danish Experience, *Policy and Politics*, **21**(2), pp. 109–20.

Anderson, J. M. (2001) Models for Retirement Policy Analysis, *Report to the Society of Actuaries*, Society of Actuaries, Schaumburg, IL.

Anderson, M. (1985) The Emergence of the Modern Life Cycle in Britain, *Social History*, **10**(1), pp. 69–87.

Anderson, R. (2004) Working Carers in the European Union, in Harper, S. (ed.) *Families in Ageing Societies: A Multi-Disciplinary Approach*, Oxford University Press, Oxford, pp. 95–113.

Anderson, W. and Cowan, N. (1956) Work and Retirement: Influences on the Health of Older Men, *Lancet*, **271**(6957), pp. 1344–8.

Andrews, G. R., Esterman, A. J., Braunack-Mayer, A. J. and Rungie, C. M. (1986) *Ageing in the Western Pacific: a Four Country Study, Western Pacific Reports and Studies No. 1*, World Health Organization, Manila.

Andrietti, V. (2001) *Occupational Pensions and Interfirm Job Mobility in the European Union: Evidence from the ECHP Survey*, Center for Research on Pensions and Welfare Policies, University of Turin, Turin.

Apt, N. A. (1971) *Socio-Economic Conditions of the Aged in Ghana*, Department of Social Welfare and Community Development, Accra.

Apt, N. A. (1972) *The Role of the Aged in the Ghanaian Family: Young People's View*, Department of Social Welfare and Community Development, Accra.

Apt, N. A. (1980) Rural Aging: The Case of Ejisu Bosmtwe District of Ashanti, Mimeo, Department of Sociology, University of Ghana, Legon.

Apt, N. A. (1986) Grandparenthood Role: An Example from the Eastern Region of Ghana, Mimeo, Department of Sociology, University of Ghana, Legon.

Apt, N. A. (1987) Aging, Health and Family Relations: A Study of Aging in the Central Region of Ghana, Mimeo, Department of Sociology, University of Ghana, Legon.

Apt, N. A. (1991) Activities, Care and Support of Ageing Women in Africa: A Ghanaian Case Study, in Hoskins, I. (ed.) *Older Women as Beneficiaries and Contributors to Development: International Perspectives*, AARP, Washington, DC.

Apt, N. A. (1992) Family Support to Elderly People in Ghana., in Kendig, H. L., Hashimoto, A. and Coppard, L. C. (eds) *Family Support for the Elderly: The International Experience*, published on behalf of the World Health Organization by Oxford University Press, Oxford, pp. 203–12.

Apt, N. A. (1993) Care for the Elderly I Ghana: An Emerging Issue, *Journal of Cross-Cultural Gerontology*, **8**, pp. 301–12.

Apt, N. A. (1996) *Coping with Old Age in a Changing Africa: Social Change and the Elderly Ghanaian*, Avebury, Aldershot.

Apt, N. A. (1997) *Ageing in Africa, Ageing and Health Programme*, World Health Organization, Geneva.

Apt, N. A. (2002) Ageing and the Changing Role of the Family and Community: An African Perspective, *International Social Security Review*, **55**(1), pp. 39–47.

Apt, N. A. and Grieco, M. (1994) Urbanization, Caring for People and the Changing African Family: The Challenge to Social Policy, *International Social Security Review*, **47**(1), pp. 3–4.

Arber, S. and Ginn, J. (1992) Class and Caring: A Forgotten Dimension, *Sociology*, **26**(4), pp. 619–34.

Arnold, R. D., Graetz, M. J. and Munnell, A. H. (1998) *Framing the Social Security Debate: Values, Politics, and Economics*, National Academy of Social Insurance and Brookings Institution Press, Washington, DC.

Arrowsmith, J. and McGoldrick, A. E. (1996) HRM Service Practices: Flexibility, Quality and Employee Strategy, *International Journal of Service Industry Management*, **7**(3), pp. 46–62.

Arrowsmith, J. and McGoldrick, A. E. (1997) A Flexible Future for Older Workers, *Personnel Review*, **26**(4), pp. 258–73.

Ashenfelter, O. and Card, D. E. (2000) How Did the Elimination of Mandatory Retirement Affect Faculty Retirement?, *NBER Working Paper No. 8378*, National Bureau of Economic Research, Cambridge, MA.

Ashenfelter, O., Rees, A. and Woodrow Wilson School of Public and International Affairs (1973) *Discrimination in Labor Markets*, Princeton University Press, Princeton, N.J.

Asher, M. G. (1998) The Future of Retirement Protection in Southeast Asia, *International SocialSecurity Review*, **51**(1), pp. 3–30.

Asher, M. G. (2000) The Pension System in Singapore, *Social Protection Discussion Paper No. 9919*, Social Protection Unit, Human Development Network, World Bank, Washington, DC.

Askham, J. (1998) Supporting Caregivers of Older People: An Overview of Problems and Priorities, paper presented at the World Congress of Gerontology "Ageing Beyond 2000: One World One Future", Adelaide, Australia, 1997.

Atkinson, A. B. (1995) *Incomes and the Welfare State: Essays on Britain and Europe*, Cambridge University Press, Cambridge.

Atkinson, A. B. and Hills, J. (1991) Social Security in Developed Countries: Are There Lessons for Developing Countries?, in Ahmad, E., Dreze, J., Hills, J. and Sen, A. (eds) *Social Security in Developing Countries*, Clarendon Press, Oxford, pp. 81–111.

Attfield, R. (1998) Environmental Ethics and Intergenerational Equity, *Inquiry*, 41(2), pp. 207–22.

Auerbach, A. J., Kotlikoff, L. J. and Leibfritz, W. (1999) *Generational Accounting around the World*, University of Chicago Press, Chicago.

Augusztinovics, M. (2002) Issues in Pension System Design, *International Social Security Review*, **55**(1), pp. 21–35.

Austad, S. (1997) Postreproductive Survival in Nature, in Wachter, K. W. and Finch, C. E. (eds) *Between Zeus and the Salmon: The Biodemography of Longevity*, National Academy Press, Washington, DC, pp. 161–74.

Australian Bureau of Statistics (1997) *Australian Social Trends*, Australian Bureau of Statistics, Canberra.

Australian Bureau of Statistics (1998) *Australian Social Trends*, Australian Bureau of Statistics, Canberra.

Australian Bureau of Statistics (1999) *Australian Social Trends*, Australian Bureau of Statistics, Canberra.

Aylaya, L. (1994) Social Needs, Inequality and the Welfare State in Spain: Trends and Prospects, *Journal of European Social Policy*, **4**(3), pp. 159–79.

Baily, M. N. and Garber, A. M. (1997) Health Care Productivity, *Brookings Papers on Economic Activity: Microeconomics*, pp. 143–202.

Banks, J., Blundell, R., Disney, R. and Emmerson, C. (2002) Retirement, Pensions and the Adequacy of Saving: A Guide to the Debate, *Briefing Note No. 29*, Institute for Fiscal Studies, London.

Banks, J. and Emmerson, C. (2000) Public and Private Pension Spending: Principles, Practice and the Need for Reform, *Fiscal Studies*, **21**, pp. 1–64.

Bardasi, E., Jenkins, S. P. and Rigg, J. A. (2000) Retirement and the Economic Well-Being of the Elderly: A British Perspective, *ISER Working Paper No. 2000–33*, Institute for Social and Economic Research University of Essex, Colchester.

Barer, M. L., Evans, R. G., Hertzman, C. and Lomas, J. (1987) Aging and Health Care Utilization: New Evidence on Old Fallacies, *Social Science and Medicine*, **24**(10), pp. 851–62.

Barham, C. (2002) Patterns of Economic Activity among Older Men, *Labour Market Trends*, **110**(June).

Bartel, A. P. and Sicherman, N. (1993) Technological Change and Retirement Decisions of Older Workers, *Journal of Labor Economics*, **11**(1), pp. 162–83.

Bassanini, A. and Scarpetta, S. (2001) Does Human Capital Matter for Growth in OECD Countries?, *Economics Letters*, **74**(3), pp. 399–402.

Bein, B., Wojszel, B., Politynska, B. and Wilmanska, J. (2001) Poland, in Philp, I. (ed.) *Family Care of Older People in Europe*, IOS Press, Amsterdam, pp. 161–88.

Belbin, E. (1958) Methods of Training Older Workers, *Ergonomics*, **1**, pp. 207–11.

Bellemare, D., Poulin-Simon, L. and Tremblay, D.-G. (1998) Le Paradoxe de l'Âgisme dans une Société Vieillissante; Enjeux et Défis de Gestion, Ed. St-Martin, Montreal.

Bengtson, V. L. (1985) Diversity and Symbolism in Grandparental Roles, in Bengtson, V. L. and Robertson, J. F. (eds) *Grandparenthood*, Sage Publications, Beverly Hills, CA, pp. 11–24.

Bengtson, V. L. (1995) Hidden Connections: Intergenerational Linkages in American Society, in Bengtson, V. L., Schaie, K. W. and Burton, L. (eds) *Adult Intergenerational Relations: Effects of Societal Change*, Springer, New York.

Bengtson, V. L. (2001) Beyond the Nuclear Family: The Increasing Importance of Multigenerational Bonds, *Journal of Marriage and the Family*, **63**, pp. 1–16.

Bengtson, V. L., Giarusso, R., Mabry, J. B. and Silverstein, M. (2002) Solidarity, Confict, and Ambivalence: Complementary or Competing Perspectives on Intergenerational Relationships ?, *Journal of Marriage and the Family*, **64**, pp. 568–76.

Bengtson, V. L. and Harootyan, R. A. (eds) (1994) *Intergenerational Linkages: Hidden Connections in American Society*, Springer, New York.

Bengtson, V. L., Rosenthal, C. and Burton, L. (1990) Families and Aging: Diversity and Heterogeneity, in Binstock, R. H. and George, L. K. (eds) *Handbook of Aging and the Social Sciences*, 3rd edn, Academic Press, San Diego, CA, pp. 263–87.

Bennington, L. A. and Wein, R. (2000) Antidiscrimination Legislation in Australia: Fair, Effective, Efficient or Irrelevant?, *International Journal of Manpower*, **21**(1), pp. 21–33.

Bernheim, B. D. (1993) Is the Baby Boom Generation Preparing Adequately for Retirement?, *Summary Report*, Merrill Lynch, Princeton, NJ.

Bhaumik, S. K. and Nugent, J. (2000) Wealth Accumulation, Fertility and Transfers to Elderly Household Heads in Peru, in Mason, A. and Tapinos, G. P. (eds) *Sharing the Wealth: Demographic Change and Economic Transfers between Generations*, Oxford University Press, Oxford, pp. 256–81.

Binstock, R. H. (1983) The Aged as a Scapegoat, *Gerontologist*, **23**, pp. 136–43.

Binstock, R. H. (2000) Older People and Voting Participation: Past and Future, *Gerontologist*, **40**(1), pp. 18–31.

Binstock, R. H. and Day, C. L. (1996) Aging and Politics, in Binstock, R. H. and George, L. K. (eds) *Handbook of Aging and the Social Sciences*, 4th edn, Academic Press, San Diego, CA, pp. 362–87.

Binstock, R. H. and Quadagno, J. (2001) Aging and Politics, in Binstock, R. H. and George, L. K. (eds) *Handbook of Aging and the Social Sciences*, 5th edn, Academic Press, San Diego, CA, pp. 333–51.

Bird, C. P. and Fisher, T. D. (1984) Thirty Years Later: Attitudes toward the Employment of Older Workers, *Journal of Applied Psychology*, **71**, pp. 515–17.

Boersch-Supan, A. and Schnabel, R. (1998) Social Security and Declining Labor Force Participation in Germany, *American Economic Review*, **82**(2), pp. 173–8.

Bornat, J., Dimmock, B., Jones, D. and Peace, S. (1998) Generational Ties in the 'New' Family: Changing Contexts for Traditional Obligations, in Silva, E. B. and Smart, C. (eds) *The 'New' Family?*, Sage, London.

Bornat, J., Dimmock, B., Jones, D. and Pearce, S. (1999) Stepfamilies and Older People: Evaluating the Implications of Family Change for an Ageing Population, *Ageing and Society*, **19**(2), pp. 239–61.

Bos, E. (1994) *World Population Projections*, World Bank, Washington, DC.

Bosworth, B. and Burtless, G. T. (eds) (1998) *Aging Societies: The Global Dimension*, Brookings Institution Press, Washington, DC.

Bourgeois-Pichat, J. (1989) From the 20th to the 21st Century: Europe and Its Population after the Year 2000, *Population: An English Selection*, **44**(1), pp. 57–90.

Brehm, S. S. (1992) *Intimate Relationships*, 2nd edn, McGraw-Hill, New York.

Breman, J. (2001) The Impact of the Asian Economic Crisis on Work and Welfare in Village Java, *Journal of Agrarian Change*, **1**(2), pp. 242–82.

Briscoe, G. and Wilson, R. A. (1991) Explanations of the Demand for Labour in the United Kingdom Engineering Sector, *Applied Economics*, **23**(5), pp. 913–26.

Buck, N. H. and Scott, J. (1994) Household and Family Change, in Buck, N. H., Gershuny, J., Rose, D. and Scott, J. (eds) *Changing Households: The British Household Panel Study 1990–1992*, ESRC Research Centre on Micro-Social Change, Colchester.

Bui, T. C., Truong, S. A., Goodkin, D., Knodel, J. and Friedman, J. (2000) Vietnamese Elderly Amidst Transformations in Social Welfare Policy, in Phillips, D. (ed.) *In Ageing in the Asia-Pacific Regions: Issues and Policies*, Routledge, London, pp. 334–59.

Bumpass, L. L., Martin, T. C. and Sweet, J. A. (1991) The Impact of Family Background and Early Marital Factors on Marital Disruption, *Journal of Family Issues*, **12**(1), pp. 22–42.

Bureau of the Census (1998) Current Population Report, U.S. Government Printing Office, Washington, DC.

Burgess, R. and Stern, N. (1991) Social Security in Developing Countries: What, Why, Who, and How, in Ahmad, E., Dreze, J., Hills, J. and Sen, A. (eds) *Social Security in Developing Countries*, Clarendon Press, Oxford, pp. 41–80.

Burgess, S. and Rees, H. (1997) Transient Jobs and Lifetime Jobs: Dualism in the British Labour, *Oxford Bulletin of Economics and Statistics*, **59**(3), pp. 309–28.

Burkhauser, R. V., Holden, K. C. and Feaster, D. (1988) Incidence, Timing, and Events Associated with Poverty: A Dynamic View of Poverty in Retirement, *Journal of Gerontology Series B: Psychological Sciences and Social Sciences*, **43**(2), pp. S46–52.

Burner, S. T., Waldo, D. R. and McKusick, D. R. (1992) National Health Expenditure Projections through 2030, *Health Care Financing Review*, **14**(1), pp. 1–29.

Burtless, G. T. and Quinn, J. F. (2000) Retirement Trends and Policies to Encourage Work among Older Americans, *Boston College Working Paper in Economics No. 436*, Boston College Department of Economics, Chestnut Hill, MA.

Butler, R. N., Austad, S. N., Barzilai, N., Braun, A., Helfand, S., Larsen, P. L., McCormick, A. M., Perls, T. T., Shuldiner, A. R., Sprott, R. L. and Warner, H. R. (2003) Longevity Genes: From Primitive Organisms to Humans, *Journal of Gerontology Series A: Biological Sciences and Medical Sciences*, **58**(7), pp. 581–4.

Caffrey, R. A. (1992) Family Care of the Elderly in Northeast Thailand: Changing Patterns, *Journal of Cross-Cultural Gerontology*, **7**, pp. 105–16.

Caldwell, J. C. (1969) *African Rural-Urban Migration: The Movement to Ghana's Towns*, Australian National University Press, Canberra.

Caldwell, J. C. (1976) Toward a Restatement of Demographic Transition Theory, *Population and Development Review*, **2**(3), pp. 321–66.

Campbell, N. (1999) The Decline in Employment among Older People in Britain, *LSE CASE Discussion Paper No. 19*, LSE, London.

Carey, J. R. and Gruenfelder, C. (1997) Population Biology of the Elderly in Human Aging, in Wachter, K. W. and Finch, C. E. (eds) *Between Zeus and the Salmon: The Biodemography of Longevity*, National Academy Press, Washington, DC, pp. 127–60.

Carins, J. and Dickens, K. (1995) Individual Rights Versus the Rights of Future Generations: Ecological Resource Distribution over Large Temporal and Spatial Scales, in Ingman, S. R., Pei, X., Ekstrom, C., Friedsam, H. and Bartlett, K. (eds) *An Aging Population, an Aging Planet, and a Sustainable Future*, Center for Texas Studies, Denton, TX.

Carnes, B. A. and Olshansky, S. J. (2001) Heterogeneity and Its Biodemographic Implications for Longevity and Mortality, *Journal of Experimental Gerontology*, **36**(3), pp. 419–30.

Carnes, B. A., Olshansky, S. J. and Grahn, D. (1996) Continuing the Search for a Law of Mortality, *Population and Development Review*, **22**(2), pp. 231–64.

Carnes, B. A., Olshansky, S. J. and Grahn, D. (2003) Biological Evidence for Limits to the Duration of Life, *Biogerontology*, **4**(1), pp. 31–45.

Caro, T. M., Sellen, D. W., Parish, A., Frank, R., Brown, D. M., Voland, E. and Borgerhoff-Mulder, M. (1995) Termination of Reproduction in Nonhuman and Human Female Primates, *International Journal of Primatology*, **16**(2), pp. 205–20.

Carter, S. B. and Sutch, R. (1996) Myth of the Industrial Scrap Heap: A Revisionist View of Turn-of-the-Century American Retirement, *Journal of Economic History*, **56**(1), pp. 5–38.

Case, A. and Deaton, A. (1998) Large Cash Transfers to the Elderly in South Africa, *Economic Journal*, **108**(405), pp. 1330–61.

Casey, B., Lakey, J. and White, M. R. M. (1992) *Payment Systems: A Look at Current Practice*, England Employment Department, Sheffield.

Cattell, M. (2001) Gender, Age and Power: Hierarchy and Liminality among the Abaluyia Women of Kenya, in Aguilar, M. (ed.) *Rethinking Age in Africa*, Africa World Press, Trenton.

Cattell, M. (2002) Gender, Age and Work among the Abaluyia of Kenya, in Makoni, S. and Stroeken, K. (eds) *Ageing in Africa: Sociolinguistic and Anthropological Approaches*, Ashgate, Aldershot, pp. 155–76.

CBI (2004) Press Release, *14 July*, Confederation of British Industry, London.

Central Office of Information (1947) *The Battle for Output: Economic Survey for 1947*, White Paper Cmd. 7046, His Majesty's Stationery Office, London, pp. 49.

Chan, C. G. and Elder, G. H. J. (2000) Matrilineal Advantage in Grandchild–Grandparent Relations, *Gerontologist*, **40**(2), pp. 179–90.

Chancellor of the Exchequer (1954) *Report of the Committee on the Economic and Financial Problems of the Provision for Old Age*, Cmd. 9333, HMSO, London.

Charlesworth, B. (1994) *Evolution in Age-Structured Populations*, 2nd edn, Cambridge University Press, Cambridge.

Cherlin, A. J. (1992) *Marriage, Divorce, Remarriage*, Rev. and enl. edn, Harvard University Press, Cambridge, MA.

Cherlin, A. J. and Furstenberg, F. F. (1985) Styles and Strategies of Grandparenting, in Bengston, V. L. and Robertson, J. F. (eds) *Grandparenthood*, Sage, Beverly Hills, CA, pp. 97–116.

Cherlin, A. J. and Furstenberg, F. F. (1986) *The New American Grandparent: A Place in the Family, a Life Apart*, Basic Books, New York.

Chwalow, J., Bagnall, A., Baudoin, C. and Elgrably, F. (2001) France, in Philp, I. (ed.) *Family Care of Older People in Europe*, IOS Press, Amsterdam, pp. 27–48.

Chye, E. (2000) Love, Money and Power in the Singaporean Household Economy, *PhD thesis*, Faculty of Anthropology and Geography, Oxford University, Oxford.

Cicirelli, V. G. (1983) A Comparison of Helping Behavior to Elderly Parents of Adult Children with Intact and Disrupted Marriages, *Gerontologist*, **23**, pp. 619–25.

CIPD (2004) *Age and Employment*, Chartered Institute of Personnel and Development (CIPD), London.

Clark, G. L. (2002) Pension Systems: A Comparative Perspective, in Lazonick, W. (ed.) *The International Encyclopedia of Business and Management: IEBM Handbook of Economics*, Thompson, London, pp. 5194–204.

Clark, G. L. (2003) 21st Century Pension (in)Security, in Clark, G. L. and Whiteside, N. (eds) *Pension Security in the 21st Century: Redrawing the Public-Private Debate*, Oxford University Press, Oxford.

Clark, G. L. and Whiteside, N. (eds) (2003) *Pension Security in the 21st Century: Redrawing the Public–Private Debate*, Oxford University Press, Oxford.

Clay, D. and Vander Haar, J. (1993) Patterns of Intergenerational Support and Childbearing in The Third World, *Population Studies*, **47**(1), pp. 67–83.

Clutton-Brock, T. H., Albon, S. D. and Guinness, F. E. (1988) Reproductive Success in Male and Female Red Deer, in Clutton-Brock, T. H. (ed.) *Reproductive Success: Studies of Individual Variation in Contrasting Breeding Systems*, University of Chicago Press, Chicago, pp. 325–53.

Coates, P. (1998) *Nature: Western Attitudes since Ancient Times*, University of California Press, Berkeley, CA.

Cole, T. R. (1992) *The Journey of Life: A Cultural History of Ageing in America*, Cambridge University Press, Cambridge.

Cole, T. R. and Gadow, S. (eds) (1986) *What Does It Mean to Grow Old?: Reflections from the Humanities*, Duke University Press, Durham, NC.

Coleman, D. (1996) *Europe's Population in the 1990s*, Oxford University Press, Oxford.

Comte, A. (1849) *Cours de Philosophie Positive*, 4, Paris.

Corbello, S. (1997) Italy: National Analysis and Outlook, in DG Employment Industrial Relations and Social Affairs (ed.) *The Outlook on Supplementary Pensions in the Context of Demographic, Economic, and Social Change: A Report by the EU Network of Experts on Supplementary Pension Provision, 1996*, Office for Official Publications of the European Communities, Luxembourg.

Corti, L. and Dex, S. (1995) Informal Carers and Employment, *Employment Gazette,* **103**, pp. 101–7.

Costa, D. L. (1998) *The Evolution of Retirement: An American Economic History, 1880–1990*, University of Chicago Press, Chicago.

Cowgill, D. O. and Holmes, L. D. (1972) *Aging and Modernization,* Appleton-Century-Crofts, New York.

Cox, D. and Jimenez, E. (1990) Achieving Social Objectives through Private Transfers: A Review, *World Bank Research Observer,* **5**(2), pp. 205–18.

Creasey, G. (1993) The Association between Divorce and Late Adolescent Grandchildren's Relations with Grandparents, *Journal of Youth and Adolescence,* **22**(5), pp. 513–29.

Crimmins, E. M., Saito, Y. and Reynolds, S. L. (1997) Further Evidence on Recent Trends in the Prevalence and Incidence of Disability among Older Americans from Two Sources: The LSOA and the NHIS, *Journal of Gerontology Series B: Psychological Sciences and Social Sciences,* **52B**, pp. S59–71.

Cunningham-Burley, S. (1986) Becoming a Grandparent, *Ageing and Society,* **6**(4), pp. 453–71.

Cutler, D. M. and Meara, E. (1999) The Concentration of Medical Spending: An Update, *NBER Working Paper No. 7279,* National Bureau of Economic Research, Cambridge, MA.

Cutright, P. (1965) Political Structure, Economic Development, and National Social Security Programs, *American Journal of Sociology,* **70**(5), pp. 537–50.

Daatland, S. O. (1997) Welfare Policies for Older People in Transition? Emerging Trends and Comparative Perspectives, *Scandinavian Journal of Social Welfare,* **6**, pp. 153–61.

Dannefer, D. (1987) Aging as Intracohort Differentiation: Accentuation, the Matthew Effect and the Life Course, *Sociological Forum,* **2**, pp. 211–36.

Dannefer, D. and Uhlenberg, P. R. (1999) Paths of the Life Course: A Typology, in Bengtson, V. L. and Schaie, K. W. (eds) *Handbook of Theories of Aging,* Springer, New York, pp. 306–26.

Darkwa, O. and Muzibuko, F. (2002) Population Ageing and Its Impact on Elderly Welfare in Africa, *International Journal of Aging and Human Development,* **54**(2), pp. 107–23.

David, H. and Pilon, A. (1990) Les Pratiques d'entreprises Manufacturières à l'égard de leur Main-d'œuvre Vieillissante, in David, H. (ed.) *Le Vieillissement au Travail: Une Question de Jugement. Actes du Colloque de l'IRAT,* IRAT, Montreal, pp. 88–91.

Davis-Friedmann, D. (1991) *Long Lives: Chinese Elderly and the Communist Revolution,* Expanded edn, Stanford University Press, Stanford, CA.

Dawkins, R. (1995) God's Utility Function, *Scientific American,* **273**, pp. 80–5.

Dawson, A. and Evans, G. (1987) Pensioners–Incomes and Expenditure 1970–1985, *Employment Gazette,* **95**(5), pp. 243–52.

Day, L. (1995) Recent Fertility Trends in Industrialized Countries: Toward a Fluctuating or a Stable Pattern?, *European Journal of Population,* **11**, pp. 275–88.

DeMaris, A. and Rao, K. V. (1992) Premarital Cohabitation and Subsequent Marital Stability in the United States: A Reassessment, *Journal of Marriage and the Family,* **54**, pp. 178–90.

Dench, D., Ogg, J. and Thomson, K. (1999) The Role of Grandparents, in Jowell, R., Curtice, J., Park, A. and Thomson, K. (eds) *British Social Attitudes: The 16th Report,* Ashgate (in association with National Centre for Social Research), Aldershot.

Department for Education and Employment (2000) Work-Life Balance: Changing Patterns in a Changing World, *Discussion document,* DfEE, London.

Department for Work and Pensions (2004) *Simplicity, Security and Choice: Informed Choices for Working and Saving,* Cm 6111, Stationery Office, London.

Department of Health (2000) *The NHS Plan,* HMSO, London.

Department of Health (2001) *National Service Framework for Older People,* HMSO, London.

Department of Health and Department of Social Security (1989) *Caring for People: Community Care in the Next Decade and Beyond,* HMSO, London.

Department of Trade and Industry (2003) *Equality and Diversity: Age Matters,* DTI, London.

Department of Trade and Industry (2004) *Fairness for All: A New Commission for Equality and Human Rights,* Cm 6185, DTI, London.

De-Shalit, A. (1995) *Why Posterity Matters: Environmental Policies and Future Generations,* Routledge, London.

DETR (2001) *Supporting People: Policy into Practice,* Department of the Environment Transport and the Regions, London.

Diamond, P. A., Lindeman, D. C. and Young, H. (1996) *Social Security: What Role for the Future?,* National Academy of Social Insurance and Brookings Institution, Washington DC.

Dietz, T., Stern, P. C. and Guagnano, G. A. (1998) Social Structural and Social Psychological Bases of Environmental Concern, *Environment and Behavior,* **30**(4), pp. 450–71.

Dilthey, W. (1875) Üeber das Studium der Geschichte der Wissenschaften vom Menschen, der Gesellschaft und dem Staat, in *Gesammelte Schriften,* Vol. 5, Teubner, Leipzig.

Dimmock, B., Bornat, J., Peace, S. and Jones, D. (2004) Intergenerational Relationships among Stepfamilies in the UK, in Harper, S. (ed.) *Families in Ageing Societies: A Multi-Disciplinary Approach,* Oxford University Press, Oxford, pp. 95–113.

Disney, R. (1996) *Can We Afford to Grow Older?: A Perspective on the Economics of Aging,* MIT Press, Cambridge, MA.

Disney, R. (1998) Social Security in the UK: A Voluntary Privatisation?, Paper presented at the Social Security Reform: International Comparisons Conference, Rome, 16–17 March, 1998.

Disney, R. and Emmerson, C. (2002) Choice of Pension Scheme and Job Mobility in Britain, *IFS Working Paper No. 02/09,* Institute for Fiscal Studies, London.

Disney, R., Emmerson, C. and Smith, S. (2004) Pension Reform and Economic Performance in Britain in the 1980s and 1990s, in Card, D. E., Blundell, R. and Freeman, R. B. (eds) *Seeking a Premier Economy: The Economic Effects of British Economic Reforms, 1980–2000*, University of Chicago Press, Chicago.

Disney, R., Emmerson, C. and Wakefield, M. (2001) Pension Reform and Saving in Britain, *Oxford Review of Economic Policy*, **17**(1), pp. 70–94.

Disney, R., Grundy, E. and Johnson, P. (1997a) *The Dynamics of Retirement: Analysis of the ONS Retirement Survey, Occasional Paper*, Department of Social Security, Washington, DC.

Disney, R., Grundy, E. M. D. and Johnson, P. (1997b) *The Dynamics of Retirement: Analyses of the Retirement Surveys*, The Stationery Office, London.

Disney, R., Meghir, C. and Whitehouse, E. (1994) Retirement Behaviour in Britain, *Fiscal Studies*, **15**(1), pp. 24–43.

Dohner, H. and Kofahl, C. (2001) Germany, in Philp, I. (ed.) *Family Care of Older People in Europe*, IOS Press, Amsterdam, pp. 49–74.

Domingo, L., Asis, M., Jose, M. and Kabamalan, M. (1993) *Living Arrangements among the Elderly on the Philippines: Qualitative Evidence, Elderly in Asia Research Report No. 93–23*, Population Studies Center, University of Michigan, Ann Arbor, MI.

Drenos, F. and Kirkwood, T. B. L. (2005) Modelling the Disposable Soma Theory of Ageing, *Mechanisms of Ageing and Development*, **126**(1), pp. 99–103.

Drerup, E. (1933) *Das Generationsproblem in der griechischen und griechisch-römischen Kultur*, F. Schoeningh, Paderborn.

Drew, L. M. and Smith, P. K. (1999) The Impact of Parental Separation/Divorce on Grandparent–Grandchild Relationships, *International Journal of Aging and Human Development*, **48**, pp. 191–215.

Dreze, J. and Sen, A. (1991) Public Action for Social Security: Foundations and Strategy, in Ahmad, E., Dreze, J., Hills, J. and Sen, A. (eds) *Social Security in Developing Countries*, Clarendon Press, Oxford, pp. 1–40.

Dromel, J. (1862) *La Loi des Revolutions, les Generations, les nationalités, Les Dynasties, les Religions*, Paris.

Dudley, N. J. and Burns, E. (1992) The Influence of Age on Policies for Admission and Thrombolysis in Coronary Care Units in the United Kingdom, *Age and Ageing*, **21**(2), pp. 95–8.

Dwyer, J. W. and Coward, R. T. (1991) A Multivariate Comparison of the Involvement of Adult Sons Versus Adult Daughters in the Care of Impaired Adults, *Journal of Gerontology Series B: Psychological Sciences and Social Sciences*, **46B**(5), pp. S259–69.

Easterlin, R. A. (1976) Population Change and Farm Settlement in the Northern United States, *Journal of Economic History*, **36**(1), pp. 45–75.

Elder, G. H. (1974) *Children of the Great Depression: Social Change in Life Experience*, University of Chicago Press, Chicago.

Elder, G. H. (1978) Family History and the Life Course, in Hareven, T. K. (ed.) *Transitions: The Family and the Life Course in Historical Perspective*, Academic Press, New York.

Elder, G. H. (1985) Perspectives on the Life Course, in Elder, G. H. (ed.) *Life Course Dynamics: Trajectories and Transitions, 1968–1980*, Cornell University Press, Ithaca, NY, pp. 23–49.

Elder, G. H. and O'Rand, A. M. (1995) Adult Lives in a Changing Society, in Cook, K. S., Fine, G. A. and House, J. S. (eds) *Sociological Perspectives on Social Psychology*, Allyn and Bacon, Boston, pp. 452–75.

Elder, G. H., Jr. (1994) Time, Human Agency, and Social Change: Perspectives on the Life Course, *Social Psychology Quarterly*, **57**(1), pp. 4–15.

Eltringham, S. K. (1982) *Elephants*, Blandford Press, Poole, Dorset.

Emerson, A. (1959) The First Years of Retirement, *Occupational Physiology*, **34**, pp. 197–208.

Emmerson, C. (2002) Pension Reform in the United Kingdom: Increasing the Role of Private Provision, Oxford Institute of Ageing, University of Oxford, available online at: http://www.ageing.ox.ac.uk

Encel, S. (2001) Age Discrimination in Australia: Law and Practice, in Hornstein, Z., Encel, S., Gunderson, M. and Neumark, D. (eds) *Outlawing Age Discrimination: Foreign Lessons, UK Choices*, Policy Press (in association with the Joseph Rowntree Foundation), Bristol, pp. 12–30.

Engineering Employers Federation (2004) *Working Brief on Age Discrimination*, EEF, London.

ESCAP (1987) *Population Ageing: Review of Emerging Issues, Asian Population Studies Series, No. 80,* ESCAP, Bangkok.

Eschtruth, A. D. and Gemus, J. (2001) Are Older Workers Responding to the Bear Market?, *Just the Facts on Retirement Issues No. 5,* Boston College Center for Retirement Research, Chestnut Hill, MA.

Esping-Andersen, G. (1990) *The Three Worlds of Welfare Capitalism*, Polity, Cambridge.

Ettner, S. L. (1996) The Opportunity Costs of Elder Care, *Journal of Human Resources,* **31**(1), pp. 189–205.

European Commission (1980) *Birth and Fortune: The Impact of Numbers on Personal Welfare*, Basic Books, New York.

European Commission (1995a) *The Demographic Situation in the European Union: 1994 Report*, Office for Official Publications of the European Communities, Luxembourg.

European Commission (1995b) *Social Protection in Europe*, Office for Official Publications of the European Communities, Luxembourg.

European Commission (1996) Working on European Social Policy: A Report, paper presented at the Social Policy Forum, Brussels, 27–30 March, Office for Official Publications of the European Communities, Luxembourg.

European Commission (1997a) Modernising and Improving Social Protection in the European Union, *Commission Communication COM(97)102,* Office for Official Publications of the European Communities, Luxembourg.

European Commission (1997b) *Social Protection in the Member States of the Union*, Office for Official Publications of the European Communities, Luxembourg.

European Commission (1998) *Demographic Report 1997, Commission Communication COM(97) 361,* Office for Official Publications of the European Communities, Luxembourg.

European Commission (1999) *Living Conditions in Europe: Statistical Pocketbook, 1999,* Office for Official Publications of the European Communities, Luxembourg.

European Commission (2000a) *Equal Opportunities for Women and Men in the European Union, Annual Report 1999,* Office for Official Publications of the European Communities, Luxembourg.

European Commission (2000b) *The Social Situation in the European Union 2000,* Office for Official Publications of the European Communities, Luxembourg.

European Commission (2002) *Public Finances in EMU – 2002,* DG Economic and Financial Affairs, Office for Official Publications of the European Communities, Luxembourg.

European Commission (2004) *Equal Rights in Practice: Key Voices 2004,* DG Employment and Social Affairs, Office for Official Publications of the European Communities, Luxembourg.

European Population Committee (2000) *Recent Demographic Developments in Europe,* EPC, Council of Europe, Strasbourg.

European Population Committee (2001) *Recent Demographic Developments in Europe,* EPC, Council of Europe, Strasbourg.

Eurostat (1998) *Social Portrait of Europe,* Office for Official Publications of the European Communities, Luxembourg.

Fairbanks, L. A. and McGuire, M. T. (1986) Age, Reproductive Value, and Dominance-Related in Vervet Monkey Females: Cross-Generational Influences on Social Relationships and Reproduction, *Animal Behavior,* **34**, pp. 1710–21.

Farkas, J. and Hogan, D. (1995) The Demography of Changing Intergenerational Relationships, in Bengtson, V. L., Schaie, K. W. and Burton, L. (eds) *Adult Intergenerational Relations: Effects of Societal Change,* Springer, New York.

Farley, R. (1996) *The New American Reality: Who We Are, How We Got Here, Where We Are Going,* Russell Sage Foundation, New York.

Feldstein, M. (1998) Social Security Pension Reform in China, *NBER Working Paper No. 6794,* National Bureau of Economic Research, Cambridge, MA.

Ferrari, G. (1874) *Teoria dei Periodi Politici,* Milan.

Ferreira, C. (1997) Portugal: National Analysis and Outlook, in DG Employment Industrial Relations and Social Affairs (ed.) *The Outlook on Supplementary Pensions in the Context of Demographic, Economic, and Social Change: A Report by the EU Network of Experts on Supplementary Pension Provision, 1996,* Office for Official Publications of the European Communities, Luxembourg.

Figueiro, D. and Sousa, L. (2001) Portugal, in Philp, I. (ed.) *Family Care of Older People in Europe,* IOS Press, Amsterdam, pp. 189–210.

Finch, C. E. (1997) Comparative Perspectives on Plasticity in Human Aging, in Wachter, K. W. and Finch, C. E. (eds) *Between Zeus and the Salmon: The Biodemography of Longevity,* National Academy Press, Washington, DC, pp. 245–68.

Finch, C. E. and Pike, M. C. (1996) Maximum Lifespan Prediction from the Gompertz Mortality Model, *Journal of Gerontology Series A: Biological Sciences and Medical Sciences,* **51A**(3), pp. B183–B94.

Finch, J. (1989) *Family Obligations and Social Change,* Polity, Cambridge.

Finch, J. (2004) Inheritance and Intergenerational Relationships in English Families, in Harper, S. (ed.) *Families in Ageing Societies: A Multi-Disciplinary Approach*, Oxford University Press, Oxford, pp. 164–76.

Finch, J. and Wallis, L. (1994) Inheritance, Care Bargain and Elderly People's Relationships with Their Children, in Challis, D., Davies, B. and Stewart, K. (eds) *Community Care: New Agendas and Challenges from the UK and Overseas*, Arena in association with the British Society of Gerontology, Aldershot.

Finley, M. I. (1984) *The Legacy of Greece: A New Appraisal*, Oxford University Press, Oxford.

Firbank, O. (1997) Early Retirement Incentive Programs (Erips): Organizational Strategies and Individual Choices, *Arbete Och Halsa,* **16**, pp. 121–37.

Fitch, C. A. and Ruggles, S. (2000) Historical Trends in Marriage Formation: The United States 1850–1990, in Waite, L. J. and Bachrach, C. (eds) *The Ties That Bind: Perspectives on Marriage and Cohabitation*, Aldine de Gruyter, New York, pp. 59–88.

Flanigan, W. H. and Zingale, N. H. (2002) Political Behavior of the American Electorate, 10th edn, CQ Press, Washington, DC.

Fleischer, D. and Kaplan, B. H. (1980) *Work and Retirement: Policy Issues*, University of Southern California Press, Los Angeles, CA.

Fogel, R. and Costa, D. L. (1997) A Theory of Techno-Physioevolution with Some Implications for Forecasting Population Health Care Costs, and Pension Costs, *Demography,* **34**, pp. 49–66.

Fogerty, J. R. (1992) Growing Old in England, 1878–1949, *PhD thesis,* Australian National University, Canberra.

Foner, A. (2000) Age Integration or Age Conflict as Society Ages?, *Gerontologist,* **40**(3), pp. 272–6.

Forte, C. S. and Hansvick, C. L. (1999) Applicant Age as a Subjective Employability Factor: A Study of Workers over and under Age Fifty, *Journal of Employment Counselling,* **36**(1), pp. 24–34.

Fortes, M. (1984) Age, Generation and Social Structure, in Kertzer, D. I. and Keith, J. (eds) *Age and Anthropological Theory*, Cornell University Press, Ithaca, NY, pp. 99–122.

Fox, G. L. and Kelly, R. F. (1995) Determinants of Child Custody Arrangements at Divorce, *Journal of Marriage and the Family,* **57**(3), pp. 693–708.

FPSC (2000) Family Change: Guide to the Issues, *Family Briefing Paper No. 12,* Family Policy Studies Centre, London.

Franco, D. (1993) *L'espansione della Spesa Pubblica in Italia (1960–1990)*, IL Mulino, Bologna.

Frank, O. (1983) Infertility in Sub-Saharan Africa: Estimates and Implications, *Population and Development Review,* **9**(1), pp. 137–44.

Freedman, V. A. and Martin, L. G. (1998) Understanding Trends in Functional Limitations among Older Americans, *American Journal of Public Health,* **88**(10), pp. 1457–62.

Friedman, B., James, E., Kane, C. and Quiesser, M. (1996) How Can China Provide Income Security for Its Rapidly Aging Population, *Policy Research Working Paper No. 1674,* Poverty and Human Resources Division, Policy Research Department, World Bank, Washington, DC.

Friedman, S. and Sarah, E. (1982) *On the Problem of Men: Two Feminist Conferences*, Women's Press, London.

Fries, J. (1980) Ageing, Natural Death and the Compression of Morbidity, *New England Journal of Medicine,* (303), pp. 130–5.

Fry, C. L. (1999) Anthropological Theories of Age and Aging., in Bengtson, V. L. and Schaie, K. W. (eds) *Handbook of Theories of Aging,* Springer, New York, pp. 271–86.

GAD and ONS (2001) *National Population Projections: 2000-Based, Series PP2 no. 23,* Government Actuary's Department and Office for National Statistics, London.

Gallie, D. (1998) *Equal Opportunities for Women and Men in Europe?: Eurobarometer 44.3 - Results of an Opinion Survey,* Office for Official Publications of the European Communities, Luxembourg.

Gaster, L. (2002) *Past It at 40?: A Grassroots View of Ageism and Discrimination in Employment: A Report,* SMA Associates and Policy Press, Bristol.

Gavrilov, L. A. and Gavrilova, N. S. (1991) The Biology of Life Span: A Quantitative Approach, Rev. and updated English edn, Harwood Academic Publishers, New York.

General Medical Council (2001) *Good Medical Practice,* GMC, London.

Gerdtham, U.-G. (1992) The Impact of Aging on Health Care Expenditure in Sweden, *Health Policy,* **24**(1), pp. 1–8.

Giarrusso, R., Silverstein, M. and Bengtson, V. L. (1996) Family Complexities and the Grandparent Role, *Generations,* **20**(1), pp. 17–23.

Gibson, C. (1993) The Four Baby Booms, *American Demographics,* **15**(11), pp. 36–40.

Gill, I., Packard, T., Pugatch, T. and Yermo, J. (2005a) Rethinking Social Security in Latin America, *International Social Security Review,* **58**(2–3), pp. 71–85.

Gill, I. S., Packard, T. and Yermo, J. (2005b) *Keeping the Promise of Social Security in Latin America,* Stanford University Press and World Bank, Palo Alto, CA.

Gillion, C. (1991) Ageing Populations: Spreading the Costs, *Journal of European Social Policy,* **1**(2), pp. 107–28.

Ginn, J. and Arber, S. (1992) Pension Systems in Three Contrasting European Welfare States, *Journal of European Social Policy,* **2**(4), pp. 255–77.

Ginn, J., Street, D. and Arber, S. (2001) *Women, Work and Pensions: International Issues and Prospects,* Open University Press, Buckingham.

Goldman, N. (1986) Effects of Mortality Levels on Kinship, in UN Dept. of International Economic and Social Affairs (ed.) *Consequences of Mortality Trends and Differentials,* United Nations, New York.

Goldscheider, F. K. and Goldscheider, C. (1994) Leaving and Returning Home in Twentieth Century America, *Population Bulletin,* **48**, pp. 1–34.

Gompertz, B. (1825) On the Nature of the Function Expressive of the Law of Human Mortality, and on a New Mode of Determining the Value of Life Contingencies, *Philosophical Transactions of the Royal Society of London,* **115**, pp. 513–85.

Gonzales-Catala, V. (1997) Spain: National Analysis and Outlook, in DG Employment Industrial Relations and Social Affairs (ed.) *The Outlook on Supplementary Pensions in the Context of Demographic, Economic, and Social Change: A Report by the EU Network of Experts on Supplementary Pension Provision, 1996,* Office for Official Publications of the European Communities, Luxembourg.

Goode, W. J. (1964) *The Family*, Prentice-Hall, Englewood Cliffs, NJ.

Gorman, M. (1999) Development and the Rights of Older People, in HAI (ed.) *The Ageing and Development Report: Poverty, Independence and the World's Older People*, Earthscan, London, pp. 3–21.

Gould, A. (1996) Sweden: The Last Bastion of Social Democracy, in George, V. and Taylor-Gooby, P. (eds) *European Welfare Policy: Squaring the Welfare Circle*, Macmillan, Basingstoke, pp. 72–94.

Gould, R. and Solem, P. E. (2000) Change from Early Exit to Late Exit. A Finland/Norway - Comparison, Paper presented at the COSTA Meeting Ageing and Work, Rome, 13–14 April, 2000.

Granick, S. (1952) Adjustment of Older People in Two Florida Communities, *Journal of Gerontology*, **7**(3), pp. 419–25.

Green, H. (1988) *Informal Carers: A Study Carried out on Behalf of the Department of Health and Social Security as Part of the 1985 General Household Survey*, UK Government Social Survey Dept., HMSO, London.

Grimley-Evans, J. (2003) *They've Had a Good Innings: Can the NHS Cope with an Ageing Population?*, Institute for the Study of Civil Society, London.

Gruber, J. and Wise, D. A. (1999) *Social Security and Retirement around the World*, University of Chicago Press, Chicago.

Grundy, E. (1987) Household Change and Migration among the Elderly in England and Wales, *Espace, Population, Societies*, **1**, pp. 109–23.

Grundy, E. (1999) Household and Family Change in Mid and Later Life in England and Wales, in McRae, S. (ed.) *Changing Britain: Families and Households in the 1990s*, Oxford University Press, Oxford, pp. 201–28.

Grundy, E. and Harrop, A. (1992) Co-Residence between Adult Children and Their Elderly Parents in England and Wales, *Journal of Social Policy*, **21**, pp. 325–48.

Guagnano, G. A. and Markee, N. (1995) Regional Differences in the Sociodemographic Determinants of Environmental Concern, *Population and Environment*, **17**, pp. 135–50.

Guarente, L. and Picard, F. (2005) Calorie Restriction—the Sir2 Connection, *Cell*, **120**(4), pp. 473–82.

Hagestad, G. and Neugarten, B. (1985) Age and the Life Course, in Binstock, R. H. and Shanas, E. (eds) *Handbook of Aging and the Social Sciences*, 2nd edn, van Nostrand Reinhold, New York, pp. 35–61.

Hagestad, G. O. (1985) Continuity and Connectedness, in Bengtson, V. L. and Robertson, J. F. (eds) *Grandparenthood*, Sage, Beverly Hills, CA.

Hagestad, G. O. (1986) Dimension of Time and the Family, *American Behavioral Scientist*, **29**, pp. 679 –94.

Hagestad, G. O. (1988) Demographic Change and the Life Course: Some Emerging Trends in the Family Realm, *Family Relations*, **37**, pp. 405–10.

HAI (1999) *The Ageing and Development Report: Poverty, Independence and the World's Older People*, Earthscan, London.

HAI (2001) *Equal Treatment, Equal Rights - Ten Actions to End Age Discrimination*, HelpAge International, London.

HAI (2002) *A Policy Framework and Plan of Action on Africa*, HelpAge International, Nairobi.

Hajnal, J. (1965) European Marriage Patterns in Perspective, in Glass, D. V. and Eversley, D. E. C. (eds) *Population in History: Essays in Historical Demography*, E. Arnold, London.

Halperin, R. (1987) Age in Cross-Cultural Perspective - an Evolutionary Approach, in Silverman, P. (ed.) *The Elderly as Modern Pioneers*, Indiana University Press, Bloomington, pp. 283–311.

Hannah, L. (1986) *Inventing Retirement: The Development of Occupational Pensions in Britain*, Cambridge University Press, Cambridge.

Hardy, M. A. and Waite, L. J. (1997) Doing Time: Reconciling Biography with History in the Study of Social Change, in Hardy, M. A. (ed.) *Studying Aging and Social Change*, Sage, Thousand Oaks, CA.

Hareven, T. K. (ed.) (1978) *Transitions: The Family and the Life Course in Historical Perspective*, Academic Press, New York.

Hareven, T. K. (1982) *Family Time and Industrial Time: The Relationship between the Family and Work in a New England Industrial Community*, Cambridge University Press, Cambridge.

Hareven, T. K. (1986) Historical Changes in the Social Construction of the Life Course, *Human Development,* **29**(3), pp. 171–80.

Hareven, T. K. (ed.) (1996) *Aging and Generational Relations: Life-Course and Cross-Cultural Perspectives*, Aldine de Gruyter, New York.

Harootyan, R. A. and Takeuchi, J. (1993) Aging of the U.S. Population: Economic and Environmental Implications, in Harootyan, R. A., Takeuchi, J. and Fri, R. (eds) *Proceedings of an Invitational Workshop Conducted by American Association of Retired Persons and Resources for the Future, November 1989*, American Association for Retired Persons, Washington, DC, pp. 1–6.

Harper, C. (1994) An Assessment of Vulnerable Groups in Mongolia: Strategies for Social Policy Planning, *World Bank Discussion Paper No. 229,* World Bank, Washington, DC.

Harper, S. (1987) The Kinship Network of the Rural Aged: A Comparison of the Indigenous Elderly and the Retired Immigrant, *Ageing and Society,* **7**, pp. 303–27.

Harper, S. (1989) The Impact of the Retirement Debate on Post-War Retirement Trends, in Gorst, A., Johnman, L. and Lucas, W. S. (eds) *Post-War Britain, 1945–64: Themes and Perspectives*, printed in association with the Institute of Contemporary British History, London, pp. 95–108.

Harper, S. (1990) The Emergence and Consolidation of the Retirement Tradition in Post-War Britain, in Bury, M. and Macnicol, J. (eds) *Aspects of Ageing: Essays on Social Policy and Old Age*, Royal Holloway and Bedford New College, Egham, Surrey, pp. 19–29.

Harper, S. (1992) Caring for China's Ageing Population: The Residential Option – a Case Study of Shanghai, *Ageing and Society,* **12**(2), pp. 157–84.

Harper, S. (2002) Social Implications of Early Retirement, paper presented at the Future of Retirement Conference, Reykjavik, 7 June, 2002, Institute of Economic Studies at the University of Iceland.

Harper, S. (2004a) The Challenge for Families of Demographic Ageing, in Harper, S. (ed.) *Families in Ageing Societies: A Multi-Disciplinary Approach*, Oxford University Press, Oxford, pp. 6–30.

Harper, S. (ed.) (2004b) *Families in Ageing Societies: A Multi-Disciplinary Approach*, Oxford University Press, Oxford.

Harper, S. (2004c) The Implications of Ageing Societies, in Oberg, B.-M. (ed.) *Changing Worlds and the Ageing Subject: Dimensions in the Study of Ageing and Later Life*, Ashgate, Burlington, VT.

Harper, S. (2005) Understanding Grandparenthood, in Johnson, M. L. and Bengston, V. L. (eds) *The Cambridge Handbook of Age and Ageing*, Cambridge University Press, New York.

Harper, S. and Laslett, P. (2005) The Puzzle of Retirement and Early Retirement, in Heath, A. F., Ermisch, J. and Gallie, D. (eds) *Understanding Social Change*, Vol. 225–54, Oxford University Press (for the British Academy), Oxford.

Harper, S. and Leeson, G. W. (2002) Active Ageing, Social Inclusion and Independence: UK, UN and European Policy Development, Oxford Institute of Ageing, University of Oxford, available online at: http://www.ageing.ox.ac.uk/

Harper, S. and Leeson, G. W. (2003) *Independent Living: Literature Review, Commissioned Report to Department for Work and Pensions,* Department for Work and Pensions, London.

Harper, S. and Lund, D. A. (1990) Wives, Husbands, and Daughters Caring for Institutionalized and Noninstitutionalized Dementia Patients: Toward a Model of Caregiver Burden, *International Journal of Ageing and Human Development,* **30**(4), pp. 241–62.

Harper, S., Smith, T., Ruicheva, I., Lectmen, Z. and Zeilig, H. (2003) *Grandmother Care: The Role of Grandmothers in Providing Child Care to Lone Parent Daughters*, Nuffield Foundation, London.

Harper, S. and Thane, P. (1986) The Social Construction of Old Age in Post-War Britain, 1945–1965, *Working Paper, Social History Series,* Goldsmiths College, University of London, London.

Harper, S. and Thane, P. (1989) The Consolidation of 'Old Age' as a Phase of Life, 1945–65, in Jefferys, M. (ed.) *Growing Old in the Twentieth Century*, Routledge, London, pp. 43–61.

Harper, S. and Vlachantoni, A. (2004) New Technological Based Firms, Late Life Work and Retirement Aspirations, paper presented at the British Society of Gerontology 33rd Annual Scientific Meeting, Roehampton, University of Surrey, 9–11 September, 2004.

Harris, J. (1972) *Unemployment and Politics: A Study in English Social Policy, 1886–1914*, Clarendon Press, Oxford.

Harris, J. (1997) The Rationing Debate: Maximising the Health of the Whole Community. The Case Against: What the Principal Objective of the NHS Should Really Be, *British Medical Journal,* **314**(7081), p. 669.

Haskey, J. (1983) Marital Status before Marriage and Age at Marriage: Their Influence on the Chance of Divorce, *Population Trends 32,* Office for National Statistics, London, pp. 4–14.

Haskey, J. (1992) Pre-Marital Cohabitation and the Probability of Subsequent Divorce, *Population Trends 32,* Office for National Statistics, London, pp. 10–19.

Haskey, J. (1998) Families: Their Historical Context, and Recent Trends in the Factors Influencing Their Formation and Dissolution, in Kiernan, K., Morgan, P. M. and David, M. E. (eds) *The Fragmenting Family: Does It Matter?*, Institute of Economic Affairs, Health and Welfare Unit, London.

Hassle, R. (2001) Sweden, in Philp, I. (ed.) *Family Care of Older People in Europe*, IOS Press, Amsterdam, pp. 237–54.

Hayflick, L. (1994) *How and Why We Age*, 1st edn, Ballantine Books, New York.

Hazelrigg, L. (1997) On the Importance of Age, in Hardy, M. A. (ed.) *Studying Aging and Social Change: Conceptual and Methodological Issues*, Sage Publications, Thousand Oaks, CA. pp. 93–128.

Heller, P. S. (2003) *Who Will Pay?: Coping with Aging Societies, Climate Change, and Other Long-Term Fiscal Challenges*, International Monetary Fund, Washington, DC.

Hellerstein, J., Neumark, D. and Troske, K. (1999) Wages, Productivity and Worker Characteristics: Evidence from Plant Level Production Functions and Wage Equations, *Journal of Labor Economics*, **17**(3), pp. 409–46.

Help the Aged (2002) *Age Discrimination in Public Policy: A Review of Evidence*, Help the Aged, London.

Henretta, J. C. (1994) Recent Trends in Retirement, *Reviews in Clinical Gerontology*, **4**, pp. 71–81.

Henretta, J. C. (1998) U.S. Kinship Patterns and Their Social Context, Paper presented at the Nuffield Foundation Conference on Intergenerational Relationships and Later Life, Oxford, January 6–8, 1998.

Henretta, J. C., Grundy, E. and Harris, S. (2001) Socioeconomic Differences in Having Living Parents and Children: A US-British Comparison of Middle-Aged Women, *Journal of Marriage and the Family Relations*, **63**(3), pp. 852–67.

Henretta, J. C., Hill, M. S., Li, W., Soldo, B. J. and Wolf, D. A. (1997) Selection of Children to Provide Care: The Effect of Earlier Parental Transfers, *Journal of Gerontology Series B: Psychological Sciences and Social Sciences*, **52B**, pp. 110–19.

Henretta, J. C., O'Rand, A. M. and Chan, C. G. (1993) Joint Role Investments and Synchronization of Retirement: A Sequential Approach to Couples' Retirement Timing, *Social Forces*, **71**, pp. 981–1000.

Hermalin, A. I. (1999) Drawing Policy Lessons from Asia on Ageing and Family Life, in HAI (ed.) *The Ageing and Development Report: Poverty, Independence and the World's Older People*, HelpAge International and Earthscan, London.

Hermalin, A. I. (2000) *Ageing in Asia: Facing the Crossroads, Comparative Study of the Elderly in Asia Research Report No. 00–55*, Population Studies Center, University of Michigan, Ann Arbor, MI.

Hermalin, A. I. and Chan, A. (2000) *Work and Retirement among the Older Population in Four Asian Countries: A Comparative Analysis, CAS Research Paper No. 22*, Center for Advanced Studies, National University of Singapore, Singapore.

Hermalin, A. I., Ofstedal, M. B. and Lee, M. L. (1992) *Characteristics of Children and Intergenerational Transfers, Comparative Study of the Elderly in Asia Research Report No. 92–21*, Population Studies Center, University of Michigan, Ann Arbor, MI.

Hermalin, A. I., Roan, C. and Perez, A. (1998) *The Emerging Role of Grandparents in Asia, Comparative Study of the Elderly in Asia Research Report No. 98–52,* Population Studies Center, University of Michigan, Ann Arbor, MI.

Heron, A. and Chown, S. M. (1961) Ageing and the Semi-Skilled: A Survey in Manufacturing Industry on Merseyside, *Medical Research Council Annual Report,* **40**, pp. 1–59.

Herz, D. (1995) Work after Early Retirement: An Increasing Trend among Men, *Monthly Labour Review,* **118**(4), pp. 13–20.

Herz, D. E. and Rones, P. L. (1989) Institutional Barriers to Employment of Older Workers, *Monthly Labor Review,* **112**(4), pp. 14–21.

Hetler, C. B. (1990) Survival Strategies, Migration and Household Headship, in Dube, L. and Palriwala, R. (eds) *Structures and Strategies: Women, Work, and Family,* Sage, New Delhi, pp. 175–99.

Hill, K. and Hurtado, A. M. (1991) The Evolution of Premature Reproductive Senescence and Menopause in Human Females: An Evaluation of the 'Grandmother Hypothesis', *Human Nature,* **2**, pp. 313–50.

Hilton, J. M. and Macari, D. (1997) Grandparent Involvement Following Divorce: A Comparison in Single-Mother and Single-Father Families, *Journal of Divorce and Remarriage,* **29**, pp. 203–24.

Himsworth, R. L. and Goldacre, M. J. (1999) Does Time Spent in Hospital in the Final 15 Years of Life Increase with Age at Death? A Population-Based Study, *British Medical Journal,* **319**(7221), pp. 1338–9.

Hirsch, B., Macpherson, D. and Hardy, M. (2000) Occupational Age Structure and Access for Older Workers: The Role of Compensation, Skills, and Working Conditions, *Industrial and Labor Relations Review,* **53**(3), pp. 401–8.

Hochschild, A. R. (1973) *The Unexpected Community,* Prentice-Hall, Englewood Cliffs, NJ.

Hodgson, L. G. (1992) Adult Grandchildren and Their Grandparents: The Enduring Bond, *International Journal of Aging and Human Development,* **34**, pp. 209–25.

Holzmann, R., Arthur, I. W. M. and Sinn, Y. (2000) Pension Systems in East Asia and the Pacific: Challenges and Opportunities, *Social Protection Discussion Paper No. 0014,* Social Protection Unit, Human Development Network, World Bank, Washington, DC.

Horiuchi, S. and Wilmoth, J. R. (1995) The Aging of Mortality Decline, paper presented at the Annual Meeting of the Population Association of America, San Franciso, USA, April 6–8.

Hoskins, D. (2002) Thinking about Ageing Issues, *International Social Security Review,* **55**(1), pp. 13–20.

Howse, K. (2005) Policies for Healthy Ageing, *Ageing Horizons,* **2**, pp. 3–13.

Hrdy, S. (1981) 'Nepotists' and 'Altruists': The Behaviour of Old Females among Macaques and Langur Monkeys, in Amoss, P. and Harrell, S. (eds) *Other Ways of Growing Old: Anthropological Perspectives,* Stanford University Press, Stanford, CA.

HRS (2004) A Longitudinal Study of Health, Retirement, and Aging, Health and Retirement Study, National Institute on Aging and Michigan University, available online at: http://hrsonline.isr.umich.edu/

Hsin, P.-L. and Mitchell, O. (1997) 1997 Managing Public Sector Pensions, in Schieber, S. J. and Shoven, J. B. (eds) *Public Policy toward Pensions*, MIT Press, Cambridge, MA.

Hu, S.-C., Chen, K.-M. and Chen, L.-T. (2000) Demographic Transition and Social Security in Taiwan, *Population and Development Review*, **26**(Supplement), pp. 117–38.

Hudson, R. B. (1997) *The Future of Age-Based Public Policy*, Johns Hopkins University Press, Baltimore, MD.

Hughes, M. E. and Waite, L. J. (2004) The American Family as a Context for Healthy Aging, in Harper, S. (ed.) *The Family in an Aging Society: A Multi-Disciplinary Approach*, Oxford University Press, Oxford, pp. 176–89.

Hugo, G. (2000) Lansia - Elderly People in Indonesia at the Turn of the Century, in Phillips, D. R. (ed.) *Ageing in the Asia-Pacific Region: Issues, Policies and Future Trends*, Routledge, London, pp. 299–321.

Hume, D. (1739) *A Treatise of Human Nature: Being an Attempt to Introduce the Experimental Method of Reasoning into Moral Subjects*, printed for John Noon, London.

Humphrey, A., Costigan, P., Pickering, K., Stratfrd, N. and Barnes, M. (2003) *Factors Affecting the Labour Market Participation of Older Workers: A Report of Research Carried out by the National Centre for Social Research, in Conjunction with the Institute of Fiscal Studies on Behalf of the Department for Work and Pensions*, Corporate Document Services, Leeds.

Hutchens, R. M. (1986) Delayed Payment Contracts and a Firm's Propensity to Hire Older Workers, *Journal of Labor Economics*, **4**(4), pp. 439–57.

Hutchens, R. M. (1988) Do Job Opportunities decline with Age?, *Industrial and Labor Relations Review*, **42**(1), pp. 89–99.

Hyde, V. and Gibbs, I. (1993) A Very Special Relationship: Granddaughters' Perceptions of Grandmothers, *Ageing and Society*, **13**, pp. 83–96.

Ikels, C. (2004) *Filial Piety: Practice and Discourse in Contemporary East Asia*, Stanford University Press, Stanford, CA.

ILO (1997) *Ageing in Asia: The Growing Need for Social Protection*, International Labour Organization, Regional Office for Asia and the Pacific, Bangkok.

Industrial Welfare Society (1951) *The Employment of Elderly Workers*, IWS, London.

Ippolito, R. (1990) *Pension Plan Choice*, Pension Benefit Guaranty Corporation, Washington, DC.

Irudaya Rajan, S. (1999) Financial and Social Security in Old Age in India, *Social Change*, **29**(1/2), pp. 90–125.

Irudaya Rajan, S., Mishra, U. S. and Sarma, P. S. (1999) *India's Elderly: Burden or Challenge*, Sage, New Dehli.

ISSA (1980) *Report of the Asian Regional Round Table, Meeting on Social Security Protection of the Rural Population in Developing Countries*, International Social Security Association, Kuala Lumpur.

Issacharoff, S. and Harris, E. W. (1997) Is Age Discrimination Really Age Discrimination?: The Adea's Unnatural Solution, *New York University Law Review*, **72**, pp. 780–840.

Jacobs, K., Kohli, M. and Rein, M. (1991) Testing the Industry-Mix Hypothesis of Early Exit, in Kohli, M. (ed.) *Time for Retirement: Comparative Studies of Early Exit from the Labor Force*, Cambridge University Press, Cambridge, pp. 67–96.

Jacobzone, S. (1999) *The Health of Older Persons in OECD Countries: Is It Improving Fast Enough to Compensate for Population Ageing?*, Directorate for Education Employment Labour and Social Affairs, Organisation for Economic Co-operation and Development, Paris.

Jaeger, H. (1985) Generations in History: Reflections on a Controversial Concept, *History and Theory*, **23**(3), pp. 273–92.

James, E. (2000) New Models for Old Age Security: How Can They Be Applied in China, Mimeo, China Country Office, World Bank, Beijing.

James, E. (2001) How Can China Solve Its Old Age Security Problem? The Interaction between Pension, Soe and Financial Market Reform, *Journal of Pension Economics and Finance*, **1**(1) State Enterprise.

James, P. D. (1992) *The Children of Men*, Faber and Faber, London.

Jani-Le Bris, H. (1993) *Care for Carers of Dependent Older Elderly in France*, European Foundation for the Improvement of Living and Working Conditions, Dublin.

Jennings, M. K. and Markus, G. B. (1988) Political Involvement in the Later Years: A Longitudinal Survey, *American Journal of Political Science*, **32**(2), pp. 302–16.

Jensen, P. H. (1999) Activation of the Unemployed in Denmark since the Early 1990s: Welfare of Workfare?, *CCWS Working Paper*, Aalborg University, Aalborg.

Jerrome, D. (1993) Intimate Relationships, in Bond, J., Coleman, P. and Peace, S. (eds) *Ageing in Society*, Sage, London, pp. 226–54.

Johnson, C. L. (1988) *Ex Familia: Grandparents, Parents, and Children Adjust to Divorce*, Rutgers University Press, New Brunswick, NJ.

Johnson, M. and Stears, G. (1998) Why Are Older Pensioners Poorer?, *Oxford Bulletin of Economics and Statistics*, **60**(3), pp. 270–91.

Johnson, P. (1994) The Employment and Retirement of Older Men in England and Wales, 1881–1981, *Economic History Review*, **47**(1), pp. 106–28.

Johnson, P. and Falkingham, J. (1988) Intergenerational Transfers and Public Expenditure on the Elderly in Modern Britain, *Ageing and Society*, **8**, pp. 129–46.

Johnson, P. and Falkingham, J. (1992) *Ageing and Economic Welfare*, Sage, London.

Johnson, P. and Stears, G. (1995) Pension Income Inequality, *Fiscal Studies*, **16**(4), pp. 69–93.

Johnson, R. W. and Lo Sasso, A. T. (2004) Family Support of the Elderly and Female Labour Supply: Trade-Offs among Caregiving, Financial Transfers, and Work: Evidence from the US Health and Retirement Survey, in Harper, S. (ed.) *Families in Ageing Societies: A Multi-Disciplinary Approach*, Oxford University Press, Oxford, pp. 114–42.

Johnson, T. E. and Shook, D. R. (1997) Identification and Mapping of Genes Determining Longevity, in Wachter, K. W. and Finch, C. E. (eds) *Between Zeus and the Salmon: The Biodemography of Longevity*, National Academy Press, Washington, DC, pp. 108–26.

Kannisto, V. (1994) *Development of Oldest Old Mortality 1950 –1990: Evidence from 28 Developed Countries*, Odense University Press, Odense, Denmark.

Kaplan, H. (1997) The Evolution of the Human Life Course, in Wachter, K. W. and Finch, C. E. (eds) *Between Zeus and the Salmon: The Biodemography of Longevity*, National Academy Press, Washington, DC, pp. 175–211.

Kapteyn, A. and de Vos, K. (1998) Social Security and Labor Force Participation in the Netherlands, *American Economic Review,* **88**(2), pp. 164–7.

Keith, J., Fry, C. L., Glascock, A. P., Ikels, C., Dickerson-Putnam, J., Harpending, H. and Draper, P. (1994) *The Aging Experience: Diversity and Commonality across Cultures*, Sage, Thousand Oaks, CA.

Kennedy, G. E. (1990) College Students' Expectations of Grandparent and Grandchild Role Behaviors, *Gerontologist,* **30**, pp. 43–5.

Kennedy, G. E. and Kennedy, C. E. (1993) Grandparents: A Special Resource for Children in Stepfamilies, *Journal of Divorce and Remarriage,* **19**, pp. 45–68.

Kertzer, D. I. (1995) Toward a Historical Demography of Aging, in Kertzer, D. I. and Laslett, P. (eds) *Aging in the Past: Demography, Society, and Old Age*, University of California Press, Berkeley, CA, pp. 363–83.

Kertzer, D. I. and Keith, J. (eds) (1984) *Age and Anthropological Theory*, Cornell University Press, Ithaca, NY.

Kertzer, D. I. and Laslett, P. (eds) (1995) *Aging in the Past: Demography, Society, and Old Age*, University of California Press, Berkeley, CA.

Kertzer, D. I. and Schaie, K. W. (eds) (1989) *Age Structuring in Comparative Perspective*, L. Erlbaum Associates, Hillsdale, NJ.

Khasiani, S. A. (1994) The Changing Role of the Family in Meeting the Needs of the Ageing Population in the Developing Countries, with Particular Focus on Eastern Africa, paper presented at the United Nations International Conference on Ageing Population in the Context of the Family (Ageing and the Family), Kitakyushu, Japan, 15–19 October, 1990, UN Dept. for Economic and Social Information and Policy Analysis, New York, pp. 121–7.

Kiernan, K. (1999) Cohabitation in Western Europe, *Population Trends 96,* Office for National Statistics, London.

Kiernan, K. (2000) European Perspectives on Union Formation, in Waite, L. J. and Bachrach, C. (eds) *The Ties That Bind: Perspectives on Marriage and Cohabitation*, Aldine de Gruyter, New York, pp. 48–58.

Kiernan, K. and Mueller, G. (1999) Who Divorces?, in McRae, S. (ed.) *Changing Britain: Families and Households in the 1990s*, Oxford University Press, Oxford.

Kilbom, A. (1999) Evidence-Based Programs for the Prevention of Early Exit from Work, *Experimental Aging Research,* **25**, pp. 291–9.

King, V. and Elder, G. H. J. (1997) The Legacy of Grandparenting: Childhood Experiences with Grandparents and Current Involvement with Grandchildren, *Journal of Marriage and the Family,* **59**, pp. 848–59.

Kinsella, K. and Gist, Y. J. (1998) Mortality and Health: Gender and Aging, *International Brief No. IB/98–2,* US Bureau of the Census, Washington DC.

Kinsella, K. G. and Velkoff, V. A. (2001) *An Aging World: 2001*, US Dept. of Commerce, Economics and Statistics Administration, Washington, DC.

Kinston, E. and Williams, J. (1993) The Generational Equity Debate: A Progressive Framing of a Conservative Issue, *Journal of Aging and Social Policy,* **5**(3), pp. 31–53.

Kirkwood, T. B. L. (1977) The Evolution of Aging, *Nature,* **270**, pp. 301–4.

Kirkwood, T. B. L. (1999) *Time of Our Lives: The Science of Human Ageing*, Weidenfeld and Nicolson, London.

Kirkwood, T. B. L. (2005a) Asymmetry and the Origins of Ageing, *Mechanisms of Ageing and Development,* **126**(5), pp. 533–4.

Kirkwood, T. B. L. (2005b) Understanding the Odd Science of Aging, *Cell,* **120**(4), pp. 437–47.

Kirkwood, T. B. L., Feder, M., Finch, C. E., Franceschi, C., Globerson, A., Klingenberg, C. P., La Marco, K., Omholt, S. and Westendorp, R. G. J. (2005) What Accounts for the Wide Variation in Life Span of Genetically Identical Organisms Reared in a Constant Environment?, *Mechanisms of Ageing and Development,* **126**(3), pp. 439–43.

Knodel, J. and Chayovan, N. (1997) Family Support and Living Arrangements of Thai Elderly, *Asia-Pacific Population Journal,* **12**(4), pp. 51–68.

Knodel, J., Chayovan, N. and Siriboon, S. (1992) The Impact of Fertility Decline on Familial Support for the Elderly: An Illustration from Thailand, *Population and Development Review,* **18**(1), pp. 79–103.

Knodel, J., Chayovan, N. and Siriboon, S. (1996) Familial Support and the Life Course of Thai Elderly and Their Children, in Hareven, T. K. (ed.) *Aging and Generational Relations: Life-Course and Cross-Cultural Perspectives*, Aldine de Gruyter, New York.

Knodel, J. and Debavalya, N. (1997) Living Arrangements and Support among the Elderly in Southeast Asia: An Introduction, *Asia-Pacific Population Journal,* **12**(4), pp. 5–16.

Knodel, J. and Saengtienchai, C. (1996) Family Care for Rural Elderly in the Midst of Rapid Social Change: The Case of Thailand, *Social Change,* **26**(2), pp. 98–115.

Knodel, J. and Saengtienchai, C. (1999) Studying Living Arrangements of the Elderly: Lessons from a Quasi-Qualitative Case Study Approach in Thailand, *Journal of Cross-Cultural Gerontology,* **14**(3), pp. 197–220.

Kodz, J., Kersley, B. and Bates, P. (1999) *The Fiftieth Revival, IES Report No. 359,* Institute of Employment Studies, Brighton.

Kohli, M. (1986) The World We Forgot: An Historical Review of the Life-Course, in Marshall, V. W. (ed.) *Later Life: The Social Psychology of Aging*, Sage, Beverly Hills, CA, pp. 271–303.

Kohli, M., Rein, M., Guillemard, A.-M. and van Gunsteren, H. (eds) (1991) *Time for Retirement: Comparative Studies of Early Exit from the Labor Force*, Cambridge University Press, Cambridge.

Kono, S. (1994) Ageing and the Family in the Developed Countries and Areas of Asia: Continuities and Transitions, paper presented at the United Nations International Conference on Ageing Populations in the Context of the Family (Ageing and the Family), Kitakyushu, Japan, 15–19 October, 1990, United Nations. Dept. for Economic and Social Information and Policy Analysis, New York.

Kornhaber, A. (1996) *Contemporary Grandparenting*, Sage Publications, Thousand Oaks, CA.

Kornhaber, A. and Woodward, K. L. (1981) *Grandparents, Grandchildren: The Vital Connection*, 1st edn, Anchor Press/Doubleday, Garden City, NY.

Kotlikoff, L. J. (1992) *Generational Accounting: Knowing Who Pays, and When, for What We Spend*, Free Press, New York.

Kotlikoff, L. J. and Smith, D. E. (1983) *Pensions in the American Economy*, University of Chicago Press, Chicago.

Kowald, A. and Kirkwood, T. B. (1993) Explaining Fruit Fly Longevity, *Science*, **260**, pp. 1664–5.

Kreager, P. (2004) Coping without Children: Comparative Historical and Cross-Cultural Perspectives, Oxford Institute of Ageing, University of Oxford, available online at: http://www.ageing.ox.ac.uk/

Kreager, P. and Schroeder-Butterfill, E. (2003) Age-Structural Dynamics and Local Models of Population Ageing in Indonesia, Oxford Institute of Ageing, University of Oxford, Available online at: http://www.ageing.ox.ac.uk/

Kruk, E. (1995) Grandparent-Grandchild Contact Loss: Finding from a Study of 'Grandparent Rights' Members, *Canadian Journal on Aging*, **14**, pp. 737–54.

Kummer, F. (1922) *Deutsche Literaturgeschichte des 19. und 20. Jahrhunderts*, Nach Generationen Dargestellt, Carl Reissner, Dresden.

Kunst, A. E., Looman, C. W. and Mackenbach, J. P. (1988) Medical Care and Regional Mortality Differences within the Countries of the European Community, *European Journal of Population*, **4**(3), pp. 223–45.

Laing and Buisson (1999) *Care of Elderly People: Market Survey 1999*, 12th ed., Nursing Home Properties plc and Laing & Buisson, London.

Lamb, S. (2000) *White Saris and Sweet Mangoes: Aging, Gender, and Body in North India*, University of California Press, Berkeley, CA.

Lamura, G., Melchiorre, M., Quattrini, S., Mengani, M. and Albertini, A. (2001) Italy, in Philp, I. (ed.) *Family Care of Older People in Europe*, IOS Press, Amsterdam, pp. 97–134.

Lancaster, J. B. and King, B. J. (1992) An Evolutionary Perspective on Menopause, in Kerns, V. and Brown, J. K. (eds) *In Her Prime: New Views of Middle-Aged Women*, 2nd edn, University of Illinois Press, Urbana, IL.

Landale, N. S. (1989) Agricultural Opportunity and Marriage: The United States at the Turn of the Century, *Demography*, **26**(2), pp. 203–18.

Landale, N. S. and Tolnay, S. (1991) Group Differences in Economic Opportunity and the Timing of Marriage: Blacks and Whites in the Rural South 1910, *American Sociological Review*, **56**(1), pp. 33–45.

Lang, F. R. (2000) Endings and Continuity of Social Relationships: Maximizing Intrinsic Benefits within Personal Networks When Feeling Near to Death, *Journal of Social and Personal Relationships*, **17**(2), pp. 155–82.

Lang, F. R. (2004) The Availability and Supportive Functions of Extended Kinship Ties in Later Life: Evidence from the Berlin Ageing Study, in Harper, S. (ed.) *Families in Ageing Societies: A Multi-Disciplinary Approach*, Oxford University Press, Oxford, pp. 64–81.

Lang, F. R., Staudinger, U. M. and Carstensen, L. L. (1998) Perspectives on Socioemotional Selectivity in Late Life: How Personality and Social Context Do (and Do Not) Make a Difference, *Journal of Gerontology Series B: Psychological Sciences and Social Sciences*, **53B**(1), pp. P21–9.

Larizgoitia-Jauregi, A. (2001) Spain, in Philp, I. (ed.) *Family Care of Older People in Europe*, IOS Press, Amsterdam, pp. 211–36.

Laslett, P. (1976) Societal Development and Aging, in Binstock, R. H. and Shanas, E. (eds) *Handbook of Aging and the Social Sciences*, Van Nostrand Reinhold, New York, pp. 87–116.

Laslett, P. and Wall, R. (eds) (1972) *Household and Family in Past Time: Comparative Studies in the Size and Structure of the Domestic Group over the Last Three Centuries in England, France, Serbia, Japan and Colonial North America, with Further Materials from Western Europe*, Cambridge University Press, Cambridge.

Lawson, R. (1996) Germany: Maintaining the Middle Way, in George, V. and Taylor-Gooby, P. (eds) *European Welfare Policy: Squaring the Welfare Circle*, Macmillan, Basingstoke, pp. 31–50.

Leavitt, T. and Schulz, J. (1983) *Pension Integration: Concepts, Issues and Proposals*, Employee Benefit Research Institute, Washington, DC.

LeBlanc, L. S. and McMullin, J. A. (1997) Falling through the Cracks: Addressing the Needs of Individuals between Employment and Retirement, *Canadian Public Policy,* **23**(3), pp. 289–304.

Lee, R. and Skinner, J. (1999) Will Ageing Baby-Boomers Bust the Federal Budget?, *Journal of Economic Perspectives,* **13**(1), pp. 117–40.

Lee, R. and Tuljapurkar, S. (2000) Population Forecasting for Fiscal Planning, in Auerbach, A. J. and Lee, R. (eds) *Demography and Fiscal Policy*, Cambridge University Press, Cambridge.

Lee, R. D. (1997) Intergenerational Relations and the Elderly, in Wachter, K. W. and Finch, C. E. (eds) *Between Zeus and the Salmon: The Biodemography of Longevity*, National Academy Press, Washington, DC, pp. 212–33.

Lee, Y.-J. and Palloni, A. (1992) Changes in the Family Status of Elderly Women in Korea, *Demography,* **29**(1), pp. 69–92.

Leeson, G. W. (1981) The Mortality of the Elderly in Denmark, 1960–80, *Ugeskrift for Laeger,* **143**, pp. 2324–7.

Leeson, G. W. (2002) Geographical Distribution, Urbanization, Depopulation and International Migration – the Changing Face of the Population of Europe, *Nordregio Working Paper 2002–2,* Nordic Centre for Spatial Development (Nordregio), Stockholm.

Leeson, G. W. (2004a) Addressing Age Discrimination in Employment Practices, paper presented at the meeting of the Engineering Employers Federation, Rutland, July, 2004, Engineering Employers Federation.

Leeson, G. W. (2004b) The Demographics and Economics of UK Health and Social Care for Older Adults, Oxford Institute of Ageing, University of Oxford, available online at: http://www.ageing.ox.ac.uk/

Leeson, G. W. (2004c) *Sociale Netwaerk, Aelder Sagen Fremtidsstudie Rapport Nr. 4,* Aelder Sagen, Copenhagen.

Leeson, G. W. (2005a) Denmark, *National Background Report,* Services for Supporting Family Carers of Elderly People in Europe: Characteristics, Coverage and Usage (EUROFAMCARE) and Oxford Institute of Ageing, Oxford.

Leeson, G. W. (2005b) The Effect of HIV/AIDS on Intergenerational Relationships in Zimbabwe: the Story of Sophie, *Working Paper No. WP305,* Oxford Institute of Ageing, University of Oxford, available online at: http://www.ageing.ox.ac.uk/

Leeson, G. W. (forthcoming) Changing Patterns of Contact with and Attitudes to the Family in Denmark, *Journal of Intergenerational Relationships.*

Le Gros Clark, F. (1959) *Age and the Working Lives of Men*, Nuffield Foundation, London.

Le Gros Clark, F. (1968) *Pensioners in Search of a Job*, Nuffield Foundation, London.

Leppel, K. and Clain, S. (1995) The Effect of Increases in the Level of Unemployment on Older Workers, *Applied Economics,* **27**(10), pp. 901–6.

Lester, A. (2001) Age Discrimination and Equality: Help the Aged Annual Lecture 2001, 25 September 2001, Help the Aged, London.

Lesthaege, R. (1992) Beyond Economic Reductionism: The Transformation of the Reproductive Regimes in France and Belgium in the 18th and 19th Centuries, in Goldscheider, C. (ed.) *Fertility Transitions, Family Structure, and Population Policy,* Westview Press, Boulder, CO.

Lesthaeghe, R. (2001) Postponement and Recuperation: Recent Fertility Trends and Forecasts in Six Western European Countries, *IPD Working Paper no. 2001–1,* Vrije Universiteit, Brussels.

Lesthaeghe, R. and Neels, K. (2000) Maps, Narratives, and Demographic Innovation, *IPD Working Paper no. 2000–8,* Vrije Universiteit, Brussels.

Lewin, B. (1992) Unmarried Cohabitation: A Marriage Form in a Changing Society, *Journal of Marriage and the Family,* **44**(3), pp. 763–73.

Liebig, P. and Rajan, S. I. (2003) *An Aging India: Perspectives, Prospects, and Policies,* Haworth Press, New York.

Lillard, L. A., Brien, M. J. and Waite, L. J. (1991) Premarital Cohabitation and Subsequent Marital Dissolution: A Matter of Self-Selection?, *Demography,* **32**(3), pp. 437–57.

Lindley, R. M. (1999) Population Ageing and the Labour Market in Europe, *Rivista Italiana di Economia, Demografia e Statistica,* **LIII**(1), pp. 167–92.

Litwak, E. (1985) *Helping the Elderly: The Complementary Roles of Informal Networks and Formal Systems,* Guilford Press, New York.

Liu, K., Manton, K. G. and Aragon, C. (2000) Changes in Home Care Use by Older People with Disabilities: 1982–1994, *Research Report No. 2000–02,* American Association of Retired Persons Public Policy Institute, Washington, DC.

Liu, S. and MacKellar, L. (2001) Key Issues of Aging and Social Security in China, *Interim Report IR–01–004/January,* International Institute for Applied Systems Analysis, Laxenburg, Austria.

Livi-Bacci, M. and Ipsen, C. (1992) *A Concise History of World Population,* Blackwell, Oxford.

Lloyd-Sherlock, P. (2001) *Old Age, Poverty and Economic Survival: Rural and Urban Case Studies from Thailand, Department for International Development Research Report,* UK Department for International Development, London.

Logan, J. R. and Spitze, G. D. (1996) *Family Ties: Enduring Relations between Parents and Their Grown Children,* Temple University Press, Philadelphia, PA.

Lopez, M. E. (1991) The Filipino Family as Home for the Aged, *Comparative Study of the Elderly in Asia Research Report No. 91–7,* Population Studies Center, University of Michigan, Ann Arbor, MI.

Lorenz, A. (1928) *Abendländische Musikgeschichte im Rhythmus der Generationen,* Max Hesses Verlag, Berlin.

Loscocco, K. (2000) Age Integration as a Solution to Work-Family Conflict, *Gerontologist,* **40**(3), pp. 292–300.

Lothian, K., McKee, K., Philp, I. and Nolan, M. (2001) United Kingdom, in Philp, I. (ed.) *Family Care of Older People in Europe,* IOS Press, Amsterdam, pp. 255–80.

Lovejoy, C. O., Meindl, R. S., Pryzbeck, T. R., Barton, T. S., Heiple, K. G. and Kotting, D. (1977) Paleodemography of the Libben Site, Ottawa County, Ohio, *Science*, **198**, pp. 291–3.

Lubitz, J. and Riley, G. F. (1993) Trends in Medicare Payments in the Last Year of Life, *New England Journal of Medicine*, **328**(15), pp. 1092–6.

Luchak, A. (1997) Retirement Plans and Pensions: An Empirical Study, *Relations Industrielles/Industrial Relations*, **52**, pp. 865–86.

Lund, F. (2002) 'Crowding in' Care, Security, and Micro-Enterprise Formation: Revisiting the Role of the State in Poverty Reduction and in Development, *Journal of International Development*, **14**(6), pp. 681–94.

Lundh, C. (1999) Marriage and Economic Change in Sweden during the 18th and 19th Century, in Devos, I. and Kennedy, L. (eds) *Marriage and Rural Economy: Western Europe since 1400*, Brepols, Turnhout.

Lundstroem, H. (1995) Record Longevity in Swedish Cohorts Born since 1700, in Jeune, B. and Vaupel, J. W. (eds) *Exceptional Longevity: From Prehistory to the Present*, Odense University Press, Odense, Denmark.

Lussier, G. and Wister, A. V. (1995) A Study of Workforce Aging of the British Columbia Public Service 1983–1991, *Canadian Journal on Aging*, **14**(3), pp. 480–97.

Lutjens, E. (1997) Netherlands: National Analysis and Outlook, in DG Employment Industrial Relations and Social Affairs (ed.) *The Outlook on Supplementary Pensions in the Context of Demographic, Economic, and Social Change: A Report by the EU Network of Experts on Supplementary Pension Provision, 1996*, Office for Official Publications of the European Communities, Luxembourg.

Lutz, W. and Prinz, C. (1993) Modelling Future Immigration and Integration, in King, R. (ed.) *The New Geography of European Migrations*, Belhaven Press, London.

Luzadis, R. A. and Mitchell, O. S. (1991) Explaining Pension Dynamics, *Journal of Human Resources*, **26**, pp. 679–703.

Ma, J. and Zhai, F. (2001) Financing the Pension Reform in China, paper presented at the Financial Sector Reform in China Conference, John F. Kennedy School of Government, Harvard University, September 11–13, 2001.

MacFarlane, A. (1978) *The Origins of English Individualism: The Family, Property and Social Transition*, Blackwell, Oxford.

MacManus, S. A. (1995) Taxing and Spending Politics: A Generational Perspective, *Journal of Politics*, **57**, pp. 607–29.

Mair, L. P. (1969) *African Marriage and Social Change*, Cass, London.

Makoni, S. and Stroeken, K. (eds) (2002) *Ageing in Africa: Sociolinguistic and Anthropological Approaches*, Ashgate, Aldershot.

Malaysian Chinese Association (1987) *The Chinese Community Towards and Beyond 1990 in Multi-Racial Malaysia*, MCA, Kuala Lumpur.

Malthus, T. R. (1798) *An Essay on the Principle of Population, as It Affects the Future Improvement of Society*, printed for J. Johnson, London.

Mangan, G. (1997) Ireland: National Analysis and Outlook, in DG Employment Industrial Relations and Social Affairs (ed.) *The Outlook on Supplementary Pensions in the Context of*

Demographic, Economic, and Social Change: A Report by the EU Network of Experts on Supplementary Pension Provision, 1996, Office for Official Publications of the European Communities, Luxembourg.

Mannheim, K. ([1929] 1964) Das Problem der Generationen, in *Wissenssoziologie, Soziologische Texte 28*, Luchterhand, Neuwied.

Manton, K. G. (2000) Gender Differences in the Cross-Sectional and Cohort Age Dependence of Cause-Specific Mortality: The United States, 1962 to 1995, *Journal of Gender-Specific Medicine,* **3**(4), pp. 47–54.

Manton, K., Corder, L. and Stallard, E. (1993) Changes in the Use of Personal Assistance and Special Equipment from 1982 to 1989: Results from the 1982 and 1989 NLTCS, *Gerontologist,* **33**(2), pp. 168–76.

Manton, K. G., Corder, L. S. and Stallard, E. (1997) Chronic Disability Trends in Elderly United States Populations: 1982–94, *Proceedings of the National Academy of Science,* **94**, pp. 2593–8.

Manton, K. G. and Land, K. C. (2000) Active Life Expectancy Estimates for the U.S. Elderly Population: A Multidimensional Continuous-Mixture Model of Functional Change Applied to Completed Cohorts, 1982–1996, *Demography,* **37**(3), pp. 253–65.

Marks, N. F. (1996) Caregiving across the Lifespan: National Prevalence and Predictors, *Family Relations,* **45**(1), pp. 27–36.

Marmot, M., Banks, J., Blundell, R., Lessof, C. and Nazroo, J. (eds) (2003) *Health, Wealth and Lifestyles of the Older Population in England: The 2002 English Longitudinal Study of Ageing,* Institute for Fiscal Studies, London.

Marshall, V. W. (1985) Aging and Dying in Pacific Societies, in Counts, D. A. and Counts, D. R. (eds) *Aging and Its Transformations: Moving toward Death in Pacific Societies,* University Press of America, Lanham, MD.

Martin, L. G. (1988) The Aging of Asia, *Gerontology,* **43**(4), pp. 99–113.

Martin, L. G. (1989) Living Arrangements of the Elderly in Fiji, Korea, Malaysia, and the Philippines, *Demography,* **26**(4), pp. 627–43.

Martin, L. G. (1990) The Status of South Asia's Growing Elderly Population, *Journal of Cross-Cultural Gerontology,* **5**(2), pp. 93–117.

Martin, L. G. and Kinsella, K. G. (1994) Research on the Demography of Aging in Developing Countries, in Martin, L. G. and Preston, S. H. (eds) *Demography of Aging,* National Academy Press, Washington, DC, pp. 356–403.

Mason, K. (1992) Family Change and Social Support of the Elderly in Asia – What Do We Know?, *Asia-Pacific Population Journal,* **7**(3), pp. 13–32.

Maule, A. J., Cliff, D. R. and Taylor, R. (1996) Early Retirement Decisions and How They Affect Later Quality of Life, *Ageing and Society,* **16**, pp. 177–204.

McAdams, D. P. and De St. Aubin, E. (eds) (1998) *Generativity and Adult Development: How and Why We Care for the Next Generation,* 1st edn, American Psychological Association, Washington, DC.

McCallum, J. (1990) Noncontributory Pensions for Less Developed Countries, *Journal of Cross-Cultural Gerontology,* **5**, pp. 255–75.

McCarthy, F. D. and Zheng, K. (1996) Population Aging and Pension Systems: Reform Options for China, *Policy Research Working Paper No. 1607*, Poverty and Human Resources Division, Policy Research Department, World Bank, Washington, DC.

McGarry, K. (1998) Caring for the Elderly: The Role of Adult Children, in Wise, D. (ed.) *Inquiries in the Economics of Aging*, University of Chicago Press, Chicago.

McGlone, F., Parks, A. and Roberts, C. (1999) Kinship and Friendships: Attitudes in Britain, in McRae, S. (ed.) *Changing Britain*, Oxford University Press, Oxford.

McGrail, K., Green, B., Barer, M. L., Evans, R. G., Hertzman, C. and Normand, C. (2000) Age, Costs of Acute and Long-Term Care and Proximity to Death: Evidence for 1987–88 and 1994–95 in British Columbia, *Age and Ageing,* **29**(3), pp. 249–53.

McKay, S. and Middleton, S. (1998) Characteristics of Older Workers: Secondary Analysis of the Family and Working Lives Survey, *Research Report No. RR45*, Department for Education and Skills, Suffolk.

McLanahan, S. S. and Casper, L. M. (1995) Growing Diversity and Inequality in the American Family, in Farley, R. (ed.) *State of the Union: America in the 1990s*, vol. 2, Russell Sage Foundation, New York, pp. 1–45.

McMahon, C. and Ford, T. (1955) Surviving the First Five Years of Retirement, *Journal of Gerontology,* **10**, pp. 212–15.

McMullin, B. (2000) John Von Neumann and the Evolutionary Growth of Complexity: Looking Backward, Looking Forward…, *Artificial Life,* **6**, pp. 347–61.

McNicol, J. (1998) *The Politics of Retirement in Britain, 1878–1948*, Cambridge University Press, Cambridge.

Mead, G. H. (1934) *Mind, Self and Society: From the Standpoint of a Social Behaviorist*, University of Chicago Press, Chicago.

Meadows, P. (2004) *The Economic Contribution of Older People*, Age Concern England, London.

Meghir, C. and Whitehouse, E. (1997) Labor Market Transitions and Retirement of Men in the UK, *Journal of Econemetrics,* **79**(2), pp. 327–54.

Meier, E. L. and Kerr, E. (1976) Capabilities of Middle-Aged and Older Workers: A Survey of the Literature, *Industrial Gerontology,* (Summer), pp. 147–55.

Mendelson, D. N. and Schwartz, W. B. (1993) The Effects of Aging and Population Growth on Health Care Costs, *Health Affairs,* **13**(1), pp. 119–25.

Merton, R. (1968) The Matthew Effect in Science, *Science,* **199**, pp. 55–63.

Mesa-Lago, C. (1989) *Ascent to Bankruptcy: Financing Social Security in Latin America*, University of Pittsburgh Press, Pittsburgh, PA.

Mesa-Lago, C. (1991) Social Security in Latin America and the Caribbean: A Comparative Assessment, in Ahmad, E. (ed.) *Social Security in Developing Countries*, Clarendon Press, Oxford.

Mesa-Lago, C. (1997) Comparative Analysis of Structural Pension Reform in Eight Latin American Countries: Description, Evaluation, and Lessons, paper presented at the ILO Regional Social Security Seminar, Lima, Peru, October, 1997.

Mesle, F. (1996) Mortality in Eastern and Western Europe: A Widening Gap, in Coleman, D. (ed.) *Europe's Population in the 1990s*, Oxford University Press, Oxford, pp. 127–43.

Mestheneos, E. and Svensson-Dianellou, A. (2004) Naming Grandparents, *Generations Review,* **14**(3), pp. 10–13.

Millar, J. (1998) Kinship Obligations in Western Europe. Ageing and the Family Conference, University of Oxford., paper presented at Nuffield Foundation Conference on Intergenerational Relationships and Later Life, Oxford, 6–8 January, 1998.

Miller, D. (1966) Age Discrimination in Employment: The Problem of the Older Worker, *New York University Law Review,* **41**, pp. 383–424.

Miniaci, R. and Stancanelli, E. (1998) Microeconomic Analysis of the Retirement Decision, *Working Paper No.206,* OECD, Paris.

Ministry of Health (1954) Unpublished memo, UK Ministry of Health, London.

Ministry of Labour (1945–55) Unpublished memos, UK Ministry of Labour, London.

Minkler, M. and Estes, C. L. (eds) (1999) *Critical Gerontology: Perspectives from Political and Moral Economy,* Baywood, Amityville, NY.

Minois, G. (1989) *History of Old Age: From Antiquity to the Renaissance,* University of Chicago Press, Chicago.

Mitchell, O. S. (1992) Trends in Pension Benefit Formulas and Retirement Provisions, in Turner, J. and Beller, D. (eds) *Trends in Pensions 1992,* US Dept. of Labor, Washington, DC, pp. 177–216.

Mkandawire, T. (2001) Social Policy in a Development Context, *Social Policy and Development Programme Paper Number 7,* United Nations Institute for Social Development, Geneva.

Moen, P. (1996) Gender, Age and the Life Course, in Binstock, R. H. and George, L. K. (eds) *Handbook of Aging and the Social Sciences,* 4th edn, Academic Press, San Diego, CA, pp. 171–87.

Mogey, J. M., Cseh-Szombathy, L. and International Sociological Association. (1990) *Aiding and Aging: The Coming Crisis in Support for the Elderly by Kin and State,* Greenwood Press, New York.

Mohai, P. and Twight, B. W. (1987) Age and Environmentalism: An Elaboration of the Buttel Model Using National Survey Evidence, *Social Science Quarterly,* **68**(4), pp. 798–815.

Moller, V. and Welch, G. J. (1990) Polygamy, Economic Security and Well-Being of Retired Zulu Migrant Workers, *Journal of Cross-Cultural Gerontology,* **5**, pp. 205–16.

Morgan, L. A. and Kunkel, S. (1998) *Aging: The Social Context,* Pine Forge Press, Thousand Oaks, CA.

Moser, C. (2001) Insecurity and Social Protection - Has the World Bank Got It Right?, *Journal of International Development,* **13**, pp. 361–8.

Mui, A. C. (1995) Caring for Frail Elderly Parents: A Comparison of Adult Sons and Daughters, *Gerontologist,* **35**, pp. 86–93.

Munnell, A. H. (2002) Restructuring Pensions for the 21st Century: The United States Debate, *Working Paper No. WP 502,* Oxford Institute of Ageing, University of Oxford, Available online at: http://www.ageing.ox.ac.uk

Munnell, A. H. (2003) Restructuring Pensions for the 21st Century: The United States Social Security Debate, in Clark, G. L. and Whiteside, N. (eds) *Pension Security in the 21st Century: Redrawing the Public–Private Debate,* Oxford University Press, Oxford.

Murphy, M. (2001) Family and Kinship Networks in the Context of Ageing Societies, paper presented at the Conference on Population Ageing in the Industrialized Countries: Challenges and Responses, Tokyo, Japan, 19–21 March, 2001, Nihon University Population Research Institute.

Murphy, M. (2004) Models of Kinship from the Developed World, in Harper, S. (ed.) *Families in Ageing Societies: A Multi-Disciplinary Approach*, Oxford University Press, Oxford, pp. 31–52.

Murphy, M. and Wang, D. (1999) Forecasting British Families into the Twenty-First Century, in McRae, S. (ed.) *Changing Britain: Families and Households in the 1990s*, Oxford University Press, Oxford.

Mutran, E. J., Reitzes, D. C. and Fernandez, M. E. (1997) Factors That Influence Attitudes toward Retirement, *Research on Aging*, **19**, pp. 251–73.

Müller, H. V. (1928) Zehn Generationen deutscher Dichter und Denker, Frankfurter Verlangsanstalt, Berlin.

Myers, D. (ed.) (1990) *Housing Demography: Linking Demographic Structure and Housing Markets*, University of Wisconsin Press, Madison, WI.

Myers, G. C. (1992) Demographic Aging and Family Support for Older Persons, in Kendig, H. L., Hashimoto, A. and Coppard, L. C. (eds) *Family Support for the Elderly: The International Experience*, published on behalf of the World Health Organization by Oxford University Press, Oxford, pp. 31–68.

Myers, G. C. and Agree, E. M. (1993) Social and Political Implications of Population Ageing: Ageing of the Electorate, paper presented at the International Population Conference, New Delhi.

Myles, J. (1995) Neither Rights nor Contracts: The New Means Testing in the US Aging Policy, *Generations Review*, **13**(3), pp. 20–4.

Natividad, J. and Cruz, G. (1997) Patterns in Living Arrangements and Familial Support for the Elderly in the Philippines, *Asia-Pacific Population Journal*, **12**(4), pp. 17–34.

Neugarten, B. L. (1982) *Age or Need?: Public Policies for Older People*, Sage Publications, Beverly Hills, CA.

Neumark, D. (2001) Age Discrimination in the US: Assessment of the Evidence, in Hornstein, Z., Encel, S., Gunderson, M. and Neumark, D. (eds) *Outlawing Age Discrimination: Foreign Lessons, UK Choices*, Policy Press (in association with the Joseph Rowntree Foundation), Bristol, pp. 43–60.

Neumark, D. and Stock, W. A. (1999) Age Discrimination Laws and Labor Market Efficiency, *Journal of Political Economy*, **107**(5), pp. 1081–125.

Niero, M. (1996) Italy: Right Turn for the Welfare State, in George, V. and Taylor-Gooby, P. (eds) *European Welfare Policy: Squaring the Welfare Circle*, Macmillan, Basingstoke, pp. 117–35.

Norgard, T. M. and Rodgers, W. L. (1997) Patterns of in-Home Care among Elderly Black and White Americans, *Journal of Gerontology Series B: Psychological Sciences and Social Sciences*, **52B**, pp. 93–101.

NSSO (1998) *The Aged in India: A Socio-Economic Profile*, India Dept. of Statistics, New Delhi.

Nugent, J. (1985) The Old-Age Security Motive for Fertility, *Population and Development Review*, **11**(1), pp. 75–97.

NZDS (1999) *Demographic Trends*, New Zealand Dept. of Statistics, Wellington, NZ.

OECD (1988) *Reforming Public Pensions, Social Policy Studies, no. 5,* Organisation for Economic Co-operation and Development, Paris.

OECD (2001a) *Ageing and Income: Financial Resources and Retirement in 9 OECD Countries,* Organisation for Economic Co-operation and Development, Paris.

OECD (2001b) *Labour Force Statistics,* Organisation for Economic Co-operation and Development, Paris.

OECD (2003a) *Ageing and Employment Policies: Sweden,* Organisation for Economic Co-operation and Development, Paris.

OECD (2003b) *Employment Outlook,* Organisation for Economic Co-operation and Development, Paris.

OECD (2003c) *European Labour Force Statistics,* Organisation for Economic Co-operation and Development, Paris.

OECD (2004a) *Ageing and Employment Policies: Japan,* Organisation for Economic Co-operation and Development, Paris.

OECD (2004b) *Ageing and Employment Policies: Norway,* Organisation for Economic Co-operation and Development, Paris.

OIA (2002) Unpublished discussion paper, Oxford Institute of Ageing, University of Oxford, Oxford.

Okemwa, S. N. (2002) Privileged Authority of Elders and the Contested Graduations of Seniority, in Makoni, S. and Stroeken, K. (eds) *Ageing in Africa: Sociolinguistic and Anthropological Approaches,* Ashgate, Aldershot.

Okraku, I. O. (1985) A Study of Ghanaian Public Service Pensioners, paper presented at the Thirteenth International Congress of Gerontology, New York.

Olshansky, S. J. and Carnes, B. A. (1997) Ever since Gompertz, *Demography,* **34**(1), pp. 1–15.

Olshansky, S. J., Carnes, B. A. and Brody, J. (2002a) A Biodemographic Interpretation of Lifespan, *Population and Development Review,* **28**(3), pp. 501–13.

Olshansky, S. J., Carnes, B. A. and Butler, R. (2003) If Humans Were Built to Last, *Scientific American,* **284**(3), pp. 50–5.

Olshansky, S. J., Carnes, B. A. and Cassel, C. (1990) In Search of Methuselah: Estimating the Upper Limits to Human Longevity, *Science,* **250**, pp. 634–40.

Olshansky, S. J., Carnes, B. A. and Cassel, C. K. (1993) Fruit Fly Aging and Mortality, *Science,* **260**, pp. 1565–6.

Olshansky, S. J., Hayflick, L. and Carnes, B. A. (2002b) Position Statement on Human Aging, *Journal of Gerontology Series A: Biological Sciences and Medical Sciences,* **57A**(8), pp. B1–6.

Ominde, S. H. and Ejiogu, C. N. (eds) (1972) *Population Growth and Economic Development in Africa,* Heinemann Educational (in association with the Population Council, New York), London.

O'Neill, C., Groom, L., Avery, A. J., Boot, D. and Thornhill, K. (2000) Age and Proximity to Death as Predictors of GP Care Costs: Results from a Study of Nursing Home Patients, *Health Economics,* **9**(8), pp. 733–8.

ONS (1997) *Social Trends,* Office for National Statistics, London.

ONS (1999) *Social Trends, 29,* Office for National Statistics, London.

ONS (2001) *Census 2001,* Office for National Statistics, available online at: http://www.statistics.gov.uk/census2001/census2001.asp

OPCS (1992) *1991 Census: Great Britain,* Office of Population Censuses and Surveys, London.

O'Rand, A. M. (1996) The Cumulative Stratification of the Life Course, in Binstock, R. H. and George, L. K. (eds) *Handbook of Aging and the Social Sciences, 4th ed.,* Academic Press, San Diego, pp. 188–207.

Ortega y Gasset, J. (1923) *El Tema de Nuestro Tiempo,* Madrid.

Osborne, T. (2004) Will the EU Directive on Equal Treatment Fulfill Its Purpose of Combatting Age Discrimination in Employment?, AARP, Available online at: http://www.age-platform.org/AGE/IMG/pdf/AARP_EN–2.pdf

Ostrup, P. (1997) Denmark: National Analysis and Outlook, in DG Employment Industrial Relations and Social Affairs (ed.) *The Outlook on Supplementary Pensions in the Context of Demographic, Economic, and Social Change: A Report by the EU Network of Experts on Supplementary Pension Provision, 1996,* Office for Official Publications of the European Communities, Luxembourg.

Packard, T. (2002) Pooling, Savings and Prevention: Mitigating the Risk of Old Age Poverty in Chile, *Background Paper for Regional Study on Social Security Reform,* Office of the Chief Economist, Latin America and Caribbean Regional Office, World Bank, Washington, DC.

Page, T. (1997) On the Problem of Achieving Efficiency and Equity, Intergenerationally, *Land Economics,* **73**, pp. 580–96.

Palacios, R. and Pallarès-Miralles, M. (2000) International Patterns of Pension Provision, *Social Protection Discussion Paper No. 0009,* Social Protection Unit, Human Development Network, World Bank, Washington, DC.

Palier, B. (2002) Facing Pension Crisis in France, *Working Paper No. WP302,* Oxford Institute of Ageing, University of Oxford, available online at: http://www.ageing.ox.ac.uk

Palme, J. (2003) Pension Reform in Sweden and the Changing Boundaries between Public and Private, in Clark, G. L. and Whiteside, N. (eds) *Pension Security in the 21st Century: Redrawing the Public–Private Debate,* Oxford University Press, Oxford.

Paoli, P. and Merllie, D. (2001) *Third European Survey on Working Conditions 2000,* European Foundation for the Improvement of Living and Working Conditions and Office for Official Publications of the European Communities, Luxembourg.

Papke, L., Peterson, M. and Poterba, J. (1996) Did 401(K)S Replace Other Employer-Provided Pensions?, in Wise, D. A. (ed.) *Advances in the Economics of Aging,* University of Chicago Press, Chicago.

Parish, F. and Peacock, A. (1954) Economics of Dependence, *Economica,* **21**, pp. 84.

Parkin, T. G. (1992) *Demography and Roman Society,* Johns Hopkins University Press, Baltimore, MD.

Partridge, L. (1997) Evolutionary Biology and Age Related Mortality, in Wachter, K. W. and Finch, C. E. (eds) *Between Zeus and the Salmon: The Biodemography of Longevity,* National Academy Press, Washington, DC, pp. 78–95.

Pebley, A. R. (1998) Demography and the Environment: Presidential Address to the Annual Meetings of the Population Association of America., *Demography*, **35**(4), pp. 377–89.

Pelling, M. and Smith, R. M. (1991) *Life, Death, and the Elderly: Historical Perspectives*, Routledge, London.

Periago, M. R. (2005) Longevity and the Quality of Life: A New Challenge for Public Health in the Americas, *Pan American Journal of Public Health/Revista Panamericana de Salud Publica*, **17**(5/6), pp. 297–8.

Perrin, G. (1969) Reflections on Fifty Years of Social Security, *International Labour Review*, **99**, pp. 242–92.

Pestieau, P. (1997) Belgium: National Analysis and Outlook, in DG Employment Industrial Relations and Social Affairs (ed.) *The Outlook on Supplementary Pensions in the Context of Demographic, Economic, and Social Change: A Report by the EU Network of Experts on Supplementary Pension Provision, 1996*, Office for Official Publications of the European Communities, Luxembourg.

Petersen, J. (1930) *Die literarischen Generationen*, Junker und Duennhaupt, Berlin.

Peterson, P. G. (1999) *Gray Dawn: How the Coming Age Wave Will Transform America—and the World*, Times Books, New York.

Petmesidou, M. (1991) Statism, Social Policy and the Middle Classes in Greece, *Journal of European Social Policy*, **1**(1), pp. 31–48.

Petridou, H. (1997) Greece: National Analysis and Outlook, in DG Employment Industrial Relations and Social Affairs (ed.) *The Outlook on Supplementary Pensions in the Context of Demographic, Economic, and Social Change: A Report by the EU Network of Experts on Supplementary Pension Provision, 1996*, Office for Official Publications of the European Communities, Luxembourg.

Petrou, S., Henderson, J., Roberts, T. and Martin, M.-A. (2000) Recent Economic Evaluations of Antenatal Screening: A Systematic Review and Critique, *Journal of Medical Screening*, **7**(2), pp. 59–73.

Philp, I. (ed.) (2001) *Family Care of Older People in Europe*, IOS Press, Amsterdam.

Pinder, W. (1926) *Das Problem der Generationen in der Kunstgeschichte Europas*, Frankfurter Verlagsanstalt, Berlin.

Platteau, J.-P. (1999) Traditional Systems of Social Security and Hunger Insurance, in Ahmad, E., Dreze, J., Hills, J. and Sen, A. (eds) *Social Security in Developing Countries*, Clarendon Press, Oxford.

Pochet, P. (2003) Pensions: The European Debate, in Clark, G. L. and Whiteside, N. (eds) *Pension Security in the 21st Century: Redrawing the Public–Private Debate*, Oxford University Press, Oxford.

Ponzetti, J. J. (1992) Bereaved Families: A Comparison of Parents' and Grandparents' Reactions to the Death of a Child, *Omega*, **25**(1), pp. 63–71.

Pool, I. (2000) Age Structural Transitions and Policy Frameworks, paper presented at the Age Structural Transitions and Policy Implications Conference, Phuket, Thailand, 8–10 November, 2004.

Popenoe, D. (1993) American Family Decline 1960 to 1990: A Review and Appraisal, *Journal of Marriage and the Family*, **55**, pp. 527–55.

Popenoe, D. (1996) *Life without Father: Compelling New Evidence that Fatherhood and Marriage Are Indispensable for the Good of Children and Society*, Martin Kessler Books, New York.

Posner, R. A. (1985) *Aging and Old Age*, University of Chicago Press, Chicago.

Poterba, J. M., Venti, S. F. and Wise, D. A. (1995) Do 401(K) Contributions Crowd out Other Personal Saving?, *Journal of Public Economics*, **58**(1), pp. 1–32.

Prescott, N. (1997) Poverty, Social Services and Social Safety Nets in Vietnam, *World Bank Discussion Paper No.376*, World Bank, Washington, DC.

Preston, S. (1984) Children and the Elderly: Divergent Paths for America's Dependents, *Demography*, **21**, pp. 435–57.

Prieler, P. (1997) Austria: National Analysis and Outlook, in DG Employment Industrial Relations and Social Affairs (ed.) *The Outlook on Supplementary Pensions in the Context of Demographic, Economic, and Social Change: A Report by the EU Network of Experts on Supplementary Pension Provision, 1996*, Office for Official Publications of the European Communities, Luxembourg.

Proctor, C. J., Soti, C., Boys, R. J., Gillespie, C. S., Shanley, D. S., Wilkinson, D. J. and Kirkwood, T. B. L. (2005) Modelling the Actions of Chaperones and Their Role in Ageing, *Mechanisms of Ageing and Development*, **126**(1), pp. 119–31.

Quinn, J. F., Burkhauser, R., Cahill, K. and Weather, R. (1998) Microeconometric Analysis of the Retirement Decision: United States, *Economics Department Working Paper No. 203*, Organisation for Economic Co-operation and Development, Paris.

Quinn, J. F. and Kozy, M. (1996) The Role of Bridge Jobs in the Retirement Transition: Gender, Race and Ethnicity, *Gerontologist*, **36**(6), pp. 363–72.

Raju, S. (2002) Meeting the Needs of the Older, Poor and Excluded in India, in UNFPA (ed.) *Situation and Voices: The Older Poor and Excluded in South Africa and India*, United Nations Population Fund (UNFPA), New York.

Raley, R. K. (2000) Recent Trends and Differentials in Marriage and Cohabitation, in Waite, L. J. and Bachrach, C. (eds) *The Ties That Bind: Perspectives on Marriage and Cohabitation*, Aldine de Gruyter, New York, pp. 19–39.

Ransom, R. L. and Sutch, R. (1986) The Labor of Older Americans: Retirement of Men on and Off the Job, 1870–1937, *Journal of Economic History*, **46**, pp. 1–30.

Rasmussen, S. J. (1997) *The Poetics and Politics of Tuareg Aging: Life Course and Personal Destiny in Niger*, Northern Illinois University Press, DeKalb.

Rattan, S. I. S. (2004) Aging, Anti-Aging, and Hormesis, *Mechanisms of Ageing and Development*, **125**(4), pp. 285–9.

Raymo, J. M. and Cornman, J. C. (1999) Labor Force Status Transitions at Older Ages in the Philippines, Singapore, Taiwan, and Thailand: 1970–1990, *Journal of Cross-Cultural Gerontology*, **14**(3), pp. 221–44.

Rees, W. (1996) Revisiting Carrying Capacity: Area-Based Indicators of Sustainability, *Population and Environment: A Journal of Interdisciplinary Studies*, **17**, pp. 195–215.

Reher, D. S. (1998) Family Ties in Western Europe: Persistent Contrasts, *Population and Development Review*, **24**(2), pp. 203–34.

Reif, K. and Melich, A. (1993) *Eurobarometer 39.0: European Community Policies and Family Life, March-April 1993*, Office for Official Publications of the European Communities, Luxembourg.

Reiss, I. L. (1960) Toward a Sociology of the Heterosexual Love Relationships, *Marriage and Family Living,* **22**, pp. 139–45.

Richardson, S. J., Senikas, V. and Nelson, J. F. (1987) Follicular Depletion During the Menopausal Transition: Evidence for Accelerated Loss and Ultimate Exhaustion, *Journal of Clinical Endocrinology and Metabolism,* **65**(6), pp. 1213–313.

Riddle, S. (1984) Age, Obsolescence and Unemployment: Old Men in the British Industrial System, *Ageing and Society,* **4**(4), pp. 517–24.

Riley, M. W. (1976) Age Strata in Social Systems, in Binstock, R. H. and Shanas, E. (eds) *The Handbook of Aging and the Social Sciences*, Van Nostrand, Reinhold, New York.

Riley, M. W. (1983) The Family in an Aging Society: A Matrix of Latent Relationships, *Journal of Family Issues,* **4**(3), pp. 439–54.

Riley, M. W. (1987) On the Significance of Age in Sociology, *American Sociological Review,* **52**(1), pp. 1–14.

Riley, M. W., Foner, A. and Riley, J. W. (1999) The Aging and Society Paradigm, in Bengtson, V. L. and Schaie, K. W. (eds) *Handbook of Theories of Aging*, Springer, New York, pp. 327–43.

Riley, M. W., Johnson, M. and Foner, A. (eds) (1972) *Aging and Society: A Sociology of Age Stratification*, vol. 3, Russell Sage Foundation, New York.

Riley, M. W. and Riley, J. (1994) Age Integration and the Lives of Older People, *Gerontologist,* **34**, pp. 110–15.

Roberto, K. and Stroes, J. (1995) Grandchildren and Grandparents: Roles, Influences and Relationships, in Hendricks, J. (ed.) *The Ties of Later Life*, Baywood, New York, pp. 141–53.

Roberts, E. (2000) Age Discrimination in Health and Social Care, *Briefing note,* King's Fund, London.

Rogers, A. R. (1993) Why Menopause?, *Evolutionary Ecology,* **7**, pp. 406–20.

Rogers, L. L. (1987) Factors Influencing Dispersal in the Black Bear, in Chepko-Sade, B. D. and Halpin, Z. T. (eds) *Mammalian Dispersal Patterns: The Effects of Social Structure on Population Genetics*, University of Chicago Press, Chicago.

Rose, M. R. (1997) Toward an Evolutionary Demography, in Wachter, K. W. and Finch, C. E. (eds) *Between Zeus and the Salmon: The Biodemography of Longevity*, National Academy Press, Washington, DC, pp. 96–107.

Rosenzweig, M. (1994) Human Capital Development, the Family, and Economic Development, in Asefa, S. and Huang, W. C. (eds) *Human Capital and Economic Development*, Upjohn Institute, Kalamazoo, MI, pp. 63–90.

Roseveare, D., Leibfritz, W., Fore, D. and Wurzel, E. (1996) Ageing Populations, Pension Systems and Government Budgets: Simulations for 20 OECD Countries, *Economics Department Working Paper No. 168,* Organisation for Economic Co-operation and Development, Paris.

Rossi, A. (1987) Parenthood in Transition: From Lineage to Child to Self-Orientation., in Lancaster, J. B., Altmann, J., Rossi, A. and Sherrod, L. (eds) *Parenting across the Life Span: Biosocial Dimensions*, Aldine de Gruyter, New York.

Rossi, A. S. and Rossi, P. H. (1990) *Of Human Bonding: Parent-Child Relations across the Life Course*, Aldine de Gruyter, New York.

Rowlands, O., Singleton, N., Maher, J. and Higgins, V. (1997) *Living in Britain: Results from the 1995 General Household Survey*, The Stationery Office, London.

Royal Commission on Population (1949) *Report*, Cmd. 7695, HM Stationery Office, London.

Rümelin, G. (1875) Über den Begriff und die Dauer einer Generation, in *Reden und Aufsätze*, H. Laupp'sche Buchhandlung, Tübingen, pp. 285–304.

Ryder, N. B. (1965) The Cohort as a Concept in the Study of Social Change, *American Sociological Review*, **30**, pp. 843–61.

Ryder, N. B. (1975) Notes on Stationary Populations, *Population Index*, **41**, pp. 3–28.

Salais, R. (2003) Work and Welfare: Towards a Capability Approach,, in Zeitlin, J. and Trubek, D. M. (eds) *Governing Work and Welfare in a New Economy: European and American Experiments*, Oxford University Press, Oxford.

Saller, R. (1991) European Family History and Roman Law, *Continuity and Change*, **36**, pp. 335–46.

Samwick, A. a. S., J. (1997) Abandoning the Nest Egg? 401(K) Plans and Inadequate Pension Saving, in Schieber, S. J. and Shoven, J. B. (eds) *Public Policy toward Pensions*, MIT Press, Cambridge, MA.

Saraceno, C. and Negri, N. (1994) The Changing Italian Welfare State, *Journal of European Social Policy*, **4**, pp. 19–34.

Sathar, Z. A. and Casterline, J. B. (1998) The Onset of Fertility Transition in Pakistan, *Population and Development Review*, **24**(4), pp. 773–96.

Scales, J. and Scase, R. (2000) *Fit and Fifty*, A Report prepared for the Economic and Social Research Council, ESRC, Swindon.

Scheidt, W. (1929) *Lebensgesetze der Kultur. Biologische Betrachtungen zum Problem der Generation in der Geistesgeschichte*, Frankfurter Verlags-Anstalt, Berlin.

Schieber, S. J. (1997) Retirement Income Adequacy at Risk: Baby Boomers' Prospects in the New Millennium, in Schieber, S. J. and Shoven, J. B. (eds) *Public Policy toward Pensions*, MIT Press, Cambridge, MA, pp. 267–312.

Schieber, S. J. and Shoven, J. B. (eds) (1997) *Public Policy toward Pensions*, MIT Press, Cambridge, MA.

Schmähl, W. (2002) A Pension System in Transition: Private Pensions as Partial Substitute to Public Pensions in Germany, Oxford Institute of Ageing, University of Oxford, Available online at: http://www.ageing.ox.ac.uk

Schmähl, W. (2003) Private Pensions as Partial Substitute for Public Pensions in Germany, in Clark, G. L. and Whiteside, N. (eds) *Pension Security in the 21st Century: Redrawing the Public–Private Debate*, Oxford University Press, Oxford.

Schneekloth, U. and Potthoff, P. (1993) Hilfe- und Pflegebedürftige in Privaten Haushalten, *Bericht: Reprasentativerhebung im Forschungsprojekt 'Möglichkeiten und Grenzen selbständiger*

Lebensfuhrung', Federal Ministry for the Family and Senior Citizens (BMFuS), Stuttgart/Berlin/Cologne.

Schoen, R. and Weinick, R. M. (1993) The Slowing Metabolism of Marriage: Figures from 1988 U.S. Marital Status Life Tables, *Demography*, **30**(4), pp. 737–46.

Schroeder, G. (1997) Luxembourg: National Analysis and Outlook, in DG Employment Industrial Relations and Social Affairs (ed.) *The Outlook on Supplementary Pensions in the Context of Demographic, Economic, and Social Change: A Report by the EU Network of Experts on Supplementary Pension Provision, 1996*, Office for Official Publications of the European Communities, Luxembourg.

Schroeder-Butterfill, E. (2003) Pillars of the Family - Support Provided by the Elderly in Indonesia, *Working Paper No. WP303*, Oxford Institute of Ageing, University of Oxford, Available online at: http://www.ageing.ox.ac.uk

Schulz, J. H. (1992) *The Economics of Aging*, 5th edn, Auburn House, New York.

Schulz, J. H. (1999) Economic Security in Old Age: A Family-Government Partnership, in Randel, J., German, T. and Ewing, D. (eds) *The Ageing and Development Report: Poverty, Independence and the World's Older People*, Earthscan, London, pp. 82–97.

Scott, E., Edin, K., London, A. and Mazelis, J. M. (1999) *My Children Come First: Welfare-Reliant Women's Post-TANF Views of Work-Family Tradeoffs, and Marriage*, Northwestern University/University of Chicago Joint Center for Poverty Research, Chicago.

Segalen, M. (1997) Introduction, in Gullestad, M. and Segalen, M. (eds) *Family and Kinship in Europe*, Pinter, London.

Seshamani, M. and Gray, A. (2002) The Impact of Ageing on Expenditures in the National Health Service, *Age and Ageing*, **31**(4), pp. 287–94.

Sgro, C. and Partridge, L. (1999) A Delayed Wave of Death from Reproduction in Drosophila, *Science*, pp. 2521–24.

Shahar, S. (1997) *Growing Old in the Middle Ages: 'Winter Clothes Us in Shadow and Pain'*, Routledge, London New York.

Shanas, E. (1980) Older People and Their Families: The New Pioneers, *Journal of Marriage and the Family*, **42**, pp. 9–15.

Sharma, M. L. and Dak, T. M. (eds) (1987) *Aging in India: Challenge for the Society*, Ajanta Publishers, New Delhi.

Shenfield, B. E. (1957) *Social Policies for Old Age*, Routledge & Kegan Paul, London.

Shoven, J. B., Topper, M. D. and Wise, D. (1994) The Impact of the Demographic Transition on Government Spending, in Wise, D. (ed.) *Studies in the Economics of Aging*, University of Chicago Press, Chicago.

Silverstein, M., Angelelli, J. and Parrott, T. (2001) Changing Attitudes Towards Aging Policy in the US During the 1980 and 1990's, *Journal of Gerontology Series B: Psychological Sciences and Social Sciences*, **56B**(1), pp. S36–43.

Silverstein, M., Burholt, V., Wenger, G. C. and Bengtson, V. L. (1998) Parent-Child Relations among Very Old Parents in Wales and the United States: A Test of Modernization Theory, *Journal of Aging Studies*, **12**(4), pp. 387–409.

Silverstein, M., Parrott, T., Angelelli, J. and Cook, F. (2000) Solidarity and Tension Age-Groups in the US: Challenge for an Aging America in the 21st Century, *International Journal of Social Welfare*, **9**, pp. 270–84.

Silverstein, M. and Waite, L. J. (1993) Are Blacks More Likely Than Whites to Receive and Provide Social Support in Middle and Old Age? Yes, No, and Maybe So, *Journal of Gerontology Series B: Psychological Sciences and Social Sciences*, **48B**(4), pp. S212–2.

Sloan, F. A., Picone, G. and Hoerger, T. J. (1997) The Supply of Children's Time to Disabled Elderly Parents, *Economic Inquiry*, pp. 295–308.

Smith, J. P., Juster, F. T. and Willis, R. J. (1999) *Wealth, Work, and Health: Innovations in Measurement in the Social Sciences: Essays in Honor of F. Thomas Juster*, University of Michigan Press, Ann Arbor, MI.

Smith, J. P. and Kington, S. (1997) Race, Socioeconomic Status, and Health in Late Life, in Martin, L. G. and Soldo, B. J. (eds) *Racial and Ethnic Differences in the Health of Older Americans*, National Academy Press, Washington, DC, pp. 105–62.

Smith, R. (1984) The Structured Dependency of the Elderly as a Recent Development: Some Sceptical Historical Thoughts, *Ageing and Society*, **4**(4), pp. 409–28.

Soldo, B. J. and Hill, M. S. (1994) Intergenerational Transfers: Economic, Demographic, and Social Perspectives, in Maddox, G. L. and Lawton, M. P. (eds) *Annual Review of Gerontology and Geriatrics: Aging, Kinship, and Social Change*, vol. 13, Springer, New York.

Soldo, B. J. and Hill, M. (1995) Family Structure and Transfer Measures in the Health and Retirement Study: Background and Overview, *Journal of Human Resources*, **30**(5), pp. S108–37.

Soulsby, J. (2000) *Learning in the Fourth Age*, National Institute of Adult Continuing Education, Leicester, England.

Spitze, G. and Logan, J. R. (1989) Gender Differences in Family Support: Is There a Payoff?, *Gerontologist*, **29**, pp. 108–13.

Spitze, G. and Logan, J. R. (1990) More Evidence on Women (and Men) in the Middle, *Research on Aging*, **12**, pp. 182–98.

Spitze, G. and Logan, J. R. (1992) Helping as a Component of Parent-Adult Child Relations, *Research on Aging*, **14**(3), pp. 291–312.

Spitzer, A. B. (1973) The Historical Problem of Generations, *American Historical Review*, **78**(5), pp. 1353–85.

SSA (1997) *Social Security Programs Throughout the World, Research Report no. 65*, U.S. Social Security Administration, Office of Policy, Office of Research, Evaluation, and Statistics, Washington, DC.

SSA (1999) Social Security Programs Throughout the World, U.S. Social Security Administration, Office of Policy, Office of Research, Evaluation, and Statistics, Washington, DC.

Stacey, J. (1996) *In the Name of the Family: Rethinking Family Values in the Postmodern Age*, Beacon Press, Boston.

Stathopoulos, P. (1996) Greece: What Future the Welfare State?, in George, V. and Taylor-Gooby, P. (eds) *European Welfare Policy: Squaring the Welfare Circle*, Macmillan, Basingstoke, pp. 136–54.

Statistics Canada (1998) *Annual Demographic Statistics*, Statistics Canada, Demography Division, Ottawa.

Stearns, S. C. (1992) *The Evolution of Life Histories*, Oxford University Press, Oxford.

Steinberg, M., Walley, L., Tyman, R. and Donald, K. (1998) Too Old to Work, in Patrickson, M. and Hartman, L. (eds) *Managing an Ageing Workforce*, NSW, Woodslane.

Stern, S. (1995) Estimating Family Long-Term Care Decisions in the Presence of Endogenous Child Characteristics, *Journal of Human Resources*, **30**(3), pp. 551–80.

Steuerle, E. and Carasso, A. (2001) A Prediction: Older Individuals Will Work More in the Future, *Straight Talk on Social Security and Retirement Policy No. 32.*, Urban Institute, Washington, DC.

Sticker, E. J. (1991) The Importance of Grandparenthood During the Life Cycle in Germany, in Smith, P. K. (ed.) *The Psychology of Grandparenthood: An International Perspective*, Routledge, London, pp. 32–49.

Stock, J. H. and Wise, D. A. (1990) The Pension Inducement to Retire: An Option Value Analysis, in Wise, D. A. (ed.) *Issues in the Economics of Aging*, University of Chicago Press, Chicago, pp. 205–24.

Stoller, A. (1962) *The Family Today: Its Role in Personal and Social Adjustment*, F. W. Cheshire, Melbourne.

Strate, J. M., Parrish, C. M., Elder, C. D. and Ford, C. I. (1989) Life Span Civic Development and Voting Participation, *American Political Science Review*, **83**, pp. 443–64.

Sutton, G. (1997) Will You Still Need Me, Will You Still Screen Me When I'm Past 64?, *British Medical Journal*, **315**(7115), pp. 1032–3.

Szinovacz, M. (1998) Grandparents Today: A Demographic Profile, *Gerontologist*, **38**, pp. 37–52.

Tamburi, G. (1997) European Overview of the Likely Evolution of Supplementary Pensions, in DG Employment Industrial Relations and Social Affairs (ed.) *The Outlook on Supplementary Pensions in the Context of Demographic, Economic, and Social Change: A Report by the EU Network of Experts on Supplementary Pension Provision, 1996*, Office for Official Publications of the European Communities, Luxembourg.

Tanner, M. and Pinera, J. (1995) The Cato Project on Social Security Privatization, Cato Institute, Washington, DC, available online at: http://www.cato.org/research/ss_prjct.html

Tanner, S. (1997) The Dynamics of Retirement Behaviour, in Disney, R., Grundy, E. M. D. and Johnson, P. (eds) *The Dynamics of Retirement: Analyses of the Retirement Surveys*, The Stationery Office, London.

Tanskanen, A. (1997) Finland: National Analysis and Outlook, in DG Employment Industrial Relations and Social Affairs (ed.) *The Outlook on Supplementary Pensions in the Context of Demographic, Economic, and Social Change: A Report by the EU Network of Experts on Supplementary Pension Provision, 1996*, Office for Official Publications of the European Communities, Luxembourg.

Taylor, P. and Walker, A. (1994) The Ageing Workforce: Employers' Attitudes Towards Older Workers, *Work, Employment and Society*, **8**, pp. 569–91.

Teague, P. (1998) Monetary Union and Social Europe, *Journal of European Social Policy*, **8**(2), pp. 117–27.

Tengan, A. (2002) Social Categories and Seniority in a House-Based Society, in Makoni, S. and Stroeken, K. (eds) *Ageing in Africa: Sociolinguistic and Anthropological Approaches*, Ashgate, Aldershot, pp. 137–54.

Thane, P. (2000) *Old Age in English History: Past Experiences, Present Issues*, Oxford University Press, Oxford.

Thatcher, A. R. (1997) Trends and Prospects at Very High Ages, in Charlton, J. and Murphy, M. (eds) *The Health of Adult Britain 1841–1994*, vol. II, The Stationery Office, London, pp. 204–10.

Thiele, L. P. (1999) *Environmentalism for a New Millennium: The Challenge of Coevolution*, Oxford University Press, New York.

Thomas, K. (1979) Age and Authority in Early Modern England, *Proceedings of the British Academy*, **42**, pp. 206–48.

Thompson, P., Itzin, C. and Abendstern, M. (1990) Grandparenthood, in Thompson, P., Itzin, C. and Abendstern, M. (eds) *I Don't Feel Old, the Experiences of Later Life.*, Oxford University Press, Oxford, pp. 174–213.

Thomson, D. (1989) The Welfare State and Generational Conflict: Winners and Losers, in Johnson, P., Conrad, C. and Thomson, D. (eds) *Workers Versus Pensioners: Intergenerational Justice in an Ageing World*, Manchester University Press in association with the Centre for Economic Policy Research, Manchester, pp. 35–56.

Thomson, D. (1993) A Lifetime of Privilege? Aging and Generations, in Bengtson, V. L. and Achenbaum, W. A. (eds) *The Changing Contract across Generations*, Aldine de Gruyter, New York, pp. 215–37.

Timpone, R. J. (1998) Structure, Behavior, and Voter Turnout in the United States, *American Political Science Review*, **92**(1), pp. 145–58.

Tinsley, B. J. and Parke, R. D. (1988) The Role of Grandfathers in the Context of the Family, in Bronstein, P. and Cowan, C. P. (eds) *Fatherhood Today: Men's Changing Role in the Family*, J. Wiley, New York.

Titmuss, R. M. (1958) *Essays on 'the Welfare State'.* Allen & Unwin, London.

Torgerson, D. and Gosden, T. (1998) Clinical and Economic Arguments Favour Extension to the Upper Age Limit for Breast Screening, *British Medical Journal*, **316**(7147), pp. 1829.

Townsend, P. (1957) *The Family Life of Old People; An Inquiry in East London*, Routledge and K. Paul, London.

Traphagan, J. W. (2000) *Taming Oblivion: Aging Bodies and the Fear of Senility in Japan*, State University of New York Press, New York.

Treas, J. and Logue, B. (1986) Economic Development and the Older Population, *Population and Development Review*, **12**(4), pp. 645–73.

Triantafillou, J. and Mestheneos, E. (2001) Greece, in Philp, I. (ed.) *Family Care of Older People in Europe*, IOS Press, Amsterdam, pp. 75–96.

Trinder, C. (1989) Employment after 55, *Discussion Paper No. 166*, National Institute for Economic and Social Research, London.

Tunaley, J. (1998) Grandparents and the Family: Support Versus Interference, paper presented at the BPS Annual Conference, London.

Turner, N. J., Haward, R. A., Mulley, G. P. and Selby, P. J. (1999) Cancer in Old Age: Is It Inadequately Investigated and Treated?, *British Medical Journal,* **319**(7205), pp. 309–12.

Twigg, J. (ed.) (1992) *Carers: Research and Practice*, HMSO, London.

Uccello, C. E. and Mix, S. E. (1998) *Factors Influencing Retirement: Their Implications for Raising Retirement Age*, AARP, Washington.

Uhlenberg, P. (1994) Implications of Being Divorced in Later Life, paper presented at the United Nations International Conference on Ageing Population in the Context of the Family (Ageing and the Family), Kitakyushu, Japan, 15–19 October, 1990, UN Dept. for Economic and Social Information and Policy Analysis, New York, pp. 121–7.

Uhlenberg, P. (1995) Demographic Influences on Intergenerational Relationships, in Bengtson, V. L., Schaie, K. W. and Burton, L. (eds) *Adult Intergenerational Relations: Effects of Societal Change*, Springer, New York.

Uhlenberg, P. (1996) Intergenerational Support in Sri Lanka, in Hareven, T. K. (ed.) *Aging and Generational Relations: Life-Course and Cross-Cultural Perspectives*, Aldine de Gruyter, New York.

Uhlenberg, P. R. and Hammill, B. G. (1998) Frequency of Grandparents Contact with Grandchild Sets: Six Factors That Make a Difference, *Gerontologist,* **38**(3), pp. 276–85.

Uhlenberg, P. and Miner, S. (1996) Life Course and Ageing: A Cohort Perspective, in Binstock, R. H. and George, L. K. (eds) *Handbook of Aging and the Social Sciences*, 4th edn, Academic Press, San Diego, pp. 208–28.

UNAIDS, UNICEF and USAID (2002) *Children on the Brink 2002: A Joint Report on Orphan Estimates and Program Strategies*, U.S. Agency for International Development, Washington, DC.

UNDP (1996) *Human Development Report 1996: Economic Growth and Human Development*, United Nations Development Programme and Oxford University Press, Oxford.

UNDP (2002) *Human Development Report 2002: Deepening Democracy in a Fragmented World*, United Nations Development Programme and Oxford University Press, Oxford.

UNFPA (1999) *The New Generations, the Family and Society, No. 5,* United Nations Population Fund (UNFPA), New York.

UNFPA (ed.) (2002) *Situation and Voices: The Older Poor and Excluded in South Africa and India*, United Nations Population Fund (UNFPA), New York.

United Nations (2000) *Replacement Migration: Is It a Solution to Declining and Ageing Populations?*, UN Dept. of Economic and Social Affairs, Population Division, New York.

United Nations (2001) *International Strategy for Action on Ageing*, UN Commission for Social Development, Economic and Social Counsil (ECOSOC), New York.

United Nations (2005) *World Population Prospects: The 2004 Revision*, UN Dept. of Economic and Social Affairs, Population Division, New York.

US Bureau of the Census (1997) *Current Population Report*, US Government Printing Office, Washington, DC.

US Bureau of the Census (1998) *Current Population Report*, US Government Printing Office, Washington, DC.

Van de Kaa, D. J. (1987) Europe's Second Demographic Transition, *Population Bulletin,* **42**(1), pp. 3–57.

van Poppel, F. and Nelissen, J. (1999) The Proper Time to Marry: Social Norms and Behavior in Nineteenth-Century Netherlands, *History of the Family,* **4**(1), pp. 51–75.

van Reil, B., Hemerijck, A. and Visser, J. (2002) Is There a Dutch Way to Pension Reform?, *Working Paper No. WP202,* Oxford Institute of Ageing, University of Oxford, available online at: http://www.ageing.ox.ac.uk/

Vatuk, S. (1982) Old Age in India, in Stearns, P. N. (ed.) *Old Age in Preindustrial Society,* Holmes and Meier, New York, pp. 70–103.

Vaupel, J. W. (1997) The Remarkable Improvements in Survival at Older Ages, *Philosophical Transactions of the Royal Society of London, ser. B: Biological Sciences,* **352**(1363), pp. 1799–804.

Vaupel, J. W. and Carey, J. R. (1993) Compositional Explanations of Medfly Mortality, *Science,* **260**, pp. 1666–7.

Vaupel, J. W. and Lundstroem, H. (1994) The Future of Mortality at Older Ages in Developed Countries, in Lutz, W. (ed.) *The Future Population of the World: What Can We Assume Today?,* Earthscan, London.

Venti, S. F. and Wise, D. (1997) The Wealth of Cohorts: Retirement Saving and the Changing Assets of Older Americans, in Schieber, S. J. and Shoven, J. B. (eds) *Public Policy toward Pensions,* MIT Press, Cambridge, MA.

Ventura, S. J., Martin, J. A., Curtin, S. C. and Mathews, T. J. (1998) *Report of Final Natality Statistics, Monthly Vital Statistics Report, Vol. 46 (11), Supplement,* National Center for Health Statistics, Washington, DC.

Vijaya Kumar, S. (1990) Old Age: A Challenge of Life, *Journal of Indian Anthropological Society,* **16**, pp. 3–4.

Vijaya Kumar, S. (2003) Economic Security for the Elderly in India: An Overview, in Liebig, P. S. and Irudaya Rajan, S. (eds) *An Ageing India: Perspectives, Prospects, and Policies,* Haworth Press, Binghamton, NY, pp. 45–66.

Vijg, J. and Papaconstantinou, J. (1990) Erage Workshop Report. Aging and Longevity Genes: Strategies for Identifying DNA Sequences in Controlling Life Span, *Journal of Gerontology,* **45**(5), pp. B179–82.

vom Saal, F. S. and Finch, C. E. (1988) Reproductive Senescence: Phenomena and Mechanisms in Selected Vertebrates, in Knobil, E. and Neill, J. D. (eds) *The Physiology of Reproduction,* Raven Press, New York.

vom Saal, F. S., Finch, C. E. and Nelson, J. F. (1994) Natural History and Mechanisms of Reproductive Aging in Humans, Laboratory Rodents, and Other Selected Vertebrates, in Knobil, E. and Neill, J. D. (eds) *The Physiology of Reproduction,* 2nd edn, Raven Press, New York, pp. 1213–313.

Wachter, K. W. (1997) Kinship Resources for the Elderly, *Philosophical transactions of the Royal Society of London, ser. B: Biological Sciences,* **352**(1363), pp. 1811–17.

Wadensjo, E. (1997) Sweden: National Analysis and Outlook, in DG Employment Industrial Relations and Social Affairs (ed.) *The Outlook on Supplementary Pensions in the Context of Demographic, Economic, and Social Change: A Report by the EU Network of Experts on Supplementary Pension Provision, 1996,* Office for Official Publications of the European Communities, Luxembourg.

Waite, L. J. (1995) Does Marriage Matter?, *Demography*, **32**(4), pp. 483–507.

Waite, L. J. and Bachrach, C. (eds) (2000) *The Ties That Bind: Perspectives on Marriage and Cohabitation*, Aldine de Gruyter, New York.

Waite, L. J. and Lillard, L. A. (1991) Children and Marital Disruption, *American Journal of Sociology*, **96**(4), pp. 930–53.

Waite, L. J. and Spitze, G. D. (1981) Young Women's Transition to Marriage, *Demography*, **18**(4), pp. 681–94.

Wakabayashi, M. and MacKellar, L. (1999) Demographic Trends and Household Saving in China, *Interim Report IR–99–057/November*, International Institute for Applied Systems Analysis, Laxenburg, Austria.

Walker, A. (1996) *The New Generational Contract: Intergenerational Relations, Old Age and Welfare*, UCL Press, London.

Wall, R. (1996) Intergenerational Relationships Past and Present, in Walker, A. (ed.) *The New Generational Contract: Intergenerational Relations, Old Age and Welfare*, UCL Press, London, pp. 37–55.

Warner, H. R. (2005) Longevity Genes: From Primitive Organisms to Humans, *Mechanisms of Ageing and Development*, **126**(2), pp. 235–42.

Warr, T. (1994) Age and Employment, in Triandis, H. C., Dunnette, M. D. and Hough, L. M. (eds) *Handbook of Industrial and Organizational Psychology*, vol. 4, 2nd edn, Consulting Psychologists Press, Palo Alto, CA, pp. 485–550.

Warshawsky, M. J. (1994) Projections of Health Care Expenditures as a Share of the GDP: Actuarial and Macroeconomic Approaches, *Health Services Research*, **29**(3), pp. 293–313.

Wechssler, E. (1930) *Die Generation als Jugendreihe und Ihr Kampf um die Denkform*, Quelle und Meyer, Leipzig.

Weiss, K. M. (1973) Demographic Models for Anthropology, *Society for American Archaeology Memoirs*, **27**, pp. 11–86.

Weiss, K. M. (1981) Evolutionary Perspectives on Human Aging, in Amoss, P. and Harrell, S. (eds) *Other Ways of Growing Old*, Stanford University Press, Stanford, CA.

Welford, A. T. (1958) *Ageing and Human Skill*, Oxford University Press, London.

Wenger, G. C. (1984) *The Supportive Network: Coping with Old Age*, Allen and Unwin, London.

Wenger, G. C. (1992) *Help in Old Age: Facing up to Change: A Longitudinal Network Study*, Liverpool University Press, Liverpool.

Whelan, J. (1998) *Equal Access to Cardiac Rehabilitation*, Age Concern England, London.

WHO (2001) Impact of AIDS on Older People in Africa: Zimbabwe Case Study, *Draft Report September 2001*, World Health Organization, Geneva.

WHO (2003) *The World Health Report 2003: Shaping the Future*, WHO, Geneva.

Williamson, J. and McNamara, T. (2001) *Why Some Workers Remain in the Laborforce Beyond the Typical Age of Retirement*, Boston College Center for Retirement Research, Chestnut Hill, MA.

Willmore, L. (2001) Universal Pensions in Low Income Countries, paper presented at the Oxford Institute of Ageing Workshop, Oxford, UK, September, 2001.

Wilmoth, J. R. (1995) Are Mortality Rates Falling at Extremely High Ages? An Investigation Based on a Model Proposed by Coale and Kisker, *Population Studies,* **49**(2), pp. 281–95.

Wilmoth, J. R. (1997) In Search of Limits, in Wachter, K. W. and Finch, C. E. (eds) *Between Zeus and the Salmon: The Biodemography of Longevity,* National Academy Press, Washington, DC, pp. 38–64.

Wilmoth, J. R. and Lundstroem, H. (1996) Extreme Longevity in Five Countries: Presentation of Trends with Special Attention to Issues of Data Quality, *European Journal of Population,* **12**(1), pp. 63–93.

Wolf, D. A., Freedman, V. A. and Soldo, B. J. (1997) The Division of Family Labor: Care for Elderly Parents, *Journal of Gerontology Series B: Psychological Sciences and Social Sciences,* **52B**(Special Issue), pp. 102–9.

Wolf, D. A. and Soldo, B. J. (1994) Married Women's Allocation of Time to Employment and Care of Elderly Parents, *Journal of Human Resources,* **29**(3), pp. 1259–76.

World Bank (1994) Averting the Old Age Crisis: Policies to Protect the Old and Promote Growth, *World Bank Policy Research Report,* Oxford University Press, Oxford.

World Bank (2000) *Making Transition Work for Everyone: Poverty and Inequality in Europe and Central Asia,* World Bank, Washington, DC.

World Bank (2001) *Brazil: Critical Issues in Social Security, A World Bank Country Study No. 22513,* World Bank, Washington, DC.

Wright, S. D. and Lund, D. A. (2000) Gray and Green: Stewardship and Sustainability in an Aging Society, *Journal of Aging Studies,* **14**(3), pp. 229–49.

Wrigley, E. A. and Schofield, R. (1981) *The Population History of England, 1541–1871: A Reconstruction,* Edward Arnold, London.

Yang, B.-M. (2001) The National Pension Scheme the Republic of Korea, *WBI Working Paper No. 22712,* World Bank Institute, Washington, DC.

Zeilig, H. and Harper, S. (2000) Locating Grandparents, *Working Paper No. WP3/00,* Oxford Centre on Population Ageing, University of Oxford, Oxford.

Zweifel, P., Felder, S. and Meiers, M. (1999) Ageing of Population and Health Care Expenditure, *Health Economics,* **8**(6), pp. 485–96.

Index